# Public Health

Also by Rob Baggott:

*Pressure Groups Today*

*Health and Health Care in Britain,* 2nd edn

# Public Health: Policy and Politics

Rob Baggott

palgrave
macmillan

Published by
PALGRAVE MACMILLAN
Houndmills, Basingstoke, Hampshire RG21 6XS and
175 Fifth Avenue, New York, N.Y. 10010
Companies and representatives throughout the world

PALGRAVE MACMILLAN is the new global academic imprint of
St. Martin's Press LLC Scholarly and Reference Division and
Palgrave Publishers Ltd (formerly Macmillan Press Ltd).

ISBN 0–333–67635–1 hardback
ISBN 0–333–67649–1 paperback

This book is printed on paper suitable for recycling and
made from fully managed and sustained forest sources.

A catalogue record for this book is available
from the British Library.

Library of Congress Cataloging-in-Publication Data

Baggott, Rob.
Public health : policy and politics /Rob Baggott
    p. cm
    Includes bibliographical references and index.
    ISBN 0–333–67635–1
1. Public health—Political aspects—United States. 2. Medical
care—Political aspects—United States. 3. Medical policy—
United States. I. Title.

RA395 .A3 B24 2000
362.1'0973—dc21                              00–033319

10   9   8   7   6
09  08  07  06  05  04

Editing and origination by
Aardvark Editorial, Mendham, Suffolk

Printed and bound in Great Britain by
Antony Rowe Ltd, Chippenham and Eastbourne

# Contents

# List of Exhibits, Figures and Tables

# Preface

Some projects have a long gestation period, and this book provides such an example. My interest in public health was first established many years ago during the early 1970s, following news coverage of an outbreak of food poisoning that had affected a group of pensioners who had up to that point being enjoying a picnic. I recall that the victims contracted botulism from some tinned fish they had eaten. It goes without saying that this particular delicacy was off the family menu for some time. Thirty years on, public health concerns have moved to centre stage. Food safety, for example, is now a permanent fixture on the political agenda rather than a matter of sporadic public alarm. The same could be said of other issues that are now more widely recognised as a having an important bearing on public health: pollution, road safety and transport, housing, poverty and socio-economic inequities, health and safety at work, alcohol, tobacco and drugs. Meanwhile, the political significance of public health today has been reflected by the appointment of a Minister for Public Health in 1997 and the adoption of public health strategies in each part of the UK. Even so, most books on the subject are rather narrowly focused on public health services (including health promotion), epidemiology or preventive medicine. Indeed, it was the political naïvety of much of the writing on public health, in particular the absence of a public policy focus, that inspired me to write this book.

What I have tried to do is to capture the key features of contemporary debates in public health in the context of the policy process. The early chapters set the scene by outlining conceptual frameworks and discussing historical background. The later chapters discuss contemporary policy debates in a range of case study areas, such as food policy. The book is aimed at a wide audience, including students undertaking politics, health and social policy courses, professionals whose work has a public health element, and that elusive creature, the general reader.

Although this work is solely my responsibility, I would like to acknowledge others who have freely and generously given me assistance during the course of the project. Several people have commented on the book, including two anonymous reviewers whose observations were extremely constructive. I do not know who you are, but thanks anyway! Helpful comments on draft chapters were also received from Professor Frank Dewhurst, Professor Judith Allsop, Dr Stephen Peckham and Nicky Drucquer. I would also like to mention those who helpfully supplied information when I asked and were happy to discuss specific points with me, including Professor Albert Weale (University of Essex), Professor Erik Millstone (University of Sussex), Eric Appleby (Alcohol Concern), Howard Price (Chartered Institute of Environmental Health), Yvonne Cornish (South East Institute of Public Health), Dr Chris Nottingham (Glasgow Caledonian University) and Holly Crossen. The following colleagues at DMU all gave their help when asked: Professor Mel Chevannes, Professor Martyn Denscombe, Professor Andrew Watterson, Dr Lorraine Culley, Dr Simon Dyson, Dr Merrill Clarke, Helen Bentley, Ellen Carter, Kay Davis, Dr John Ehiri, Dr Alison Hann, Dr Mark Johnson, Dr Kathryn Jones, Jackie Leatham, Julie Prowse, Dr Lawrence Pratchett, Dr Sally Ruane, Paul Rigby, Melvin Wingfield and Ceri Lilley. I am grateful to members of the PSA Health Policy Group, particularly Bruce Wood (Manchester University), Fiona O'Neill (University of Leeds), Dr Stephen Peckham (Oxford Brookes University) and Dr Martin Powell (University of Bath) for their observations on an earlier conference paper that set out a conceptual framework for the study. The paper was subsequently published as a chapter in Alison Hann's edited volume *Analysing Health Policy* (Ashgate Press, 2000), and I must acknowledge that Chapter 1 of this book draws to some extent on this material. In addition, Crown copyright material is reproduced with the permission of the controller of HMSO in Exhibit 4.1 and Appendix 1. Other acknowledgements and permissions are given *in situ*. Thanks to Tracey Dodman who typed up corrections to some of the later chapters and helped to compile the dreaded bibliography section as the deadline loomed large, and also to Dr Kathryn Jones, Sue Dewing, Julie Conroy and Sue Smith, and to Ceri Laing of Scraptoft campus library, who helped me to track down some of the more obscure publications and reports.

I also had some contact with people involved in the public health policy process, including some former and current civil servants. All were helpful, but two observers in particular, Roy Cunningham and Dr David Player, gave me some particularly useful insights. My head of department, Professor David Wilson, and Dean of the Faculty of Business and Law, Professor John Coyne, have continued to support my research programme. Professor Mike Saks, Dean of Health and Community Studies, has also been a strong supporter of health policy research at De Montfort University and deserves mention. On a lighter note, I would like to thank all the participants in the Scraptoft Campus Staff Badminton Challenge for providing a welcome distraction from my academic labours. Thanks to Steven Kennedy at the publishers for prompting me to write the book in the first place. Also, my editors, first Catherine Gray and more recently Houri Alavi, have been extremely supportive throughout. I would like to thank Aardvark Editorial for their sterling efforts in steering me through the final treacherous stages of the publication process. But above all I would like once again to thank my

# Acknowledgements

The author and publishers wish to thank the following for permission to use copyright material:

Ashgate Publishing Limited for extracts from *Analysing Health Policy*, edited by Alison Hann (ISBN 0–7546–1153–1).

HMSO for extracts from Independent Inquiry into Inequalities in Health (the Acheson Report; see the Appendix) and Cm 1986 *(The Health of the Nation: A Strategy for Health in England)*. Crown copyright material is reproduced with the permission of the Controller of Her Majesty's Stationery Office.

The World Health Organization for the text of the WHO European regional targets adapted from *Health 2: The Health Policy Framework for the WHO European Region* (European Health for All Series No. 5, 1999).

Every effort has been made to trace all the copyright holders but, if any have been inadvertently overlooked, the publishers will be pleased to make the necessary arrangements at the first opportunity.

# 1

# Analysing Public Health

## What is Public Health?

In a narrow sense, public health refers to the health of a population, the longevity of its individual members and the extent to which they are free from disease. Alternatively, public health can be seen as a philosophy of intervention aimed at protecting and promoting the health of the population. According to Smith and Jacobson (1988, p. 3), for example, public health 'involves the promotion of health, the prevention of disease, the treatment of illness, the care of those who are disabled, and the continuous development of the technical and social means for the pursuit of these objectives'. In terms of this broader conception, public health is anticipatory, geared to the prevention of illness rather than simply the provision of care and treatment services. It is also rooted in a positive conception of health (see WHO, 1946) and is concerned with promotion of health and social wellbeing in its widest sense. Moreover, this concept of public health has a strong collective focus, echoing Rosen's (1993, p. 1) observation that 'throughout human history, the major problems of health... have been concerned with community life'. It also incorporates methods that connect collective action to these broader aims, as reflected in Winslow's (1920, p. 23) classic definition:

> Public health is the science and art of preventing disease, prolonging life and promoting physical health and efficiency through organised community efforts for the sanitation of the environment, the control of community infections, the education of the individual in principles of personal hygiene, the organisation of medical and nursing service for the early diagnosis and preventive treatment of disease, and the development of social machinery which will ensure to every individual in the community a standard of living adequate for the maintenance of health.

Public health is therefore a very broad church indeed. This is seen as problematic because, as Griffiths and Hunter (1999, p. 1) have observed, if public health can encapsulate so many things, it risks being nothing more than a confusing and diffuse collection of ideas that cannot deliver a concrete product.

1

Another perceived problem is that public health often lacks coherence because of the range of competing perspectives, which emphasise different priorities and modes of intervention. Some – particularly those adopting an orthodox medical model – focus on the prevention of specific diseases, through immunisation, health screening and surveillance, and the treatment of the early stages of disease. Some place their faith in health education and in improving the flow of information to the public in the hope that this will lead to healthier lifestyles. Others see a much greater role for government in regulating economic, social and environmental factors linked to ill health.

Different interests favour their own particular interpretations of public health, and their interplay establishes its meaning. The interpretation of public health is therefore an essentially political process. But this is not all, as the various public health perspectives also connect with wider political debates, such as those surrounding the role of the state and the protection of individual liberty. Furthermore, public health strategies and policies are themselves shaped by the interplay of political forces in government and in society at large. Clearly then, a political analysis of public health is entirely appropriate.

This book adopts such an approach. It is primarily concerned with the political debates surrounding public health and their implications for the emergence, formation and implementation of public health strategies and policies. One must, however, devise a coherent analytical framework in order to avoid a purely descriptive account. Several alternative frameworks exist (see Signal, 1998, for an example of the applied political analysis of health promotion). Of these, three approaches seem particularly appropriate to this study: ideological perspectives on the role of the state and the individual; models of the policy process; and theories of risk and expertise. Each will now be discussed in turn.

# Ideologies

Public health reflects key ideological debates regarding the freedom of the individual, the authority of the state and the balance between individual and collective responsibilities (see Mills and Saward, 1993). Three broad ideological perspectives are relevant here: collectivism/socialism; individualism/ libertarianism; and environmental/green ideology.

## *Collectivist and Socialist Perspectives*

Collectivists and socialists place great emphasis on the role of the state and other collective arrangements (such as voluntary mutual societies and co-operative efforts) and are highly critical of self-centred individualism. They are particularly cynical about the ability of isolated individuals to produce their own solutions to complex social problems. There is certainly some foundation for this cynicism in the field of public health, where, according to Rose (1985, p. 138), 'a preventive measure which brings much benefit to the population offers little to each participating individual'. This 'prevention paradox' implies that, left to their own devices, individuals have little incentive to contribute towards activities that improve public health. Collectivists have long argued that state intervention is the principal means of social improvement (see Berki, 1975; Crick, 1987). More recently, however, a specific concern about the adverse effects of state intervention has influenced both collectivist thought and the views of practising politicians who claim to hold this creed. In the UK, this was reflected in the endorsement by the Labour Party leadership of alternative ideas about the state intervention that claimed to accommodate greater individual choice and responsibility (see Jones, 1996; Tam, 1998).

'Public health', as Sears (1992, p. 65) has observed, 'was identified with the state from the outset'. The broader definition of public health discussed earlier certainly justifies a key role for the state in protecting citizens' health while providing a rationale for specific health policy interventions. From a collectivist standpoint, this includes ameliorating the health-damaging consequences of individualism and tackling the socio-economic causes of ill health generated by capitalism (Navarro, 1976; Doyal, 1979; Allsop, 1990). Indeed, as Beauchamp (1988) has argued, the protection of health depends in part on preventing the market from invading other spheres. Furthermore, the appeal to resist the market on grounds of health is a powerful one. As Dicey (quoted in Weale, 1983, p. 806) has observed, 'a collectivist never holds a stronger position than when he advocates the best ascertained laws of health'. From a socialist or collectivist perspective, equity in health is a key element of social justice. Intervention is justified not merely to protect individuals from specific threats to health, such as junk food or noxious emissions from factories, but to promote the health of everyone, irrespective of social class, income, gender or ethnic background. As will become clear, these notions of equity are an integral part of the *Health for All* perspective.

Finally, socialist and collectivist perspectives on liberty are used to justify certain types of public health intervention. In contrast to the conventional liberal approach, discussed below, positive liberty (Green, 1911; Berlin, 1969) is given greater weight than negative liberty, the freedom from interference. Positive liberty concerns the extent to which individuals are in control of their own fate and free from circumstances that limit their opportunities. Hence state intervention and other forms of collective action can be justified on the grounds that such restrictions actually empower individuals to take control of their lives and make informed choices. This view is articulated by Beauchamp (1988), for example, who argues that advances in public health and prevention can actually expand the liberties of citizens. Labonte (1998) pursues a similar line in relation to health promotion. He contends that arguments for social justice, which strongly reflect notions of positive liberty, are more consistent with the historical practice of public health, with contemporary international health accords, and with current evidence on the impact of economic equality and environmental sustainability upon health. They therefore outweigh considerations about individual (that is, negative) liberties. Labonte stresses, however, that libertarian theory offers an important caution against the under-mining of individual autonomy by the state and that a social justice approach must be complemented by 'deliberative democratic practice' in order to avoid interventions that marginalise and exclude socially disadvantaged groups.

## Liberal Individualist Perspectives

As already suggested, the liberal individualist perspective places a much greater emphasis on negative liberty, the freedom to pursue one's activities without interference from the state, providing others are not harmed as a result (Berlin, 1969; Mill, 1974). Those adopting this perspective argue that the collectivist state is not a benign or even neutral force, but a hostile entity that coerces and disempowers citizens (Hayek, 1976, 1988). They argue that individuals are in greater need of protection from the state than from the vagaries of the market. Individual liberty can be saved only by strengthening the market sphere and increasing self-reliance among ordinary citizens. Neo-liberalism – the revitalised version of this philosophy (Green, 1987; King, 1987) – provided a blueprint for political action to reverse the tide of collectivism and had a major ideological influence on British governments during the 1980s and 90s (see Gamble, 1994).

Specifically in relation to public health, liberal individualists argue that it is unfair for the majority of individuals to sacrifice their personal freedom for an illusory common good. The prevention paradox, noted earlier, is from this point of view an illustration of this unfairness. Proponents of this view call for an increase in individual responsibility for health and believe that individuals should make their own informed choices rather than be told what to do by the 'nanny state' or the 'food and drink police' (Bennett and DiLorenzo, 1999; see also Appleyard, 1994).

According to the liberal individualist critique, the state bureaucracy has a vested interest in regulating and controlling certain activities, and consequently has an incentive to exaggerate certain risks. It is argued that budgets, careers and status depend on an expansion of bureaucratic and regulatory functions (see Berger, 1991; Booker and North, 1994). But there is a high price to pay: regulatory overkill imposes high social costs, including restricting liberties, discouraging risk taking and enterprise, and reducing the efficiency and profitability of corporations (Neal and Davies, 1998). According to Skrabanek (1994) this can give rise to 'healthism', in which the promotion of health through collective means becomes a part of state ideology. He notes that an extreme form of this existed in Nazi Germany, where fascism was intimately connected with a set of beliefs about the state's role in public health (see Procter, 1988). Ideas about racial purity and the quality of 'human stock' have not, however, been confined to Fascists. At the beginning of the twentieth century, such ideas had wide currency in liberal democratic states and were seen as providing a solution to the problem of national efficiency (see Searle, 1976; Nottingham, 1999).

It has also been argued that the elevation of health over other considerations facilitates the domination of individuals by 'health experts', particularly the medical profession. According to Skrabanek (1994), again, 'healthism' is driven by a desire for power and control by doctors. Echoing Illich (1977), he perceives a medicalisation process whereby the medical profession seeks to extend its expertise to other spheres of social and economic life. Liberal individualists are particularly fearful of the incorporation of such expertise into government, leading to the creation of an 'expert bureaucracy' that can dictate to and dominate individuals. The role of experts in identifying and disseminating knowledge about health risks is discussed in more detail later in the context of social and cultural models of risk and expertise.

## *Environmental and Green Ideology*

Those adopting a Green perspective oppose the destructiveness of industrial society, in particular its pursuit of economic growth at all costs. They reject both previously discussed ideologies, although they are arguably closer to the socialist/collectivist perspective, particularly in relation to concepts of social justice and the countervailing power of collectivism (see Ryle, 1988). Greens are suspicious of individual libertarian arguments, seeing them as a cynical means of justifying non-interventionism and corporate exploitation, but are at the same time wary of state power, believing that large state bureaucracies can be equally oppressive towards individuals and as damaging to the environment as private corporations. Hence they place an emphasis on the role of individuals and small, local groups in promoting a sustainable environment (see Porritt and Winner, 1989; Dobson, 1990). However, as Adams (1993, p. 318) has observed, 'while there is a good deal of consensus about what Greens are against, there is much less agreement about what Greens are for'. There are in practice many shades of green, which differ considerably in their aims, ideas and prescriptions for change.

Green perspectives adopt an ecological model of health (Hançock, 1985; Draper, 1991; Pietroni, 1991). This places an emphasis on the complex and multiple sources of illness arising from the environment in which people live.

In particular, mankind's interaction with the natural environment and other species is seen as a crucial factor in the maintenance of health. Hence many of the major health problems of our time, such as foodborne illness and diseases linked to pollution, are viewed as a product of the human exploitation of the environment. Greens believe that the social and economic structure of industrial society is also damaging in view of its tendency to create unhealthy lifestyles and working patterns, as well as to produce socio-economic inequalities that undermine health.

Greens argue for an holistic solution to the environmental and public health problems of industrial societies. They argue for sustainable development, balancing economic, social and environmental considerations. They also support 'precautionary' principles – believing that early intervention on the basis of limited information, rather than waiting for concrete evidence of irreversible and widespread harm, is warranted to prevent serious damage to environment and health (see O' Riordan and Cameron, 1994, for a comprehensive discussion of this principle). However, despite criticism that their views are Utopian, those adopting a Green perspective are prepared to endorse specific practical solutions (such as a ban on lead additives in petrol, for example) that they believe can contribute in a small but significant way to a healthier environment.

In summary, public health can be seen as an arena in which the various ideological perspectives discussed in this section compete for supremacy. When framing policy, decision-makers and those seeking to influence them may draw to some extent on these sets of ideas. It is therefore important that this study explores the extent to which these perspectives have prevailed, particularly within governing institutions, as well as in society at large, in order to assess their impact on public health policy.

# Models of the Policy Process

Another possible framework involves an examination of how public health strategies and policies have emerged and developed within the policy process. It is helpful to analyse these processes by using models of policy making (see, for example, Howlett and Ramesh, 1995; Parsons, 1995; John, 1998). Three main approaches are particularly useful in analysing public health policy.

## *Institutional Politics*

One way of explaining public health policy is to see it as a product of interaction within and between different political institutions. These include central government departments and agencies, Parliament and the media, as well as subnational institutions such as local government and NHS health authorities, and supranational institutions such as the European Commission and the World Health Organization (WHO).

An institutional approach focuses on the processes of agenda setting, policy formation and policy implementation, and the ways in which these processes are influenced by relationships and procedures within and between institutions. One can also include within the realm of institutional politics informal arrangements such as policy networks (Marsh and Rhodes, 1992; Marsh, 1998a). These networks encompass pressure groups, government agencies and other participants having an interest in a specific policy area. The configuration of policy networks varies: some, known as policy communities, are exclusive, stable, highly integrated and involve a high degree of interdependence between the participants. Others, known as issue networks, are less integrated, more open and more unstable, and their members are not interdependent. It has been argued that the configuration of these networks has a major influence on the development of policy (see Marsh, 1998b). Others disagree, although they accept that policy networks provide a metaphor for the policy process (Dowding, 1995). Empirical work in this field has led to suggestions that policy networks vary and change over time and that this can have implications for policy development (Baumgartner and Jones, 1993; Heinz *et al.*, 1993; Marsh, 1998a).

## Pressure-group Politics

Another way of conceptualising public health policy is to view it as the product of interaction between different interests articulated by pressure groups. This is likely to be fruitful given the range of groups involved in this field: business organisations such as the alcohol and tobacco industry; professional organisations such as the Royal Colleges and the British Medical Association (BMA); as well as welfare groups and environmental pressure groups. In addition, there are single issue groups campaigning on specific public health issues, such as Action on Smoking and Health, the Campaign Against Drinking and Driving, and the Food Commission, as well as umbrella groups such as the UK Public Health Alliance.

A pressure group is an organisation that seeks to represent interests or preferences in society, has a certain degree of independence from government and is not a recognised political party (see Baggott, 1995 pp. 2–3). There are several different approaches to the study of pressure-group politics but most seek to explore how groups' resources, political contacts and status within the political process relate to their influence over policy. Studies of pressure groups also examine the environment within which groups interact with each other and with government, and how this affects their influence. Grant's (1989) distinction between insider and outsider groups is based on an acknowledgement that insider groups are given privileged access to decision makers in government and that this enhances their potential influence over policy. Modifications to this model have since been proposed by others, including Maloney, Jordan and McLaughlin (1994), who argue that insider status (conferred by government) should not be confused with insider strategy (when a group decides for itself how it will pursue its campaign) and that insider status is further differentiated (into core, specialist and peripheral insider status, each of which carries different weight in the policy process).

Pressure-group analysis is also concerned with how public support is mobilised (Jordan and Maloney, 1997; Ridley and Jordan, 1998) and how pressure groups relate to other 'pressure points' in the political system, such as Parliament (Rush, 1990), supranational decision makers (Mazey and Richardson, 1992) and the media (Baggott, 1995; see Chapter 8). Finally, pressure-group analysts are interested in how groups, often with a very different background and ethos, collaborate with each other and form coalitions to press for a common policy.

## *Policy Knowledge and Policy Learning*

Alternatively, public health policy can be seen as emerging from the interplay of ideas and knowledge. One can fashion a rather simple model in which policy is implemented in response to a perceived social problem on the basis of advice from experts and other interested parties. This is, however, rather unrealistic. In practice, the movement of an issue on to the political agenda is a complex process. Kingdon (1984) has explained how the prospects of a policy reaching the agenda are shaped by several factors. Policy development is probable when there is coincidence between (a) the processes that identify problems, (b) the processes that promote ideas on how to tackle problems, and (c) the processes of decision making and public debate (for example, government organisations, Parliament, pressure groups and the media). Kingdon adopts the term 'policy window' to describe such a state of affairs.

Opportunities to promote policy change are, however, limited. According to Baumgartner and Jones (1993), institutional arrangements can restrict access and inhibit the intrusion of new ideas. In effect, a 'policy monopoly' is created, which is resistant to certain interests and ideas. Such a monopoly can be challenged by redefining policy problems and setting new agendas in such a way that excluded interests have to be incorporated. Similarly, Majone (1989) has argued that discussion and argument are institutionalised and, as a result, the choice of policy options is constrained. Furthermore, like Baumgartner and Jones, he acknowledges that institutional arrangements are not immutable. Actors can seek to change institutional arrangements 'that either give them new resources or increase the value of those they already have' (pp. 102–3).

Persuasion is also an important weapon within the policy process, but, as Majone observes, some policies are more highly resistant to change than others. Much seems to depend on how deeply rooted such policies are in the core beliefs of political actors. This view is endorsed by Sabatier (1987; see also Jenkins-Smith and Sabatier, 1993), who has attempted to explain policy change in terms of advocacy coalitions. Advocacy coalitions comprise actors within the policy process who share a set of beliefs about policy and who often act in concert. According to Sabatier, policy change can occur as a result of a change in the beliefs of advocacy coalitions, a change in the composition of a coalition or a change in the relative strength of competing coalitions (which is in turn dependent upon resources such as money, expertise, the number of supporters and legal authority). In the absence of external 'perturbations' (such as broader political or socio-economic changes) fundamental policy beliefs are, however, unlikely to change, and this means that, in practice, the core policies of government are relatively consistent over time.

The work of Sabatier and Majone is a refreshing response to simplistic models of policy making that assume the adoption of rational solutions to policy problems. Meanwhile, empirical work on the role of expert policy advisors has confirmed that that scientific findings are not automatically translated into policy, but are filtered through a political process (Jasanoff, 1990; Collingridge and Reeve, 1986; Barker and Peters, 1993a). Experts are valued by politicians not merely for their knowledge and advice, but because they give legitimacy to government decisions (Barker and Peters, 1993b). Indeed, as Fischer (1990) observed, as politics becomes a more technologically oriented task, the expertise of technocrats becomes a key resource in governance. For example, politicians may use their scientific findings to justify action or inaction, to gain public support for new policy initiatives or to reassure the public that all is well. Alternatively, the government may attempt to suppress findings, and in such situations doctors or other scientific experts may find themselves engaging in wider public debate in order to bring about policy change.

Finally, any study of public policy, even if undertaken primarily within one country, must be aware of the comparative dimension, in particular the tendency for policy makers in one country to borrow ideas from others. This can occur by drawing lessons (such as on drug decriminalisation) from particular countries. Alternatively, supranational organisations, such as multinational companies, international pressure groups or European or United Nations (UN) institutions, may be directly involved in promoting particular policies at the global or regional level. By the same token, it is also possible for policies in one country to be rejected or discouraged as result of adverse experiences elsewhere or because of opposition from international players. Given that public health has an important international dimension – disease does not respect borders – these transmission and inhibition mechanisms are likely to be important.

Having examined relevant policy models, it appears that the key questions for this study are as follows. First, it needs to examine the extent to which public health policies in the UK have been developed or inhibited by initiatives from international organisations, networks or institutions, or by policies transmitted from other countries. Second, it must look at the interaction of pressure groups with regard to public health policies, in particular whether policies have been advanced (or blocked) by relatively powerful interests with insider status. It is also important to explore how groups have mobilised public opinion, the media or Parliament in order to influence policy. Third, the study must consider how public health experts have operated within the political process and the extent to which their findings have influenced policy. Fourth, the impact of policy networks and political institutions must be examined in order to assess their effect on public health policy. Finally, the study needs to see if political actors have learned from their participation in the policy process and the implications of this.

# Risk and Expertise

A third approach reflects the important role played by technical experts in the field of public health. Their role has often gone beyond that discussed earlier of advising government, legitimising policy or even campaigning directly for policy change. Experts, and the concepts they employ, appear to have a much broader social and cultural influence over the parameters of political debate, policy agenda and policy outcome, with important consequences for the autonomy and liberty of the individual. A number of writers have explored the influence of technical experts over the concept of risk in contemporary societies. Similar themes can be found in their work – the shaping of public perceptions of risk by experts, variations in the level of public awareness and fear of risks, and a tendency for 'risk expertise' to promote a greater regulation of human activities. These contributions, however, also differ in several important respects, as will become clear.

## Risk Society

It has been argued by Giddens (1991) and Beck (1992) that we live in a 'risk society', in which political conflict is increasingly defined by high-consequence risks linked to industrialisation and globalisation (see also Lash *et al.*, 1996). There is a declining faith in scientific experts as individuals become ever more anxious about the hazards of everyday life. Scientific calculations of risk lose credibility as they seem to be inconsistent with individuals' own perceptions, partly shaped by direct experience and partly indirectly, through the media. Meanwhile, a declining consensus among technical experts further under-mines their public credibility. As conventional science loses its dominant posi-tion in relation to other explanations of risk, it is transformed by the opening up of critical debates about scientific purpose and ethos.

Other writers have focused on the processes by which risks are identified and pay particular attention to the use of risk identification and prevention as a means of social control. Castel (1991) explicitly applied Foucault's work on governmentality to prevention strategies in health and social policy. He argued that there had been a shift in emphasis over the past century from 'dangerousness' to 'risk', shifting the focus of policy away from individuals manifesting signs and symptoms of impending illness, abnormality or social deviance, towards anticipating and preventing problems. Meanwhile, specifi-cally in relation to health, Skrabanek (1994) coined the term 'anticipatory medicine' to describe a new mode of surveillance involving the scrutiny of risk factors in the population as a whole as a basis for intervention.

According to Castel, the wider political ramification of a preventive approach was the erosion of professional power by administrators, who control the technologies of health surveillance and the flow of information and resources. He also noted that these new strategies for administering populations were consistent with a plan of governability appropriate to the needs of advanced industrial societies. This is underlined by Freeman's (1992, 1995) point that prevention policies and processes of risk identification are useful in the management of health and social problems even though they may not actually ameliorate these problems.

A further point made by Castel is that the preventive approach gives rise to greater social exclusion, as he argues that such a regime provides the basis for differential modes of treatment for populations, which aim to 'maximise the returns on doing what is possible and to marginalise the unprofitable' (p. 294). In order to achieve this, individuals can be assigned different social destinies according to their ability to contribute to economic competitiveness and profitability. In addition, he suggests that modern ideologies of prevention are oppressive. These arguments echo those articu-lated earlier by Stone (1989), who saw preventive strategies as a sinister tool of government that threatened liberty and social cohesion by adopting puni-tive and exclusionary forms of control.

## Other Critiques of Prevention

Armstrong (1993) and Petersen and Lupton (see Lupton, 1995; Petersen and Lupton, 1996; Petersen, 1997) adopt a similarly critical approach towards prevention. Armstrong examined the way in which four different regimes of public health delineated spaces in which individual identity is located, these being quarantine, sanitary science, personal hygiene and new public health. Each of these was identified as being dominant in a particular historical period and linked to a mode of control: quarantine represents a simple line of inclusion and exclusion; sanitary science regulates the movement between different spaces; and personal hygiene regulates a psychosocial space regarding attitudes and behaviours. According to Armstrong, the fourth regime – new public health – can be distinguished from previous regulatory approaches in the way in which it generalises danger, increases the scope of surveillance and attempts to gear many aspects of behaviour to health objectives.

Petersen and Lupton take a similar line, arguing that 'the new public health can be seen as but the most recent of a series of regimes of power and knowledge that are oriented to the regulation and surveillance of individual bodies and the social body as a whole' (Petersen and Lupton, 1996, p. 3). They contend that, in modern societies, public health is comprehensive in its scope, providing opportunities for the state to engage in moral regulation aimed at making subjects more self-regulating and productive in order to serve society's broader interests. This point is enthusiastically made by others, including Bennett and DiLorenzo (1999), who argue that public health policies, especially in the realm of food and drink, reflect efforts by 'nannies and busybodies' to impose moral regulation on the masses.

While accepting Castel's point about the growing power of administrators, Petersen and Lupton argue that preventive strategies also enhance the power of professionals (in particular doctors and epidemiologists) as the scope of expert surveillance, assessment and intervention is extended. Epidemiology, for example, is held to perform several crucial regulatory roles in relation to the discovery of disease, the evaluation of intervention and the identification of priorities and risk factors. They are particularly interested in the ways in which public health science is socially constructed. They argue that epidemiology constructs patterns of causation through particular expectations and processes of investigation, not to mention the selective use of evidence. Similar concerns about the exaggeration of risk by epidemiological studies have been raised by Lee (1994), Skrabanek (1994), Beaver (1997), Bennett and DiLorenzo (1999) and Feinstein (1999); see also Le Fanu (1994a) and Bate (1999). These studies agree that risk is a social construct, often dominated by dubious epidemiological concepts.

## Trust and Uncertainty

The above approach seems to contradict the Beck/Giddens standpoint maintaining that the experts' monopoly of rationality is broken as people lose faith in conventional science. Even Furedi (1997), who leans towards the Beck/Giddens position by acknowledging declining levels of trust in certain traditional forms of technical expertise, observes that new forms of expertise play a key role in the social construction of environmental, social and public health risks. These might include experts in the application of the precautionary principle, those with a vested interest in identifying new risks and potential victims. Like some of the writers mentioned above, Furedi also identifies the crucial role of experts in constructing public health and is similarly critical of the quality of their knowledge base, challenging the grounds on which epidemiological models of causation are based. He notes the tendency of the professions most closely associated with the new public health philosophy to exaggerate risks and manipulate information, while prioritising certain health risks that are not necessarily the greatest hazards facing individuals and society.

Furedi shares Petersen and Lupton's (1996) concern about the moral regulation implicit in modern public health, but goes further in some respects by delineating what he sees as the debilitating and damaging impact of this philosophy upon innovation, experimentation and human intellectual activity. He also argues that the breakdown of trust in society is a symptom rather than a cause of the heightened awareness of risks, maintaining that 'a culture of fear', inspired by professionals with a vested interest in identifying risks and victims in the context of an increasingly individualised society, has been a crucial factor in the decline of trust in traditional forms of expertise and institutions.

In contrast, Wynne (1996) argues that unqualified public trust in scientific experts has never in fact prevailed. In his view, science has been regarded with much suspicion in the past, and with good reason. Far from being objective, scientific knowledge is pervaded with indeterminate practices, is uncertain, and produces unanticipated consequences (see also Adams (1995) who is similarly critical of the contribution of science to the understanding of problems involving uncertainty). Even so, scientific models have been imposed on lay people despite the fact that the latter have much to contribute to the understanding of risks and hazards.

Wildavsky (1988, 1991) (see also Douglas and Wildavsky, 1982) also challenges claims made by scientists about the risks of modern society. He believes that science is dominated in such a way that risks are exaggerated and that the benefits of technology are not fully appreciated. Douglas and Wildavsky (1982) further argue that cultural factors play a major role in the growth of risk perceptions, and that, in particular, the growth of voluntary egalitarian associations (including environmental and public health campaign groups) has created incentives for the state (and scientists) to identify and respond to risks. Wildavsky, like Beck and Giddens, places faith in reformed science (and reformed decision-making institutions generally) to clear up misunderstandings and uncertainties, while taking a different view on the actual magnitude of risk.

In spite of the different positions taken on science and risk, it is clear that the identification and assessment of risk is a social process. All too often, as Horlick-Jones (1998, p. 87) has argued, the debate is seen in terms of bridging the gap between hard scientific approaches to risk and soft judgemental and value-laden perspectives. Horlick-Jones goes on to argue for an approach that allows the 'contextualisation of scientific knowledge and the integration of knowledges' in order to find ways of effectively managing complex risks.

The above discussion has identified a number of controversies that are relevant to this study of public health and which it must focus upon. It needs to explore whether public health risks are increasing or whether they are merely *perceived* to be increasing. The study must also examine why the public appears to be losing faith in public health experts and government with regard to public health issues and consider the relevance of lay perspectives on public health issues. It is also important to ask what, if anything, should be done to restore public confidence in the management of health risks and the promotion of health. In addition, the study will examine the effect that some believe health concerns have had on the power of expert groups and the implications of this for individual liberty.

The questions and themes identified in this chapter will be explored in the context of a wide range of public health issues and will be returned to in the concluding chapter. In Chapters 2 and 3, the history of public health is outlined, focusing on the factors that have shaped public health intervention in the UK up to the 1990s. In Chapter 4, the development of health strategies in the 1990s is examined. Chapters 5 and 6 explore the public health functions of the National Health Service (NHS): the former considers public health medicine along with the public health aspects of primary care, while the latter examines cancer screening policy. In Chapter 7, the focus is upon environmental health in its widest sense, and this is followed by a discussion of food policy in Chapter 8. The public health problems associated with alcohol, tobacco and other drugs are examined in Chapter 9, while Chapter 10 analyses the broader socio-economic context of public health.

# 2

# The Historical Context of Public Health

As Rosen's (1993) impressive history of public health demonstrated, efforts to promote health and prevent disease were undertaken even by the earliest civilisations. Evidence from ancient sites in what is now part of India indicates that the importance of water and sewerage systems, paved streets and town planning was recognised as long ago as 2000 BC. Archaeological evidence also confirms that other ancient civilisations such as the Egyptians and the Incas understood the importance of urban planning and sanitation. It also appears that some ancient civilisations sought to impose rules in an effort to promote health. The Babylonians, for example, drew up strict public health regulations governing personal behaviour, while the Egyptians promoted the value of good diet and hygiene among their people (Inglis, 1965).

As Rosen explains, many of the ancient civilisations were concerned about cleanliness because of religious beliefs and practices. This was particularly true of the Egyptians, Mesopotamians and Hebrews. Disease was often associated in ancient cultures with the cosmos and divine retribution. It was not until fifth century BC in Ancient Greece that evidence of a more rational, scientific approach to public health began to emerge (for a further discussion, see Kitto, 1957). *Airs, Waters and Places*, attributed to Hippocrates, discussed the importance of the ecological balance between man and the environment, as well as the role of climate, soil, water and nutrition in the maintenance of good health. In so doing, it provided not only an explanation for ill health, but also practical recommendations for avoiding disease. Hence rivers were diverted to dry out marshland in an effort to prevent malaria. In fact, as Rosen points out, although the observed association between marshland and malaria provided a sound basis for their intervention, the Greeks got the precise causal process wrong in this particular case as they believed that the disease was caused by drinking swamp water.

The Romans were also aware of the health implications of the environment, in particular sanitation. They not only built impressive aqueducts, public bathing facilities and sewerage systems, but additionally devised new techniques to purify water supplies. They were also aware of other links between environment and health, documenting the association between occupation and illness, for example. The poorer classes, however, never really benefited from these advances in knowledge. Notably, as Inglis (1965) observed, the Romans were unable to prevent the outbreak of epidemics such as smallpox and plague. Indeed, the Roman Empire, especially the movement of goods and people it generated, provided ideal conditions for the spread of infectious disease across a large geographical area (McNeill, 1976).

As the Roman Empire declined, its system of public health decayed, and the knowledge built up by the classic civilisations was either lost or fell into abeyance. In the Middle Ages, epidemics struck regularly and often with terrifying severity, the Black Death of the fourteenth century being a prime example. The main response to such outbreaks was to isolate those infected. This was rarely undertaken with any clear plan in mind, although, as Rosen (1993) notes, quarantine methods began to improve from the middle of the fourteenth century, large commercial ports such as Venice leading the way.

Once an epidemic spread beyond the major ports, each settlement responded in its own way. The methods adopted were crude, often brutal. Those suspected of being infected were incarcerated in their own homes in an effort to halt the spread of infection. The corpses of the dead were either buried in mass graves outside the town or city, or burned. Victims' belongings were usually incinerated and their homes fumigated. Harsh regimes of isolation were also imposed on those suffering from chronic diseases, where there was a fear of contamination. Leprosy sufferers, for example, were banished from society to live in isolated colonies. Before an individual was removed, a religious service would be held to signify their 'social death' (Rosen, 1993, p. 41).

Yet isolation was not the only method used to combat disease during the Middle Ages. As Simon (1890) indicated, limited public health measures were introduced in some cities from the twelfth and thirteenth centuries onwards. In London, for example, regulations were introduced in the latter part of the twelfth and the early-thirteenth century to control a range of activities believed to be hazardous to health. These included restrictions on pigsties and stray animals, regulations for 'offensive trades', street cleaning and the dumping of waste, and rules concerning the slaughter of animals. Some European cities, such as Paris and Prague, sought to improve the local environment by paving their streets, making them easier to cleanse. Some cities established municipal abattoirs in an effort to prevent offal littering the streets, while others established food inspection and market regulations to try to protect citizens from contaminated or dirty food. Such rules were apparently enforced quite vigorously, with severe penalties for those who transgressed them (Rosen, 1993).

In the centuries following the Black Death, societies responded to the threat of disease in a piecemeal and reactive fashion. For example, a syphilis epidemic in Europe at the end of the fifteenth century led to the closure of brothels, the medical examination of prostitutes and compulsory 'treatment' for sufferers. The basis for a more systematic approach to public health nevertheless grew, albeit slowly, as a result of important studies such as Fracastoro's enquiry into contagion and epidemics in the sixteenth century and that of Sydenham into the causes of acute fever in the next century. There were also studies of particular sections of the population, such as Agricola's study of illness in miners in the sixteenth century and Graunt's work on variations in death rates, which appeared in the 1660s.

Efforts to analyse the underlying causes of disease increased during the Enlightenment period, and a number of significant public health interventions also emerged around this time. The Gin Act of 1751, for example, imposed a high tax on the product and restricted its availability. Cheap gin had, from the 1720s onwards, been held responsible for a range of social ills (consequences depicted famously by Hogarth's etching *Gin Lane*), not least of which was a rising death rate. Around the middle of the eighteenth century, there was also much interest in possible ways of improving the health of seamen and soldiers (Inglis, 1965). James Lind demonstrated that scurvy – a seemingly unavoidable consequence of long sea voyages – was caused by an inadequate diet and could be prevented by issuing fresh fruit rations. Captain Cook successfully tested his thesis, but the Admiralty was not convinced until the early years of the following century. Sir John Pringle's analysis of epidemics in the army had a similar fate. Pringle identified a range of conditions – overcrowded accommodation, inadequate ventilation, poor sanitation – that were associated with common epidemics such as typhus, although the military authorities ignored his recommendations for many years.

As the eighteenth century came to a close, it appeared that public health was being taken more seriously by those in power. Rosen (1993) notes that some municipal corporations began to take more interest in improving the civic environment and obtained private Improvement Acts to this end. Some also began to tackle specific problems, such as polluted water supplies and offensive trades. But the extent to which powers were used and rules were enforced was another matter. Towns and cities lacked a coherent system of public health administration, and efforts to introduce such a system (as in Manchester, which established a Board of Health in 1796) were rare and enjoyed limited success. During the eighteenth century, concern for public health also arose out of the prison reform movement. Indeed, the work of John Howard and others is credited with giving an important impetus to the public health movement (Patterson, 1948). Campaigners began to examine the causes of disease, for example, typhus in jails, and identified possible ways of preventing illness, such as improved hygiene, ventilation and sanitation, and the segregation of sick and healthy prisoners.

No account of the history of public health would be complete without mentioning the work of Edward Jenner (Fisher, 1991). In the last years of the eighteenth century, Jenner famously discovered that cowpox vaccination gave protection against smallpox. This represented an advance on an earlier discovery, which had been publicised by Lady Mary Wortley Montagu in the 1720s. While resident in Turkey as the wife of the English Ambassador, Lady Montagu learned of a process called variolation, in which pus taken from a smallpox sufferer was injected into a healthy person. Although this procedure could save lives, it was risky and time consuming as the patient required a long period of preparation and convalescence. Jenner took this a stage further by suggesting that infection with cowpox, a milder illness than smallpox, could provide protection against the more serious disease. He subsequently proved this through experimentation, inoculating a child first with cowpox and then with smallpox. Although the initial reaction of the scientific community was not positive, other doctors soon took an interest in vaccination. By Victorian times, vaccination against smallpox was commonplace, becoming compulsory in the 1850s.

The above discussion hopefully goes some way to correcting a common misunderstanding that public health began (and ended) with the Victorians. It is, however, undeniable that the Victorians introduced many important public health reforms, and these will now be discussed. The intention is not to provide a detailed history of Victorian public health – for this the reader is directed to comprehensive historical accounts such as those of Simon (1890), Flinn (1968), Smith (1979) and Wohl (1984). Instead, the aim is to conduct a more general analysis of public health in Victorian times, focusing particularly on the political context.

Two main phases of public health during the nineteenth century are usually identified (Kickbusch, 1986; Fee and Porter, 1992; Armstrong, 1993). The first and earlier phase is known as the sanitary revolution, the main aim of reformers being to improve health through a better physical environment. The second and subsequent phase emphasised personal health and hygiene, and involved the development of specific health and welfare services to promote health and prevent disease.

## The Victorian Sanitary Revolution

As has been indicated, some towns and cities were beginning to take action to improve the local environment long before the Victorians began their sanitary crusade. It is therefore reasonable to conclude that at least some communities had good intentions regarding public health, but were unable to cope with the tide of problems that industrialisation brought in its wake. The influx of people to the newly industrialised towns and cities (Figure 2.1) created problems that even the most enlightened of local administrations would have found difficult to handle.

It is difficult to believe that early nineteenth century political élites were completely oblivious to the social consequences of industrialisation. There was at this time little political will to deal with these problems, although attempts were made to confront the worst practices. A number of Acts concerning factories and workplaces were, for example, introduced before the dawn of the Victorian era. However, as Trevelyan (1973, p. 484) observed, they 'were not only very limited in scope, but remained dead letters for want of any machinery to enforce them'. An awareness of the health and social problems associated with industrialisation was clearly not enough: cause and effect had to be clearly established, feasible solutions identified and, of course, the case for reform accepted by political élites. This was a tall order in an era dominated by liberal free market ideas.

Yet reformers had one thing in their favour: the Victorians' obsession with rational solutions and facts (Fraser, 1973). Research findings provided much of the impetus for sanitary reform. Local studies had been undertaken in several towns from the late eighteenth century onwards. The pioneering work of Haygarth (in Chester) and Heysham (in Carlisle) led the way for

**Figure 2.1**    Population growth in the early nineteenth century

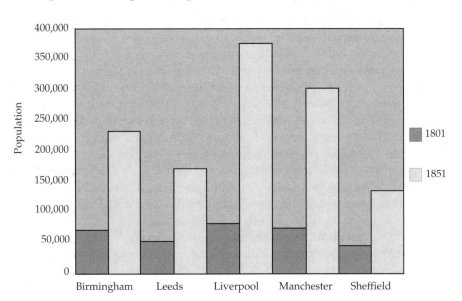

subsequent enquiries into the condition of the people in the newly industrialised districts, such as Kay's (1832) study of the Manchester slums. These
documented high levels of illness among the poor and attracted the attention
of the Poor Law Commission, the body responsible for the system of relief to
those in poverty. The Poor Law Commission was established in 1834 by the
Poor Law Amendment Act, the main intention of which had been to reform
the system of poor relief in order to reduce the burden on local rate payers.
The key principle of this new system was ' less eligibility': poor relief for the
able-bodied would be given in conditions that deterred all but the absolutely
destitute. Workhouses were built for this purpose, outdoor relief being
restricted to those who were aged, infirm or ill (although many of these actually ended up in the workhouse). The regime was harsh and led to
widespread protest. Although some of its worst aspects were tackled in 1847,
key elements of this system continued well into the next century.

Keen to explore any avenues that would reduce the burden that the poor
placed on rate payers, and would provide a more productive labouring population, the Poor Law Commission (prompted by Edwin Chadwick, the Secretary to the Commission, who was to play a major role in sanitary reform)
supported further studies into the possible link between illness and poverty.
In 1838, three doctors – Kay, Southwood Smith and Arnott – were appointed
to study conditions affecting public health in London. These findings
prompted further investigations culminating in Chadwick's report on *The
Sanitary Condition of the Labouring Population of Great Britain* (Chadwick, 1842).[1]
The publication of this report ensured that the research findings reached a
wide audience, around 20,000 copies apparently being sold in the fortnight
following publication and a further 3000 being given away free (Flinn, 1965).

Chadwick's report set the terms of the debate by clarifying the link
between physical environment and disease. Subsequent reports by the Royal
Commission on the State of Large Towns and Populous Districts (1844/1970,
1845/1970), in which the ubiquitous Chadwick was also involved, provided
detailed recommendations on sanitation and public health administration,
many of which were subsequently enshrined in law. The impact of the documentation of physical conditions and their health consequences was
augmented by reports from the Registrar-General's office, created in 1837. Its
driving force was William Farr, a statistician with a medical background. Farr
employed the vital statistics acquired through the registration process to illustrate the need for improvements in public health. In particular, the mortality
rates of poorer areas were highlighted in comparison with healthier areas,
giving further ammunition to public health reformers.

Mounting concern about the link between environment and ill health was
given a sharper focus by the death toll resulting from infectious diseases (see
Exhibit 2.1 below). Epidemics were particularly effective in drawing attention to
the need for reform. According to Hodgkinson (1967, p. 658), 'the chief impor-

tance of epidemics from the Public Health point of view was that they gave impetus to sanitary reform, for real panics made an ineffaceable impression'. Wohl (1984, p. 125) agreed, observing that fever drew attention to filthy conditions and to poverty, forcing the authorities to come to terms with public health.

---

Exhibit 2.1

---

## Infectious diseases

During the middle of the nineteenth century, infectious diseases were responsible for a third of all deaths in England and Wales (Logan, 1950), compared with less than 1 per cent today. Infectious diseases are, however, still among the biggest killers in poor countries. Worldwide, such diseases account for a third of all deaths, diarrhoea, tuberculosis, measles and malaria alone accounting for 10 million deaths every year (WHO, 1999a). There a number of other reasons, apart from concern about the health of people in the Third World, why industrialised countries such as the UK must continue to take infectious diseases seriously:

- The cost (both human and economic) of morbidity resulting from infections is significant. Consider, for example, food poisoning for which around 100,000 cases are notified each year in the UK.

- Infectious diseases disproportionately affect children, resulting in a significant loss of life years through premature death and in some cases a legacy of ill health over the lifetime of those who survive.

- In recent years, a range of chronic diseases have been linked to infectious agents (Parsonnet, 1999). These include stomach cancer (Parsonnet *et al.*, 1991), cervical cancer (see Chapter 6), childhood leukaemia (Kinlen, 1988, 1995; Stiller and Boyle, 1996), Kawasaki disease, a form of heart disease (Taubert and Shulman, 1999), multiple sclerosis (Skegg, 1991) and new variant CJD (see Chapter 8). This suggests that infectious diseases may today be responsible for a greater level of illness and mortality than official statistics suggest.

- Although the burden of infectious disease seems much less than it once was, the threat from epidemics remains, particularly in view of their potentially catastrophic consequences. The past is full of examples of large-scale epidemics, such as the Black Death, which carried off around a third of the English population in the fourteenth century, or, nearer our own time, the influenza epidemic of 1918/19, which was blamed for at least 20 million deaths (see Kolata, 2000). While alarming predictions of plague and pestilence in the new millennium may be exaggerated, one should not dismiss genuine concerns about the revival of longstanding infectious diseases and the emergence of new ones that pose a serious threat to human health.

Exhibit 2.1 *(cont'd)*

There is no doubt that diseases once thought to be conquered are more threatening. Tuberculosis notifications in England rose by 20 per cent between 1988 and 1998. There is particular concern about the emergence of forms of tuberculosis that are resistant to conventional treatment, part of a broader fear concerning microbial resistance to antibiotics. Johnson *et al.* (1996), for example, found that pneumococcal resistance to penicillin increased from 1.5 per cent to 3.9 per cent between 1990 and 1995, and that over the same period resistance to erythromycin rose from 2.8 to 8.6 per cent. The number of reported cases of methicillin-resistant *Staphylococcus aureus* meanwhile has also grown, adding to the problem of hospital-acquired infections. In addition, there are new infectious diseases, notably HIV/AIDS (see Exhibit 3.1), which infected around 30,000 in the UK up to the year 2000. Other infectious diseases causing concern are meningitis (almost 2000 cases and 242 deaths in England in 1998), viral hepatitis (almost 3000 cases and 165 deaths in the same year) and intestinal infections (384 deaths in 1998). On top of this are worries about the emergence of new strains of the influenza virus, an even more deadly form of the cholera bacteria and the spread of resistant strains of malaria, not to mention other more exotic agents such as the Ebola virus, which kills 90 per cent of those infected (see Garrett, 1994; Preston, 1994; Krause, 1998).

There are several reasons why infectious diseases may have begun to flourish. The indiscriminate use of antibiotics has undoubtedly been a key factor. Antibiotics are often used inappropriately to treat illnesses for which they have no therapeutic effect. As a result, microbial resistance increases and new strains may develop (DoH/SMAC, 1998; House of Lords, 1998a). Furthermore, antibiotics are also used in animals, to promote growth, despite evidence that this creates antimicrobial resistance here too. Even worse, it is known that these bacteria are transmitted through the food chain to humans, raising the possibility of infecting humans with resistant strains and the transfer of resistance to other organisms (see Glynn *et al.*, 1998; MAFF, 1998a; DoH/UK Advisory Committee on the Microbiological Safety of Food, 1999).

Other possible causes can also be found (see Wilson, 1995). Environmental factors, such as pollution, the thinning of the ozone layer and global warming, are all relevant. There is a belief that pollution may increase the potency of infective agents, although the precise mechanism is not known. The ozone layer protects humans and animals from ultraviolet rays, and any damage to it is likely to lead to a greater vulnerability to infection (see Chapter 7). Climatic change, however, poses the greatest threat of all. Hotter temperatures create ideal conditions for outbreaks of infectious disease. Malaria, for example, is likely to become a serious threat to public health in countries that were previously unaffected by the disease. It is also predicted that climate change will bring extreme weather conditions such as hurricanes, floods and other catastrophes, the aftermath of which will be extremely hospitable for the transmission of infectious agents.

Exhibit 2.1 *(cont'd)*

Other factors include increased trade and greater mobility, which increase the opportunity for the transport of microbes and their vectors. The greater mixing of populations, through new settlement patterns and migration, can also encourage the spread of infectious agents (see Wilson, 1995). Poverty is another factor in the development of infectious disease, not just in the Third World but in industrialised countries as well. Tuberculosis, for example, is clearly associated with poverty and deprivation rather than increased immigration, to which it is often attributed (Bhatti *et al.*, 1995; Mangtani *et al.*, 1995).

Media interest in infectious disease – particularly in the prospects of a large-scale epidemic – is guaranteed. This is sometimes misplaced, as in the coverage of the so-called 'flesh-eating bug' during 1994 (Gwyn, 1999). Nevertheless, as this exhibit suggests, there are genuine public concerns that cannot be lightly dismissed, not to mention doubts raised by scientists, doctors and pressure groups. The UK government has responded in a number of ways. In 1999, guidance was issued to the NHS to combat the overprescribing of antibiotics (DoH/NHSE, 1999). A public education campaign was also launched in the winter 1999/2000. Meanwhile, the Chief Medical Officer undertook a review of communicable disease strategy, due to report in the year 2000. This may lead to new legislation, although it should be pointed out that a recommendation in the Acheson Report on public health (Cm 289, 1988, p. 73) for a revised legislative framework for infectious disease was not pursued. More positively, in 1998, a new surveillance unit was established within the Public Health Laboratory Service to monitor the spread of antibiotic resistance. It should also be mentioned in this context that the World Health Assembly in 1999 resolved to counter the threat posed by the overuse of antibiotics and, in the previous year, the European Union took steps to tackle one aspect of this problem by banning four antibiotics used on animals (see Chapter 8).

Of all the Victorian epidemics, cholera made the greatest impression (Longmate, 1966; Morris, 1976), according to Wohl (1984) out of all proportion to its statistical importance (see Table 2.1). Other infectious diseases certainly killed more people (Creighton, 1965, p. 614). Between 1837 and the end of the century, smallpox killed over 200,000 people in England and Wales (44,000 in the period 1871–73 alone), measles over half a million (including 16,765 in 1887) and scarlet fever over three-quarters of a million (including 32,543 in 1870). Indeed, an analysis of data from the period 1848–72 has shown that the average mortality rates in Britain for men and women from typhus, smallpox, measles, scarlet fever, whooping cough and tuberculosis were all higher than those for cholera (Logan, 1950). Moreover, over the

**Table 2.1**    Cholera deaths in England and Wales:
main epidemics in the nineteenth century

| Year(s) of outbreak | Number of deaths |
| --- | --- |
| 1831–32 | 21,866 |
| 1848–49 | 53,293 |
| 1853–54 | 20,097 |
| 1866 | 14,378 |

*Source of data:* C. Creighton (1965) *A History of Epidemics*, Vol. 2,
London, Frank Cass

century, these diseases, along with typhoid, diphtheria and influenza, arguably represented a greater threat to health than cholera in terms of the number of people affected. But cholera epidemics induced a climate of fear that surpassed them all. It was the classic 'dread disease', striking quickly, often killing people within hours. The belief that cholera was caused by filthy living conditions and a poor physical environment added to the pressure for sanitary reform. The threat of further epidemics kept reform on the agenda when other political issues, such as the repeal of the corn laws and Chartist agitation, might have removed it. The outbreak of cholera in 1848, as Trevelyan noted, 'scared society into the tardy beginnings of sanitary self-defence' (1973, p. 529).

These 'tardy beginnings' took the form of the 1848 Public Health Act, which permitted localities outside London to establish health boards responsible for regulating practices and conditions that could harm health (such as offensive trades and houses unfit for human occupation), and for managing sanitation, waste disposal and other services such as burial grounds, backed up with the power to levy rates. The Act also established a central authority – the General Board of Health – which could in certain circumstances compel localities to establish health boards. The impact of this new framework is discussed later.

Cholera aside, other circumstances played a part in the emergence of the new legislation. The Reform Act of 1832 widened the franchise and in theory made governments slightly more vulnerable to pressure from the electorate. The effect of this should, however, not be exaggerated, as the vote was still restricted to a tiny minority of adults and only around one in twenty adults were eligible. More significant perhaps was the Chartist agitation of the 1830s and 40s, which forced an awareness of the grievances of the working classes on both government and Parliament. Wohl (1984) has pointed out that the Chartists were not particularly interested in public health and in fact opposed some of the sanitary measures proposed by reformers. Nevertheless, as Woodward (1962, p. 147) correctly observed, 'this agitation of the poor compelled other classes to think about the condition of England', and it certainly strengthened the hand of those seeking to promote public health reform.

Battles were also being fought on other fronts, notably with regard to working conditions. Here a similar story unfolded, the collection of evidence and organised pressure producing public outcry and legislation to curb some of the worst evils. Legislation governing factories and mines provided a further example of how reforms developed a momentum of their own. The 1833 Factory Act was the first effective Act regulating hours at work, although its achievements were in retrospect limited (adult hours of work, for example, not being covered by the Act), only a small number of inspectors was appointed to enforce the law, and they were granted limited powers. The activities of the inspectors, however, maintained the focus on working conditions not only in factories covered by the Act (the textile factories), but also in other places of work. In 1840, a commission was established to examine child labour in mines and factories. Its first report in 1842 had a major impact: the public was shocked by the revelations of children and women working in barbaric conditions down the mines. This created a favourable political climate for the passage of the Mines and Collieries Act (1842), which, although vigorously contested by the mine owners, prohibited the employment of women and boys under 10 years of age underground, set an age limit for tending machinery and created a mines inspectorate.

Finally in this section, mention must be made of the Victorians' campaign against the evils of drink (Harrison, 1971; Dingle, 1980). Although not a central concern of the public health movement (Wohl, 1984), the health and social implications of a high level of alcohol consumption were widely acknowledged. A Select Committee of 1834 found:

> That [the] following are only a few of the evils directly springing from this baneful source; destruction of health, disease in every form and shape, premature decrepitude in the old, stunted growth, and general debility and decay in the young, loss of life by paroxysms, apoplexies, drownings, burnings, and accidents of various kinds, delirium tremens..., paralysis, idiotcy (sic), madness and violent death. (Select Commitee on Drunkenness, 1834/1968, p. iv)

To place the Victorian consumption level in perspective, it should be noted that, in Britain in 1870, the amount of alcohol consumed per person aged 15 and over was more than double that of the 1960s (for a discussion of Victorian attitudes to drink, see Harrison, 1971). The temperance movement, initially a non-conformist-based movement concerned mainly with the immorality of drunkenness and its social consequences, focused on 'moral suasion' to persuade individuals to abstain from drinking (Dingle, 1980). The movement later expanded to include members of the established church, the Liberal Party and the medical profession. The temperance movement then began to campaign for 'legislative suppression' to restrict the alcohol trade by such devices as an age limit for children, restricting the hours of sale, higher taxes and imposing stricter conditions for licensing retail outlets and restrictions on the number of outlets in a locality. Some of these measures were enacted in the late Victorian period, and most of the remainder either during the Edwardian period or as emergency regulations during the First World War. Many of the latter (such as permitted hours) were retained in some form after hostilities ceased, although, as will be discussed in Chapter 9, there has been some relaxation of these controls in recent years.

## Ideas, Values and Ideologies

The aims of the public health reformers were at odds with two key principles of the Victorian age: *laissez-faire* in economic matters and local self-government (Fraser, 1973). The opponents of reform were able to mount a defence of the *status quo* from these two standpoints, arguing that government interference would damage the economy or undermine the rights of local communities to make their own decisions. Such arguments often barely covered the naked self-interest of industrialists and powerful local élites. However, they carried considerable weight at this time and required a cautious response from reformers.

The fact that many reformers, including Chadwick, Arnott and Southwood Smith, were inspired by Bentham's utilitarian principles undoubtedly helped their cause. Bentham's key principle that 'the greatest happiness of the greatest number is the foundation of morals and legislation' was often used to justify the *laissez-faire* approach to economic and social matters, but, as Marquand (1988, p. 223) has perceptively remarked, 'the reaction against full-blooded market liberalism took place under the same philosophical aegis as the movement towards it'. Hence Edwin Chadwick's brand of utilitarianism was based on a desire to maximise public benefit. If it could be demonstrated that the market did not achieve this, an enlightened bureaucracy would have to intervene. As Finer (1952, p. 3) observed, 'Chadwick, was instantly fired by any and every feature that caused unnecessary suffering, disease, and economic waste' and he realised that 'it was good economy to prevent the evils' (p. 152).

But to see Victorian public health as simply a utilitarian response is far too crude. There are indeed those who argue that Benthamite utilitarianism was less significant than 'administrative momentum' (see Fraser, 1973, pp. 103–8, and MacDonagh, 1977, for a further discussion). From this perspective, state bureaucracies that had been established as a response to revelations about social problems developed their own agendas for reform and gradually acquired greater powers of intervention. This, it is argued, occurred in an incremental and pragmatic manner rather than being determined by an ideological 'master plan' of social reform. Moreover, one should not forget the humanitarian motive, as reflected in the participation in the public health movement of philanthropists such as Lord Ashley, the Earl of Shaftsbury. Yet it has been argued that the importance of such actors should not be exaggerated. Tesh (1982, p. 339), for example, has stated that 'the argument for sanitary reform was not... primarily a humanitarian one'. Indeed, as Flinn (1965, p. 29) noted, aside from factory reform, most of the great Victorian philanthropists did not show much interest in public health. Yet as the public health movement developed, it reached an accommodation with the broader notion of 'improvement', which was a major influence in the Victorian era (see Briggs, 1959; Walvin, 1987). As Wohl (1984) notes, the public health movement became a moral crusade to eliminate the visible signs of filth, physical cleanliness and good health being viewed as a precondition for both social and spiritual progress.

As these ideas and values became entrenched in the latter half of the Victorian period, the resistance to state intervention in the field of public health began to weaken. Meanwhile, a number of defenders of local self-government became transformed from the enemies of public health to its staunchest supporters. The reason for this was the desire of local politicians to create a civic identity by improving the physical environment of their towns and cities. The classic example was Birmingham, which, under its Mayor, Joseph Chamberlain, developed a local strategy of social reform in the 1870s (see Judd, 1977). Chamberlain's motto – 'high rates and a healthy city' (Longmate, 1966) – was reflected in a range of programmes including the municipal provision of gas and water, housing improvements and welfare services.

## Political Agents and Institutions

The public health legislation and local improvements of the Victorian age did not occur simply because circumstances were favourable or because certain ideas and values prevailed. Political agents had to employ these ideas, promote such values and take advantage of the circumstances. In today's political system, political parties play a key role in campaigning, selecting candidates and leaders, marshalling parliamentary majorities for and against legislation, and shaping the political agenda. In the period before the second Reform Act of 1867, however, parties were much weaker. There was more dissent within them than occurs today, when a rebellion by backbench MPs is infrequent enough to be newsworthy. During this period, coalitions of support for legislation often cut across party lines, and public health issues were no exception. As MacDonagh (1977) observed, the political allegiance of those involved in the public health movement did not lie exclusively with any particular party.

In the early Victorian period, pressure groups rather than parties were the main rallying point for those seeking to influence government. The Health of Towns Association, for example, was extremely active in promoting public health reform among the middle classes, in Parliament, in the press and within the government itself (Patterson, 1948; Hollis, 1974). After achieving its main objective – the passage of the 1848 Public Health Act – the association was dissolved, although local associations continued to press for further reform. Other organised groups later became more actively involved in the public health debate, including the Social Science Association (SSA), the (BMA), the Metropolitan Association of Medical Officers of Health (MAMOH) and the Sanitary Institute.

The SSA and the BMA were particularly influential in the establishment of the Royal Sanitary Commission in 1869. The Commission's recommendations (C 281, 1871) led to the reorganisation of public health responsibilities (under the Local Government Board in 1871) and paved the way for the Public Health Acts of 1872 and 1875, which set the framework for modern public health administration. MAMOH (and its successor, the Society of Medical Officers of Health) was also involved at a high level, helping to draft the public health legislation and lobbying successfully for stricter requirements on the notification of diseases. Meanwhile, the Sanitary Institute, which acted as a professional body for sanitary inspectors, was regarded as an influential lobby group in the late Victorian period (Frazer, 1950, p. 233), deriving its authority from the growing expertise of its members.

Other potential supporters did not, however, play a major role. As Porter (1995, p. 59) has argued, 'the medical colleges never gave an impetus to the public health movement'. More generally, he maintains that 'the organised medical profession played a surprisingly secondary and desultory role in the vast expansion of the Victorian state provision'. Indeed, medical professional bodies often took a negative view of public health measures, as exemplified by the criticism of the General Board of Health by the Royal College of Physicians (RCP). This should not, however, obscure the fact that many doctors were concerned about public health and participated in other organisations that sought improvement. Also, as mentioned above, the BMA was active in the late Victorian period in pressing for reform.

Pressure groups were important actors, but the role of public servants, furthering the cause from the inside, was crucial. Flinn (1965, pp. 30–1) suggests that professional administrators within government played a key role in promoting public debate and government intervention. In the early Victorian period, the name of Edwin Chadwick looms large. He held a number of influential positions: secretary of the Poor Law Commission, secretary to the Health of Towns Commission, member of the General Board of Health. Southwood Smith was also a key figure in this period, playing a key role in the inquiries into urban conditions of the 1830s. He was also a leading member of the Health of Towns Association and sat alongside Chadwick on the General Board of Health. In the later phase of reform, the key figure was Sir John Simon, a founding member of the Health of Towns Association, the first Medical Officer for London and the nation's first Medical Officer (Lambert, 1963). His achievement was to consolidate the earlier victories of the public health movement while advancing state intervention into new areas. Simon's role is discussed in more detail later in this chapter.

Politicians also played an important role in initiating legislation and steering it through Parliament; these included Morpeth and Disraeli, both members of the Health of Towns Association. Morpeth, who was a member of the Whig cabinet during the 1840s, worked closely with Chadwick in framing public health legislation, including the 1848 Act. It has been argued that the contribution of some politicians to public health reform has been exaggerated. The landmark Public Health Act of 1875, introduced by Disraeli, was, for example, strongly influenced by the policies of the previous Liberal government. Moreover, it has been argued that Disraeli's government could have done more to promote public health but was inhibited by an ideological commitment to local independence and private property rights (Smith, 1967).

Throughout the Victorian period, politicians and the vested interests they represented – such as the water companies – mounted a strong rearguard action against public health reform. They were, for example, successful in securing the abolition of the General Board of Health. There are many other historical examples of business interests opposing public health reforms during the nineteenth century. One striking example occurred during the outbreak of cholera in Sunderland in 1831, the local business community being so concerned about the impact of a possible quarantine on trade that they forced the doctors to retract their diagnoses (Longmate, 1966, pp. 27–32). A group of antiquarantine businessmen later secured control of the Sunderland Board of Health and were able for a time to prevent the publication of details of new cases of the disease in a vain effort to prevent quarantine being imposed. Local interests also resisted attempts from central government to impose public health measures. For example, powerful London interests, and the MPs representing London constituencies, opposed central direction in public health matters and were successful in the exclusion of the metropolis from the provisions of the 1848 Act. However, the City of London did appoint its own Medical Officer in the same year, partly in response to a fresh outbreak of cholera, and as the century wore on, the powerful interests within the capital became more responsive to the need to introduce public health measures.

Other opposition came from civil liberties groups, particularly on the question of vaccination. Antivaccination groups flourished in the latter part of the nineteenth century following the imposition of compulsory vaccination against smallpox in 1853. Strong local campaigns in over 50 cities and towns made it difficult to enforce the law, and by 1896 around a fifth of districts failed to do so. In the 1890s, the law was modified to allow conscientious objectors the right to decline vaccination. The Contagious Diseases Acts, passed between 1866 and 1869, also raised concerns about the intrusiveness of public health reform and its disregard for civil liberties. These Acts enabled the authorities to undertake the compulsory medical examination of alleged prostitutes in naval and military towns. Women found to be infected with venereal disease were subjected to compulsory detention and treatment. Venereal disease was a growing problem, particularly in towns where soldiers or sailors were stationed. Liverpool, for example, was described as 'a hot bed of syphilis' (Frazer, 1950, p. 200). Some, including members of the medical profession, wanted to see the Acts extended to other localities, and a pressure group was formed with this aim, but there was strong opposition from the National Association for the Repeal of the Contagious Diseases Acts, led by Josephine Butler. This organisation, as its name suggests, not only opposed the extension of these Acts, but also called for repeal of the existing legislation, achieving this in 1886.

The press often saw itself as the guardian of individual liberty against the intrusion of the public health reformers, particularly in the 1840s and 50s. The defeat of the General Board of Health in 1854 was, for example, greeted with glee in *The Times*:

> The British nation abhors absolute power. We prefer to take our chance with cholera and the rest than be bullied into health. (quoted by Longmate, 1966, p. 188)

From the 1860s onwards, however, as public opinion shifted strongly in favour of reform, the press became generally more supportive of intervention.

In the Victorian era, although Parliament was a key battleground between public health reformers and their opponents, local government was also an important arena. The 1848 Act was permissive in all but the most exceptional circumstances. This meant that decisions about public health were largely delegated to local communities, which mirrored political divisions on these issues. Efforts to impose a central framework for regulation were resisted, but in the longer term, the impetus proved too powerful. The crucial change was the 1866 Sanitary Act, which imposed obligations on localities to cleanse their communities, although local communities continued to have considerable autonomy within this framework.

The Public Health Act of 1875 represented the culmination of the sanitary reformers' campaign. Although a consolidating measure, it set a clear framework for public health for the next 50 years. It also signalled the end of an era, for although legislation would still be used to improve the physical environment, attention was shifting towards other means of intervention aimed at improving social welfare generally and personal hygiene in particular.

## Victorian Public Health: The Second Phase

In the latter part of the Victorian period, 'preventive medicine' replaced the 'sanitary idea' as the dominant philosophy of public health (see Kickbusch, 1986; Fee and Porter, 1992; Lewis, 1992; Armstrong, 1993). This was manifested in a number of ways: by the 'medicalisation' of public health, by a shift in the focus of attention from the general population towards specific subgroups and individuals, and by an increasing emphasis on access to health services. At the same time, the activities of the sanitary movement, while still contributing to public health debates, became more closely integrated with broader issues of social welfare.

Individual members of the medical profession were an important driving force behind the sanitary revolution. Much of the early evidence on the extent of the problem was documented by individuals with a medical background, such as Farr, Southwood Smith and Simon. As has been mentioned, medical professional bodies were less than enthusiastic about central government intervention, but, as the century wore on, and as central government increasingly began to incorporate medical expertise, these attitudes began to change.

Doctors, alongside inspectors of nuisances and surveyors, played an important role in the improvement of public health after the 1848 Act. The Act permitted the appointment of a local Medical Officer of Health (MOH), although this did not become compulsory until later (1855, in the case of metropolitan boroughs, 1872 for other local sanitary authorities and 1909 for county councils). As more and more localities employed MOHs, their influence grew, although they initially had a rather precarious existence. In some places, opposition to sanitary reform led to the ousting of the local MOH (see Wohl, 1984). In addition, posts were often part time, salaries hardly generous and the duties often onerous. But the MOH began to exert leadership in health matters at local level, partly due to the growing status of medicine in general, to be discussed below. MOHs also began to exert a greater influence at national level. They formed their own separate association in 1856 and lobbied for improvements in legislation. As noted earlier, the MAMOH (and its successor, the Society of Medical Officers, formed in 1889) helped to draft public health legislation. Meanwhile, other professional organisations, the BMA in particular, became increasingly involved in campaigning on public health issues, both in relation to specific issues (such as vaccination) and with regard to reforming the system of public health administration (Bartrip, 1996).

The medical profession also began to exert a greater influence over public health matters within government. The appointment of a Medical Officer to the Board of Health in 1855 was a significant development. The holder of this post, Sir John Simon, documented the main threats to health, such as cholera, diphtheria and tuberculosis, and the principal causes of disease: bad housing, overcrowding, insanitary conditions, poor nutrition and difficult and dangerous working conditions. Simon's achievement was to place public health on a sounder scientific footing by establishing a link between health and a range of social factors. This helped to establish a case for further government intervention in areas such as food quality, housing and sanitary reform. In a broader sense, Simon also helped to promote within government the influence of the medical profession and its representative organisations (Lambert, 1963).

The growing influence of the medical profession over debates about the future direction of public health provides only a partial explanation of the medicalisation of public health. The other main reason was that medical knowledge was advancing, and this, along with the rising status of the profession (Parry and Parry, 1976), strengthened medical authority. The value of medical knowledge in relation to public health was demonstrated in two fields: epidemiology and bacteriology.

First is epidemiology, exemplified by Snow's work on the cholera epidemic of 1854, which showed how the causes of ill health could be identified and measured (Snow, 1936). Snow discovered, by marking reported cases on a map of the area, that water supplies were associated with an outbreak of cholera in the Soho area of London. The resulting cluster highlighted a particular source of drinking water – the Broad Street pump. Further investigation revealed that a common factor in the deaths was that victims drank from this particular source. At the time, the medical establishment was reluctant to acknowledge Snow's findings, there being much controversy within the profession over whether diseases such as cholera were caused by noxious substances carried in the air or by contagion (Pelling, 1978). The discovery was, however, subsequently hailed as a classic example of epidemiological detection.

Public health intervention has often anticipated scientific findings on the precise nature of disease causation. Snow's work provided compelling evidence on the causes of cholera and endorsed efforts to improve sanitation, but it preceded the identification of the disease agent (the cholera vibrio, discovered by Koch) by about 30 years. There are many other examples of this: the London County Council registered a nil return for typhus in their annual statistics three years before the transmission route of the disease – lice – was identified (Shryock, in Inglis, 1965, p. 169). Furthermore, Lind's discovery of the link between diet and scurvy, discussed earlier in this chapter, preceded the identification of vitamin C deficiency by over a century.

Epidemiologists such as Snow, and others such as William Budd (who developed a theory of causation regarding cholera similar to Snow's and established that human excreta were associated with the spread of typhoid), legitimised improvements in sanitation that were already taking place and added further weight to the arguments of reformers. Yet it was only with the bacterial revolution of the 1880s that the scientific achievements of Snow, Budd and others came to be fully appreciated. The discovery of the bacteriological causes of infectious diseases placed preventive medicine on a sounder scientific basis. However, the endorsement of 'germ theory' had a number of other implications (see Fee and Porter, 1992; Lewis, 1992). First, it pinpointed the laboratory rather than society as the workshop for public health medicine. In future, public health would be the province of scientifically trained professionals. By implication, scientific knowledge would carry greater weight than other competing forms of knowledge. This in turn implied that public health intervention could no longer be justified solely on the basis of detective work and circumstantial evidence but required hard, scientific evidence. This favoured laboratory studies over and above circumstantial evidence and qualitative studies. It also emphasised the importance of medical intervention, which could be more easily measured and quantified, over social intervention, which was more difficult to evaluate.

Another consequence of the growing dominance of germ theory was a sharper focus on the manifestation of disease in particular individuals and subgroups within the population, rather than on the health of the population as a whole. As Starr (1982), in an American context, notes, the concept of 'dirt' was in effect narrowed by bacteriological discoveries. It would, however, be wrong to see the emphasis on individuals and subgroups as entirely new. For example, much of impetus for the sanitary movement arose out from studies of the condition of the poor and other vulnerable groups. Moreover, personal health, particularly regarding hygiene, had long been an important focus for the movement. Local sanitary associations emphasised the importance of cleanliness and from the 1860s employed 'visitors' (the forerunners of today's health visitors) to provide advice and education on health matters. Other groups, such as the Ladies' Association for Diffusion of Sanitary Knowledge, also disseminated advice to the lower classes. Meanwhile, the Association for Promoting Cleanliness among the Poor lobbied successfully for legislation (the Baths and Washhouses Act 1846) to improve the public provision of washing and bathing facilities in poorer communities.

The emphasis on personal health nonetheless shifted attention away from environmental health concerns. This was associated with a debate about the financing and organisation of health services, which became prominent in the latter part of the Victorian era. Indeed, the state's role in funding and providing preventive and treatment services came to be seen as one of the central health issues as the turn of the century approached. Yet concern about social and environmental causes of ill health did not subside in the late Victorian period. It was rather that the energies of the sanitarians became absorbed into a broader movement to improve social welfare. This was in part reflected by the growing demands for improved access to specific health services, particularly for vulnerable people, such as mothers and children. It was also evident in the campaign to promote better housing and lay behind pressures for further state intervention to tackle poverty and destitution.

According to Wohl (1984), Victorian public health reformers failed to challenge the fabric of society. He does not blame them, believing that to have done so would have risked jeopardising their position, thereby undermining the system of public health they had so carefully constructed. In the earlier phase of reform, as Shryock (1979) remarks, sanitarians had sought to break the cycle of poverty and disease, but, as noted above, it was possible to bring about only limited change to alleviate the worst conditions, given the prevailing values of early Victorian society. In the later phase of reform, those seeking to advance public health – such as Sir John Simon – readily acknowledged the role played by poverty in disease, and indeed regarded it as among the worst of the sanitary evils. In his role as Medical Officer, he sought to draw attention to the health consequences of poverty. However, within central government, as Webster (1990) observed, the public health response was overshadowed by the Poor Law administration. The creation of a Local Government Board (LGB) in 1871, which incorporated the Poor Law Board and the Medical Department of the Privy Council, rather than integrating health and local government, merely made it more difficult for those concerned about public health to initiate change. As Honigsbaum (1970, p. 9) noted, 'with few exceptions, the LGB's Poor Law functions smothered its concern for public health'. Eventually, in 1876, Simon resigned his post 'in frustration at the low status afforded to scientific authority in the Local Government Board' (Webster, 1990, p. 11).

The Poor Law system shaped public health at local level as well. Hodgkinson (1967) documents longstanding divisions between Poor Law Medical Officers and MOHs. Apart from temporary co-operation brought on by the exigencies of epidemics, Hodgkinson (1967, p. 679) claims that 'Poor Law and public health continued side by side, each according to its own principles and ignoring the effect on the other'. Poor Law officers were mainly concerned with providing care for the poor, but they had an important public health role. They were particularly active in preventing the spread of disease during epidemics. Poor Law Medical Officers also acquired powers to recommend the removal of nuisances injurious to health. In some areas, they were appointed to MOH posts on a part-time basis. Despite these overlaps, however, the preventive work of the Poor Law Medical Officers and the MOHs was restricted by the continuation of different administrative systems. This was not addressed by the reforms of 1871, mentioned earlier, which brought the Poor Law and the sanitary authorities together under the LGB. Indeed, according to Hodgkinson (1967) the gulf between the public health and the Poor Law widened further after this date.

The system of Poor Law administration continued to influence public health in the early part of the twentieth century in ways that will be examined in the next chapter, alongside efforts to tackle the social and economic roots of ill health and provide more accessible services for the prevention and treatment of illness. But, to complete this chapter, it is important to explore the main areas in which the reformers endeavoured to make a difference to the social and economic conditions of the latter half of the nineteenth century: housing improvement and factory legislation.

According to Wohl (1984, p. 327), 'Healthy housing was one of the cornerstones of the sanitary reformers philosophy and programme.' Yet, apart from regulations on cellar dwellings and provisions for adequate drains for new houses, it was not until the late Victorian period that local authorities acquired significant power to deal with problems of overcrowding and poor-quality housing. Even then, much was left to voluntary activity, such as the housing schemes initiated by Octavia Hill (a grand-daughter of Southwood Smith). An Act of 1868 gave municipal authorities powers to force owners to repair or rebuild insanitary housing. This was followed by the Cross Act (Artisans' Dwellings Act 1875), which enabled local authorities to undertake programmes of slum clearance, compensate owners and rehouse people. This legislation, however, did not compel authorities to do so, and few took up the challenge as the costs were prohibitively high. Moreover, local authorities were not permitted to adopt a landlord role until the later legislation of 1885, 1890 and 1909. So although cities such as Liverpool and Birmingham set an example, municipal housing was by no means widespread by the end of the century, and, as Wohl observed, the problem of poor housing remained unresolved.

## Factories

Legislation to deal with some of the worst working conditions came as the result of many years of hard campaigning. The early Acts – the Factory Act of 1833 and the Mines and Collieries Act of 1842 – have already been mentioned. A further Act of 1844 limited the working hours of women and children in textile factories and set out regulations regarding the safety of machinery. The Ten Hours Act of 1847 placed a limit on the number of hours worked by women and young people (and, by implication, on the working hours of men too) in the textile industry. Meanwhile, a further Mines Act was passed in 1850, enabling the appointment of inspectors to enforce the law. Acts in 1864 and two others in 1867 extended regulation to other industries and made provisions regarding the health and safety of the working environment. Although the legislation was consolidated in 1878, there remained exceptions, such as the notorious 'sweated trades', aspects of which were regulated in 1891, more comprehensive legislation following in 1909. By the turn of the century, regulations had begun to address the problems of the working environment, as well as those associated with long hours of work. There was a growing interest in particular occupational diseases, but little was done to address these problems at the time. As Wohl (1984) notes, physical conditions at work at the end of the Victorian era were still harmful to health in spite of these improvements.

## Conclusion

This chapter has shown that the perceived importance of public health intervention has varied considerably both over time and between different societies. Furthermore, although strong similarities in public health intervention can be found – the emphasis on sanitation by both the Romans and Victorians being an example – there has been much variation in the approach used to promote and protect public health. In Britain, for example, from the Middle Ages up to the twentieth century, interventions fall into several phases, each of which emphasises a particular model of public health: quarantine, sanitary science and personal hygiene. On closer inspection, however, these phases are, as this chapter has shown, not as clear cut as they first appear, different models co-existing in the same time period. It is therefore more appropriate to view each period as being subject to different emphases, one particular model having a stronger influence over public health policy and practice but coexisting to some extent with others.

Why public health appears to have greater priority in some societies and in some eras compared with others requires some explanation. Equally importantly, one needs to explore why certain models of public health seem to have more influence in some periods than others. Towards the end of the next chapter, possible explanations will be discussed with reference to the analytical framework set out in Chapter 1. First, however, it is necessary to move closer to the present by exploring the development of public health in the first part of the twentieth century and the subsequent emergence of the so-called 'new public health'.

### Note

1.  Chadwick was identified as the sole author of the report by default because the Poor Law Commission as a whole was unable to endorse it.

# 3

# Public Health in the Twentieth Century

By the end of the Victorian era, the public health movement had bifurcated into two main elements: the first committed to the promotion of general improvements in social conditions, the second more concerned with the provision of specific preventive and curative health services. This chapter examines how these elements influenced public health reform during the first half of the twentieth century and then goes on to discuss developments following the creation of the NHS in 1948, the impact of subsequent reorganisations and the revival of interest in public health strategies from the 1970s onwards.

## Public Health before the NHS

### Living Conditions

Social surveys, such as Charles Booth's study of London and Benjamin Seebohm Rowntree's of York, did much to stimulate an awareness of the extent of poverty in late Victorian and Edwardian Britain. Their findings reinforced arguments articulated by the national efficiency movement (see Searle, 1971) regarding Britain's ability to compete at an international level, economically, technologically and militarily, because of the poor physical health, inadequate skills and limited educational ability of the British people. Such fears came to a head during the Boer War, when evidence came to light of poor physical health among recruits. Subsequently, the report of the Interdepartmental Committee on Physical Deterioration (Cd 2175, 1904), along with the Royal Commission on Physical Training in Scotland (Cd 1507, 1903), called for a range of measures, including systematic school medical inspections and facilities for the feeding of malnourished children to ensure that the health of schoolchildren was improved. In 1906, local authorities were

granted the power to feed children in need, and a year later the Board of
Education established a system of medical inspection in schools. This was
followed by the Children's Act of 1908, which codified the law relating to
children's health and welfare. As we shall see shortly, this period witnessed
local authorities beginning to provide a range of health and welfare services
for children.

The People's Budget of 1909, which introduced a more progressive tax
system, made it possible for the state to finance social policies that were likely
to improve health through better material conditions. State pensions for the
elderly were introduced in 1908. This was followed by the National Insurance
scheme, which provided financial benefit in times of unemployment for
insured workers in specified industries on a non-means-tested basis (that is,
outside the realm of the Poor Law system of relief), cash benefits for all
insured workers when they became ill and health insurance for general
medical services provided by GPs.

National Health Insurance (NHI) was a compulsory insurance scheme
financed by employers, the state and the worker. It heralded a system of state-
funded health care based on contributions and operated outside the Poor
Law system of health care. On the negative side, dependants – non-working
wives and children – were excluded from the scheme, and apart from treatment for tuberculosis, specialist services lay outside its remit. Furthermore,
because it dealt with people who were already ill, it was a very limited
measure in terms of preventing illness.

The introduction of NHI effectively outmanoeuvred two competing
lobbies: those wanting to retain the Poor Law in a modified form and those
clamouring for its abolition. In 1909, a Royal Commission had reported on
this issue, but the divisions between abolitionists and reformists ran so deep
that two separate reports were issued, each of which represented a different
vision of social welfare and public health (Cd 4499, 1909; see also Bruce,
1968). The Commission's majority report was critical of aspects of the Poor
Law but believed that it could be refashioned. The stigma attached to the
Poor Law was identified as a particular problem, although it was believed
that this could be overcome by renaming it 'public assistance' and transferring responsibility for its administration to local authorities. Another 20 years
passed before this proposal was enshrined in law. Some of the majority
report's other recommendations, such as the creation of labour exchanges and
unemployment insurance, were, however, acted upon rather more quickly .

The majority report called for a more humane system of health care, recommending that sick people treated under the Poor Law should be
accommodated in separate institutions from able-bodied persons, and
acknowledging that an individual's need for medical care should be assessed
prior to an assessment of means. However, it opposed free medical care as of
right, albeit endorsing a scheme enabling poor people to have greater access

to medical care in the community, funded by state subscriptions to existing provident schemes. To administer health services for the poor, it was envisaged that there would be a medical assistance committee under the auspices of each public assistance authority at local level.

In contrast, the minority report sought to address the causes of poverty and ill health by recommending that central government be responsible for the management of the labour market and in particular reducing unemployment. It recommended that Poor Law health services be combined with sanitary authorities to create a unified state health service. At local level, it proposed a health committee with wide responsibility for illness prevention as well as service provision. The minority report also called for services to be free at the point of delivery, the assessment of means taking place only after treatment had been received, the poor being exempt from payment.

Although both reports were critical of the Poor Law, this system continued as the principal form of state assistance. It was not until the 1929 Local Government Act, according to Frazer (1950, p. 393) 'one of the important landmarks in the history of public health', that the Poor Law boards were replaced by local authority assistance committees – as recommended 20 years earlier by the Royal Commission majority report. The Act also gave local authorities discretion over the allocation of cases to specialist committees such as education, health and so on (echoing a recommendation in the Poor Law Commission minority report), transferred public health services provided by boards of guardians to local authorities and allowed local health committees to take responsibility for Poor Law hospitals. Yet, despite these important legislative and administrative changes, the remnants of the Poor Law system continued to influence health care and public health during the inter-war period. One notes, for example, that on the eve of the Second World War, the majority of chronically ill people were still being cared for institutions controlled by public assistance committees (Abel-Smith, 1964).

As the previous chapter demonstrated, the origins of public health reform in the Victorian period lay in the Poor Law system. Throughout its long history, however, this system adversely affected public health in a number of ways. First, the philosophy that underpinned the Poor Law was often inconsistent with the sanitary idea. As Hodgkinson (1967, p. 637) notes, 'the Poor Law was a deterrent aimed at reducing costs and the Public Health movement by its obvious insistence on prevention, entailing large expenditure, was incompatible with Poor Law principles'. Indeed, prevention was not really a concern of those who administered the Poor Law, except during major epidemics (see also Chapter 1).

Second, the Poor Law deterred those needing treatment who were reluctant to submit to the workhouse test. Yet a system of relief that promoted earlier intervention would probably have had a significant advantage in terms of an improvement in public health. Even so, during the late Victorian period, the conditions for medical relief were relaxed, and as a result it was given to those not technically destitute (Hodgkinson, 1967). Furthermore, in 1885, sick people were exempted from the strict Poor Law requirements by the Medical Relief Act. Despite these developments, the social stigma of medical relief provided under the auspices of the Poor Law persisted.

Third, the system of medical relief added to the complexity of health administration and, given the disinterest of Poor Law authorities in preventing illness, seriously inhibited efforts to promote public health. Even when the Poor Law authorities subsequently developed public health functions (in relation to sanitation, vaccination and the treatment of diseases such as tuberculosis and venereal disease, for example), these developed separately from the activities of local authorities.

Fourth, even where limited integration occurred, the Poor Law philosophy tended to dominate, to the detriment of public health. As noted in the previous chapter, the organisation of public health and the Poor Law under the auspices of the LGB in 1871 inhibited public health initiatives. This continued well into the early years of the twentieth century (Honigsbaum, 1970). The development of schemes with a strong public health element – such as the inspection and treatment of schoolchildren – forced the LGB to take a greater interest in public health. This, however, did not occur until the second decade of the twentieth century and was at any rate short-lived – the LGB's functions were taken over in 1919 by a new Ministry of Health, discussed later in this chapter.

## Health and Welfare Services

One of the main reasons for the decline of the Poor Law was the emergence of health and welfare schemes beyond its remit. These included the NHI scheme, which challenged Poor Law principles by offering free services at the point of delivery without a corresponding workhouse test. The first two decades of the twentieth century also saw the development of a range of health and welfare services for babies and young children. These services, established by local authorities and voluntary organisations, included milk supplies and infant welfare centres. Local authorities also began to organise a network of community health services such as midwifery, district nursing and health visiting, working closely with voluntary associations and self-employed professionals in these fields. In addition, from 1912 onwards, the school medical service began to move beyond inspection and diagnosis towards the development of services such as school nursing, dental clinics and the provision of spectacles. In 1918, following the Education Act of that year, a duty was placed on local authorities to provide treatment facilities for certain diseases, such as skin complaints and dental problems, in schoolchildren. In the same year, the

Maternity and Child Welfare Act clarified the law relating to the local authority provision of services to expectant and nursing mothers and preschool children, facilitating the extension of schemes in this field (Frazer, 1950, p. 412).

During the 1920s and 30s, local authorities' responsibilities for health care continued to grow. As mentioned earlier, the 1929 Local Government Act enabled them to bring Poor Law hospitals under the control of their health committee, and transferred other responsibilities of the boards of guardians relating to maternity and child welfare, tuberculosis, immunisation, blind people and mental deficiency to the local authorities, enabling them to develop a more comprehensive range of services in these areas. The expanding remit of local health committees and MOHs in the inter-war period explains why some see it as a golden age of public health (Chave, 1974; Godber, 1986; Holland and Stewart, 1998). These developments were seen by MOHs themselves in a positive light as possibly leading to a highly integrated public health service. Others, however, have argued that the acquisition of responsibility adversely affected public health. Lewis (1986, p. 16) observed that 'the public health departments added to their domain without questioning what was distinctive about public health'. She claims that the failure to develop a coherent public health philosophy had two consequences: public health doctors became preoccupied with their service delivery role at the expense of their traditional community watchdog role, and 'turf battles' developed, notably between public health doctors and GPs.

Lewis's argument about the decline of the community watchdog role is based partly on the failure of MOHs to take up immunisation as readily as they might have done. She suggested that they and local health committees placed greater emphasis on the use of treatment facilities as a means of dealing with infectious disease (Lewis, 1986). Lewis also argues that the MOHs neglected their community watchdog role by failing to highlight the effects of long-term unemployment in the 1930s on nutritional standards and levels of morbidity and mortality. This is supported by Webster (1990, p. 15), who has stated that, in the inter-war period 'the public health mechanism failed to respond appropriately and showed itself incapable of resisting political pressures for falsification of the evidence relating to ill health and malnutrition'.

Webster refers to the dismal performance of the public health profession in this period (see also Webster, 1986), but is this a fair assessment? After all, local health authorities, to which MOHs were accountable, operated in a political environment and faced powerful vested interests opposed to public health measures on commercial grounds. Although full-time MOHs could not be dismissed without the approval of the Minister of Health, they were often under great pressure not to upset their employing authorities, and it is hardly surprising that some succumbed. But this was hardly unprecedented: from its inception, the post of MOH was subject to political pressure (Wohl, 1984).

While it may be true that some MOHs were pusillanimous, others were not bound by these constraints. The case of M'Gonigle, the MOH for Stockton on Tees in the 1930s, who painstakingly collected evidence on the impact of malnutrition on health, illustrated how far some were prepared to go in highlighting the socio-economic causes of illness (Holland and Stewart, 1998). Similarly, Welshman's (1997) study of MOHs in Leicester found that although some were complacent, others were innovative and imaginative, particularly in view of the national and local constraints they faced.

Such examples lead others, such as Holland and Stewart (1998), to take a more favourable view of the inter-war period. They argue that the 'period between the two World Wars was one of substantial progress for public health – a proud era' (p. 58). Indeed, there were other positive developments in this period that should not be overlooked, for example the rationalisation of services, such as maternal and child welfare services, made possible by the 1929 Local Government Act. There was also the growing interest in health education: the Central Council on Health Education was established in 1927, and from 1936 local authorities were given wider power to provide information to the public on health and disease. Other social reforms of the inter-war period, such as housing improvement, discussed later in this chapter, had a positive implication for public health.

Let us turn now to the turf wars within the medical profession, which, as Lewis (1986) correctly observes, exerted a strong influence on the direction of public health in the inter-war period. The local authorities' involvement in primary care alarmed some doctors, particularly GPs, who feared the prospect of a salaried general medical service under state control. GPs were extremely vigilant towards the 'encroachment' (see Lewis, 1986, p. 10) of local authority services and saw themselves playing the principal role in the development of personal health services. This GP-centred model of primary care was central to the Dawson report, issued by the Central Council on Medical and Allied Services under the auspices of the Ministry of Health (Cmd 693, 1920). This report envisaged the creation of a system of primary health centres focused on the maintenance of health rather than simply the treatment of illness. These centres would provide an accessible range of preventive and curative services, including community health services such as prenatal care, school medical services and health promotional activities. They would bring together independent GPs, supported by nursing staff and technicians, who would have access to a range of diagnostic and treatment facilities. In addition GPs would be assisted by visiting consultants and specialists, enabling a greater range of treatment to take place in this setting.

Although the Dawson Report was never officially endorsed, not least because of the costs of implementation, it nevertheless had some impact. A number of local experiments reflected the report's emphasis on positive health and its desire to bring services under one roof. For example, the

Peckham Centre, begun in 1926, went beyond a narrow medical approach and sought to establish health centres as an integral part of community life (Stallibrass, 1989). More importantly, however, the Dawson Report had an impact on debates within the medical profession, sending out an important signal to GPs to stake their claim to this territory.

Throughout the 1920s and 30s, the tensions between the GPs and MOHs intensified, resulting in a fracturing of traditional medical solidarities (Porter, 1990). This struggle revolved around status. In this period, neither branch of the profession had much prestige though the status of GPs had risen following the introduction of NHI. By the outbreak of the Second World War, it was general practice rather than public health medicine that had the edge. GPs also had greater political clout, subsequently reflected in the organis-ation of the NHS, which preserved their independent contractor status while at the same time removing key services from the jurisdiction of the MOH.

## The Ministry of Health

The public health implications of the NHS will be considered later in this chapter. First, however, it is necessary to discuss an earlier development, the creation of a Ministry of Health in 1919, seen at the time as a major advance for public health. Calls to establish such a ministry can be traced to the early part of the previous century, when Bentham proposed a health ministry responsible for sanitation, communicable disease and the administration of medical care (Rosen and Burns, 1983). Although this suggestion was repeated on several occasions throughout the nineteenth century, the closest Britain came was the short-lived General Board of Health (see Chapter 1).

During the second decade of the twentieth century, the case for a ministry of health intensified. It was argued that such a ministry would be able to clarify aims regarding health policy and would overcome rivalries concerning health matters, for example between the insurance commissioners, the LGB and the Board of Education. It was also believed that health ministry could co-ordinate the network of public health services that had developed some-what haphazardly: sanitation, the Poor Law, the municipal health services, the school health service and the NHI scheme. Finally, for reasons discussed earlier, it was endorsed as a means of freeing public health from the shadow of the Poor Law system.

The creation of a health ministry proved difficult, largely because of the political differences between the vested interests involved (see Gilbert, 1970; Honigsbaum, 1970). Indeed, the process by which the new ministry emerged was extremely complex. Briefly, however, four factors were crucial. The First World War, rather like the Boer War, exposed the poor physical health of recruits and produced similar calls for a more coherent approach to health matters. Second, the alleged mishandling of a major influenza epidemic in 1918/19 by the LGB was heavily criticised, adding to the pressure for change. A third factor was that government had to respond more sensitively to the demands of women's organisations following the enfranchisement of females over the age of 30 in 1918. These groups had campaigned for better services, particularly in the field of maternity and infant welfare, and argued that a health ministry would help to secure such improvements. Fourth, the government was willing to make concessions to powerful interests such as the local councils, boards of guardians, friendly societies and insurance companies (as well as to other government departments) so that the ministry would not appear as threatening to them. Hence an explicit commitment to abolish the Poor Law was shelved yet again, insurance companies received special rights of representation under the new arrangements, and the Board of Education retained its responsibilities for the school medical service. The biggest loser was the LGB, even though it was not totally opposed to the creation of a health ministry providing it was based on its own existing organisation. In the event, its functions were absorbed into the Ministry of Health, and its chief officers were discharged (Gilbert, 1970, p. 133).

The Ministry of Health was given a statutory duty 'to take all steps as may be desirable to secure the preparation, effective carrying out and co-ordination of measures conducive to the health of the people' (Ministry of Health Act 1919). It had specific responsibilities for environmental health, child and maternal welfare, water supply and sanitation, housing, local government, the NHI scheme and the Poor Law. Although other health-related functions, such as industrial hygiene (the Home Office), health and safety at work (the Board of Trade) and the school health service (the Board of Education) were the responsibility of other departments, the health ministry did have responsibility for the overall co-ordination of health policies.

Despite an initial enthusiasm, early initiatives came to little. This was partly because some of the key proponents behind the ministry's creation either died, retired or moved on, and partly because of restrictions imposed by the economic conditions of the 1920s. As Webster (1988, p. 19) commented, 'the Ministry of Health fell into a cautious and routine mode of operation consistent with the growing pessimism of the times'. Yet some reforms were introduced, much inspired by Neville Chamberlain's three spells as health minister between 1923 and 1931 (Hyde, 1976). The most significant changes in this period concerned the Poor Law, mentioned earlier, and housing. Legislation in 1923 and 1924 permitted subsidies to facilitate improvements in the housing stock. In 1930, the Greenwood Act required local authorities to draw up slum clearance plans and gave additional subsidies for this purpose, while the Housing Act of 1935 made overcrowding an offence for local authorities. As a result of these changes, the housing stock was expanded and improved, particularly in the latter part of the 1930s. Yet the problem of poor housing remained significant. As Gilbert (1970, p. 201) observed, the improved statistics for housing provision could not obscure the fact that 'the poor section of the population was probably little better housed at the end of the inter-war period than it had been at the beginning'.

# Public Health and the NHS

## The NHS

The creation of the NHS in 1948 can be regarded as a major public health achievement. The new service was comprehensive, inclusive and (until the introduction of charges for prescriptions and appliances) free at the point of delivery. From a public health perspective, it had a number of advantages over the previous system. As a national service, it emphasised the importance of public health as a national priority and responsibility. Also, by bringing together the whole range of health services within a national system, it raised the possibility of a more coherent and efficient health service. Furthermore, the NHS extended access to health services for those not covered by state insurance schemes: workers' dependants, the poor and those requiring specialist services (see Vetter, 1998).

Some, however, were concerned that the NHS was a sickness rather than a health service (see Lewis, 1992). Much criticism came from MOHs contemplating the loss of municipal hospital services to the NHS, yet some pointed out a silver lining: that the loss of responsibility for hospital services could liberate them from administrative burdens and enable them to concentrate on their traditional 'community watchdog role'. This proved an optimistic view as MOHs focused instead on administering community health and social services (Frazer, 1950; Lewis, 1986).

## The Changing Role of the MOH

According to Ottewill and Wall (1990, pp. 85, 88), the overall performance of MOHs with regard to the acquisition of resources and the expansion of services was impressive. The amount of money spent on local health and social services rose by 170 per cent in real terms between 1949/50 and 1970/71, and by the end of this period, accounted for a larger share of total NHS revenue expenditure: 11.8 per cent compared with 8.5 per cent. Much of this increase was associated with the provision of social welfare services, which grew considerably in the 1950s and 60s. This expansion, however, created a momentum for further change. Social workers believed that medical control was inappropriate, inhibiting their own claims for professional status. The Seebohm Committee, which reported on the organisation of personal social services in 1968, agreed and recommended the creation of unified social service departments outside the control of the MOH (Cmnd 3703, 1968). The implementation of this measure in 1970 removed a large part of the MOH's administrative responsibilities and undermined the future viability of the post (Webster, 1996, p. 296).

Alongside the claims of social workers for emancipation, public health doctors also faced increasing competition from GPs (see Lewis, 1986). During the post-war period, clinical work undertaken by public health doctors in the community was increasingly taken over by them. The position of GPs was further strengthened by government support for family medicine, which emphasised their pivotal role in the field of primary care. From the 1960s onwards, the encouragement of Primary Health Care Teams (PHCTs), in which nurses and health visitors employed by the local health authorities were attached to general practices, further emphasised the leadership role of the GP at the expense of the MOH.

## NHS Reorganisation

Public health medicine was in effect caught in a pincer movement between the GPs and the Seebohm reforms, and its future looked bleak. One solution was to redefine public health medicine as 'community medicine' and give practitioners specialist status, as envisaged by the Royal Commission on Medical Education (Cmnd 3569, 1968). In the event, changes were prompted by a reorganisation of the NHS, which abolished the post of MOH, and transferred the responsibility for community health services to new health authorities. The role of the public health doctor in this new structure was set out by the Hunter Report (DHSS, 1972), which recommended that specialists in community medicine should promote the effective integration of health and related services while acting as link between administrators and the medical profession. It was envisaged that they would bring specialist skills, such as epidemiology and needs assessment, to enhance the planning and management function at all levels.

In 1974, community physicians were appointed to regional, area and district management teams. In addition, specialists in community medicine were appointed to advise local authorities on a range of issues, such as child health and environmental health matters (Lewis, 1986). However, this brave new world proved cruel. There was much confusion concerning the role of community physicians, not least among the post holders themselves. The granting of specialist status to community physicians did little to raise their status. Indeed, there is evidence that their skills and knowledge were inadequate for the tasks they were given (Strong and Robinson, 1990). Moreover, the management role of the community physicians, particularly when associated with budget restrictions and service cutbacks, had a detrimental effect on their professional standing (Lewis, 1986). Their hospital colleagues regarded them with suspicion, and, rather than bridging the gap between medicine and management, community physicians became isolated from the rest of the profession (Lewis, 1986). Managers too distrusted them, believing that they had greater loyalty to the profession than to the management team (Strong and Robinson, 1990).

The position of community medicine deteriorated further with subsequent reorganisations of the NHS in the 1980s. In 1982, area health authorities were abolished, and the community physicians they employed were forced to seek posts elsewhere, usually in district health authorities, regarded by most as a downward career move (Lewis, 1986). Then came the Griffiths management reforms, which led to the reconstitution of management boards. A consequence was that, in many authorities, community physicians were retained as advisors rather than in a managerial capacity and consequently lost their places on the senior management boards.

## The Acheson Report

The parlous state of community medicine, underlined by a number of high-profile failures of the public health function at local level during the mid-1980s, discussed later in this chapter, led to the appointment of a committee of inquiry, chaired by the Chief Medical Officer, Donald Acheson. The Acheson Report placed some of the blame on the confusion surrounding the role of the specialty. It called for community medicine to be renamed 'public health medicine' and recommended that each health authority should appoint a Director of Public Health (DPH) to lead the public health function. The DPH would act as a chief medical advisor and would advise on priorities, planning and evaluation, co-ordinate the control of communicable disease and develop policy on prevention and health promotion.

However, the report accepted that the shortcomings of public health were to some degree also attributable to the failure of strategic management by acknowledging that health authorities did not prioritise public health and that their responsibilities in this area were not clearly defined. It suggested a number of changes (Cm 289, 1988), which are discussed more fully in Chapter 5. These included the establishment of a public health unit within the Department of Health (DoH) and a new responsibility on health authorities to safeguard the health of their resident populations. It also envisaged that improvements in the health of the local population would be used as an indicator of health authority performance.

## The Need for a Strategy

The Acheson Report, however, failed to acknowledge the magnitude of the strategic failure in central government. Co-ordination on public health matters at national level was weak. Indeed, the broader public health and welfare responsibilities of the Ministry of Health had long ago been transferred. By 1951, it had ceded to other departments responsibilities for financial assistance to the poor, pensions, town and country planning, environmental health, water supply, sewerage, land use, local government, housing and rent control. This divestment was not, however, bemoaned by all. For example, as a report from Political and Economic Planning (PEP, 1937, quoted in Gilbert, 1970, p. 234) stated, 'the Ministry of Health has too often allowed the non-health functions which it inherited from the Local Government Board to overshadow its public health duties'.

Even so, the transfer of functions to other government departments had a number of adverse effects (see Webster, 1996). First, it reduced the size and status of the Ministry of Health. Over the next 20 years, it was often not represented directly in Cabinet, and as a result decisions were made in the absence of health ministers. Second, its low status meant that (with one or two exceptions) it was difficult to attract ambitious ministers who might have given a stronger lead. Third, the removal of wider public health responsibilities (and the retention of community health services by local government) concentrated the ministry's focus on hospital services. As Macleod, a Conservative health minister of the 1950s, commented, it was 'a ministry not for health, but for the NHS' (Webster, 1996, p. 39). This sentiment has subsequently been echoed by others, notably Klein (1980) – who remarked that Britain 'has a health service but no policy for health' – and by former senior Department of Health and Social Security (DHSS) civil servant Kenneth Stowe (1989), who acknowledged the overwhelming power of the hospital lobby within the NHS.

As Webster's official history suggests, the Ministry of Health was in the 1950s largely a non-interventionist department. This began to change in the following decade with the emergence of national plans for hospitals and community health services. Efforts were also made to widen the focus of the department, a Department of Social Welfare at one stage being proposed (Webster, 1996). Eventually, in 1968, the health department was merged with the Ministry of Pensions and National Insurance to form the DHSS. This arrangement, however, did little to restore the focus upon public health: ministerial attention was dominated by NHS reorganisation and plans for specific client groups such as elderly, mentally ill and disabled people.

Nonetheless, some important public health measures were introduced in the 1950s and 60s (Yarrow, 1986; Webster, 1996), including an immunisation programme against childhood diseases (see Exhibit 5.3). The government was persuaded to intervene to protect health by legislation. For example, the

Clean Air Act was passed in 1956 in an attempt to reduce urban smog – a major cause of respiratory problems in industrial areas. Another significant measure, the Road Safety Act of 1967, introduced alcohol breath tests for motorists and led to a fall in the number of alcohol-related motor accidents (Baggott, 1990). Two years earlier, the government had responded to the growing evidence of smoking-related illness by banning cigarette advertisements on television. However, such legislative interventions were rare, and it was not until the 1970s and 80s that pressures for a more strategic approach to public health began to emerge.

# The New Public Health

The revival of public health – often called the new public health – can be traced to a number of sources: intellectual debates about the role of medicine and the future costs of health care, high-profile failures in public health, a change in the public perception of health risks, policy initiatives at the international and the local level, and lobbying by pressure groups.

## Dissenting Voices

In the 1970s, critics questioned the efficiency and the efficacy of modern health care. Particularly important was Cochrane's (1971) call for a rigorous evaluation of health services and McKeown's (1976) critique of the contribution of modern medicine. But while Cochrane reinforced the medical model, by emphasising the scientific evaluation of interventions, McKeown's thesis challenged it. McKeown argued that modern medicine was too individualised and disease oriented, and ignored the wider social, economic and environmental influences on health. He contended that the contribution of medicine to the decline of disease had been exaggerated, supporting this with historical evidence that the decline of major diseases such as measles, whooping cough and tuberculosis occurred well before the advent of immunisation and effective medical treatment. McKeown identified an improvement in nutrition and a rising standard of living as the key factors in the reduction of morbidity and mortality since the late nineteenth century, and accepted that improved hygiene was also partly responsible for the reduction in the death rate from the mid-nineteenth century onwards (see also, Wohl, 1984). Furthermore, he pointed out that the major causes of ill health in industrial societies – cancer, heart disease and circulatory disease – resulted largely from individual behaviour and environmental factors and could therefore be prevented. In contrast, orthodox medicine could offer only an inadequate and belated response following conclusive evidence of specific disease processes.

Many of McKeown's conclusions attracted support (see Burkitt, 1973; Powles, 1973; Illich, 1977; McKinlay, 1979), although some challenged aspects of his thesis. Szreter (1988) disputed that rising nutritional and living standards were mainly responsible for the declining mortality rate. He argued that key actors within the medical profession played a key role in preventing illness by participating in the Victorian public health movement and promoting community health services at a local level.

Sagan (1987), while sharing McKeown's cynicism about the impact of medical care, meanwhile rejected the argument that public health measures or improvements in standards of living and nutrition were primarily responsible for declining mortality. He argued that the improvement in health resulted from a higher level of resistance to disease that was determined by social factors. In particular, he identified a reduction in family size and modern parenting behaviour as the main reasons for the improvement in health. In Sagan's own words, 'the smaller and more affectionate modern family has been a powerful factor contributing to improved health of individuals and to the historic fall in mortality rates' (p. 102). By the same token, he suggests that recent trends – marital instability, divorce and single parenting – have an adverse implication for both mental and physical health today.

McKeown's thesis was also attacked for failing to appreciate the full contribution of modern medicine. While scientific medicine in the Victorian period did little for patients at the time, there were some important innovations – such as chloroform anaesthesia and the development of diphtheria antitoxin – that laid the foundation for later discoveries and made possible the development of new and more effective forms of treatment (see Bynum, 1994). In addition, many improvements in medical treatment not only saved lives, but also improved the quality of life for many, even though such advances were not necessarily reflected in mortality and morbidity indicators (Morris, 1980). Furthermore, it is clear that treatment does 'add years to life'. Bunker *et al.* (1994), examining the impact of medical care in the USA, found that the current effect of curative medicine added between 44 and 45 months to life expectancy, an additional 18–19 months being added by preventive medicine.

Although McKeown's original thesis was disputed, it served to focus attention on the wider causes of ill health and created a broader awareness of social and environmental factors. This had implications for two key policy debates: the use of resources by the health care system and the need for a broader strategy to promote health and prevent disease.

## Health Care Resources

The preoccupation of successive governments with the funding of the NHS intensified in the adverse economic circumstances of the 1970s and the neo-liberal ideological climate of the following decade. The desire to secure economies in the public sector budget led them to consider measures to prevent illness in the hope of saving treatment costs in the longer term. Indeed, as Lewis (1992) has argued, the interest in prevention was prompted more by a desire to save money than to improve medical care. Not surprisingly, the idea of prevention, particularly as it related to individuals taking greater responsibility for their own health, was endorsed by the Treasury in this period (Webster, 1996).

Yet it is by no means certain that prevention is less costly to the public purse compared with expanding treatment facilities. Indeed, as Cairns (1995) has observed, there is very little evidence on the cost effectiveness of prevention strategies. It may well be that prevention is actually a less cost-effective strategy compared with expanding treatment services. In particular, prevention strategies often have longer-term costs that weigh heavily in the future. For example, if more people live longer because they give up smoking, this may have an impact on health care cost, not to mention the costs of pensions and long-term care (unless these can be shifted back onto individuals, as recent UK governments have tried to do).

## Towards a Health Strategy

In the 1970s, the Labour government sought to raise the profile of prevention and health promotion issues by publishing a consultative document, *Prevention and Health: Everybody's Business* (DHSS, 1976). This identified the following as key areas for future intervention: inequalities in health status, heart disease, road accidents, smoking-related diseases, alcoholism, mental illness, drugs, diet and venereal disease. The document aimed to promote discussion rather than to outline a programme of action, and it was expected that the government's subsequent White Paper, *Prevention and Health* (Cmnd 7047, 1977), would be more strategic, although this turned out to be a rather cautious document. Apart from an increase in resources for health education, which still remained poorly resourced, the government did little to alter the balance between prevention and treatment services.

The British government's interest in prevention and health promotion reflected a broader international movement. During the 1970s, several governments examined the potential for placing a greater emphasis on these elements of health policy. In Canada, for example, the Lalonde Report (Lalonde, 1974) called for a government strategy incorporating an awareness that health could be promoted in a range of fields, such as lifestyle and the environment, rather than just within the boundaries of health service provision. Over the next two decades, health strategies were adopted in a number of other countries, including the USA, Australia and New Zealand. These initiatives took place in the context of the *Health for All* strategy (WHO, 1981) and *Healthy Cities* initiative (Davies and Kelly, 1992), discussed in Chapter 4.

Throughout the 1980s, the UK government, led by Margaret Thatcher, was vehemently opposed to any form of central health strategy, despite being out of step with international developments. The Thatcher government favoured prevention policies that were consistent with its ideological predisposition – saving public money, promoting managerialism in public services and encouraging individual responsibility. More pragmatically, certain schemes were endorsed if they promised reassurance to voters that the NHS was safe in the hands of the Conservative Government. This partly explains the extension of cancer screening programmes, mass health education campaigns and health promotion in general practice during this period.

Faced with the refusal to formulate a national strategy, many local authorities bypassed central government and set up their own *Health for All* strategies. Many built on the experience of the *Healthy Cities* initiative, which sought to develop comprehensive strategies to improve health among cities with some of the worst problems. These initiatives also attracted the attention of some health authorities, which made a real effort to work with local authorities to promote public health. However, as we shall see in the following chapter, a lack of central direction and funding inhibited the development of local strategies to combat the causes of ill health. In other parts of the UK outside England, there was more support for the development of public health strategies. In Wales, for example, an attempt was made in 1989 to develop a clear health strategy along the lines of *Health for All* (see Exhibit 4.2). Both Scotland and Northern Ireland launched plans to promote health during the following year. England eventually followed suit with its *Health of the Nation* strategy in 1992, discussed in some detail in Chapter 4.

The English strategy resulted from additional pressure during the late 1980s. This took the form of pressure-group lobbying as well as a broader public concern about health issues. The pressure groups fell into two main categories: those campaigning across the range of environmental and public health issues and those more sharply focused on a specific illness or cause of ill health. The latter included 'single issue' groups such as Action on Smoking and Health (ASH) and Alcohol Concern. The former category included groups such as the Public Health Alliance, formed in 1987, which brought together a range of individuals and organisations concerned with public health. This category also included environmental pressure groups, such as Greenpeace and Friends of the Earth, as well as professional organisations, such as the BMA, the RCP, and the Faculty of Community Medicine (now the Faculty of Public Health Medicine).

The professional organisations used their contacts with the DoH and other relevant government departments to raise concerns about public health policy. Most pressure groups in the field of public health were, however, 'outsider groups' (see Chapter 1) and lacked a close and continuous relationship with government, but these groups were able to develop links with

Parliament: individual MPs and peers were lobbied on specific issues such as food safety, smoking and alcohol abuse. In addition, both insider and outsider groups submitted evidence to Select Committees – in particular the Committee of Public Accounts, the Agriculture Committee and the Health (formerly Social Services) Committee – when they investigated aspects of public health policy (see, for example, Public Accounts Committee, 1989, 1992, 1997; Agriculture Committee, 1989, 1990, 1998).

The activities of pressure groups also shaped public perception by publicising environmental and public health matters during the 1980s. The media played a crucial role, covering public health issues in depth and highlighting failures of policy and shortcomings in service provision. During the 1980s and 90s, public health was rarely out of the news given the high-profile coverage of issues such as AIDS (see Exhibit 3.1), drug and alcohol abuse, smoking, food poisoning, bovine spongiform encephalopathy (BSE), and environmental pollution.

Particularly important was the media coverage of two major outbreaks of infectious disease during the mid-1980s: the food poisoning incident at the Stanley Royd Hospital in Wakefield, which resulted in 19 deaths (Cmnd 9716, 1986), and the outbreak of Legionnaire's disease at Stafford General Hospital, where 39 people died (Cmnd 9772, 1986). Both exposed failures of public health planning at a local level and a shortage of medical expertise in environmental health, leading to the establishment of the Acheson inquiry, discussed earlier.

---

Exhibit 3.1

---

### AIDS, sexual health and public health

Predictions of a worldwide AIDS epidemic in the 1980s forced governments to take the issue of sexual health far more seriously than had previously been the case. In the UK, the Thatcher government's ideological position on family values and sexual morality (see Durham, 1991) initially predisposed it against health promotion strategies in this field. Indeed, despite the potential consequences of inaction on the AIDS issue, there was much hostility to an awareness campaign, both within the Cabinet and in the Conservative Party at large (Day and Klein, 1989; Garfield, 1994). Yet by 1985, the Chief Medical Officer, Donald Acheson, and the Secretary of State for Health, Sir Norman Fowler, had been authorised to issue advertisements in national newspapers, publicising the dangers of AIDS. This was a step forward, although ,as Garfield (1994) noted, the initial advertisement was considerably delayed by internal wrangling and was heavily censored by those in government who believed it might offend the public.

Exhibit 3.1 *(cont'd)*

A high-profile publicity campaign was subsequently launched, largely as a result of the persuasiveness of DoH ministers and civil servants, and Thatcher's own senior advisors, in particular the Cabinet Secretary, Robert Armstrong. Another factor was the creation of a separate Cabinet committee on AIDS, which comprised some of the more liberal members of the Thatcher Cabinet and was able to facilitate a more enlightened policy (see Berridge, 1996). At the same time, responsibility for devising a programme of action was delegated to the medical profession and public health experts, which, as Day and Klein (1989) observed, insulated the policy process from disruptive populist pressures, articulated chiefly by the tabloid press. The Thatcher government's policy was, as a result, surprisingly liberal: increased funding for research into HIV/AIDs and support services for those suffering from the illness, as well as relatively generous budgets for health promotion in this field. Some things were, however, clearly beyond the pale: in 1989, Prime Minister Margaret Thatcher refused to fund a survey of the nation's sexual habits, which some argued would provide useful information on which to base future policies and campaigns. In the event, the survey proceeded thanks to the Wellcome Trust. The Thatcher government was also opposed to needle-exchange schemes to prevent HIV transmission among drug users, although such schemes were also eventually introduced (see Chapter 9).

The Major government included HIV/AIDS as one of its five target areas within *The Health of the Nation* strategy (Cm 1986, 1992). Two main targets were set, neither relating directly to HIV infection: to reduce the incidence of gonorrhoea by at least 20 per cent between 1990 and 1995, and to reduce by at least half the rate of conception among the under-16s by the year 2000 (baseline 1989). A further risk factor target – to reduce the percentage of injecting drug misusers sharing injecting equipment – was widely welcomed. In other respects, however, the Major government's policy on AIDS and sexual health was less enlightened. Following a campaign by 'family values' campaigners on the right of the Conservative Party, the 1993 Education Act contained a clause that inhibited sex education and contraceptive advice in schools by enabling parents to withdraw their children from sex education classes. In an attempt to appease the 'family values' lobby, ministers began to be more openly critical of 'explicit' sex education campaigns. In 1994, for example, a booklet on sexual matters for teenagers produced by the Health Education Authority (HEA) was withdrawn on the orders of the health minister, Brian Mawhinney. In addition, the Major government was criticised for scrapping a £2m AIDS awareness campaign in 1994 and for cutting funding for AIDS prevention and treatment in 1996.

The impact of *The Health of the Nation* strategy on sexual health was mixed. There was criticism that the target for the reduction in gonorrhoea infection, which was achieved earlier than expected, masked other, less favourable trends in sexual health (see Adler, 1997). The HIV infection rate, for example, continued to rise during the 1990s, while the rate of infection for other sexually transmitted diseases, such as genital warts, chlamydia infections and herpes, increased. Chlamydia infections rose

Exhibit 3.1 *(cont'd)*

almost a fifth, herpes by over a third and wart virus by over a quarter between 1990 and 1996. Furthermore, it was unlikely that the other main target would be achieved, relating to the reduction of under-age pregnancies, as the rate had fallen by around a third of that required by 1996.

Finally, the Blair government launched a 10-year sexual health initiative in 1999. This aimed to improve the links between health services, schools and families in an effort to cut the high levels of teenage pregnancy (by half), sexually transmitted disease, and abortion. Additional funding has been announced for new advisory services and publicity campaigns, and fresh guidance on sex education will be provided.

Meanwhile, the number of reported cases of HIV infection has continued to increase, although, at around 2500 a year, at much less than was predicted back in the early 1980s. Nevertheless, between 1990 and 1997, over 9000 people in the UK died from AIDS (ONS, 1999). It is currently estimated that around 30,000 people in the UK are carrying the HIV virus, although, because of improved therapy (see below), the number of deaths from AIDS in England and Wales fell from 1200 in 1996 to 395 in 1998. Worldwide, over 32 million adults and 1.2 million children are believed to be infected with HIV/AIDS. It was estimated that there would be 6 million new infections in 1999 and 2.6 million deaths (UNAIDS, 1999). It is estimated that the vast majority of currently HIV-infected people live in sub-Saharan Africa (approximately 23 million) and South East Asia (6 million) (UNAIDS, 1999).

On a more positive note, the survival rate has improved where treatment with antiretroviral drugs is available. Notably, the death rate from AIDS fell by two-thirds in the USA between 1995 and 1997, largely as a result of improved drug therapy.

Although the media played an important role in publicising perceived threats to public health, some sections of it – in particular the tabloid press – took a rather cynical view of public health campaigners. Despite the fact that they were able to tap into a 'fatalistic' strand of public opinion, these newspapers operated against the tide of public opinion, which became more rather than less concerned with lifestyle and environmental threats to public health. Evidence from successive British Social Attitudes surveys indicated a high level of public concern about such issues. The 1987 survey, for example, reported that a large majority of people – 70 per cent of respondents – believed that they could alter their lifestyle to avoid heart disease, younger people being on average less fatalistic than their elders (Sheiham *et al.*, 1987). The 1990 survey found a significant level of public concern surrounding pollution and environmental health: 94 per cent of respondents were concerned about the disposal of sewage, 91 per cent about insecticides, fertilisers and chemical sprays, and 82 per cent about the quality of drinking water (Young, 1991; see also Young, 1985).

# Explaining Historical Variations

Returning to the questions posed at the end of the previous chapter, why has public health varied in importance over time, and why have particular approaches to public health predominated in certain historical periods? Taking ideological factors first, it appears that dominant ideologies within government have exerted much influence on both the priority given to public health and the choice of policy options. Historically, the entrenchment of *laissez-faire* and individualistic libertarian principles has been associated with a downgrading of health considerations relative to other priorities, such as promoting trade, and has been linked to the rejection of certain policy options, such as tighter regulations on commercial activities that harm health or welfare policies that actively promote health.

It has, however, also been shown that prevailing ideologies can generate approaches that conflict with their own basic principles. Hence in Victorian and Edwardian times, although *laissez-faire* principles remained strong, a collectivist approach to public health nevertheless emerged. Similarly, it was under the neo-liberal governments of Thatcher and Major that the adoption of new public health strategies were considered and then implemented. This apparent paradox can perhaps be explained in terms of the desire of such governments to curb the state's responsibilities: certain interventionist strategies are endorsed because it is believed that they will produce a net reduction in the responsibilities of the state. Hence in the Victorian period, improved sanitation was viewed as a means of reducing the burden of the Poor Law, while in the Edwardian period, it was argued that public health interventions could improve Britain's national efficiency and competitiveness. Moreover, during the 1990s, public health strategies were endorsed by governments as means of reducing the cost of illness to the state and increasing individual responsibility for health. It is similarly ironic that the pursuit of collectivist policies to improve state welfare, including the creation of the NHS, apparently did little to support a more comprehensive approach to public health focused on tackling the underlying causes of ill health. Indeed, by emphasising the importance of specific state-funded treatment services rather than the promotion of health, the case for this broader approach was apparently undermined.

Another point is that one should not focus on the influence of ideologies within government to the extent that the interplay of ideological forces in society is ignored. Even those supporting collectivist solutions to public health problems in various historical periods faced opposition from key sections of public opinion, not to mention commercial interests. As has been shown, this was particularly evident in the Victorian period, but even during the first few decades of the early twentieth century, the entrenchment of these ideologies inhibited radical reform, which partly explains the slow progress made on issues such as Poor Law reform and housing improvement. In contrast, during the 1980s and 90s, it was the entrenchment of ideological values in society rather than in government that supported a more progressive approach to public health. The growth of Green ideologies within society, coupled with the persistence of collectivist values, appears to have to some extent deterred neo-liberal governments from pursuing approaches placing less emphasis on state intervention. Indeed, public health strategies can be seen as a means by which these governments sought to reassure the public of their stewardship of health and the NHS, while environmental legislation (see Chapter 7) represented an attempt to show their Green credentials.

Institutional factors have also been shown to be crucial to the prioritisation of public health and the adoption and rejection of certain modes of intervention. As was shown in the previous chapter, the administration of the Poor Law, although on one hand providing a rationale for sanitary improvement in the early Victorian era, nevertheless prevented the emergence of social policies that could have significantly improved public health. One reason for this was that, until the creation of the Ministry of Health in 1919, public health was governed within an institutional framework dominated by the Poor Law ethos. The inclusion of public health within the brief of the LGB underlined its subservience to these principles. Even when the Ministry of Health was created, it proved a relatively weak ministry within the structure of government, and this effectively undermined its potential contribution. It did have wide-ranging responsibilities enabling it to consider a broad spread of factors that affected health, but important functions lay outside its direct control and fragmented efforts aimed at improving public health. Furthermore, the loss of non-health service functions after the Second World War narrowed the focus of the Ministry, so it became primarily concerned with health service provision rather than with public health in its wider sense. Meanwhile the responsibility for public health issues became fragmented between different departments, making it difficult to incorporate health into the wider decision-making process.

This historical review has also shown that individuals have played a key role in the form of public health intervention. Figures such as Chadwick and Simon were obviously influential, but it must not be forgotten that they operated within an institutional setting, holding positions within government bureaucracies, and employed ideas that attracted much wider support. In the modern era, there have been fewer 'giants'. Instead, many significant individuals have been active behind the scenes, in government departments and agencies, in the professions and in academia, although this is not to say that their collective impact has been less important.

The activities of pressure groups and their interaction with institutions of decision making has influenced public health over the years. Public health legislation in the nineteenth century was due in no small part to the agitation of groups that drew their support from a wide range of professional back-grounds, including the medical profession, sanitary inspectors, engineers, statisticians and social scientists. Support from individual doctors for public health intervention was extremely helpful to the campaigns of the nineteenth century, even though medical organisations such as the Royal Colleges were unsupportive and in some respects hostile. The growing status of medicine added greatly to its political clout and strengthened the hand of the public health lobby, particularly during the late Victorian period.

During the twentieth century, the medical profession was allowed to domi-nate the public health lobby as many other interests began to focus more upon social justice and welfare provision. At the same time, although the impor-tance of preventive medicine was not forgotten, the medical profession became more concerned with the provision of treatment services, particularly those associated with new technology. This was to some extent redressed from the 1960s onwards, when doctors and their representative organisations began to highlight once again the role of social and economic factors in ill health. Later, they also began to build links with other groups concerned with public health issues, environmental organisations for example. The lesson appears to be that although doctors and their representative organisations have – in view of their considerable political resources, status and contacts – played a vital role in public health policy making, their domination of this policy community has in the past led to a greater emphasis on clinical intervention rather than social, economic or environmental action. Conversely, when public health lobbies are more broadly based, with the medical profession as a powerful ally rather than a leader, they tend to favour the latter type of intervention.

Finally, explanations related to the perception of risk and the role of scientific experts are extremely relevant. Particular events and circumstances, such as epidemics, have played an important role in highlighting the need for public health measures. Hence cholera and HIV/AIDS did much to provoke action in their respective historical periods. But the magnitude of a health problem is much less important than the perception of the threat it poses. As we have seen, cholera was by no means the biggest cause of death in the nine-teenth century, and the same could so far be said of HIV/AIDS in industri-alised countries in our own time. Much has therefore depended on the publicity surrounding certain threats to health, public attitudes to risk, the documentation of disease trends and efforts to establish a link between illness and particular social, economic and environmental circumstances in ways that evoke a policy response.

Scientific factors are also important in shaping both public perceptions and government policies. Developments in medical science from the late Victorian period onwards facilitated the shift away from crude public health interventions such as quarantine, and to some extent from sanitary measures, towards an approach geared more to individualised clinical intervention. The location of new technology in the hospital sector enhanced the status of the medical professionals working there, eclipsing their colleagues working in general practice and public health medicine. Hospital medicine also dominated the research agenda, resulting in limited resources for the analysis of the social and environmental causes of modern illness, placing even greater emphasis on clinical intervention at the individual level. This was in turn reinforced by the growing status of GPs, who focused on individual and family health, at the expense of public health medicine, though even the latter concentrated more on the provision of services than on promoting healthy communities. These trends also encouraged an emphasis on clinical interventions such as mass screening. However, criticism of the cost effectiveness of medical interventions, the contribution of medicine to the decline of diseases, and research into the impact of social and environmental factors led to a renewed emphasis on comprehensive public health strategies, though, as will be shown in the next chapter, this new agenda remained focused primarily on the reduction of disease and remained dominated by medical expertise.

# 4

# Health Strategies

As shown in the previous chapter, the British government faced increasing pressure from the 1970s onwards to adopt formal health strategies. This chapter begins by examining the introduction of the health strategy for England by the Major government, its impact and its subsequent amendment by the Blair government. It also discusses the similarities and differences between England and the rest of the UK. The latter part of the chapter explores the development of international health strategies and in particular the role played by the WHO and the European Union, and also discusses the adoption of local health strategies in the UK.

## *The Health of the Nation* Strategy for England

### A U-turn for the Conservatives?

In 1991, despite its earlier hostility to the idea, the Conservative government published a Green Paper, *The Health of the Nation* (Cm 1523, 1991), proposing a health strategy for England. A number of factors lay behind this. The replacement in 1990 of Margaret Thatcher as Prime Minister by the seemingly more pragmatic John Major suggested that the strategy would be less likely to be vetoed on ideological grounds. In addition, William Waldegrave, appointed by Thatcher as Secretary of State for Health before her departure and retained by Major, apparently supported the development of health targets and encouraged efforts already underway to establish a strategy based on this.

The stated aim of the strategy was to secure a continuing improvement in the health of the population by 'adding years to life' – increasing life expectancy and reducing premature death – and by 'adding life to years' – increasing the quality of life and minimising illness. This was to be achieved through the selection of key health areas, based on the following criteria: that the health problem in question must be a major cause of premature death or avoidable ill health, responsive to effective intervention and amenable to the setting of objectives, targets and methods of monitoring.

The Green Paper set out potential key areas for the strategy. These included causes of substantial mortality, such as coronary heart disease, stroke, cancer and accidents, and causes of substantial ill health, for example mental health problems, diabetes and asthma. Also covered were factors contributing to both mortality and morbidity, such as smoking, alcohol consumption and a lack of exercise. Areas where there was considerable scope for improving health were also identified: the health of the elderly, the care of pregnant women, the health of infants and children, dental health, rehabilitation of physically disabled people, back pain, drug misuse and the environment. Finally, the Green Paper identified a number of other health problems where there was great potential for harm, such as HIV/AIDS, other communicable diseases, such as hospital-acquired infections, and food safety.

The Green Paper was a basis for discussion with a range of experts and interested parties. Following consultation, a White Paper was issued (Cm 1986, 1992) that finalised the strategy. In this document, several of the potential target areas mentioned in the Green Paper were discarded. Some – childhood immunisation, maternal and child health, oral health and food safety – were excluded because the government argued that they were already sufficiently well developed. Other possible key areas, including rehabilitation, the health of the elderly, asthma, back pain and drug misuse, were rejected on the grounds that further research would be needed before national targets could be set. A further three potential areas – diabetes, hospital-acquired infection and breastfeeding – were acknowledged as areas in which improvement should occur but were not accredited with key area status. The remaining five areas – cancer, heart disease and stroke, mental illness, HIV/AIDS and sexual health, and accidents – were regarded as suitable. Two types of target were identified for each category: main targets, setting out a reduction in the incidence of illness and mortality in various key areas, and risk factor targets, aimed at tackling some of the causes of these illnesses. These are detailed in Exhibit 4.1.

The White Paper set out how different organisations and agencies could help to achieve these priorities. Central government's main contribution was to co-ordinate the activities of the various departments of state. Guidance on policy appraisal was proposed as a means of assessing policies in terms of their consequences for health. A ministerial Cabinet committee (involving ministers drawn from 11 government departments) was established to oversee the implementation of the strategy for England and to co-ordinate health issues across the UK as a whole. A number of other committees were set up to support the ministerial committee: the Wider Health Working Group (chaired by a Health Minister), the Health Priorities Working Group (chaired by the government's Chief Medical Officer) and the Working Group on Implementation in the NHS (chaired by the Chief Executive of the NHS). In addition the Chief Medical Officer chaired an interdepartmental group comprising officials from all government departments whose activities were relevant to public health.

The NHS was expected to operate within this strategic framework. Health authorities were to collaborate with other agencies in an attempt to tackle the main health problems identified by national strategy as well as priorities identified in local plans. Regional co-ordinators were appointed to assist with the implementation process by disseminating good practice, and focus groups were established for each key area to emphasise their importance within the NHS. Furthermore, in an effort to promote collaboration between the NHS and other agencies, task forces were formed incorporating individuals from government, business, the NHS and academia. Their purpose was to draw up co-ordinated programmes of action for specific areas of the strategy, to promote co-operation between the parties involved and to ensure effective implementation.

---

Exhibit 4.1

---

### *The Health of the Nation*: original main targets and risk factor targets

**1. Main targets**

*Coronary heart disease and stroke:*

- To reduce death rates in the under-65 age group for both coronary heart disease (CHD) and stroke by 40 per cent by the year 2000 (1990 baseline).

- To reduce the death rate for CHD in people aged 65–74 by at least 30 per cent by the year 2000 (1990 baseline).

- To reduce the death rate for stroke in people aged 65–74 by at least 40 per cent by the year 2000 (1990 baseline).

*Cancer:*

- To reduce the death rate from breast cancer in the screened population by at least 25 per cent by the year 2000 (1990 baseline).

- To reduce the incidence of invasive cervical cancer by at least 20 per cent by the year 2000 (1986 baseline).

- To reduce the death rate for lung cancer in the under-75s by at least 30 per cent in men and at least 15 per cent in women by 2010 (1990 baseline).

- To halt the year-on-year increase in skin cancer by 2005.

Exhibit 4.1 *(cont'd)*

---

*Mental health:*

- To improve significantly the health and social functioning of mentally ill people.
- To reduce the overall suicide rate by at least 15 per cent by the year 2000 (1990 baseline).
- To reduce the suicide rate of severely mentally ill people by at least 33 per cent by the year 2000 (1990 baseline).

*HIV/AIDS and sexual health:*

- To reduce the incidence of gonorrhoea by at least 20 per cent by 1995 (1990 baseline) as an indicator of HIV/AIDS trends.
- To reduce by at least 50 per cent the rate of conception among the under-16s by the year 2000 (1989 baseline).

*Accidents:*

- To reduce the death rate for accidents among children aged under 15 by at least 33 per cent by 2005 (1990 baseline).
- To reduce the death rate for accidents among young people aged 15–24 by at least 25 per cent by 2005 (1990 baseline).
- To reduce the death rate for accidents among people aged 65 and over by at least 33 per cent by 2005 (1990 baseline).

**2. Risk factor targets**

*Diet and nutrition:*

- To reduce the proportion of men drinking more than 21 units of alcohol (approximately equivalent to 10.5 pints of beer) per week, and the proportion of women drinking more than 14 units per week, by 30 per cent by 2005 (1990 baseline).
- To reduce the proportion of obese men and women in the 16–64 age group by 25 per cent and 33 per cent respectively by 2005 (1986/87 baseline).
- To reduce the average percentage of food energy derived by the population from saturated fat by at least 35 per cent by 2005 (1990 baseline).
- To reduce the average percentage of food energy derived from total fat by the population by at least 12 per cent by 2005 (1990 baseline).

Exhibit 4.1 *(cont'd)*

*Smoking:*

● To reduce the prevalence of men and women smoking cigarettes to no more than 20 per cent by the year 2000 (1990 baseline).

● To reduce the consumption of cigarettes by 40 per cent by the year 2000 (1990 baseline).

● To reduce the prevalence of smoking among 11–15-year-olds by at least 33 per cent by 1994 (1988 baseline).

● To reduce smoking among women at the start of pregnancy by at least 33 per cent by the year 2000.

*Blood pressure:*

● To reduce the mean systolic blood pressure in the adult population by at least 5 mmHg by 2005 (baseline to be established by a new national survey).

*HIV/AIDS:*

● To reduce the percentage of injecting drug misusers who report sharing injecting equipment in the previous four weeks from 20 per cent in 1990 to no more than 10 per cent by 1997 and no more than 5 per cent by the year 2000.

*Source:* Adapted from Cm 1986 (1992) *The Health of the Nation*, pp. 18–21, London, HMSO.

A central theme of the strategy was collaboration. It was envisaged that local authorities, the HEA, the voluntary sector, the media and employers would co-operate with the strategy. The government promoted the formation of 'healthy alliances' to improve health in the key areas. Several settings were also identified as possible arenas where healthy alliances could flourish: 'healthy cities', 'healthy schools', 'healthy hospitals', 'healthy homes', 'healthy workplaces', 'healthy prisons' and 'healthy environments'. Finally, a series of measures was announced in an effort to improve the information base for public health decision making. These included more surveys of health and illness, a public health information strategy and new research and development priorities to reflect the health strategy.

## *The Impact of* The Health of the Nation *Strategy*

Although most observers welcomed the Major government's strategy as being long overdue, specific aspects of its design and content, and subsequently the implementation of the policy, attracted criticism. It was pointed out that the health strategy was inconsistent with other health care reforms, in particular the NHS internal market introduced in the early 1990s (Moran, 1989; Ewles, 1993). Although the internal market gave health authorities clearer responsibility for the health of their resident populations, it made it more difficult to achieve improvements in public health by introducing competition. This, it was argued, fragmented systems of service delivery and diverted resources away from health promotion into service provision (see Chapter 5).

It was later found that the health strategy had a symbolic effect and in some cases stimulated health promotion activity. For example, a review of the strategy's impact in the North Thames region found a 'widespread commitment to local health strategies and to *Health of the Nation* across the NHS and beyond'. The study also discovered 'a great deal of activity' within the five key areas and in healthy settings such as workplaces and hospitals. In addition, it found evidence of joint working to promote health between NHS trusts, local authorities and primary health care teams (PHCTs) (Cornish *et al.*, 1997, pp. 4–5). However, it identified several factors that inhibited implementation, including the clash of different organisational cultures and agendas, tension between different public health perspectives and between rival professional groups, and the conflict between the public health agenda and the need to 'balance the books'.

Further research commissioned by the DoH also found that the initiative had a symbolic effect of placing health improvement and the prevention of illness on the agenda (DoH, 1998b). However, these researchers found that 'it did not change significantly the perspective and behaviour of health authorities and did not fundamentally alter the context within which the dialogue between health purchasers and providers and other partners took place' and that 'by 1997, its impact on local policymaking was negligible' (DoH, 1998b, p. 13). A number of reasons were suggested to explain this, one of the most significant being that health authorities perceived the strategy to be less important than other priorities and pressures, such as reducing waiting lists and implementing further reorganisations.

Other critics of *The Health of the Nation* had earlier challenged the use of targets on the grounds that they downgraded health problems that could not easily be quantified (Faculty of Public Health Medicine, 1991). It was also argued that many of the targets were based on inadequate scientific evidence (Akehurst *et al.*, 1991). Furthermore, the targets were said to reflect a medical rather than a broader social perspective (Radical Statistics Health Group, 1991). Indeed, they related more to the prevention of specific diseases rather than to the promotion of health in the community as a whole or to any improvement in the health of specific groups such as elderly people, children and those in poverty. The Faculty of Public Health Medicine had argued for an approach based on factors that caused ill health rather than on disease (Holland and Stewart, 1998). Although risk factor targets were included in the government's strategy, they were clearly secondary to the main disease targets and reflected individual rather than environmental or socio-economic factors. By neglecting the underlying socio-economic causes of ill health, the strategy alienated potential supporters and partners, in particular the local authorities (DoH, 1998b).

Some said that the targets were too ambitious. Bosanquet and Hockley (1998), for example, claimed that the government had little influence over the targets and that too many targets had been adopted. They called for fewer core targets combined with a less directive and more inclusive approach bringing together a range of organisations (including non-government organisations) while harnessing consumer power to raise health and safety standards. They also identified the need to improve information systems as a prerequisite to effective decision-making in the field of public health. Others, however, argued that the targets were too easy to achieve and that many would be met simply by the continuation of current trends (see, for example, Mooney and Healey, 1991). This may partly explain why, only three years after the introduction of the strategy, the government was able to state that it was on course for achieving most of the targets (DoH, 1995b).

Yet subsequent reports proved less optimistic. A report from the National Audit Office (NAO, 1996a) discovered good progress in only 11 out of the 27 of target areas and found poor progress in three areas: women's alcohol consumption, smoking among children and obesity in both men and women. The proportion of women drinking above 14 units per week rose from 11 per cent to 13 per cent between 1990 and 1994. Smoking among 11–15-year-olds increased from 8 per cent to 12 per cent over the period 1988–94. Meanwhile, the proportion of obese adult males of working age rose from 7 per cent in 1986 to 13 per cent by 1994. Over the same period, obesity among women rose from 12 per cent to 16 per cent.

The failure to meet these targets revealed the limits of the Major government's health promotion policy. Like its predecessor, this government resisted the strong pressure to ban tobacco advertising in spite of evidence that it could reduce smoking (see Chapter 9). It was reluctant to take on the alcohol industry and, in 1995, actually relaxed the 'sensible drinking' limits for alcohol in spite of warnings from the majority of medical opinion, charities dealing with alcohol abuse and other organisations, including the WHO (Chapter 9). Furthermore, it was keen to avoid confrontation with the food industry lobby, refusing to establish an independent food standards agency (see Chapter 8). The Major government also refused to incorporate environmental factors into its health strategy, which, given the association between environment and health, was seen as a crucial omission (see Chapter 7). In 1996, however, it did respond to these critics by proposing that the environment be included as an additional key area.

The failure to consider inequality and social deprivation as part of the health strategy was also widely condemned. In the Appendix to the Green Paper, the government admitted that the WHO European Region target of reducing health inequalities by at least 25 per cent by the year 2000 would probably not be achieved. The relationship between poverty and ill health was not explicitly discussed in either the Green or the White Paper, and a section on housing and ill health was omitted from the published version of the Green Paper. In the White Paper, 'healthy homes' were identified as a 'setting' on which to focus, but no clear commitment made to improving poor housing conditions.

Those who were cynical about the impact of the health strategy on the co-ordination on public health matters within central government were largely proved correct. Other government departments refused to subvert their policy objectives to health priorities, and it was found that the initiative failed to generate cross-departmental commitment and ownership (DoH, 1998b). Although guidance on policy appraisal and health was issued by the DoH, other departments were not compelled to adopt it. Moreover, it fell far short of the comprehensive health impact assessment procedure called for by some (see Exhibit 7.2). The ministerial committee on public health was not perceived as being active or effective, and it had a very low profile (DoH, 1998b). Calls for a Minister for Public Health to co-ordinate the health aspects of policy making across government were resisted (see Public Health Alliance, 1988), although the Blair government did create such a post on taking office in 1997.

## Our Healthier Nation

Senior Labour Party politicians endorsed the idea of a national health strategy while in opposition during the 1990s. Even so, they were critical of several aspects of *The Health of the Nation*, above all its failure to acknowledge the impact of social, economic and environmental factors. They made it clear that, once in office, their health strategy would be significantly different both in its content and in the manner of its implementation. Shortly after the Blair government took office, the DoH commissioned research into the impact of the previous government's strategy (DoH, 1998b). The aim of this exercise was ostensibly to create a knowledge base for the revision of the strategy. However, it also served to expose the shortcomings of *The Health of the Nation*, thereby legitimising further reforms in this field. The Blair government, as mentioned earlier, also created a new post with responsibility for the revised strategy: the Minister for Public Health. Some observers were unhappy that this was not a Cabinet-level post: the first appointee, Tessa Jowell, held the rank of Minister of State. The level of disappointment increased when, in 1999, Jowell was replaced by a minister holding the lower rank of Parliamentary Under Secretary of State.

The Blair government's public health strategy was set out in a 1998 Green Paper entitled *Our Healthier Nation* (Cm 3852, 1998). Following a long period of delay – invariably an indicator of conflict between different factions or departments within government – a White Paper was published (Cm 4386, 1999). It should be noted that, not for the first time, separate public health policy statements were set out for Wales, Scotland and Northern Ireland (Exhibit 4.2).

---

Exhibit 4.2

### Other national health strategies in the UK

Public health policies have often varied between different parts of the UK. During the early 1990s, for example, Wales was at the forefront of developing innovative public health plans, other parts of the UK – notably England – lagging behind. Differences in approach were also reflected in policy documents issued in England, Wales, Scotland and Northern Ireland during that decade. Devolved government, in the form of the Scottish Parliament and the Welsh and Northern Ireland Assemblies, has opened up the prospect of further divergence in future.

Wales became the first part of the UK to launch a public health strategy when, in 1989, the Welsh Office introduced its *Strategic Intent and Direction* document (Welsh Office, NHS Directorate, 1989). This set out 10 priority areas for achieving a sustained improvement in health status or, in the terminology used, a 'health gain'. These areas were cancer, maternal and child health, mental handicap, mental distress and illness, injury, emotional health, respiratory illness, cardiovascular disease, a healthy environment, and physical disability/discomfort. It was intended that protocols in each area would highlight priorities for the investment and disinvestment of NHS resources. Plans were also introduced to involve other stakeholders, such as local authorities, the voluntary sector and service users, in the development of local health strategies. In practice, however, this ambitious plan did not achieve its aims. In an evaluation of the strategy, the National Audit Office (NAO, 1996b) found that it had only a marginal impact as a result of several factors: a lack of leadership from the Welsh Office (which was partly due to ministerial changes and a consequent cooling of interest in the strategy), too many targets being set, an inadequate monitoring of performance and a difficulty in releasing resources to invest in areas where health gain could be maximised.

The change of government in 1997 presented a further opportunity for Wales to develop a distinctive approach. The Blair government not only appeared to be more

Exhibit 4.2 *(cont'd)*

willing to acknowledge the social and economic roots of ill health, but was also committed to giving Wales a degree of self-government, subject to a referendum. In 1998, both these developments were reflected in a revised health strategy for Wales (Cm 3922, 1998) and a subsequent strategic framework (National Assembly for Wales, 1998). The Welsh strategy appeared to focus more sharply on the economic and social context of health than did the English strategy. It also suggested a stronger commitment to reducing health inequality. The Welsh strategy identified health gain targets, incorporating the 15 targets already set out the previous year (Welsh Office, 1997). These targets – to be achieved by 2002 – covered a much broader range than those identified in the English strategy and included targets for back pain, arthritis, dental health and the consumption of fruit and vegetables. The Welsh Strategy also retained specific health gain targets relating to alcohol consumption, smoking and breast, cervical and lung cancer, while the revised English national strategy focused on four main targets for cancer, heart disease and stroke, accidents and mental illness. In addition, the Welsh strategic document set out separate targets for improving children's health and wellbeing. There are also differences in the implementation of the English and Welsh strategies. In Wales, local authorities are to lead the health alliances, which are expected to advance the public health agenda and promote an improvement in health at this level.

In Scotland, there is even more scope for divergence, given the greater self-governing powers vested in the Scottish Parliament. The Scottish strategy was outlined initially in consultative document (Cm 3854, 1998) and subsequently in a White Paper, *Towards a Healthier Scotland* (Cm 4269, 1999). The Scottish approach differed from that of England in a number of ways. First, targets for dental health, smoking, alcohol and teenage pregnancy featured alongside coronary heart disease and cancer in the headline targets set by the strategy. Secondary targets were also set, relating to diet, smoking, alcohol, physical activity, strokes and dental health. Mental health (which was not identified as a key area in the Green Paper) was mentioned as a priority in the White Paper, although (in contrast to the English strategy) no target was set. Accidents were identified as an important area for intervention, and a commitment was made to develop a new target for this. As in Wales, the Scottish strategy indicated a stronger desire to tackling health inequality than was seen in the English strategy, and an explicit commitment was made to monitor inequality within the target areas. Furthermore, the Scottish strategy proposed the inclusion of health inequality in health impact assessment (HIA) (see Exhibit 7.2). In addition, four demonstration projects, at a cost of £15m, were announced in the Scottish White Paper: 'Healthy Respect', to promote sexual health; 'The Heart of Scotland', aimed at reducing coronary heart disease; 'Cancer Challenge', which included a new screening programme for colorectal cancer; and 'Starting Well', a programme promoting children's health through to the age of school entry. Like the Welsh strategy, the Scottish White Paper was explicit in highlighting the importance of improving children's health.

Exhibit 4.2 *(cont'd)*

In Northern Ireland, two key documents were published in the late 1990s outlining the public health strategy for the province. *Well into 2000: A Positive Agenda for Health and Wellbeing* (Northern Ireland Department of Health and Social Services, 1997), like the Welsh and Scottish strategies, placed an emphasis on tackling health inequality. It also favoured a more comprehensive version of HIA than that proposed in England. As in the Scottish strategy, the importance of measuring the health impact of policies on specific subgroups within the population was highlighted. In addition, the Irish version of HIA indicated an audit of existing departmental policies on health rather than being applied only to new and emerging policies, as implied by the White Papers of Scotland, England and Wales. *Well into 2000* also endorsed regional targets for public health, the fourth version of which had earlier been outlined in *Health and Wellbeing: Into the Next Millennium,* published by the Northern Ireland Department of Health and Social Services (1996). These targets differed from the new English strategy by including smoking, breastfeeding, physical activity, sexual health, immunisation, the needs of elderly people, stillbirth, child hospitalisation, child protection and learning disability alongside targets for accidents, cancer and circulatory disease.

Finally, other differences of approach in managing and implementing these strategies should be briefly noted. The Welsh strategy is supported by the Wales Centre for Health, which provides multidisciplinary advice to the Assembly. A reorganisation of Welsh departments has also been proposed to improve co-ordination on public health issues and to ensure that health aspects are taken into account when public policies are formulated. In Scotland, a ministerial group with representatives from all relevant departments seeks to ensure that the Scottish Executive incorporates a consideration of health in all its policies. A further committee, also chaired by the Minister of Health and incorporating representatives drawn from the public, private, community and voluntary sectors, has been proposed to monitor the implementation of the public health strategy. Meanwhile, in Northern Ireland, an interdepartmental group of ministers drawn from the various departments of the Northern Ireland Office co-ordinates public health policy in the province.

The first main theme of the revised English health strategy was a 'new contract' between the state and the individual, involving government, local communities and individuals in a partnership to improve health. This was portrayed as a 'third way' between a 'nanny-state' and 'victim-blaming' approach, which the new government identified as features of previous public health policies. Second, the Blair government proposed simplifying and reducing the number of national targets. For England, only four main targets were set out in the Green Paper, each of which was meant to be achieved by 2010 using 1996 as a baseline. These targets were altered in the subsequent White Paper as follows:

- To reduce the death rate from heart disease and stroke and related illnesses among people under 75 years old by at least two-fifths (the original Green Paper having proposed a reduction in the death rate in the under-65s by a third).

- To reduce the death rate from accidents by at least a fifth and to reduce the rate of serious injury by at least a tenth (the Green Paper target having been to reduce accidents by a fifth).

- To reduce the death rate from cancer among people aged under 75 years by at least a fifth (the target in the Green Paper having been to reduce the death rate in under-65s by a fifth).

- To reduce the death rate from suicide and undetermined injury by at least a fifth (that in the Green Paper having been to reduce the death rate by a sixth).

Third, the revised public health strategy for England incorporated a greater awareness of the role of social, economic and environmental factors in ill health compared with *The Health of the Nation*. The relevance of health inequality, a taboo subject under the previous government, was reflected in the two goals stated in *Saving Lives: Our Healthier Nation*: 'to improve the health of the population as a whole by increasing the length of people's lives and the number of years people spend free from illness; and to improve the health of the worst off in society and to narrow the health gap' (Cm 4386, 1999, p. 5). Specific policies, such as Health Action Zones and Healthy Living Centres (HLCs), were advanced as a means of promoting health in specific areas where need was greatest and had considerable potential to reduce health inequality (see Chapter 5). Moreover, the importance of cutting health inequality was highlighted in DoH guidance (DoH, 1998c). Nevertheless, to the disappointment of some observers, the English strategy did not set national targets for reducing health inequality.

Fourth, ways of improving the co-ordination of public health matters both within central government and at local level were outlined in the new strategy. Within central government, health was highlighted as a key element of government policy. A Minister of Public Health had already been appointed as a means of improving the co-ordination of policy across government departments. A dedicated Cabinet committee of ministers drawn from 12 departments was created to develop health policy across the government, although this was to some extent a continuation of previous practice: as noted earlier, the Major government had established a similar ministerial subcommittee. In addition, the government expressed an intention to gear other policies – in fields such as welfare, housing, crime, education, transport and the environment – to the achievement of public health objectives. Health impact assessment (see Chapter 7) was endorsed for key government policies, a strengthening of the previous government's stated intention to take into account health implications when formulating policies.

At local level, the Blair government sought to advance public health by identifying a number of settings in which health promotion initiatives could develop: schools, workplaces and neighbourhoods. This once again built on its predecessor's approach, which identified similar settings as a focus for health promotion initiatives. But to place a greater emphasis on this activity, the government announced Health Improvement Programmes (HImPs), local action plans led by health authorities and agreed with other stakeholders, such as NHS Trusts, primary care groups, local authorities and voluntary organisations. The government also stated its intention to give local authorities statutory powers to promote the economic, social and environmental wellbeing of their localities. Both health and local authorities were expected to work more closely together on health-related issues, alongside other relevant organisations such as voluntary organisations and business. This was underlined in the Health Act of 1999, which required NHS bodies and local authorities to co-operate on health and welfare matters, and placed a statutory duty on local authorities to participate in HImPs. Local strategies on public health are discussed further in the final section of this chapter.

Finally, the Blair government sought to improve the public health function by creating a Health Development Agency to maintain and disseminate an evidence base for health improvement, to advise on standards for public health and health promotion, and to commission and carry out health promotion campaigns. It was proposed that this new agency would replace the Health Education Authority. This was criticised in some quarters, as the HEA (and its predecessor the Health Education Council) had often campaigned on public health issues, often in the teeth of hostility from commercial interests and government. Certainly the abolition of the HEA would make for a quieter life, but few believed that this move would improve public health policy-making. Furthermore, each region would have a public health observatory, linked with universities, to monitor health, highlight areas for action and evaluate progress by local agencies to improve health and reduce inequality. Proposals were also set out to improve training in public health, to strengthen the public health roles of nurses, midwives and health visitors, and to create a new post of Specialist in Public Health open to professionals outside medicine. This latter proposal distressed many doctors in public health, and indeed, reassurances were sought from the Department that this development would not damage the already fragile specialism.

# International Strategies

National health strategies must be seen in a broader, global context. As indicated in the previous chapter, national plans have been stimulated and shaped by initiatives at the international level. The WHO, for example, has long played a significant role in promoting public health strategies, while, more recently, European Union institutions have increased their involvement in this field. In this section, the role of these supranational institutions is further explored.

## The WHO

The WHO *Health for All* principles, endorsed at international conferences such as Alma Ata (WHO, 1978), Ottawa (WHO, 1986a), Adelaide (WHO, 1988), Sundsvall (WHO, 1991) and Jakarta (WHO, 1997a), are as follows.

1. Health is a fundamental human right and a social goal. Health is defined in a positive sense, in line with the classic WHO definition, and includes mental, physical and social wellbeing, not just the absence of illness or disease (WHO, 1946). Policies should be reoriented to focus on maintaining and improving health.

2. An equitable distribution of health resources, both within and between countries, should be a fundamental goal.

3. Health is shaped by many factors: social, economic, lifestyle and environmental. Policy makers must construct 'holistic' and 'intersectoral' policies that take account of other sectors of decision making that impinge upon health. Governments should adopt 'healthy public policies' that strongly reflect health priorities, co-ordinate the actions of government agencies and are based on assessments of their health impact (Milio, 1986).

4. Health policies must be pre-emptive and precautionary, the aim being to prevent the problems arising at the earliest possible stage.

5. Health improvements require a community-wide response. This involves a partnership between agencies drawn from all relevant sectors and at all levels. Health promotion must include and involve the community, responding to its concerns, while at the same time promoting healthy lifestyles and supportive environments.

6. Health services must be reoriented towards primary health care and geared to promoting health rather than simply treating illness.

7. Clear performance targets and review mechanisms must be adopted in order to guide health strategies and achieve their objectives.

The original *Health for All* strategy, which set global targets for the year 2000 (WHO, 1981), has since been revised for the twenty-first century (see WHO, 1998a). In addition, the WHO Regional Office for Europe (1985b) devised specific *Health for All* targets, which were updated in 1991 (WHO Regional Office for Europe, 1993a) and revised in 1998 (WHO Regional Office for Europe, 1998a). The revised main targets are shown in Exhibit 4.3. It should be noted that further detailed targets accompany these. Target 12, for example, includes three specific targets to be attained by 2015: that the proportion of non-smokers should be at least over 80 per cent (and close to 100 per cent in under-15-year-olds), that the per capita alcohol consumption should not exceed 6 litres per annum (and should be close to zero in under-15-year-olds), and that the prevalence of illicit psychoactive drug use should be reduced by at least a quarter and mortality by half. The WHO periodically monitors progress towards these health targets and the efforts of member nations to incorporate *Health for All* principles in their policies (see Tarimo and Creese, 1990; WHO, 1995).

Although the basic principles of *Health for All* have remained intact, the emphasis of the strategy has changed in recent years. There is now a much greater emphasis on sustainable development and the link between health and the environment (see Chapter 7). In addition, the WHO now takes a much broader view of equity than previously, recent strategy documents focusing more upon gender inequality than once was the case. Finally, as will become clear in later chapters, the WHO has become more proactive in recent years in promoting policies at the global and regional level to combat specific threats to health, covering issues such as the environment, diet, health inequality and alcohol and tobacco use.

The WHO has done much to focus attention on the key factors that influence health and illness. It has, however, been criticised in the past for its shortcomings (Beaglehole and Bonita, 1997, p. 227–9; Godlee, 1995; Walt, 1993). The bureaucratic nature of the WHO has come under attack on many occasions and it has been regarded as a relatively ineffective organisation, particularly when compared to other international institutions such as the World Bank and the International Monetary Fund (see Walt, 1996. p. 125–30). It is also recognised that the WHO has lacked the resources and the political clout to drive forward the new public health agenda. Indeed, the plethora of priorities and programmes it has devised over the years has led to criticism that it lacks focus and this has been blamed in part on poor leadership. It remains to be seen whether the appointment in 1998 of the internationally respected stateswoman and former Norwegian Prime Minister Gro Harlem Brundtland as WHO Director General will enable the organisation to reverse the decline in its status and effectiveness. Brundtland, who chaired an influential inquiry into sustainable development in the 1980s (see Chapter 7), certainly has the credentials and appears to be well aware of what must be done. Her tenure began with a call for a much sharper focus on the core business of WHO, and stressed the need to integrate the various programmes that sought to deliver key objectives. She also emphasised the need to reduce bureaucracy and to work with other organisations and stakeholders. As a result, existing programmes were grouped into four areas: building healthy communities and populations, combatting ill health, sustaining health activities, and a fourth area supporting WHO's internal work and external relations.

## The European Union

The involvement of the European Union (and, prior to this, the European Community) in health matters has increased since the early 1990s. Hitherto, aside from isolated initiatives related to occupational health and safety, cancer prevention, food standards, HIV/AIDS and drug abuse, public health was viewed as a matter for member governments. One reason was that the original Treaty of Rome contained no explicit health provisions. Community action was, however, permitted under the Single European Act of 1987, which stated that the harmonisation of trade must be based on regulations offering a high level of health protection. This had implications for policy in a number of areas, including food hygiene and health and safety at work. The Maastricht Treaty of 1992 subsequently created a new community responsibility for public health, Article 129 stating that 'the Community shall contribute towards ensuring a high level of human health protection by encouraging co-operation between the member states and, if necessary, lending support to their action' (Council of the European Communities/Commission of the European Communities, 1992). The legitimate areas for Community action were the prevention of disease through research, information and education. Paragraph 4 of the Article excluded the use of harmonisation of public health legislation, although incentive measures (grants, for example) were permitted. This was seen as strengthening European institutions' role in public health (McCarthy and Rees, 1992).

Following the ratification of the Maastricht Treaty, the European Union developed a framework for action on public health. On the basis of this, a network for the control and surveillance of communicable diseases was established. In addition, the Council of Health Ministers in 1995 agreed plans to initiate programmes in several areas: cancer prevention, HIV/AIDS and other communicable diseases, drug addiction and health monitoring. Approval was subsequently given for programmes in three further areas: pollution-related disease, injury prevention and rare diseases. The emphasis on the provision of funds, research and information rather than on regulation remained. This was hardly surprising given the desire of member governments to retain control over health matters and the existence of powerful commercial lobbies intent on resisting public health policies that might adversely affect their interests. However, a tougher regulatory approach did begin to emerge in some areas, notably smoking (see Chapter 9) and food safety (see Chapter 8).

The pressure for a more comprehensive European Union approach to public health has, however, increased in recent years. A major factor was the BSE crisis, which revealed how the European Union had neglected its public health brief (see Chapter 8). This led to a reallocation of responsibilities for public health matters within the European Commission, responsibility for food and veterinary inspection being removed from the agriculture and industry departments to a new consumer and health department. The Amsterdam Treaty of 1997 subsequently increased the powers of the European Union with regard to health. It stated that 'a high level of human health protection shall be ensured in the definition and implementation of community policies and activities' (European Union, 1997, p. 39). Community action was extended to include measures 'directed towards improving public health' as well as 'preventing human illness and diseases.' The Treaty also included powers to introduce new minimum standards for blood and human organ donation and measures relating to veterinary and phytosanitary (plant health) practices directly related to public health. In addition, greater co-operation was agreed in a number of areas, including health monitoring and the epidemiological surveillance of infectious disease. However, the Treaty continued to exclude 'the harmonisation of laws and regulations of member states' as a means of improving public health (European Union, 1997, p. 40).

These changes did not satisfy some Members of the European Parliament, who argued for a special health directorate (headed by a Commissioner) to ensure that health issues are taken into account in all areas of European Union policy making. They also called for the European Union to adopt a more active role in relation to health promotion and disease prevention (Needle, 1999). These recommendations followed the European Commission's own review of the European Union's public health functions (European Commission, 1998), which concluded that future policy should focus upon improving information for public health, reacting rapidly to threats to health and tackling health determinants through health promotion and disease prevention. The Commission also raised the possibility of an integrated framework of action on public health, superseding the current separate programmes and initiatives, and discussed possible ways of building health considerations into European Union decision making. The resignation of the European Commissioners in March 1999 presented an opportunity to restructure the Commission and its various directorates. One important development was the creation of the Health and Consumer Protection portfolio, which aimed to integrate the departments concerned with consumer policy, food and veterinary matter, animal and plant health, and public health. One of the stated objectives of this directorate was to 'assure a high level of human health protection in the development of all Community policies' (European Commission, 2000).

These institutional changes suggest that public health will have a much higher profile within European Union decision making and raise the possibility of the development of a comprehensive health strategy at this level. This, however, remains a remote possibility, for a number of reasons. First, member states have jealously guarded their sovereignty on health issues, and this is unlikely to change. Second, the expansion of the European Union is likely to make agreement on health issues even more difficult, given the increased diversity of interests that this will generate. Third, economic interests will continue to exert a powerful influence over decision making in such a way as to frustrate health campaigners.

# Local Strategies

## International Influences

Health strategies are also found at the local level. In the past, local health strategies have been influenced by international initiatives, such as the *Healthy Cities* (Davies and Kelly, 1992) project. This project emerged out of a conference held in Toronto in 1984, when the idea of using cities as the focal point for a range of health promotion interventions was discussed (see Duhl, 1986). Two years later, the *Healthy Cities* initiative was launched by the WHO European Regional Office. Its three main elements were (Ashton, 1992): a focus on improving the health of the poor and disadvantaged, a need to reorientate medical services and health systems away from hospitals and towards primary care, and an emphasis on public involvement and partnerships between the public, private and voluntary sectors. Eleven cities were initially chosen as pilot sites for the new initiative; by 1991, 30 cities had joined the programme. Of these, four – Belfast, Glasgow, Liverpool and the London Borough of Camden – were established in the UK.

Cities participating in the initiative were expected to adopt specific interventions based on *Health for All* (WHO, 1981) principles, to monitor and evaluate these interventions and to share their experiences. It was made clear that such interventions must be based on an investigation of the nature of health problems at the small area level, should reflect the need to tackle inequality in health and should be based on data from a range of sources, including public perceptions of community and personal health. Participating cities also agreed to establish a common organisational framework comprising a high level intersectoral group that would enable decision makers from all agencies involved to devise strategies and co-ordinate their activities, and a supporting technical group consisting of officers drawn from the various agencies. Further requirements included: that effective working relationships be established between the city and schools, colleges and universities; that all agencies involved should undertake reviews of their impact on health and their potential for promoting health; and that cities should encourage an open debate about health.

Other cities that were not officially part of the programme soon began to adopt similar strategies based on *Health For All* and *Healthy Cities*. As a result,

---

Exhibit 4.3

---

### WHO European Region targets for the twenty-first century

1. By the year 2020, the present gap in health status between member states of the European Region should be reduced by at least one third.

2. By the year 2020, the health gap between socio-economic groups within countries should be reduced by at least one fourth in all member states, by substantially improving the level of health of disadvantaged groups.

3. By the year 2020, all newborn babies, infants and pre-school children in the Region should have better health, ensuring a healthy start in life.

4. By the year 2020, young people in the Region should be healthier and better able to fulfil their roles in society.

5. By the year 2020, people over 65 years should have the opportunity of enjoying their full health potential and playing an active social role.

6. By the year 2020, people's psychosocial wellbeing should be improved and better, comprehensive services should be available to and accessible by people with mental health problems.

7. By the year 2020, the adverse health effects of communicable diseases should be substantially diminished through systematically applied programmes to eradicate, eliminate, or control infectious diseases of public health importance.

8. By the year 2020, morbidity, disability and premature mortality due to major chronic diseases should be reduced to the lowest feasible levels throughout the Region.

9. By the year 2020, there should be a significant and sustainable decrease in injuries, disability and death, arising from accidents and violence in the Region.

Exhibit 4.3 *(cont'd)*

10. By the year 2015, people in the Region should live in a safer physical environment, with exposure to contaminants hazardous to health at levels not exceeding internationally agreed standards.

11. By the year 2015, people across society should have adopted healthier patterns of living.

12 By the year 2015, the adverse health effects from the consumption of addictive substances such as tobacco, alcohol, and psychoactive drugs should have been significantly reduced in all member states.

13. By the year 2015, people in the Region should have greater opportunities to live in healthy physical and social environments at home, at school, and in the local community.

14. By the year 2020, all sectors should have recognised and accepted their responsibility for health.

15. By the year 2010, people in the Region should have much better access to family- and community-oriented primary health care, supported by a flexible and responsive hospital system.

16. By the year 2010, member states should ensure that the management of the health sector, from population-based health programmes to individual patient care at the clinical level, is oriented towards health outcomes.

17. By the year 2010, member states should have sustainable financing and resource allocation mechanisms for health care systems based on the principles of equal access, cost effectiveness, solidarity and optimum quality.

18. By the year 2010, all member states should have ensured that health professionals and professionals in other sectors have acquired appropriate knowledge, attitudes and skills to protect and promote health.

19. By the year 2005, all member states should have health research, information and communication systems that better support the acquisition, effective utilisation, and dissemination of knowledge to support *Health for All*.

20. By the year 2005, implementation of policies for *Health for All* should engage individuals, groups and organisations throughout the public and private sectors, and civil society, in alliances and partnerships for health.

21. By the year 2010, all member states should have and be implementing policies for *Health for All* at country, regional and local levels, supported by appropriate institutional infrastructures, managerial processes and innovative leadership.

*Source:* WHO European Region (1999) *Health 2: The Health Policy Framework for the WHO European Region,* Copenhagen, WHO Regional Office for Europe.

the initiative to establish local health strategies became a movement rather than merely a collection of pilot projects (Tsouros, 1990; Ashton, 1992). By 1991, more than 300 cities in the European region had to some degree accepted the concepts and principles of *Healthy Cities* (Tsouros and Draper, 1992). In the UK, cities such as Oxford, Sheffield, Nottingham, Manchester, Leeds and Coventry began to devise their own local strategies based on *Health for All* principles. By the late 1980s, it was estimated that 50 health authorities and 70 local authorities were actively involved in devising local health strategies (Adams, 1989).

Other researchers, however, discovered that, for many authorities, the development of local health strategies was not a priority. Disken (1990) found that although three-quarters of health authorities had established local priorities in line with *Health for All*, fewer than a third had allocated resources accordingly, and only half had appointed a specific individual to co-ordinate and lead the strategy. A later survey by Rathwell (1992) found a higher proportion (84 per cent) of health authorities in Britain indicating that they had incorporated either *Health for All* concepts or targets in some form into their plans. However, only 8 per cent actually used the targets as a means of measuring progress against particular policy objectives, and even where this occurred, targets were used selectively rather than as a complete package. Over half of the health authorities that responded to this survey stated that their short-term programmes did not contain *Health for All* targets. A more recent survey, undertaken after the introduction of the Major government's health strategy, discovered that the majority of health authorities responding had set public health targets (Harvey and Fralick, 1997), although only 40 per cent of health authorities accepted the government's *Health of the Nation* targets as a basis for their own strategy.

Furthermore, case studies of individual projects revealed problems with the implementation of health strategies at local level. In Liverpool, one of the *Healthy Cities* pilots, difficulties emerged at an early stage in co-ordinating the activities of the health authority and local government (Green, 1992). In Sheffield, problems included staff shortage and a local lack of support for the WHO European region targets (Thoms, 1992). Both sites, however, claimed success. In Liverpool, significant achievements included the establishment of health action areas to improve health status in deprived localities, a project to combat accidental poisoning in children and health and fitness testing schemes. In Sheffield, health strategists responded to negative reactions by seeking to involve local people in decision making and by refining their strategy in accordance with these concerns.

It is true that many case studies are of an 'evangelical' nature, written by those closely committed to the development of local health strategies, who not surprisingly tend to accentuate the positive. The lack of good research in this area has been noted (see Tsouros, 1990; Curtice, 1992; Hancock, 1992), the

main problem being that the impact of the *Healthy Cities* approach in particular, and local strategies in general, is likely to be diffuse, long term and
subjective, shaping a wide range of perceptions and actions that are difficult
to detect in the short run. For this very reason, research in this field must
avoid the trap of using conventional models of scientific research and rational
administration (Kelly *et al.*,1992). Indeed, researchers must utilise a range of
disciplines and recognise the complex nature of social and physical reality
when evaluating the development of local health initiatives and their impact.
As Costongs and Springett (1997) argue in their study of the Liverpool City
Health Plan, research that focuses upon formal interorganisational structures
may fail to detect the achievements of informal processes.

While *Healthy Cities* and *Health for All* provided an important stimulus for
local health strategies, other factors have also been influential in their emergence and development. During the 1980s, many local authorities in cities
such as Liverpool, Manchester and Sheffield became increasingly concerned
about the health of their communities and began to devise strategies (see
Harrow, 1991). This was a reaction to deteriorating urban conditions such as
deprivation and industrial decline and was stimulated to some extent by local
dissatisfaction with national policies on unemployment, welfare and urban
regeneration. Even relatively prosperous cities such as Oxford contained
areas of significant deprivation and harboured discontent with central policies to such an extent that local action was stimulated.

## Central Government and Local Strategies

For its own part, central government encouraged the development of local
strategies during the 1990s. As noted already, health authorities were given
the task of identifying health needs at the local level and commissioning
services to meet them. Meanwhile, the Acheson Report (see Chapters 3 and 5)
prompted a clarification of public health responsibilities at the local level. The
*Health of the Nation* strategy subsequently provided central guidance for local
strategies, although, as noted earlier, this was often ignored. Nevertheless,
central government's encouragement of 'healthy alliances' between the NHS
and local agencies and organisations such as local government, the voluntary
sector and employers promoted local strategies with regard to specific health
problems, such as heart disease and child accident prevention (DoH, 1998b,
pp. 101, 121–34). In some areas, alliances appeared to work well (Exhibit 4.4),
particularly where good relationships already existed between local authorities and health authorities, where activities took place against the background
of high-profile national campaigns such as on AIDS awareness, heart disease
prevention, road accident prevention and stopping smoking, and where
funding was available (see DoH, 1993a; Scriven, 1998).

But healthy alliances were not as effective as some had hoped, and several difficulties arose (Ewles, 1993; Nocon, 1993; Delaney, 1994; Cornish *et al.*, 1997; DoH, 1998b). The fragmentation of responsibility was problematic, particularly where a large number of authorities and organisations were involved. In some cases, this situation has been exacerbated by a fundamental disagreement between organisations – often of a longstanding nature – regarding their respective roles. There was also concern that most healthy alliances were not central to the processes of health service commissioning and contracting, and that this undermined their effectiveness. Finally, a lack of resources for

---

Exhibit 4.4

### Joint working on public health

Studies have revealed many examples of joint arrangements in which NHS bodies, local authorities and others such as voluntary organisations have worked together in an effort to improve public health:

1. The Life project was established in 1992 to tackle the high rate of heart disease on the Wirral (Trevett, 1997). This project – which operated a range of schemes offering health and lifestyle checks and advice for local people – was strongly endorsed by both the local health authority and the local council, obtaining finance from the Department of the Environment's City Challenge initiative. It was later incorporated as a specialist health promotion service, operated by a joint commissioning group drawn from the authorities involved.

2. The Healthy Islington initiative was established as an intersectoral agency in 1989 by the district health authority and Islington Borough Council. The initiative also included the voluntary sector and the local community health trust. The programme of work, which emphasises community development, has focused on women's health, accidents, health and race, refugees, children with home responsibilities, accident prevention for the elderly and homelessness (Cornish *et al.*, 1997).

3. In the North Staffordshire strategy health alliances were established in 1994 between the health authority and three local authorities. A number of other partners, including businesses, voluntary organisations, NHS trusts, the police and consumer bodies such as the Citizen's Advice Bureau and the Community Health Council, also became involved. Alliances were seen as being central to the implementation of health strategy, and specific projects in a range of topic areas, including smoking and physical activity, were launched. Community development work was regarded as important, each alliance setting up a rolling programme in this field (Levenson *et al.*, 1997).

joint initiatives inhibited collaboration in some areas. Not all authorities earmarked resources for the development of alliances, and even where budgets were allocated, the sums tended to be small (DoH, 1998b).

## *The Rio Summit*

The development of local health strategies during the 1990s was further stimulated by a concern for the environment. In 1992, the Rio Summit set out an international programme of sustainable development in the form of Agenda 21, which encouraged local authorities to draw up their own local agenda 21 (LA21) plan in consultation with their community. Although LA21 was primarily concerned with the environment, the decision-making processes it sought to encourage potentially held wide implications for all sectors, including public health. The impact of LA21 on public health is discussed more fully in Chapter 7.

At the very least, LA21 underlined the importance of local authorities working with other agencies on issues of common concern. In health matters, this implied a cross-sectoral approach focusing on the environmental and socio-economic causes of ill health, in partnership with organisations such as health authorities and the voluntary sector. As noted earlier, this was reinforced in the late 1990s by proposals to impose a statutory duty on local authorities to promote the social, economic and environmental wellbeing of their areas, a requirement to co-operate with local health improvement plans, and plans to encourage joint initiatives between health and local government on issues such as regeneration (see Chapter 10). The advent of devolved government, not just in Scotland, Wales and Northern Ireland, but additionally in London and the regions, also suggested a greater role for cross-sectoral public health planning. For example, the legislation for an elected mayor and assembly for London included a responsibility to promote an improvement in health.

Even so, health authorities retain the key responsibility for developing health improvement plans. Public health expertise is also concentrated in the health sector. Some have argued that local authorities are better placed to assess and respond to health needs (Harrison *et al.*, 1994), or that, at the very least, the public health function should be returned to local government (Environmental Health Commission, 1997). This issue is discussed further in the next chapter.

# Conclusion

Health strategies operate at a number of levels: national, international and local. They do not operate in isolation but interact with each other. Hence

local and national strategies have been influenced by international developments, while national and international developments are in turn shaped by
local experiences. Strategies are undoubtedly a useful guide for action. The
very fact that they exist is an important development in itself, indicating a
shift in emphasis from the provision of health care services to promoting
public health, but the extent of this shift should not be exaggerated. Health
strategies have been criticised on a number of grounds, including design
flaws, implementation failure, an unwillingness to tackle vested interests,
problems of co-ordination, a refusal to address fully the social, economic and
environmental causes of ill health, and inadequate resourcing. Strategy alone
is meaningless without the will to achieve objectives. Goals and targets can
only set a direction; they cannot guarantee success. Much more depends on
specific activities in a wide range of policy areas – the NHS, food policy,
addictive substances, environmental policy and social welfare – areas
explored in greater detail in the chapters that follow. It is on these crucial
battlegrounds that the commitment to the new public health perspective has
been most severely tested.

# 5

# Public Health and the NHS

Although the NHS has been criticised for being primarily a 'sickness service', it has considerable potential to protect, maintain and improve public health. In this chapter, its actual contribution to public health is explored, beginning with an analysis of public health medicine over the past two decades. This is followed by an assessment of the impact of NHS reforms on public health, looking first at the consequences of health care commissioning and then at the implications of changes in primary care, both of which were introduced by the Conservative governments of the 1980s and 90s. Finally, the impact on public health of the Blair government's NHS reform programme is discussed.

## Public Health Medicine

By the late 1980s, it was acknowledged that the speciality of community medicine was in crisis. Following high-profile failures of the public health function, referred to in Chapter 3, a Committee of Inquiry chaired by the Chief Medical Officer, Sir Donald Acheson, was appointed. Its main recommendations are set out in Exhibit 5.1.

The Acheson inquiry was seen as an effort to restore the status of public health medicine. Its report was acknowledged by the Thatcher government, which agreed to implement the main recommendations, although the proposed changes in the law relating to the control of infectious disease, and the recommended expansion of public health consultant posts both failed to materialise (Kisely and Jones, 1997). The Acheson reforms cannot, however, be seen isolation. During this period, a number of other reforms also affected the public health function, including the introduction of contracting and commissioning, and the implementation of important changes in the field of primary care. The impact of these developments will be discussed in more detail later in this chapter. The public health function was also affected by initiatives stemming from *The Health of the Nation* strategy (Cm 1986, 1992, see also Chapter 4), by reorganisation and by changes in health authority management structures. Together, these changes did little to address four key problems

Exhibit 5.1

## The Acheson Report on the future development of the public health function and community medicine
### Summary of main findings

1. Community medicine should be renamed public health medicine, with the aim of clarifying the role of doctors in this speciality and enhancing their status and profile both in the public eye and within the medical profession.

2. Within the Department of Health a small unit should be established to bring together relevant disciplines and skills to monitor the health of the public.

3. Guidance should be issued to health authorities reminding them of their public health responsibilities.

4. Health authorities should appoint a Director of Public Health (DPH) to lead the public health function. This person would act as a chief medical adviser, advise on planning, priorities and evaluation, co-ordinate control of communicable disease, develop policy on prevention and health promotion.

5. Health authorities should be required to commission an annual report on public health from their DPH.

6. Directors of Public Health and Chief Environmental Health Officers should meet regularly and encourage communication and collaboration between their organisations.

7. Clearer responsibilities at local level for dealing with outbreaks of infectious disease should exist, with a named District Control of Infection Officer responsible for linking the work of microbiologists and infection control teams and for disseminating public information on communicable disease control.

8. Improved communication between the national agencies responsible for monitoring outbreaks of disease is required: namely, between the Public Health Laboratory Service and the Communicable Disease Surveillance Centre.

9. Regional and District Health authorities should review manpower and training requirements in the light of other recommendations. Each region should aim to reach a national rate of 15.8 consultants in public health medicine per million population by 1998.

10. Government should revise current public health legislation with a view to producing a more up to date and relevant statutory backing for the control of communicable disease and infection.

*Source*: Cm 289 (1988) *Public Health in England,* London, HMSO

facing public health medicine: the confusion surrounding its role, its failure to integrate with other forms of public health expertise, its perceived lack of independence and the low status and morale of its practitioners.

## Confusion of Roles

Public health doctors are expected to fulfil a number of roles (see Goraya and Scambler, 1998). They act as *health strategists*, providing advice to health authorities on priority setting, service planning and the evaluation of outcomes; *health promoters*, developing and evaluating disease prevention and health promotion services; *health experts*, monitoring and managing outbreaks of infectious disease; *health advisors* to decision makers and the wider population regarding risks and threats to public health; and *health bureaucrats*, managing clinical services.

Having multiple roles is not intrinsically a problem providing the tasks involved are not too complex or onerous, although it is recognised that difficulties can arise when roles conflict, and when less important tasks impede the achievement of priorities. It does appear, however, that there are such problems: according to Goraya and Scambler (1998 p. 149), 'there exist seemingly intractable tensions, and perhaps contradictions, within and between clusters of tasks, a recipe for acute role strain'. In addition, it seems that the involvement of public health doctors in the management of clinical services has drawn them away from what is seen as their primary role of promoting health and preventing illness (Holland and Stewart, 1998). Similarly, Beaglehole and Bonita (1997) argue that the involvement of public health doctors in the organisation of medical services has been at the expense of their broader public health functions. Moreover, as will be discussed shortly, some observers believe that public health doctors have become more closely bound to management, to the detriment of their health promotion role.

## Medical Leadership and Multidisciplinary Working

Hunter (1996, p. 15) has argued that 'public health is not to be equated with public health medicine... It is perhaps best to think of public health as a field of inquiry or an arena where a range of skills and experiences come together.' This perspective envisages a role for a range of professionals such as statisticians, health economists and health promotion specialists. It also suggests a closer relationship between public health doctors and others with a longstanding interest in this field, such as environmental health officers (EHOs) (McCarthy, 1996) and health visitors (Health Visitors' Association, 1996), and assumes a key public health role for other caring professionals, for example

GPs, midwives and nurses working in the community. In addition, the broader concept of public health would include others with relevant expertise and skills, such as community leaders and voluntary workers.

The DoH has acknowledged the importance of multidisciplinary working in the field of public health (DoH, 1994a, 1998a), and during the 1990s, the creation of multidisciplinary public health departments at district level was encouraged. There is evidence of effective multidisciplinary working in some areas (see Levenson *et al.*, 1997), but it is recognised that the medical profession still assume the leadership role and that this can be a barrier to effective multidisciplinary working. Many observers now believe that a power-sharing model, in which professionals and others pool their skills and expertise to tackle the social, economic and environmental factors affecting health, is more appropriate to the new public health and should replace approaches based on medical leadership, focused on the disease model.

Any such changes will, however, have to be handled carefully since anything that causes friction is likely to undermine the effectiveness of the public health function (Cornell, 1996). In particular, public health doctors fear that other forms of expertise are encroaching on their territory and that this has consequences for their future career prospects (Scally, 1996). This has led to a defensive and isolationist response by some, reflected in the decision in 1995 not to extend membership of the Faculty of Public Health Medicine to those outside the profession (Crown, 1999). Notably, at its 1998 AGM, a new category of membership for all professional groups was approved. Given the need to work with other professional groups, both within and outside the NHS, an aloof approach is no longer tenable. Moreover, according to Kisely and Jones (1997), the added value of medically qualified practitioners in multidisciplinary health teams is being increasingly questioned. They argue that if the confusion surrounding the role of public health medicine in multidisciplinary teams is not addressed, the specialty will be further marginalised and fragmented, jeopardising its future. Another factor here is the growing interest of GPs in public health issues, which has added to the sense of insecurity felt by specialists in public health medicine. The role of GPs in this area is discussed in more detail later in this chapter.

The dominant medical role is to some extent being challenged. Interestingly, the Blair government's White Paper *Saving Lives: Our Healthier Nation* (Cm 4386, 1999) proposed the creation of public health specialist posts of a status equivalent to that of medically qualified consultants in public health medicine, who would subsequently be allowed to become DPHs. Medical expertise is, however, still extremely influential in the field of public health. As Levenson *et al.*, (1997) have argued, although other professions possess qualities that would enable them to lead public health, there are strong reasons for retaining medical leadership, including the need to maintain the confidence of the medical profession as a whole and of the general public.

Moreover, it should be noted that public health doctors are increasingly appearing in different guises, in trusts, as advisors to primary care organisations and even in local government (see Dent, 1999), suggesting that it is perhaps far too early to write off this branch of the profession.

## Independence

In Chapter 2, it was shown that although public health medicine enjoyed a strong tradition of independence, the former MOHs were never completely free from political pressures and administrative constraints, which in practice limited their independence. In the modern era, critics have pointed out that DPHs do not possess even this limited autonomy (Public Health Alliance, 1988) as DPHs are directly responsible to the Chief Executive of their employing health authority and are members of the health authority management board, therefore having collective responsibility for service provision. The effect of this, it is argued, has been to displace the role of promoting and protecting health with managerial functions associated with commissioning and contracting (Whitty and Jones, 1992; McCallum, 1997), while at the same time limiting their role as the advocate of the population's health (Gatherer, 1991; Davies, 1997; Goraya and Scambler, 1998; Holland and Stewart, 1998).

The abolition of regional health authorities in 1996 was viewed as further restricting the independence of public health medicine. As a result of this reorganisation, regional DPHs became civil servants with a brief to ensure the effective management of the public health function in their region. Their independence was circumscribed: they were prohibited from becoming directly involved in public health campaigns. Some post holders expressed concern about the implications of becoming civil servants (Chadda, 1996), although the actual impact of these changes has yet to be fully evaluated.

## Status and Morale

The morale of public health doctors is intimately connected with their professional status. Given the relatively low status of public health medicine, it comes as no surprise to find that morale has remained low in recent years (see Holland and Stewart, 1998). Declining status and poor morale also affect recruitment and have a knock-on effect on the quality of practitioners in the longer term (see Scally, 1996). In order to break this vicious cycle, public health medicine must clarify its role not only within the NHS, but also with regard to the rest of the medical profession, which has played no small part in its declining status.

According to most observers, public health medicine is at a critical point in its history. Much will hang on how opportunities, which undoubtedly exist (see Scally, 1996; Dent, 1999), can be taken. As Salter noted some time ago (1993), much depends on how this branch of the profession markets its particular core skills within the health care system. Others point out the opportunities that lie in building effective multidisciplinary initiatives with other professionals in the public health field (Beaglehole and Bonita, 1997). Opportunities may also arise through collaboration with lay activists who mobilise public opinion on social, economic and environmental issues related to health (Goraya and Scambler, 1998).

## Improving the Public Health Function

A number of suggestions have been made to improve the role and status of public health within the NHS (see Holland and Stewart, 1998). These include proposals to give the public health function more independence. This could take the form of a public health commission (Public Health Alliance, 1988; Sram and Ashton, 1998) that would operate independently from government departments. Its main functions would be to set national strategies, supply specialist public health services and accredit relevant training programmes. It would be multidisciplinary, integrating public health expertise, and the relevant professional groups would have a clearly defined role. At local level, public health experts would be located in health authorities but would be independent of them. The problems with this approach include a lack of accountability and the potential that a strong central authority might stifle initiatives generated by communities at local level (Holland and Stewart, 1998). But these pitfalls are theoretical, and much would depend on the precise relationship between the independent commission, government and Parliament on the one hand, and the interface between the commission and local organisations. There may also be unforeseen problems. Experience from New Zealand, where a separate commission had a short and unsuccessful life, indicates that an independent central authority can suffer from political isolation and a lack of political leverage (Scally, 1996).

Another suggestion is to return the public health function to local government. There is some logic to this, given the role that local authorities can play in improving the social, economic and environmental context of health (see Chapters 4, 7 and 10). There have been suggestions that public health functions could be transferred to local government (Cooper *et al.*, 1995, p. 25; Environmental Health Commission, 1997), although this is not without problems (see Holland and Stewart, 1998), including the likelihood of the further estrangement of public health doctors from the rest of the medical profession. Moreover, as McCallum (1997) has observed, there is a possibility that the independence of public health doctors might be even further constrained as local authority employees. Another problem is that expanded local authority responsibilities for public health could lead to an increased variation in the quality of the public health function. Some authorities might be unwilling or unable (because of financial constraints, for example) to prioritise public health, while others might become far more proactive in this field. The extent to which such a variation would be tolerated would of course depend enormously on the policy and regulatory framework adopted by central government.

Aside from these radical reforms, suggestions have been put forward to improve the public health function through incremental changes. Taylor *et al.* (1998) argue that ways should be found whereby public health would no longer be solely a health authority function but instead be jointly owned by a range of agencies at local level. Indeed, Armitage *et al.* (1998) identify a wide range of issues – concerning transport, sustainable development, nutrition, housing, education, work and leisure, social care, planning, regeneration, pollution, poverty and communicable disease – that could form a joint agenda for heath and local government collaboration. Davies (1997) has suggested the creation of local public health commissions as a means of integrating stakeholders such as health and local authorities, the voluntary sector and other agencies with an interest in public health. These can be seen as building in a more systematic way on successful healthy alliances, such as those described in Chapter 4. Notably, some health authorities have already formed joint health promotion agencies with local government and other stakeholders. Another idea that has been put forward as a means of promoting greater co-operation between health and local authorities is the joint appointment of public health professionals. This has already occurred in some authorities, Solihull for example, where the DPH was appointed jointly by the health authority and the local council (Donnelly, 1998).

At a national level, the Chief Medical Officer's interim report on the public health function (DoH, 1998a) suggested the establishment of a national forum for public health to involve the broad range of interests in this field. The need for improved expertise and a better monitoring of public health was reflected in Holland and Stewart's (1998) call for an expert national institute of public health combined with regional centres (echoing an earlier recommendation from the Public Health Alliance, 1988). This was to some extent taken up by the Blair government's White Paper on public health (Cm 4386, 1999), which proposed that, at a national level, the HEA would be replaced by a Health Development Agency in an effort to improve the quality and standing of public health. The new agency will be responsible for producing evidence-based guidelines for intervention and evaluating public health research, while regional 'observatories' will monitor trends and advise on interventions at the subnational level. Finally, another suggestion has been to establish a Royal Commission on Public Health (Olson, 1997). This would be a permanent, independent body set up along lines similar to those of the Royal Commission on Environmental Pollution. It is envisaged that this institution could commission research, undertake inquiries into public health issues, present evidence on the effectiveness of interventions, recommend policies where appropriate and disseminate good practice.

## Public Health and the Commissioning Process

As noted at the beginning of this chapter, the NHS has been criticised for not giving sufficient priority to health promotion and the prevention of illness. In 1979, the Royal Commission on the National Health Service concluded that 'only a small proportion of NHS resources is devoted to prevention' and recommended an expansion of health education and screening programmes (Cmnd 7615, 1979, p. 41). A few years earlier, the House of Commons Select Committee on Expenditure noted an estimate that less than 2 per cent of NHS resources was spent on specific preventive services (Select Committee on Expenditure, 1977). This was viewed as an underestimate by the National Audit Office (NAO, 1986), which estimated that around 5 per cent of NHS resources were devoted to preventive medicine in the 1981/82 financial year.

During the 1980s and 90s, additional funds were allocated to screening programmes (see Chapter 6) and mass media health campaigns (Whitehead, 1989a, 1989b). In addition, changes to the GP contract, discussed later in this chapter, introduced new payments for specific preventive and health promotion work. There was, however, no evidence to suggest that the balance of spending had changed significantly. Indeed, an analysis of expenditure in eight health authorities showed that, between 1991/92 and 1996/97, the proportion of the budget allocated to health promotion and education, health promotion by GPs, family planning and cancer screening actually fell from 1.62 per cent to 1.45 per cent (DoH, 1998b). It should be noted that these figures excluded centrally funded health promotion and disease prevention programmes. Furthermore, the bias towards cure and treatment has been evident in specific policy areas, such as heart disease (see NAO, 1989; Public Accounts Committee, 1989) and mental health (Exhibit 5.2).

### The NHS Internal Market and 'Health Gain'

The NHS internal market, introduced by the Conservative government in the early 1990s, was supposed to help to address the bias against prevention and health promotion. The division of commissioning from service provision brought in by the internal market was heralded as forcing health authorities to

Exhibit 5.2

## Mental health

In the past, public health policies have mainly addressed physical disease. This no longer seems sensible given the rising toll of mental illness in industrial societies, including the UK. Around one in six people have some symptoms of mental illness, mainly neuroses, fewer than 1 per cent suffering from a severe psychiatric disorder (Meltzer *et al.*, 1995). It has also been estimated that depression will affect a quarter of men and almost half of the female population before the age of 70 (Rorsman *et al.*, 1990). Moreover, there is much evidence linking mental health to physical morbidity and mortality such as death from suicide and other self-inflicted injuries. Although the suicide rate for the population as a whole has been stable for around 20 years, this is now the second most common cause of death in people under 35. Groups that are particularly at risk include young men, unemployed people, prisoners, young women originating from the Indian subcontinent and certain occupational groups, including doctors, pharmacists, vets and farmers. Poor adult mental health is also reflected in often less dramatic but nevertheless serious ways, such as alcohol and drug-related problems and stress-related illness. Furthermore, there is concern about the poor level of mental health among children and young people, arising from the neglect of emotional needs, family breakdown, bullying, abuse and even modern schooling methods, and it has been estimated that 20 per cent of children and adolescents suffer from a behavioural or emotional disorder (Mental Health Foundation, 1999). Obviously a failure to address these issues could produce a deteriorating level of adult mental health in the next generation.

In the UK, recent governments have recognised the need to incorporate mental health within public health strategies. The emphasis has, however, been mainly upon secondary prevention, that is, the early detection of mental illness and treatment. The principal focus has been on reducing the number of suicides – a particularly tragic consequence of mental illness, but disputed as an accurate indicator of mental health and wellbeing. The English *Health of the Nation* strategy (Cm 1986, 1992) introduced a target for suicide reduction in England. This was continued by the Blair government's health strategy *Saving Lives: Our Healthier Nation* (Cm 4386, 1999), which introduced a new target of reducing the number of suicides by a fifth by 2010. In Wales, however, an additional target was set, based on measurement of the mental health status of the population, while in Scotland no targets were set for mental health, even though it remained a priority area.

The continued emphasis on mental illness rather than mental health was further illus-trated by the Blair government's initial mental health strategy (DoH, 1998e). Additional resources were allocated to mental health services – £700m over the years from 1999 – to increase the number of secure beds and to fund outreach teams. Further resources were also allocated to encourage specific improvements in mental health services for children and young people. Other policy proposals, such as the preventive detention of those with a psychiatric disorder, also highlighted the continued preoccupation with

Exhibit 5.2 *(cont'd)*

mental illness rather than mental health. However, the National Service Framework for mental health, published in 1999, set a standard of promoting mental health for all and combatting discrimination against people with mental health problems, as well as continuing the commitment to reduce the suicide rate. The other standards relate mainly to care and treatment but do have important preventive aspects: to identify needs and offer effective treatment, to ensure that services are available at all times, to provide hospital beds and suitable alternatives when needed and close to home, to assess carers' needs every year, and to ensure that service users receive care that prevents crisis and reduces risk.

Mental health promotion, tackling those factors which undermine mental health, has been relatively neglected in the past (see Rogers and Pilgrim, 1996; Tudor, 1996). Poor mental health is rooted in the everyday life struggles that people face. Stress at work, a poor social environment and family breakdown can all contribute to poor mental health. Deprivation is also an important factor, and there is evidence of a class gradient in mental health, suggested by the fact that the male suicide rate is four times higher for social class V than class I (Drever and Bunting, 1997). There is also further evidence to suggest that rates of suicide, attempted suicide and deprivation are linked (see Gunnell *et al.*, 1995). Mental health can be promoted by establishing the means through which individuals (and wider communities) can gain the strength to cope with the pressures of modern life. This may involve, for example, promoting self-esteem among individuals or building civic pride within communities.

The lesson, it seems, is to combine an improvement in services with broader community action to minimise the underlying causes of mental illness and to promote mental health. This implies the sort of community-wide interventions that the Blair government has already introduced, such as New Deal, housing and regeneration programmes (see Chapter 10). Also relevant are government policies on crime and alcohol and drug abuse (see Chapter 9). Crime is linked to a poor level of mental health (see Robinson *et al.*, 1998). Not only do victims of crime suffer from a lower level of mental health, but also the fear of crime has a wider effect on the mental wellbeing of individuals, especially vulnerable people such as the elderly. Crime prevention and community safety are therefore important components of mental health promotion. Similarly, efforts to combat the adverse effects of alcohol and drug abuse must be included in any action plan to improve mental health. All these approaches require the kind of 'joined-up solutions' that the Blair government has tried to promote. For example, mental health has been identified as a priority in the local HImPs that health and local government and other stakeholders are expected to formulate. Local partnerships have also been formed to tackle community safety and regeneration issues. These are promising developments, and it will be interesting to see to what extent they not only prevent specific episodes of mental illness, but also actually improve the level of mental health and wellbeing.

focus on the wider health needs of their populations. This was reiterated by *The Health of the Nation* strategy in 1992 (Cm 1986, 1992; see Chapter 4), which set targets for health authorities to pursue, and endorsed by the Abrams Committee, which examined the public health function in the light of the changes brought by the internal market (DoH, 1993b). Others also believed that health authorities, freed from the constraints of providing services, could 'think radically and imaginatively about the community's needs' (Ham and Mitchell, 1990, p. 164). This view was endorsed by many DPHs, the majority of whom believed that commissioning improved the ability of the NHS to respond more flexibly to the needs of the population (Marks, 1995). Many public health professionals believed that if interventions could be proved to be more cost effective, they would be seen as good investments in terms of 'health gain' and that resources would flow from curative and treatment services into prevention and health promotion.

A committee chaired by the Chief Executive of the NHS was established to carry forward the implementation of the health strategy throughout the service. Specific projects to take this agenda forward were established in three key areas: purchasing, providing health care and primary care. Public health targets also came under scrutiny within the framework of performance management, although it was not until 1997 that the move towards an integrated review of health strategy and health care began. An obstacle to performance review was the lack of information about health needs. To address this, an annual survey of the health of the population was established, accompanied by similar exercises at local level. Meanwhile, efforts continued to improve the availability of information on health needs and outcomes, in order to support decisions about the allocation of resources and service provision. Although health authorities had carried out their own needs assessments for some years, systematic epidemiologically based needs assessment reviews became available to purchasers from the mid-1990s (Stevens and Raftery, 1994, 1997). In 1993, a set of population-based health outcome indicators were produced, and these were also subsequently revised (DoH, 1993c, 1996a). These tools were, however, used mainly to support the commissioning of clinical services rather than to evaluate the probable impact of public health interventions (Taylor *et al.*, 1998) and the data related mainly to the impact of health care on health; there was very little information about how NHS activity affected public health in a wider sense.

Another factor was the emphasis on evidence-based intervention, which added to the entrenched bias towards treatment services. It is easier to demonstrate the effectiveness of such services in terms of accepted evaluation methodologies compared with public health interventions. Hence a new drug or surgical procedure can be evaluated through randomised controlled trials, while public health interventions, particularly those involving a range of agencies, are much more difficult to evaluate and are, in the vast majority of cases, not suitable for such trials. Although the emphasis on evaluating health outcomes did open up the prospect of comparing preventive and curative interventions with a view to choosing the most cost-effective mix, relatively little in the way of resources was allocated to research and evaluation in this area. Indeed, research and development funding continued to be dominated by conventional medicine (Hunter, 1996). It remains to be seen whether recent efforts, by the DoH and the research councils, to promote more research into health, rather than health care, will have a significant effect on this imbalance.

## A Narrow View of Health Gain?

From one point of view then, the internal market was an advance in public health terms, the division between purchasing and provision facilitating an emphasis on health gain. It was conceded that the initiative was limited by several factors, such as the lack of a good information and research base, but that these could in time be overcome. Others were more cynical, claiming that the division between commissioning and providing services undermined rather than advanced the case for public health intervention (Moran, 1989; Whitty and Jones, 1992). They argued that commissioning invoked a narrow conception of health gain, based on the achievement of greater cost effectiveness in health services rather than a community-wide approach to tackle the social, economic or environmental causes of ill health. Indeed, although health authorities were now expected to commission services more appropriate to the health needs of the public, they faced difficulties because insufficient resources were available for assessing these needs and undertaking service reconfiguration on the scale required to promote health gain (see Flynn *et al.*, 1996; Cornish *et al.*, 1997; Levenson *et al.*, 1997; DoH, 1998b). Interestingly, Watt and Freemantle (1994) found that health authorities that had received additional resources were often the most innovative in seeking health gain. This contrasted with those experiencing little or no growth, whose efforts to produce an improvement in health were limited, largely because powerful clinical interests inhibited the effort to shift resources in the context of a static budget.

A further study by Davies (1997) explored the influence of public health in terms of the annual report produced by the DPHs. In summarising this evidence, she was careful to point out the difficulties inherent in trying to evaluate the impact of these reports, given that they are one of a range of influences. The studies she cited did not suggest that the reports alone had an enormous effect on local commissioning, although they could herald a significant change in local services (see Fulop and McKee, 1996). In one authority, for example, funds were ring-fenced to advance local strategies on *Health of the Nation* issues.

## Fragmentation

It was further pointed out (see Moran, 1989) that the internal market actually inhibited public health strategy by fragmenting the NHS into commissioners and providers, making it difficult to take a broad overview of the population's health needs and adding to the problems of collaboration between the NHS and other agencies on public health matters. The separation of these functions, for example, compounded the difficulty faced by public health doctors seeking to influence aspects of service provision (Crown, 1999). In the case of community health services, Flynn and colleagues (1996) described the lack of a structured relationship between health needs assessment, health promotion, purchasing plans and service specification, exacerbated by the contractual relationship. Furthermore, they noted that the currency of contracts – contacts with patients – was crude and failed to reflect the public health aspects of professionals' work. For example, according to McCallum (1997), health visitors tended to be drawn away from their public health role through the prioritisation of measurable tasks that were more suited to the contract culture. This was not, however, always the case as some purchasers used contracts to specify the proportion of time that health visitors should spend on public health activities. Finally, the division between purchasers and providers also apparently impeded a more strategic approach to health promotion as services were increasingly located into provider settings (Nettleton and Burrows, 1997).

## Rival Commissioners

In addition to these problems, the internal market was heavily criticised for maintaining and in some respects increasing health inequality, to the detriment of public health. As will shortly be discussed in more detail, GP fundholding was criticised for creating an inequality in access to both primary and secondary care. It was also argued that, by creating rival purchasers, the overview needed for an effective public health strategy at local level was lost. The delegation of commissioning decisions to GP fundholders and other local commissioning groups had an important but ambiguous effect on public health. In one sense, it undercut the public health function of the health authority by creating rival commissioning bodies who could undermine strategic plans and priorities. On the other hand, in combination with other developments in primary care, to be discussed in the remainder of this chapter, it raised the possibility of an increased awareness among GPs and other professionals of the public health implications of their work.

# Primary Care and Public Health

Primary care, like public health, can be defined in different ways (see Taylor *et al.*, 1998). In its broadest sense, primary care is a philosophy that places emphasis on moving health care out of large institutions and into community-based settings, with the aim of making services more responsive to the needs of individuals and communities, and facilitating closer co-operation with other agencies on issues of common concern. On a practical level, however, primary care is usually equated with one or more of the following: *health care settings* outside large institutions, such as doctors' surgeries, health centres, patients' homes and so on; *health functions* such as disease prevention, screening and rehabilitation; and *health services* provided by a group of *professionals*, such as GPs, dentists, pharmacists, community nurses and midwives, and health visitors.

The broad philosophy of primary care is highly compatible with public health principles. This is reflected in the consistency between the WHO's *Health For All* (WHO, 1981) and primary care initiatives, which share an emphasis on the positive definition of health, intersectoral strategies and community participation. Meanwhile, on a more practical level, the functions, professional services and settings included within the ambit of primary care are widely recognised as being crucial to the achievement of specific public health objectives. Primary care services such as screening can detect the early signs of illness, while immunisation, advice on lifestyle and health education can help to prevent it. Furthermore, the management of illness within a primary care setting can help to prevent conditions deteriorating. Added to this, primary care professionals can help to improve public health by feeding information about health needs into planning processes, thereby facilitating a more appropriate pattern and range of interventions not just within the NHS but across all sectors that affect health.

Notwithstanding the above, it is the case that primary care has been dominated by GPs, who have tended to adopt a much narrower perspective and one that has been less geared to the new public health philosophy. GPs have been strongly influenced by the orthodox medical model and as a result have focused mainly on disease processes rather than health promotion, on the care and treatment of individuals rather than the prevention of illness at the community level, and on clinical intervention rather than broader social and environmental action. This is not to say that all GPs have adopted a narrow orthodox view. Nor are they unaware of the social, economic and environmental influences on health. Indeed, GPs are increasingly concerned about such matters and have taken a much greater interest in health promotion in recent years. The point is rather that by reiterating the dominant role of GPs, which, as will become clear, has been the main thrust of government policy in primary care in recent years, a potentially more productive approach rooted more firmly in the new public health philosophy has not been fully exploited.

## Promoting Better Health

Up until the mid-1980s, primary care, like public health, was regarded as a backwater of the NHS. Two policy documents, however – the Green Paper on primary care (Cmnd 9771, 1986) and the Cumberlege Report on community nursing (DHSS, 1986) – played a crucial role in raising its profile. Following consultation, the government produced a White Paper, *Promoting Better Health* (Cm 249, 1987), which strongly reflected the themes set out in the earlier Green Paper. One was to give primary care professionals, in particular GPs, a greater incentive to promote health. Another idea was to reconstitute the Family Practitioner Committees (FPCs), the bodies then responsible for administering the professional contracts of GPs, dentists, pharmacists and opticians, into managerial bodies geared towards the improvement of primary care and health promotion.

A further aspect of government policy at this time was to seek to raise the charge for health services. As a result, new fees for eye tests and dental checks were introduced. Dentists and opticians argued that this would deter people from having regular checks and that, as a consequence, serious illnesses such as glaucoma and oral cancer would not be detected at an early stage. The government responded by granting an exemption from the eye test fee for those with a family history of particular diseases such as glaucoma and diabetes. Exemptions from both dental and eye checks were granted to low-income groups. Although the proportion of adults having sight tests and dental checks each year rose in the six years after the charge was imposed, it was not possible to determine accurately whether the frequency of tests had been maintained for each individual. Subsequently, following a change of government in 1997, the free sight test was restored for people over 60.

The organisational changes accompanying the new charges were also difficult to evaluate. The reconstituted FPCs attempted to become more proactive in the field of health promotion, particularly after the change in the GP contract (see below) in 1990. In principle, they now had more discretion over the budget for GP staff and premises, and in some circumstances they used these to encourage greater accountability and to promote new service developments (Huntingdon, 1993). There was a great potential for FPCs (subsequently renamed Family Health Service Authorities – FHSAs) to become more involved in assessing and planning for their population's health needs and measuring the performance of primary care services. In reality, however, the new regime exposed their weakness, in particular their lack of purchasing power and their limited leverage over the professions (Audit Commission, 1993). They increasingly joined forces with district health authorities and, following a review of the NHS structure, were formally merged with them in 1996.

Meanwhile, the implementation of the contractual changes heralded by *Promoting Better Health* (Cm 249, 1987) had already taken place. The GPs accepted the stated objectives of the new contract – to promote health and to improve the overall quality of family doctor services – but they believed that the measures introduced to achieve this were crude and unnecessarily bureaucratic. They rejected the new contract, only to have it imposed on them by government. Several aspects of the contract related directly to illness prevention and health promotion, including new payments for screening (see Chapter 6) and immunisation (Exhibit 5.3), triggered when a practice had covered a particular proportion of the population. There were also payments for health checks (including annual checks for the over-75s) and for specific health promotion activities, such as special clinics for advice on healthy lifestyle.

The contract remained a major source of dissatisfaction among GPs throughout the 1990s, even though the most contentious elements were subsequently amended. Concern about the administrative workload of GPs added to the pressure for a new system. The case for reform was strengthened by evidence that the existing scheme was not promoting health efficiently (Family Heart Study Group, 1994; Field *et al.*, 1995; Imperial Cancer Research Fund, 1995; Florin, 1999). Consequently, health promotion payments were replaced by a banded system targetted at the prevention of smoking, heart disease and stroke. Dissatisfaction with this scheme continued, resulting in a further change, a streamlined system in which GPs were paid on the basis of locally agreed health promotion activities (see Le Touze and Calnan, 1996). Although GPs were broadly happy with these new arrangements, concern was expressed that the revised scheme involved little monitoring of health promotion activities and did not give health authorities much influence over practices in this field (Baeza and Calnan, 1998). There were some exceptions, however, notably in Stockport where the health authority obtained special dispensation to introduce a scheme which specified that local GPs had to undertake at least one community-based health promotion intervention.

Government policy gave GPs a key role in relation to health promotion and illness prevention. While no one doubted that GPs should become more active in these areas, they did not seem particularly well placed to take on a strategic role. According to Ashton (1990), GPs tended to take a narrow view of health promotion, focusing on preventing disease in individual patients rather than on the health needs of the wider community. Studies found that this persisted into the 1990s, GPs continuing to focus on disease prevention rather than

Exhibit 5.3

## Immunisation

Immunisation has for many years been one of the major weapons against infectious disease (see Exhibit 2.1). The eradication of smallpox and the prevention of diseases such as whooping cough, measles and polio that were once a major threat to human health make it difficult to challenge the apparent efficacy of vaccination programmes and their application to other diseases, such as influenza and meningitis. A high vaccination rate is a key policy objective. (In 1998, for example, 96 per cent of children in England had been immunised against diphtheria, tetanus and polio, 94 per cent against whooping cough, 91 per cent against measles, mumps and rubella (MMR) and 95 per cent against *Haemophilus influenzae* type B (Hib) meningitis by their second birthday).

The longer-term impact of vaccination is, however, not well understood. Some studies have found that childhood infection seems to give some protection from other diseases. A Swedish study (Alm *et al.*, 1999) found that a group of children who took fewer antibiotics, had a lower rate of immunisation and ate fermented vegetables had a lower prevalence of atopy (multiple allergies including asthma, eczema and hay fever) than controls. In another study, a specific inverse relationship was found between contracting measles and atopic disease (Shaheen *et al.*, 1996). Other researchers revealed that measles infection and vaccination appeared to reduce the risk of hay fever (Lewis and Britton, 1998). Furthermore, a New Zealand study discovered that a small sample of children who did not have a diphtheria, pertussis, tetanus or polio immunisation did not suffer from asthma or other allergic illnesses (compared with 23 per cent of the main sample who suffered asthma episodes and 30 per cent other allergic illnesses) (Kemp *et al.*, 1997). Finally, a further study by Gibbon *et al.* (1997) found that children who suffered infections in the first year of life were less likely to develop insulin-dependent diabetes. Others, however, have cast some doubt on these findings. Bodner *et al.* (1998) discovered that while measles may give a protective effect against asthma, those with a larger number of childhood infections were more rather than less likely to have atopic disease. In Sweden, Nilsson *et al.* (1998) found no support for the hypothesis that a drastic increase in atopic disease occurs after pertussis vaccination. Moreover, British researchers found no relationship between pertussis vaccination and wheezing illnesses (Henderson *et al.*, 1999).

Vaccines have also been blamed for immediate adverse consequences, including brain damage and convulsions. Doctors have long argued that such cases are rare enough to justify mass vaccination. In the late 1990s, there was much controversy over a suggested link between MMR vaccination, autism and Crohn's disease, a chronic bowel condition (Wakefield *et al.*, 1998). These suggestions were dismissed by the medical establishment following a further study that found no link between autism and the MMR vaccine (Taylor *et al.*, 1999).

health promotion (DoH, 1998b; Taylor *et al.*, 1998). It was true that some GP practices did adopt a more positive approach to health promotion (see Cornish *et al.*, 1997), some undertaking an assessment of the health needs of their practice population and building closer links with local public health departments, but this was the exception rather than the rule.

## GP Fundholding

The introduction of GP fundholding during the 1990s had an implication for public health over and above the contractual changes previously mentioned. Initially, a small proportion of GPs were given a budget to enable them to purchase a limited range of hospital services on behalf of their patients. The scheme was subsequently expanded, over half the population eventually being covered by fundholding practices. Meanwhile, new services were added until the standard scheme covered virtually all elective and community health services. In addition, new schemes were devised, such as community fundholding, which enabled smaller practices to purchase community health services, and total fundholding, in which groups of practices were potentially able to purchase the whole range of hospital and community health services.

Fundholding was credited with two main potential advantages from a public health perspective. First, it raised the prospect that health services could be more closely aligned to the needs of the practice population, although, as the Audit Commission (1996, p. 54) noted, a formal approach to needs assessment was slow to develop. Second, the scheme was associated with innovations such as outreach clinics and the management by GPs of waiting lists, which could improve early detection and treatment for individual patients (Audit Commission, 1996). Furthermore, it was argued that added influence and the development of new services were not confined to fundholders alone. This was partly because non-fundholders and health authorities established arrangements designed to counterbalance the influence of fundholders and create a more coherent system of planning. As a result, commissioning groups involving local GPs were established in a number of health authority areas (Graffy and Williams, 1994).

Critics of fundholding pointed out several disadvantages from a public health perspective. First, fundholders could act in isolation without regard for local health priorities. Guidance was consequently introduced to strengthen planning processes and the accountability framework for fundholders. Second, there was no systematic evidence to suggest that GPs were allocating significant resources towards health promotion and disease prevention. Contracts tended to reinforce existing service patterns, and treatment rather than prevention remained the main focus of activity. It was, however, shown that some fundholders were providing 'non-standard' community health services, some of which – such as clinics for people with alcohol problems – were geared to health promotion (Audit Commission, 1996). Third, fundholding was heavily criticised on public health grounds for institutionalising inequalities. It was claimed that fundholders' patients were given priority and 'fast-tracked' into diagnostic and treatment services. Although this was difficult to prove in the absence of controlled studies, the circumstantial evidence was very strong, patients of fundholders obtaining a quicker access to outpatient clinics than those on non-fundholders' lists (see Kammerling and Kinnear, 1996; Dowling, 1997).

Finally, fundholding was criticised for encouraging the domination of primary care by GPs. The scheme, coupled with the other contractual changes set in motion by *Promoting Better Health* (Cm 249, 1987), enabled GPs to have more discretion over the employment of practice staff. The number of practice nurses, for example, more than trebled between 1987 and 1997. Furthermore, through the commissioning process, GPs could exert a greater control over the work of other professionals in primary care, such as community nurses, in a way that could undermine the effectiveness of interprofessional collaboration (Tinsley and Luck, 1998).

## Teamwork in Primary Care

The contribution of primary care to public health depends on a good working relationship between several professions. Since the 1960s, the concept of the PHCT has been promoted as a means of improving this relationship (see Chapter 3). The PHCT consists of GPs, practice nurses, midwives, health visitors, district nurses and community midwives (as well as in some cases other professionals such as social workers). Although presented as a method of integrated working based on teamwork, GPs have tended to dominate these arrangements. Furthermore, there has been confusion over the role of the participants and their responsibilities, each professional group operating independently, leading to duplication and overlap (DHSS, 1986; Hasler, 1992; Audit Commission, 1993; Wiles and Robison, 1994; Taylor *et al.*, 1998).

Yet considerable benefits arise when members of the PHCT work together effectively. Studies have revealed that, in such cases, health needs assessment, interagency working, community development activities and public health initiatives tend to flourish (Levenson *et al.*, 1997; see also Colin-Thome, 1999). It is nevertheless clear that the wider public health benefits of effective multidisciplinary working are not fully realised (Taylor *et al.*, 1998). In particular, there has been a failure to maximise the contribution of the nursing professions. Indeed, as a report from the Standing Nursing and Midwifery Advisory Committee (SNMAC) noted, their potential has been 'underused, unfocused and poorly integrated into the main responsibilities for commissioning and providing health care' (DoH/SNMAC, 1995, p. 32).

The nursing profession can participate in public health in a number of ways (see De Witt and Carnell, 1999; Cm 4386, 1999). It can network with other professionals and interface with other agencies, contribute to health needs assessment, help to detect illnesses at an early stage and participate in the development of public health strategies. Health visitors, for example, can contribute to health strategies providing information on health needs. They are also experienced in networking across health care, social services and the voluntary sector and can utilise their skills and contacts to build alliances and multisectoral initiatives aimed at improving the health of the community. Midwives, too, have an important public health role in view of their proximity to expectant and nursing mothers. In addition, they have a surveillance role with regard to the health of pregnant women and their unborn children that offers many opportunities to prevent illness.

Other specialist nurses have a great potential to contribute to health promotion and disease prevention; these include district nurses, practice nurses, occupational health nurses (who specialise in health in the workplace) and nurses specialising in the care of patients with particular diseases (such as diabetes, cancer and asthma). Meanwhile, school nurses are increasingly seen as the lead professionals with regard to school health functions (Audit Commission, 1994) and in recent years have developed a more proactive role in relation to health promotion, health education and counselling (DoH, 1996b). Their involvement in child protection has grown, as reflected by their role in investigating non-accidental injury and their participation in case conferences (Clarke, 1997).

In addition, nurses undertake specific public health functions. In some areas, for example, Communicable Disease Control Nurses (CDCNs) are concerned with the surveillance, prevention and control of infection, planning and the investigation of outbreaks of infectious disease. CDCNs interface with a range of agencies in public and environmental health, primary care and the hospital sector and promote a co-ordinated approach to infectious disease. In recent years, their work has expanded to cover non-infectious environmental hazards as well as communicable disease. Trusts and health authorities also employ Community Infection Control Nurses, whose main function is to provide clinical advice and support on infection control and prevention in primary care. In some areas, their role has expanded to include advice to local authorities and other agencies on infection control. It should also be noted that nurses are members of hospital infection control teams, which in some parts of the country also provide infection control services in the community.

Finally, the nurse practitioner role has implications for public health. Nurse practitioners are highly qualified nurses who take a lead role in diagnosis and treatment. The creation of such posts implies a greater role for nurses in the early detection of illness and if expanded may pave the way for new models of primary care, led by nurses (Wiles and Robison, 1994; Lawson and Emmerson, 1995).

Although the potential contribution of nurses to public health is great, there are several reasons why this is not fully realised in practice. First, the public health focus is fragmented among a range of nursing groups and is not part of mainstream nursing practice (Billingham and Perkins, 1997). Second, information about health needs collected by nurses is often not shared. Third, tensions between different nursing professionals can inhibit co-ordinated action.

One possible solution is the creation of specialist public health nurse posts to plan and co-ordinate services such as health promotion in family health, parental support and child protection (Billingham, 1991). This role involves developing plans on the basis of health needs and interfacing with a range of organisations whose activities affect health in a broad sense, such as local authorities and voluntary agencies. Another potential answer lies in the creation of integrated primary care nursing teams (DHSS, 1986; Lawson and Emerson, 1995; Audit Commission, 1999) that bring together district nurses, health visitors, practice nurses and nurse practitioners (see White *et al.*, 1996; Dix, 1997) and could be used to develop a broader public health philosophy among community-based nurses.

Recent policy initiatives have emphasised the public health aspects of health visitors and nurses. The White Paper on public health (Cm 4386, 1999) highlighted a key role for health visitors, encouraging them to focus on the public health needs of families and communities. It was envisaged that health visitors would lead teams of nurses at local level including other nurses, nursery nurses and community workers, which would be responsible for providing health improvement activities including child health programmes, parent support and education, developing support networks and health promotion programmes. School nurses were also given a leadership role in the assessment of health needs, the development of school health plans and the building of multidisciplinary partnerships with teachers, GPs, health visitors and others. The White Paper also referred to the importance of occupational health nurses, communicable disease nurses and midwives with regard to public health role, although it was less specific on how these roles should be developed.

## *Other Professions and Agencies*

Other professionals can make an important contribution to primary care and public health. The ability of opticians and dentists to detect serious illness at an early stage has already been mentioned, although this forms only part of their preventive role. Dentists, for example, can make a key contribution to public health through health education and early intervention, not to mention campaigning for community-level interventions such as fluoridation (see Exhibit 7.1). Other health professionals working in the community, including pharmacists and chiropodists, also have the opportunity to promote health and prevent illness. Furthermore, a range of other professionals, such as teachers and social workers, have a role to play in promoting public health through their contact with children and other vulnerable groups.

But although many professionals have the potential to promote public health, not all will necessarily do this. There are problems in getting them to recognise the importance of public health, to communicate with each other, to exchange information and to develop collaborative ways of working. The problem lies partly in traditional professional boundaries and partly in organisational and managerial structures that have failed to enhance collaboration (see Taylor *et al.*, 1998). Another problem lies in the information systems used by different professionals and agencies, which are often incompatible and restricted to a narrow set of requirements. The information revolution may help to make such information more widely accessible, although there is little to suggest that it has made much of an impact so far. Indeed, a number of studies have commented generally on the poor quality of information systems at the primary care/public health interface and have pointed out that the potential for sharing such information both between professions in the field and between planning and operational levels is simply not realised in practice (McDonald *et al.*, 1997; DoH, 1998b).

The problem of promoting collaboration to improve public health has been exacerbated by the failure to establish an effective system of health need assessment (see Kilduff *et al.*, 1998; Stevens and Gillam, 1998; Wright *et al.*, 1998; Cornell, 1999). As noted earlier, systematic health care needs assessments have been available to commissioning bodies since the mid-1990s, but these are geared to the commissioning of clinical services rather the promotion of health. In theory, public health departments, health promotion specialists, primary care professions and other stakeholders should work together to combine their assessments of what a community needs in terms of health care and other interventions to protect and promote health. In practice, however, there are many obstacles, including poor-quality data and methodology, a lack of resources or commitment by the various parties involved, a reluctance on the part of some potential participants to collaborate and a failure to integrate the findings of assessment within the planning processes. Recently, however, there has been greater pressure from central government to address these problems, as will become clear in the next section.

# The Blair Government's NHS Reforms and Public Health

In its White Paper *The New NHS: Modern, Dependable* (Cm 3807, 1997), the Blair government set out a programme of NHS reform that promised an improvement in public health as well as better-quality health services. Although the reform programme covered many aspects of NHS activity relevant to public health, three elements were particularly significant.

## Health Improvement

First, the importance of health improvement was emphasised. As noted in the previous chapter, health authorities were, under the Health Act of 1999, required to develop HImPs. HImPs are plans to improve the health of the whole population and specific sections of the community whose needs are particularly pressing, their purpose being to guide health care contracts and agreements, as well as the activities of other agencies, such as local government and the voluntary sector. A statutory duty was placed on NHS bodies and local government authorities to co-operate in improving health and welfare. A further statutory duty was imposed on local authorities to participate in the preparation or review of plans to improve health and health care. In addition, the government gave local authorities an additional duty to promote the economic, social and environmental wellbeing of their areas. The focus on health improvement was also emphasised in planning guidance and new performance assessment processes. A new set of priorities was announced that placed greater stress on the collaboration between the NHS and local authorities, and on the need to tackle the underlying causes of ill health while reducing health inequality (DoH, 1998c; see also Chapter 10). Meanwhile, the new NHS performance assessment framework identified health improvement as one of six key criteria, alongside health outcomes of care, fair access to services, efficiency, effectiveness and the patient/carer experience (DoH, 1999b).

The Blair government also altered the commissioning process. To guide the development of health improvement programmes, a rolling programme of National Service Frameworks (NSFs) was announced, each of which will set service standards in a particular field, such as mental health (see Exhibit 5.2). The NSFs are also expected to shape long-term service agreements, which, it is envisaged, will replace short-term contracts in an effort to reduce transaction costs and create a more stable condition for planning and resource allocation. The Blair government also abolished GP fundholding, although the principle of primary care-led commissioning was retained.

*Primary Care Groups*

In England, GP fundholders and other commissioning arrangements were replaced with primary care groups (PCGs). These organisations, established in April 1999, consist of all GP practices in a particular area and cover populations of around 100,000. PCGs are led by boards containing a majority of GPs along with community nurses, social service representatives, health authority representatives and lay people. Their main functions are to improve the health of their community, to develop primary and community health services in their area, to improve the quality of care and the level of integration of services and to advise on (and in some cases directly undertake) the commissioning of hospital services. Several levels of independence were envisaged for PCGs (see Hudson, 1999). At the most basic level, the PCG advises the relevant health authority on commissioning. Alternatively, PCGs can take on a devolved responsibility for managing health authority budgets for health care or may become free-standing commissioning bodies accountable to a health authority. Furthermore, the government envisaged that the latter could eventually take over the provision of community health services. Free-standing PCGs would be given Primary Care Trust (PCT) status, and indeed, 17 such organisations were created in April 2000 .

The government has stressed that health authorities will continue to retain overall responsibility for public health (NHSE, 1999). Their specific roles are to bring together all those agencies, including PCGs, PCTs, and local authorities, in an effort to promote and protect public health. In short, the health authority has a leadership role, identifying health and health care needs, setting overall objectives and targets, promoting action to achieve health improvement, facilitating alliances and promoting collaboration between the various agencies that can contribute to health improvement.

The impact of these organisational changes remains to be seen. Although past experience is not always a good guide to the future, the persistence of a rather narrow vision of health promotion among those who dominate in primary care – the GPs – does not augur well. One group of researchers studying emerging PCGs, however, expressed their surprise at the commitment to a broader vision of public health and the level of enthusiasm for interagency working and community involvement (Meads *et al.*, 1999). Others have also highlighted good practice in primary care from which others can learn, community development initiatives in particular being seen as an effective approach (see Levenson *et al.*, 1997; Fisher *et al.*, 1999). Community development involves working with communities, incorporating the views of ordinary people and voluntary groups in the assessment of needs and the development of appropriate responses (Bracht, 1999). Examples include improved community safety schemes, food co-operatives, improved transport schemes and mentoring schemes for parents.

But, as with the kinds of healthy alliance noted in the previous chapter (see Exhibit 4.4), more needs to be done to encourage across-the-board improvements rather than simply acknowledging specific arrangements and interventions that appear to have been effective. Moreover, as Meads *et al.*, (1999) noted, there is, in spite of the opportunities, no guarantee that the creation of PCGs and PCTs will automatically lead to a sharper focus on health improvement and, to this end, better interagency working. Much will depend on their ability to develop a shared perception of health improvement and to build an effective working relationship between stakeholders at local level. Another concern expressed is that PCGs (notwithstanding their lay board member) are not geared to user participation (see Taylor *et al.*, 1998; Fisher *et al.*, 1999), and much will depend on their willingness and ability to develop mechanisms for lay involvement.

It should be noted that different arrangements were introduced in other parts of Britain. In Wales, for example, local health groups based on local authority areas were established to plan and commission services. In Scotland, meanwhile, GPs were formed into local health care co-operatives under the auspices of PCTs. But while the detail of the reforms differed from that in England, and could vary even more with the advent of devolution (see also Exhibit 4.2), the policy was in essence the same: to replace GP fundholding with a system focused on health improvement and promoting a greater collaboration with agencies whose activities affected public health.

## New Programmes

A third area of reform relevant to public health has been the introduction of several programmes designed to develop innovative models of service delivery. The first of these, the personal medical services pilots, aimed to create new forms of service provision in primary care. Using the 1997 Primary Care Act, passed by the Major government, the Blair government introduced a number of new arrangements, such as salaried GPs employed by trusts and nurse-led primary care services. The public health implications of these projects varied. Some aimed to achieve a greater integration into primary care services and raised the prospect of a more coherent approach to public health. Others were also relevant because they focused on meeting the health needs of deprived communities and groups, such as homeless people.

The Health Action Zones (HAZ) programme began in April 1998. HAZs focus on improving interagency collaboration at a local level with a view to improving health and health services. They have three main strategic objectives: to identify and address the health needs of the area, to improve services, making them more responsive to needs, and to develop partnerships between various agencies at a local level. HAZ projects concentrate on those whose needs are greatest and aim to reduce health inequality. Their strategic framework emphasises the importance of public involvement in activities that meet these needs. HAZs are expected to plan services around the needs of people by considering the development and organisation of services such as primary, hospital and community care. They are also required to promote health by improving the quality of life of individuals and the wider economic and social wellbeing of the area. HAZ projects have included plans to provide integrated services to meet the health needs of specific client groups, such as the elderly, people with mental health problems, parents and children, and ethnic minorities. Examples include a project focusing on the health needs of Asian women, a community-based diabetes service and a scheme to improve the health of elderly people through services such as transport and housing.

A third programme, a network of HLCs, partly funded from the National Lottery's New Opportunities Fund, was announced in 1997. HLCs are community-based health promotion initiatives that aim to tackle the social, economic and environmental factors inhibiting good health. Once established, they will provide facilities and services that promote health and wellbeing, as well as laying the foundation for local initiatives to target specific factors such as crime, poor transport and the availability of illegal drugs, which undermine the health of communities. Like HAZs, HLCs are expected to involve local people in the assessment of needs and are expected to emerge from partnerships between different agencies and organisations at a local level. Similarly, they have been endorsed as a means of reducing health inequality, and will be established in the most deprived areas. Indeed, it is anticipated that many of the HLCs will be located within existing HAZs.

## Conclusion

Although the NHS remains primarily a treatment-oriented service, and still focuses strongly on providing health care to individuals rather than promoting the health of populations, it would be wrong to state that nothing had changed in recent years. There is now a more explicit emphasis on health improvement, reinforced by recent policy initiatives. This agenda has resulted in considerably more opportunities for those working in the NHS to contribute to public health. However, as has been suggested, it would be naïve to believe that such opportunities will automatically be taken. Indeed, there are several factors that will continue to inhibit efforts to develop a coherent approach to public health. These include the persistence of different perspectives on health improvement, both within and between various stakeholder organisations and among professional groups. Barriers to cooperation on public health between NHS bodies and local authorities also remain, although they are increasingly being challenged by recent reforms.

Finally, it is unlikely that the broader vision of public health will in the near future counteract the existing biases within the NHS, in particular the dominant medical model which remains focused on the manifestation of disease in individual patients. Most health professionals and agencies remain overwhelmingly concerned with the care and treatment of individual patients. Moreover, even when considering public health, they still tend to place greater faith on clinical interventions to prevent disease rather than broader socio-economic or environmental approaches to promote health, as illustrated by the next chapter.

# 6

# Screening and Public Health

Over the past two decades, much faith has been placed in screening programmes as a means of preventing disease. Screening, defined by Holland and Stewart (1990, pp. 1–2) as 'actively seeking to identify a disease or pre-disease condition in people who are presumed and presume themselves to be healthy', is undertaken for range of diseases and disorders, for example Down's syndrome, sensory impairments in children, bladder cancer in workers in the dye manufacturing and rubber industries, breast cancer and cervical cancer. This chapter examines the development of screening services in the UK, although in order to facilitate an in-depth analysis, it focuses mainly upon cancer screening, in particular the cervical and breast cancer programmes, which are often held up as examples for other mass screening programmes to follow. A number of general conclusions about screening policies and programmes are, however, discussed towards the end of the chapter.

## Cancer Screening

### The Impact of Cancer

Cancer is the second largest cause of mortality, responsible for a quarter of all deaths in the UK. It is also a significant cause of morbidity: 280,000 new cases are diagnosed each year in England and Wales, and it has been estimated that one in three people will develop some form of cancer during their lifetime (ONS, 1997a). Given that at any time around a tenth of hospital inpatients are being treated for cancer (ONS, 1997b), the disease has substantial resource implications, and it has been estimated that cancer treatment accounts for approximately 6 per cent of the NHS budget each year (DoH/Welsh Office, 1995). Yet cancer is also a preventable disease: lung cancer is caused mainly by smoking tobacco, skin cancer is linked to exposure to the sun, and bowel cancer is associated with diet. Although many forms of cancer may be prevented by primary prevention – such as smoking cessation, dietary change and protection from the sun's rays – secondary prevention is also regarded as being important on the grounds that treatment is likely to be more effective when the disease is detected at an early stage.

Early signs of cancer may be detected by GPs and other professionals (such as dentists in the case of oral cancer), but much depends on the patient's own realisation that there is a potentially serious problem and the ability of the practitioner to spot something unusual, order tests and refer to specialists. Early detection is in practice difficult, particularly with regard to cancers in which the symptoms are ambiguous or the patient is reluctant to present them. It is hardly surprising that a more systematic approach to cancer detection has attracted support from medical profession, the public at large and in particular women's organisations (with regard to cancers specific to females or from which they suffer disproportionately), not to mention the commercial providers of screening devices (see Batt, 1994; Sheldon, 1997).

## Principles of Screening

Before moving on to discuss the development of specific screening programmes in the field of cervical and breast cancer, as well as proposals to screen for prostate and bowel cancer, one must be aware of certain conditions and criteria for evaluating such programmes. Although screening for life-threatening diseases such as cancer has been presented as being unambiguously beneficial, it should, like any other intervention, be based on clear principles and evidence. In particular, it should only be undertaken where the following conditions hold (Wilson and Jungner, 1968; Cuckle and Wald, 1984; Holland and Stewart, 1990; Charny, 1994):

● The disease must be common and serious.

● It should have a recognised latent stage during which early symptoms can be detected.

● Its natural history (that is, its causes and development) is well understood.

● The test for the disease is acceptable and effective.

● The cost of detection should be balanced against the benefits provided.

● Physical or psychological harm to those screened should be less than the benefits of the programme.

● Treatment for the disease at an early stage should be of more benefit than treatment started at a later stage and should be acceptable, effective and available to all who need it.

Another approach (see Chamberlain, 1984) is to draw up a list of the potential costs and benefits of screening programmes. Advantages include improved prognosis, the possibility of less radical treatment, net resource savings and reassurance for those found to be clear of disease. Disadvantages include longer morbidity for those screened whose prognosis is unaltered, overtreatment for those with questionable abnormalities, the resource costs of screening plus the extra costs of meeting additional health needs, misleading reassurance for those who have received false negative results, anxiety and in some cases unnecessary treatment for those with false positive results and, finally, hazards arising directly from the screening process itself.

# Cervical Cancer

Cancer of the cervix kills approximately 1400 women each year in the UK. Although the majority of cases occur in middle-aged and older women, the disease is regarded as a serious threat to the health of younger women (Austoker, 1994a) and is responsible for one in four cancer deaths among women under 35. The rationale for screening is that cervical cancer is a significant cause of death, is more effectively treated at an early stage, and can be detected by conducting 'smear' tests at regular intervals. The test itself involves taking material from the cervix that is then examined under a microscope for abnormal changes; if these are found, further investigations will be undertaken. If the diagnosis is confirmed, treatment depends on the extent of the problem and includes laser treatment, cryocautery (the destruction of tissue by the application of extremely cold temperatures) and surgery.

Cervical cancer screening was first encouraged by a national initiative during the 1960s for women aged 35 and over, but this initiative was not implemented in a consistent way. By the mid-1970s, the response rate remained low in some localities, at around 20 per cent of the eligible female population, whereas effective local schemes achieved a response of around 80 per cent. In 1981, the Committee on Gynaecological Cytology reviewed the service and recommended the introduction of schemes that would 'call' women not previously screened and 'recall' at regular intervals those who had been screened before. The DHSS subsequently requested district health authorities to establish 'call–recall' schemes at local level by 1983. This initially had little effect, largely because of the difficulties that many district health authorities encountered trying to secure co-operation from FPCs, which at the time held patients' medical notes and details of GP's lists.

## A National Screening Programme?

During the 1980s, concerns about the service were heightened by individual cases highlighted by the media. Pressure groups, particularly women's organisations and some trade unions, argued for an improved national system and pointed to the government's approval of a national breast cancer programme in 1987, discussed later in this chapter, as a possible model. It was pointed out that two-thirds of women who had invasive cervical cancer had never been screened. Furthermore, those with the highest risk of the disease, older women and working-class women (the death rate for cervical cancer being five times greater for women in social class V than those in social class I) were least likely to have had a smear test (see Austoker, 1994a). The medical profession also recognised these shortcomings and endorsed a more systematic screening procedure for the disease. The BMA produced a report that, among other things, called for a better co-ordination of local programmes, a shorter interval between smear tests and the introduction of call–recall systems by all health authorities (BMA, 1986b). This was accompanied by criticism in Parliament, including a report from the House of Commons' Public Accounts Committee (1986, p. xi), which commented that the delay in introducing comprehensive arrangements for an effective screening programme was 'deplorable'.

At the beginning of 1986, the DHSS instructed district health authorities to install, no later than March 1988, computerised call–recall systems to screen women at least every five years. Although over four-fifths eventually met the deadline, the pressure continued. An implementation team was established, headed by the Prime Minister's advisor on the NHS. In addition, extra funds for computer equipment were provided. In 1987, the DHSS announced that the scheme would be extended to cover women aged 20–64 and instructed district health authorities to designate an individual responsible locally for the organisation of the cervical screening programme. In 1988, the DHSS promoted a new system of quality control, by establishing a national co-ordination network for monitoring and improving standards within the programme.

A change to the GP contract in 1990 – under which GPs were offered a payment for achieving new targets for cervical cytology – presented a further opportunity to improve the coverage of the system. If 80 per cent of the eligible female patients on their list in the previous five years had had a cervical smear, GPs would receive a payment of £2000; if they achieved a lower threshold of 50 per cent, they would receive £700. A similar target was also set for health authorities: they were expected to screen 80 per cent of their eligible female population within a five-year period. The Major government's *The Health of the Nation* strategy in 1992 (Cm 1986, 1992) subsequently established a target to reduce the incidence of invasive cervical cancer from 15 to 12 cases per 100,000 population by the year 2000, using the 1986 level as a baseline. Finally, during the 1990s, further reforms were introduced, including the appointment in 1994 of a full-time national co-ordinator to set common standards and encourage different parts of the NHS to co-operate more fully in improving the quality of the service.

## The Impact of the Screening Programme

These policies together increased the coverage of the screening programme. In England, fewer than half the women in the target age group were screened in 1988, rising to 83 per cent in 1992 and 87 per cent by 1994, a figure that has since hovered around the 85–90 per cent level. In addition, some of the groups most at risk from the disease – older women and working-class women – were being reached to a greater extent than before (Austoker, 1994a). Furthermore, between 1986 and 1995, the incidence of cervical cancer fell by more than the government had aimed for, declining to 11.2 per 100,000, with the result that the target set for the year 2000 was achieved five years early. In addition, there was a downward trend in the overall number of cervical cancer deaths: the mortality rates in England and Wales declined from 67.6 to 43 per million between 1990 and 1998.

But the decline in mortality provided only circumstantial evidence of the effectiveness of the programme. Indeed, as we shall see later, there has been a controversial debate over the actual number of lives saved as a result of screening. Furthermore, doubts about the degree of quality control and the standard of screening persisted (see, for example, Public Accounts Committee, 1992), stimulated by a series of high-profile service failures.

## Service Failures

One of the most significant cases in recent years occurred at the Kent and Canterbury NHS trust. Following a review of 91,000 cases, it was revealed that, between 1990 and 1995, the trust's cytology department had failed to spot minor abnormalities in 1861 women. In a further 333 cases, high-grade abnormalities were not detected and urgent treatment was required. It was alleged that eight of these patients had died from cervical cancer, although the trust initially admitted liability in only three cases (Wells, 1997). Compensation was paid to those who had suffered from a serious shortcoming in the service. The issue, however, raised important legal issues, particularly over the rights of patients to a certain standard of service. Three women with a less common form of cervical cancer, recognised as being more difficult to detect through screening, subsequently won their cases for compensation in the High Court and (following an appeal by the health authority) in the Court of Appeal.

This case and other failures in cervical screening services captured media attention, exposing errors associated with inadequate training, incompetence, inefficient management, a lack of resources and poor organisation. The major incidents also provoked inquiries and resulted in fresh guidance for service providers on how to improve the quality of service (see McGoogan, 1993; Wells, 1997). Other reports added to the pressure to improve service standards. The NAO (1998a), for example, revealed that around half the laboratories undertaking cervical cytology did not meet the national standard for accurately reading smears and that mistakes were putting lives at risk. The Public Accounts Committee (1998) subsequently issued a highly critical report stating that the system was failing those most vulnerable. It noted that 13 (around one in eight) health authorities failed to reach the national target of screening 80 per cent of women in the 25–64-year age group and called for a clear timetable of action to improve standards. Meanwhile, in its own review, the DoH found that 45 per cent of cervical screening laboratories still failed to meet the national quality standards for the service.

A range of measures was introduced aimed at restoring public confidence in the service, including a review of cervical screening programmes, action plans to improve standards, an external accreditation of all laboratories providing screening services and the transfer of responsibility and resources for cervical screening quality assurance from commissioning bodies to the NHS regional offices. In addition, a Cervical Screening Action Team was established to monitor progress and make further recommendations where necessary (Cervical Screening Action Team, 1998). Health authorities were subsequently set a deadline of March 2002 to achieve the target of screening 80 per cent of their eligible female population.

Aside from the problems illustrated by such high-profile fiascos, other concerns have been raised about the way in which the service is provided. It has been argued that cervical screening remains insensitive to women's needs in several respects (see Posner and Vessey, 1988; Milburn and MacAskill, 1994; NAO, 1998a; Public Accounts Committee, 1998). Issues raised include a lack of counselling on the interpretation of test results that can cause anxiety; poor communication between patients and professionals; inadequate attention to the pain and discomfort suffered by patients when undergoing cervical tests, investigations and treatments; and a failure to take into account social and cultural factors, such as ethnic background. Moreover, although coverage has improved, the service is still failing to reach working-class women and those from ethnic minorities. The participation rates of these groups are still significantly lower than average (Majeed *et al.*, 1994; NAO,

1998a; Public Accounts Committee, 1998). Not surprisingly, health authorities in inner city areas, where these social groups are concentrated, find it difficult to achieve the national target (NAO, 1998a).

Criticisms about the quality, sensitivity and coverage of the service presuppose, however, that the cervical cancer screening is, if properly organised, a cost-effective intervention. This assumption is shared by policy makers, most health professionals, the media and presumably most women (although the decision to comply with screening is complex – see Howson, 1999). This perhaps explains why the emphasis has been upon improving the management of the service. But there is a more radical critique of cervical cancer screening that challenges the fundamental assumptions on which it is based (see Foster, 1995; Hann, 1999), as described below.

## Radical Critiques

The effectiveness of the smear test has been challenged on a number of grounds. Skrabanek (1987) argued that the decline in the cervical cancer death rate was part of a long-term downward trend (see also Murphy *et al.*, 1987). He claimed that the benefits of organised mass screening programmes, which attribute the 40–70 per cent fall in mortality rate to early detection (see Austoker, 1994a), were therefore exaggerated. Studies have subsequently tried to provide more systematic evidence, although the controversy remains. One study (Quinn *et al.*, 1999) estimated that the programme saved 800 lives a year and pointed out that the age-standardised incidence rate fell dramatically after the introduction of the national call–recall system, while another (Sasieni and Adams, 1999) estimated that 1300 lives annually had been saved. But these findings have been contested on the grounds that the decline in the death rate from cervical cancer came too soon to be realistically attributed to the extension of the screening programme in 1988 (Raffle, 1997; Leung, 1999). Some have argued that the number of lives saved is exaggerated by researchers' calculations of expected mortality (Vaidya and Baum, 1999), although others believe that the effects of screening have actually been underestimated (Herbert, 1997).

The reliability of the smear test has also been challenged (Skrabanek, 1987; McCormick, 1989). It must be acknowledged that the smear test is a screening rather than a diagnostic test and therefore involves a margin of error (see Wells, 1997). Hence it is always possible that women with 'false positive' results will not develop cervical cancer, while some of those with 'false negatives' will later be diagnosed with the disease. However, for any screening programme, the extent of such results must be within acceptable limits, otherwise it will lose credibility. Studies indicate that false positive results in cervical cancer screening are substantial, between half and three-quarters of women with minor abnormalities not developing cervical cancer (see Nash *et al.*, 1987; Montz *et al.*, 1992). False negative rates are also evident, one study finding a rate as high as 14 per cent (see Slater *et al.*, 1994). False negatives are a particular problem because they give a false sense of security, possibly even to the point of deterring women from subsequently presenting with early clinical signs of disease. This particular criticism may of course be challenged by the development of more effective screening techniques, and several new tests are currently being pioneered that are geared to improving accuracy (see, for example, PRISMATIC Project Management Team, 1999).

Concerns have also been raised about the cost effectiveness of the programme (see, for example, Public Accounts Committee, 1992). Indeed, some commentators (Skrabanek, 1987; McCormick, 1989) have maintained that the cost is underestimated. The cost of smear tests and the call–recall system is substantial – at the time of writing around £150m per annum – but there are also resources associated with further investigations arising from a positive result. There are, moreover, other 'hidden' costs, which should also be taken into account, including the anxiety suffered by women who have positive smear tests but who only receive the all-clear following further investigations.

Finally, screening has been criticised for diverting attention and resources from the underlying causes of cervical cancer. By placing faith in a screening test, the search for the primary causes of cervical cancer is given less priority. Yet resources may be better employed in researching these factors. After all, the UK has one of the highest rates of cervical cancer mortality (and an above-average level of its incidence) among comparable industrialised societies, and it is reasonable to ask why this is so. Several factors associated with cervical cancer, including age and social class, have already been discussed. Others include smoking, identified by most (Lyon *et al.*, 1983; Trevethan *et al.*, 1983; Brinton *et al.*, 1986a; de Vet and Sturmans, 1994; Szarewski *et al.*, 1996) although not all studies (see Stone *et al.*, 1995), raising the possibility of some preventive effect through smoking cessation. The use of oral contraceptives has been associated with cervical cancer (Schiffman and Brinton, 1995), although the relative risk is higher only for current and recent users (Beral *et al.*, 1999). Oestrogen replacement therapy has also been proposed as a possible risk factor. Some researchers have cast doubt on this, suggesting that exogenous oestrogens might actually reduce the risk of cervical cancer (Parazzini *et al.*, 1997).

In contrast, aspects of sexual lifestyle – first sexual intercourse at a younger age, a higher number of previous male sexual partners and a higher number of sexual contacts of these partners – are acknowledged to be risk factors (Harris *et al.*, 1980; Buckley *et al.*, 1981; Brinton and Fraumeni, 1986; Zunzunegui *et al.*, 1986; Kjaer *et al.*, 1992; de Vet *et al.*, 1993; Stone *et al.*, 1995). More specifically, human papillomavirus type 16 and 18 (HPV16/18), transmitted between sexual partners, has been identified as a significant risk factor (Brinton *et al.*, 1989; Schiffman *et al.*, 1993; Lehtinen *et al.*, 1996). This implies possible primary prevention through altering sexual practice, notably by the increased use of barrier methods of contraception (de Vet and Sturmans, 1994). If further research confirms the extent of the risk associated with HPV infection (see Wallin *et al.*, 1999), it may lead to the prevention of cervical cancer being as much an issue for men as it currently is for women. Furthermore, recent research has also suggested that genetic factors may be relevant, and that some women may be more at risk of developing cervical cancer as a result of HPV infection (Storey, 1998), raising the possibility of a more targetted and efficient screening system in conjunction with other prevention initiatives. As a footnote to this, it should be noted that in the UK from summer 2000, pilot schemes will screen women for HPV if they have a borderline cervical smear.

## Breast Cancer

Breast cancer, now the largest cause of death in women aged under 65, kills around 15,000 women in the UK each year. Its significance arises not only from its being the main cause of death from cancer among women, but also from the dread it inspires. Even where treatment has been successful, survivors can be mentally and physically scarred by their experience and may face years of pain and disability. In view of this, it is hardly surprising that studies showing that the disease was preventable were enthusiastically received. Such evidence emerged during the 1960s and 70s from two major studies of screening programmes in the USA and Sweden (see Shapiro *et al.*, 1982; Tabar *et al.*, 1985), which found that around 30 per cent of breast cancer deaths could be prevented by the early detection of tumours through regular mammography (X-ray imaging of the breast). It was believed that mass programmes targetted at older women would pick up the early signs of the disease and that, given that the survival rate for the earlier stages of the disease is believed to be four times higher than that for the later stages, treatment would be more successful.

As Hann (1996) has shown, there was enormous political pressure during the 1970s and 80s for a national breast cancer screening programme in the UK. Women's organisations, trade unions and cancer charities campaigned vociferously on this issue. There was also support from within the medical profession, and a number of trials were established to assess the effectiveness of such a programme. In 1985, Sir Patrick Forrest – who was at the forefront of research in this field (see Forrest, 1990) – was appointed by the DHSS to chair a working group to assess the need for a national screening programme. When it reported the following year, the working party concluded that there was a convincing clinical case for screening women aged 50–64. As Hann points out, this outcome was hardly surprising given that the committee was dominated by those who already had a favourable view of breast screening. Presented with the working party's report in the run-up to the 1987 general election, the government agreed to introduce a national call–recall breast cancer screening programme (Currie, 1989, p. 124). Unlike the cervical cancer scheme, which had attracted much criticism, this was centrally funded, quality assurance lying in the hands of the regional health authorities. Furthermore, the breast screening scheme was introduced with a national co-ordinating body for training, information systems and quality assurance already in place.

The breast screening programme began in 1988 and achieved national coverage in 1990. Women aged 50–64 were invited for mammography at three-year intervals. Initially, only around two-thirds attended, but this figure later rose over the minimum target level of 70 per cent, and by 1996 over three-quarters of those invited were screened. Further impetus was added by the target for breast cancer set by *The Health of the Nation* strategy, which aimed to reduce the mortality rate by 25 per cent in the population invited for screening by the year 2000 (using 1990 as a baseline). The mortality rate from breast cancer, which had risen in the previous two decades, fell substantially in the 1990s. According to Quinn and Allen (1995), it declined by 12 per cent between 1987 and 1995. However, given that the national programme had by the end of this period been running for only five years (and that some women in the target group did not receive their first invitation until as late as 1993), it is difficult to attribute the decline directly to the introduction of the scheme (see Beral *et al.*, 1995). Indeed, improvements in treatment provide a better explanation for the continuing fall in breast cancer mortality. According to the latest available figures, the crude death rate from breast cancer fell from 49.9 per 100,000 (1990) to 44.2 (1998), a fall of around 12 per cent.

## Criticisms of the Breast Cancer Screening Programme

Criticism of the breast screening programme, like that of cervical screening, has fallen into two main camps: a criticism of service standards and coverage, and a more fundamental attack on the rationale behind the service. Proponents believe that the programme is generally good in both principle and practice, but needs to be improved and extended. Some maintain that the scheme should be extended to other groups, in particular those with a genetic predisposition to breast cancer, and to other age groups (Health Committee, 1995; Age Concern, 1996). A related concern is that the service is not as accessible as it should be to certain social groups, such as working-class women and ethnic minorities. This was reflected in the finding in 1996 that seven health authorities, each covering inner city areas, had a screening rate equivalent to less than half the eligible population. Another issue relates to the time interval for mammography. In the third year after screening, 82 per cent of breast cancers are 'interval cancers', which have not been picked up by the screening process (Woodman *et al.*, 1995). This seriously undermines the effectiveness of the programme, and as around half of interval cancers occur in the third year after screening, it has been argued that the gap between episodes of screening should be reduced to two years (see Woodman *et al.*, 1995; Asbury *et al.*, 1996).

More rigorous screening standards have also been urged. In 1995, following the publication of studies suggesting that 'two-view' mammography (that is, two different X-rays of the breast) could improve the detection rate by as much as 24 per cent and was in the longer term more cost effective (Anderson *et al.*, 1994; Wald *et al.*, 1995), the DoH ordered screening units to adopt this for women attending their first screening appointment. It has also been suggested that mammographs should be reviewed by two people, a process known as 'double-reading'. Although there is some evidence to suggest that this could be more cost effective than the conventional approach (Brown *et al.*, 1996), it is not at the time of writing recommended in official guidance to screening units.

As noted earlier, the programme was established with a strong central lead, and the regional health authorities were given a key role in quality assurance (see Public Accounts Committee, 1992). This initially enabled the breast cancer programme to avoid some of the problems of the cervical cancer screening service, which lacked central direction and common standards. However, the creation of the NHS internal market in 1991 was seen in some quarters as undermining these achievements by making the funding of breast screening services and the monitoring of quality more of a local responsibility. This was compounded by the replacement of the regional health authorities in 1996 with regional offices of the NHS Executive. Although the regional offices retained the responsibility for co-ordinating services such as breast screening and were expected to ensure that health authorities tackled government priorities – such as the national target for the reduction of breast cancer deaths – they did not have a direct monitoring role. Instead, quality assurance became the responsibility of a 'lead purchaser' (a designated health authority within each region), an arrangement subsequently criticised by the House of Commons Health Committee (1995) and the DoH's own review (DoH, 1997a).

The fears expressed by critics were realised in one particularly bad case. Unlike cervical screening services, breast cancer services tended to avoid leading to high-profile fiascos, but in 1997, it came to light that 229 women screened by the East Devon screening service should have been recalled. Twelve women were wrongly given negative results, two of whom allegedly died as result. The DoH review of breast cancer, mentioned above, was highly critical of the management arrangements within the trust concerned, as well as with national and regional arrangements that had apparently allowed a substandard service to continue. It recommended strengthening external quality assurance mechanisms and stating a clearer commitment to national standards. In particular, the committee recommended that the aims of the programme should feature in the annual priorities and planning guidance issued by the DoH. It also recommended a more proactive role for the national breast screening co-ordinator in developing and monitoring the effectiveness of systems of quality assurance. A stronger regional role in quality assurance was also recommended, funding being allocated to the regional offices of the NHS. Regional DPHs were to be given explicit responsibility to ensure that proper arrangements were in place and would delegate matters to a director of quality assurance. Finally, the report recommended an explicit requirement that health authorities and trusts should commission and deliver breast screening to national standards, raising the possibility that units failing to meet these standards would be closed. Following this report, the DoH ordered NHS trusts with cancer screening units to review their quality assurance procedures. Health authorities, trusts and regional offices were required to develop action programmes to ensure that national standards were being met. It was also announced that, from 1999, the regional offices would have overall responsibility for monitoring service quality.

Criticism has also centred on the procedures that follow screening. Women with a positive result face further investigation and, if necessary, treatment. This process is, however, often slow, causing considerable anxiety and even serious psychological problems for women (see Lovestone and Fahey, 1991; Cuckburn *et al.*, 1994). Possible strategies to minimise this include counselling and better information for women (Saidi, 1993), but a crucial factor is the length of time that women have to wait for the results of further tests and for treatment. In this context, a review of studies worldwide (Richards *et al.*, 1999) identified a worse survival rate among women who experienced a delay in treatment, although others (Hainsworth *et al.*, 1993; Sainsbury *et al.*, 1999) have challenged these findings. Nevertheless, in 1997 the government responded to concerns about delays by providing additional funding to establish 'one-stop clinics', where results could be available within a few hours rather than weeks. This was followed in 1999 by a requirement that all urgent referrals from GPs for suspected breast cancer had to be seen by specialists within 14 days.

Even where results are transmitted quickly, however, there is no guarantee that the treatment offered will be adequate. This point was forcefully made by the Health Committee in 1995, which observed that the breast cancer survival rate in the UK was relatively poor and that there was a wide regional difference in treatment. Moreover, the committee noted that the women who were treated in specialist centres tended to survive longer than those treated in smaller hospitals by general surgeons, and called for all women to receive the best available treatment in the specialist units. This concurred with other inquiries, such as that commissioned by the Royal College of Radiologists into the side effects of radiotherapy in breast cancer treatment (Bates and Evans, 1995), which recommended that 'where possible patients should be cared for by a multidisciplinary team of breast specialists with a wide knowledge of the disease' (p. 30).

Government policy was already moving in this direction. In 1995, the review of cancer services – the Calman–Hine report – proposed a three-tier system of cancer care comprising primary care teams focusing on referral and management in the community, designated hospital units for treating the most common cancers, and centres that would also treat rarer cancers and those who required highly specialised treatment (DoH/Welsh Office, 1995). It was believed that breast cancer treatment would improve as a result of this reconfiguration of services. However, some evidence of adverse effects emerged from the review of breast screening that followed the Devon case. It was found that, in some areas, resources for breast screening were being diverted into services for women presenting symptoms of breast cancer and that attempts were being made to reconfigure breast screening programmes into smaller and non-viable units in order to enhance claims for designation as a breast cancer unit (DoH, 1997a).

## Radical Critiques

There are, however, other fundamental criticisms that strike at the underlying rationale of the programme. It has been argued that evidence of the cost effectiveness of the breast screening programme is equivocal. Critics such as Wright (1986), Skrabanek (1988a), Rodgers (1990) and Watmough *et al.* (1997) have pointed out that the two main studies that provided the impetus to establish a screening programme in the UK – the Swedish and USA studies mentioned earlier – exaggerated the benefits of screening. They argue that the claimed 30 per cent reduction in death rate in the screened population refers to a relative difference in the death rate between the screened group and the control group. When this reduction is expressed as a proportion of the total number of women screened, however, the benefit is much smaller, less than 1 per cent (Wright, 1986; Rodgers, 1990). Put in this way, it is more evident that huge numbers of women are screened, and some subjected to further unnecessary investigations and treatment, for each death prevented. Furthermore, as Rodgers has noted, these deaths are postponed rather than avoided, and the screened population tends to catch up with controls after a period of time. The idea that one in three possible cancer deaths is avoided by screening is somewhat misleading. It should also be pointed out that some trials were unable to demonstrate that statistically significant benefits arose from mass screening (see Miller, 1980; Verbeek *et al.*, 1984; UK Trial of Early Detection Cancer Group, 1988; Andersson, 1988).

In 1998, further controversy was caused by the results of a large-scale study of breast screening in Sweden, which revealed that, between 1986 and 1996, breast cancer mortality was reduced by only 0.8 per cent (Mayor, 1999; Sjonell and Stahle, 1999). The research methods adopted were, however, criticised by Swedish epidemiologists (Rosen and Rhenquist, 1999). The result was also countered by further evidence from UK trials, again using relative mortality statistics, which found that the number of breast cancer deaths in the screened population was 27 per cent less than would have been expected had screening not taken place (UK Trial of Early Detection Cancer Group, 1999). In a further study of a randomised trial in Edinburgh (Alexander *et al.*, 1999), breast cancer mortality in the screened group was four-fifths that of the control group, which had not been screened. Both studies indicated that younger women aged 45–49 who were not included in the national screening programme could benefit, raising the possibility that breast screening could be extended to this group. The controversy continued, however, when a meta-analysis of clinical trials by Danish researchers found that breast cancer screening was not justi-fied. Of the eight clinical trials examined by the researchers, six were found to be methodologically flawed. The other two trials found no evidence of effect of screening on mortality (Gotzsche and Olsen, 2000).

Defenders of breast screening reject allegations of methodological bias and continue to maintain that the relative rate of mortality reduction is the most relevant indicator of effectiveness (see DoH, 1991). They have also estimated that, in Britain by the year 2000, 1250 lives and (on the basis that each survivor will live for a further 20 years) 25,000 years of life will have been saved by the programme. Others, however, have pointed out the likelihood of diminishing returns from such programmes. Watmough and colleagues (1997) found that the reduction of risk of dying from breast cancer achieved by screening appears to have declined by 10–15 per cent over time. This finding is consistent with the observation that national screening programmes tend not to achieve the kind of result attained by trials (Holland and Stewart, 1990; Sjonell and Stahle, 1999). One reason for this is that trials invariably take place in 'centres of excellence' whose performance is difficult emulate nationwide (Witcombe, 1988).

But even if one accepts that significant benefit arises from breast screening, there is scope for further criticism. Some have challenged the idea that early intervention is necessarily the best response, given the uncertainty over how to treat small invasive cancers (Moritz *et al.*, 1997). Furthermore, as already noted, there is disagreement over the impact of a delay in diagnosis or referral for treatment. Even some of those associated with the breast screening trials have acknowledged that mammography gives rise to a high false positive rate (Roberts, 1989). Patients who are eventually given the 'all-clear' represent around 90 per cent those recalled for further investigation. Another study in the USA by Elmore *et al.* (1998) revealed that around a quarter of women had at least one false positive mammogram over a 10-year period, and a further 13 per cent had a false positive breast examination. This greatly adds to the cost of screening and also means that additional follow-up costs are unnecessarily incurred. Elmore and colleagues also found that for every $100 spent on screening, an additional $33 was spent evaluating false positive results, while according to Lidbrink *et al.* (1996), 500 false positives in one Swedish trial incurred £334,000 in follow-up costs. It should be noted that the Forrest committee underestimated the cost of screening by excluding the cost of both necessary and unnecessary treatment from their calculations. Studies that have incorporated these costs have found that screening involves a far higher cost, as much as twice the Forrest estimates: Clarke and Fraser (1991) estimated the cost of breast screening to be £8638 per life year saved. For this and other reasons, it has been argued that the money may be better spent on treating symptomatic women rather than screening (see Baum, 1999).

But other, less obvious, costs are also imposed by breast screening. False positives cause unnecessary anxiety among the women involved and therefore impose a large subjective cost, notwithstanding efforts noted earlier aimed at reducing the level of anxiety (Brett *et al.*, 1998). In addition, unnecessary treatment may occur, which, given the nature of the treatment, is a serious matter for those diagnosed, particularly when surgeons err on the side of caution and subject the patient to radical surgery. Finally, the diagnostic procedures may themselves cause harm. It should be noted that mammography is painful, as many as three-quarters of women who undergo it experiencing pain (Bruyinckx *et al.*, 1999). It may be argued that other procedures beneficial to patients can also cause pain or extreme discomfort, but it has been suggested that the process of X-raying healthy breasts may cause damage as well as pain (Epstein, 1992). Furthermore, the process of compressing the breast to get a clearer image is also thought by some to be harmful (Watmough *et al.*, 1997), although others have dismissed these fears as groundless (Yeoman *et al.*, 1994).

As with cervical cancer, screening for breast cancer has been criticised for diverting resources and attention away from possible underlying causes of the disease, which might be preventable (Batt, 1994; Read, 1994). Although the aetiology of breast cancer is complex, a number of environmental and lifestyle factors have been implicated. Breast cancer is undoubtedly linked to hormonal factors: it is more common in women who begin menstruation at an earlier age, in those who have a later menopause and in those who delay having their first child. It has also been suggested that disease is associated with the use of the contraceptive pill and hormone replacement therapy (HRT). A reanalysis of research into the effect of oral contraceptives indicated a slight increase in risk associated with breast cancer. This relative risk has been estimated to be 1.24 for current users and 1.16 for women who stopped using the pill 1–4 years previously (Collaborative Group on Hormonal Factors in Breast Cancer, 1996). Little, however, is known about the longer-term risks of breast cancer resulting from oral contraception, nor about the relative risks of the pill compared with other methods (Hemminki, 1996). A similar reanalysis of the effects of HRT found that this therapy increased the relative risk of breast cancer by 1.023 for each year of use. For those who had used HRT for five years, the relative risk was higher, at 1.35 (Collaborative Group on Hormonal Factors in Breast Cancer, 1997). HRT was also associated with a slightly increased risk of breast cancer in a further study (O'Connor *et al.*, 1998), which also suggested, somewhat paradoxically, that this therapy may slow the growth of tumours. Nevertheless, it should be pointed out that the level of risk associated with HRT is relatively small and is similar to that found in women whose menopause is naturally delayed.

Diet has also been suggested as a possible factor in breast cancer, possible links having been identified between breast cancer and the consumption of certain fats – trans-fatty acids – which are found in biscuits, cakes and some margarines (Kohlmeier *et al.*, 1997). The contamination of food by pesticides and other chemicals has also been suggested to be a causal factor (Epstein, 1992; Watterson, 1995; Potts, 1999). In particular, the organochlorines, such as aldrin, dieldrin, DDT (dicophane) and hexachlorocyclohexanes (HCHs) such as lindane, and polychlorinated biphenyls (PCBs) have been identified as posing a potentially serious risk, including breast cancer, to human health.

Hard evidence of causal links is, however, difficult to find. One American study (Wolff *et al.*, 1993) did find a link between breast cancer and DDE (a residue of the pesticide DDT), but this was not confirmed by other researchers in the USA or in Europe (Krieger *et al.*, 1994; van't Veer *et al.*, 1997). Even if the case against DDE is not proven, however, it is possible that other chemicals are involved. In Israel, for example, a high concentration of HCHs in dairy products has been linked with breast cancer (Westin, 1993). Following a ban on pesticides containing these chemicals, the breast cancer rate fell markedly. In a further study (Falck *et al.*, 1992), elevated levels of PCBs and other chlorinated hydrocarbons were found in fat samples taken from women with breast cancer, suggesting a role for these compounds in the disease. A Danish study (Hoyer *et al.*, 1998) did not find an association between breast cancer and either DDT or PCBs, but it did identify a significantly increased, dose-related risk of breast cancer for the pesticide dieldrin and a slightly positive (although not statistically significant) association with beta-hexachlorocyclohexane, which led the research team to conclude that an exposure to these organochlorine compounds may increase the risk of breast cancer. Furthermore, in the UK, the Committee on the Carcinogenicity of Chemicals in Food, Consumer Products and the Environment (2000) also found no evidence of a link between breast cancer and DDT, DDE, dieldrin and lindane, although it did suggest that published literature on beta-hexachlorocyclohexane be kept under review.

There is also concern that pollutants such as DDT and PCBs have a much larger impact on breast cancer, and on public health generally, than is commonly supposed. As Arnold *et al.* (1996) note, although the low potencies of compounds studied in isolation suggest little impact on biological systems, their synergistic effect may be much greater. In other words, the interaction of multiple chemicals with humans, the food chain and the environment may have significant and unforeseen implications for cancer of the breast, as well as testicular cancer and other diseases. The review by the Committee on Carcinogenicity, mentioned above, did not find any evidence of synergistic interaction. But it did note that epidemiological research was ongoing in this field and would have to be taken into account when published.

Finally, researchers have linked breast cancer to adverse life events. Chen *et al.* (1995) examined a small sample of women with the disease and found that, after adjusting for possible confounding factors including the menopause and age, severe life events such as redundancy and bereavement significantly increased the risk of breast cancer. The suggestion that emotional and psychological factors might play an important role in the development of breast cancer has, however, been challenged by other research findings. A study by Protheroe *et al.* (1999) of 332 women attending breast clinics did not find an association between severe life events and the onset of breast cancer. However, this remains a relatively under-researched area, and a further investigation of these factors is certainly worthwhile.

## Prostate and Bowel Cancer

The problems associated with breast and cervical cancer screening have not deterred those who believe that screening is the main weapon in the battle against these diseases. Indeed, in recent years there have been calls to establish other screening programmes, notably for cancers of the prostate and bowel. Prostate cancer predominantly affects middle-aged and elderly men. Around 10,000 men in the UK die from the disease each year, representing approximately 10 per cent of male cancer deaths. It is clearly a significant problem, but is screening justified?

Despite enthusiasm in some quarters of the medical profession, the majority view is that the test for abnormality – the PSA (prostatic-specific antigen) test – is not sufficiently accurate. Two-thirds of men who demonstrate a positive PSA result are subsequently found to be free from the illness.

Also, many of those with prostate cancer will die of something else, partly because sufferers are middle-aged and elderly, and partly because the disease is often slow to develop and can take up to 20 years to kill the patient. A Canadian study (Labrie *et al.*, 1999) did find evidence that the PSA screening of men aged over 50 years was effective in identifying those at high risk of prostate cancer. It should, however, be noted that only a minority of those invited for screening, less than a quarter, actually accepted, raising questions about the representativeness of the sample (Charatan, 1998).

A further reason for caution is that there are doubts about the efficacy and cost effectiveness of treatment for prostate cancer (Office of Health Economics, 1995; Chamberlain *et al.*, 1996; Selly *et al.*, 1996), so much so that 'watchful waiting' is regarded as a reasonable alternative to treatment (Fleming *et al.*, 1993; Coley *et al.*, 1997). The side effects of surgery include impotence, incontinence and, in about 1 in 200 cases, death. Meanwhile, radiation therapy has been associated with impotence, incontinence and damage to other tissues nearby. It should be noted that new treatment techniques have been developed, which, when available, may lead to fewer and less serious side effects, making screening more beneficial (Stuttaford, 1997). Nonetheless, the UK government was advised in 1997 by the National Screening Committee (discussed further below) that a national screening programme for prostate cancer would not benefit patients and could indeed cause considerable harm.

Although calls for prostate cancer screening may for the time being have abated, pressure for a screening programme for bowel cancer has strengthened in recent years. Bowel cancer is undoubtedly a serious problem, around 19,000 people each year in Britain dying from the disease. The disease affects both men and women in equal measure, being in fact the second largest cause of death from cancer in both sexes. It affects younger-middle-aged people as well as the elderly: around a quarter of deaths from bowel cancer, compared with less than a tenth of prostate cancer deaths, occur in those aged under 65. If caught at an early stage, treatment can be effective, but because most cases are not found quickly, the disease has a high death rate: only one in three people diagnosed with bowel cancer currently survives. Although bowel cancer is a major disease, it has not until fairly recently received the attention it perhaps deserves. This is largely because of the well-known taboos surrounding bowel disorders and diseases, which, although not exclusively 'British', do seem to be an important part of our health culture (see Payer, 1989). The fact that bowel cancer – and bowel cancer screening – is now attracting greater public attention is to some extent due to an effective media campaign waged by those who believe that its profile should be raised. Their efforts were undoubtedly assisted by the publicity surrounding tragic cases such as that of Bobby Moore, the former England soccer captain, who died of cancer of the colon in 1993.

The DoH responded to these pressures by launching an initiative to improve colorectal cancer services. This involved the publication in 1997 of guidance on how to improve the outcome for people suffering from the disease, and in particular emphasised the importance of access to specialist, multidisciplinary care (DoH, 1997b). The following year, an extra £10m was allocated to bowel cancer treatment and a pilot screening study was launched. Meanwhile, in Scotland, bowel cancer screening is the subject of one of the four demonstration projects that form part of the public health strategy north of the border (see Exhibit 4.2). These moves have been to some extent prompted by evidence of the effectiveness of the faecal occult blood test, which involves an analysis of stool samples so that they can be tested for early signs of the disease. In one study of people aged 45–74 in Nottingham, it was discovered that, eight years on, there was 15 per cent lower death rate among those screened (Hardcastle *et al.*, 1996), while a Danish study of a similar age group found an 18 per cent reduction in relative mortality over a 10-year period (Kronborg *et al.*, 1996).

The faecal occult blood test is a relatively acceptable test from the patient's point of view. It can also be self-administered, which is a further advantage in minimising cost. However, only around one in seven of those with positive results will actually have cancer, raising the familiar story of unnecessary anxiety among 'false positive' candidates. There are other tests that can be used: the colon can be inspected for signs of premalignancy using a colonoscope or a sigmoidoscope, which may also be used to inspect the rectum. It is, however, unlikely that these procedures would be used for first-stage screening in a mass programme because they are costly, are unpleasant for patients and can cause damage to the bowel. In trials, colonoscopy has been used as a follow-up test for those with a positive result on faecal occult blood testing, but if patients are subsequently found to be free from disease, they have in effect been subjected to unnecessary risk and this should be acknowledged. Indeed, a study of the Nottingham trial found some investigation-related morbidity, amounting to 0.5 per cent of those investigated, but reported no mortality and little evidence to support overdiagnosis (Robinson, *et al.*, 1999). Finally, it should be noted that the cost effectiveness of bowel cancer screening has been shown to be similar to that of breast cancer screening in the short term, although estimates of bowel cancer screening appear to be superior in the longer term (Whynes *et al.*, 1998). As noted earlier, however, the results of such studies depend a great deal on what is included in the cost and benefit calculations.

# Genetic Screening

The debate surrounding mass screening programmes for cancer has become more intense as a result of developments in the field of genetics (Pianezza *et al.*,

1998). Research has identified genes that appear to predispose individuals to particular diseases, including cancer (Yates, 1996). Given that some cancers – notably breast cancer and bowel cancer – are associated with a family history of the disease, this raises the prospect of screening the population for genetic characteristics. Two genes have been identified for hereditary breast and ovarian cancer – *BRCA1* and *BRCA2*. Together, they account for around 80 per cent of 'inherited' cases of breast cancer. A further genetic factor was identified in 1999 when researchers identified a possible link between a variant of the apolipoprotein E gene and breast cancer (Hopkins, 1999). Other genes have been found for colonic cancer, mutations in *MSH2* and *MLH1* being identified as responsible for some hereditary cases. Furthermore, scientists have discovered a single gene that appears to give protection against certain cancerous chemicals in the environment. Experiments on mice revealed that those lacking the *GstP* gene cluster were more likely to develop skin cancer induced by polycyclic aromatic hydrocarbons, which are found in, for example, cigarette smoke (Henderson *et al.*, 1998).

The prospect of genetic testing for cancer, as well as for other diseases, presents a number of advantages. These include a degree of reassurance for those with a family history of the disease but who are found not to have a genetic predisposition. Those unfortunate enough to have genetic predisposition could benefit from closer surveillance and, if early signs of the disease emerge, clinical intervention at a much earlier stage than would normally have been the case. Another benefit is that such individuals may be able to make choices about work and lifestyle that reflect their higher risk of cancer. Hence in the future, those with genetic predisposition to bladder cancer may be counselled to avoid working in industries where this is a known risk. Similarly, those with genetic factors associated with bowel cancer may be more willing to accept dietary changes as a means of preventing the disease. One should not, however, be too optimistic about the latter point since it may well be that individuals adopt a fatalistic approach once they have learned of their genetic predisposition, believing that lifestyle will have little effect on the final outcome. The final advantage credited to genetic screening is that new therapies will eventually emerge, enabling doctors to alter the genes responsible for cancer. There is, however, likely to be a long time lag – known as the therapeutic gap (Holtzman and Shapiro, 1998) – between the availability of tests and the introduction of genetic therapies.

Critics of genetic technology believe that tests, for cancer and for other diseases, should not be offered if no effective treatment is available. To do otherwise goes against certain principles of screening set out at the beginning of this chapter. Telling someone that they are likely to develop a life-threatening illness without offering treatment seems, to most people, unethical. Even if treatment does become available, the knowledge that one is predisposed to a potentially fatal disease is likely to place a high psychological cost on the individual. There is also a concern that the tests are unreliable as a predictor of the onset of disease. This could lead to unnecessary treatment, which, in the case of breast cancer, for example, is particularly serious given the effects associated with radical treatment. But even if the tests are accurate, the response of the public to this information is difficult to predict and may be counterproductive from a health promotion perspective. The potentially fatalistic response of those testing positive has already been noted, but a similarly adverse response could be generated among those testing negative, who may feel that they can reject advice about healthy lifestyle because they have been told that their genes do not predispose them to a particular disease.

Moreover, genetic testing carries a range of other adverse social implications, which need to be carefully examined (see Davison *et al.*, 1994). Those tested positive for cancer and other diseased could find themselves discriminated against – by employers and by financial corporations such as banks and insurance companies. There is also the related question of confidentiality: how will the information be handled and who will see test results? A further problem, critics argue, is that the emphasis on genetic screening shifts attention away from the underlying causes of cancer. Many cancers are associated with environmental and lifestyle factors. Even when genetic factors are involved, there is an interaction with these other elements. Nevertheless, if the importance of genetic screening is overemphasised, there may be less emphasis on a collective response to prevention, including tackling powerful commercial interests whose activities are harmful to public health (Clarke, 1995; Willis, 1998).

Governments have been slow to react to the implications of the new genetics. There has been a reluctance to regulate in this field, largely because of the power of the scientific and commercial interests involved. Genetic screening is potentially a hugely lucrative industry, and governments have not wished to discourage enterprise in this area, irrespective of the consequences for ordinary people. Only after pressure from Parliament did the British government in 1996 set up an advisory commission – the Human Genetics Advisory Commission – to review scientific progress, to report on issues with social, ethical and economic consequences in relation to public health, insurance, patents and employment, and to advise on ways of improving public confidence and understanding of the new genetics. In 1999, however, it was proposed that the Human Genetics Advisory Committee, along with two other bodies, the Advisory Committee on Genetic Testing and the Advisory Committee on Scientific Advances in Genetics, would be absorbed into a new body, the Human Genetics Commission, which will report to ministers on the range of issues covered by the original bodies.

# Conclusion

This discussion of cancer screening has generated various common themes, some of which have a broader relevance for screening programmes and preventive medicine generally. The first point is that screening has an important ethical dimension often overlooked by scientists, commercial interests and decision makers. For some, such as Skrabanek (1988b) and Rodgers (1990), screening as currently practised is unethical because people are not informed about the inherent risks involved, such as the side effects of screening tests, incorrect diagnosis and unnecessary treatment. Second, there has been an assumption that screening is unambiguously good and therefore worthwhile. This has been based on poor evidence in some cases, particularly the cervical cancer screening programme, which was established by assertion rather than an assessment of its effectiveness. But even where schemes have been evaluated and found to be effective, findings have been challenged, as with breast screening. In addition, there is the question of cost, which has in the past been underestimated, particularly with regard to the unnecessary psychological cost imposed on participants who have been found falsely positive. As Stewart-Brown and Farmer (1997) argue, full account must be taken of such costs and of the wider social effect of screening, particularly the way in which it affects health behaviour.

In recent years, there has been more scepticism about screening in official circles, and new procedures have been established to evaluate the cost effectiveness of screening. In 1996, a National Screening Committee (NSC) was established to advise government on new screening programmes and to review, modify and, if necessary, terminate existing programmes. As noted earlier, the NSC advised against the adoption of a prostate cancer screening programme.

The creation of the NSC was an important step forward, although it cannot guarantee that screening is limited to areas where is cost effective. There are powerful scientific and commercial interests engaged in lobbying for the expansion of such schemes, who have the resources to ensure that the necessary 'evidence' emerges. What is needed is a wider understanding – among the public, the clinical professions and policy makers – that screening has its limitations. They would do well to heed the comments of Holland and Stewart (1990, p. 18), whose excellent review did much to stimulate debate about the screening process:

> we would contend that screening by itself can provide no answer to anything. Only if it is carried out efficiently and humanely, leads to an improved outcome in those concerned and is properly monitored and evaluated should it be contemplated.

# 7

# Health and the Environment

Until fairly recently, health policy makers showed little interest in environmental issues (Hume Hall, 1990), and, by the same token, health rarely received priority in environmental policies (WHO, 1992). Indeed, to some extent health and environmental problems still occupy different worlds. This is reflected in the separation of responsibility for these matters between agencies at local, national and international level, and by poor communication and co-ordination on what should be issues of mutual concern (Environmental Health Commission, 1997). These organisational constraints have been compounded by a failure to conceptualise environmental health and a reluctance to evaluate the impact of environmental factors upon health.

One of the main difficulties in conceptualising the link between environment and health has been that 'the environment is everything' (Lawson, 1997, p. 119). This is reflected in standard definitions, such as that employed by Lindheim and Syme (1983, p. 337), who define the environment as 'the condition or influences under which any person or thing lives or is developed'. The catch-all nature of 'the environment' is similarly reflected in definitions of environmental health. Last (1987, p. 131), for example, has defined environmental health as 'the aspect of public health concerned with all the factors, circumstances, and conditions in the environment or surroundings of humans that can exert an influence on human health and well-being'.

In addition to the problems of defining environmental health, measuring the impact of the environment on health is problematic. Although, worldwide, poor environmental health is responsible for 25 per cent of preventable ill health (WHO, 1997b), it is often difficult to prove causal links. However, although health problems are influenced by a variety of environmental factors, some of which cannot be manipulated in the short or even medium term, epidemiological evidence may pinpoint those amenable to policy intervention. Alternatively, if potential consequences are considered serious enough to warrant immediate preventive action, policy makers may be persuaded to intervene on the basis of circumstantial evidence or even in the light of theoretical risks.

This chapter identifies some of the main environmental threats to health and discusses actual and potential policy responses. The topics covered are pollution, depletion and sustainable development, accidents, and health and safety at work. Other aspects of the human environment that affect health are considered elsewhere: food and diet (Chapter 8), lifestyle (Chapter 9 and Exhibit 3.1), economic and social structure (Chapter 10) and housing (Chapter 10).

# Pollution and Depletion

Worries about pollution of the environment and the depletion of earth's resources have grown steadily since the early 1960s. From time to time, there have been 'surges' of public anxiety, the most recent being in the late 1980s in response to the twin threats of global warming and ozone layer depletion. In this period, concern for the environment became a mainstream political issue, prompting national and local governments, as well as international agencies, to develop strategies to reassure the public. However, with the exception of nuclear power, in which human health and safety considerations have always loomed large, environmental issues have been mainly dominated by concerns about the extinction of species and habitats, and the availability of resources to meet future needs, rather than about human health. The latter has nonetheless become much more prominent in recent years, exemplified by anxiety surrounding specific diseases, such as asthma linked to air pollution, and skin cancer attributed to ozone depletion, in addition to general threats to health posed by water pollution, toxic waste disposal and global warming.

## Pollution

Industrial processes release many different chemicals on land, in water and into the air. Although many chemicals are potentially harmful, the damage caused depends on the ability of the environment to cope with the level of contamination. There is currently much concern about chemicals that persist in the environment for long periods, such as organochlorine compounds and dioxins, which are believed to be harmful to human health (Crombie, 1995; see also Chapters 6 and 8). Meanwhile, the disposal of toxic waste has been blamed for many health problems, including cancer, heart disease and birth defects, even though it is hard to identify significant associations between specific pollutants and increased levels of illness because of the difficulty in tracing previous exposure to waste products (BMA, 1989; Walker, 1992). Studies presenting evidence of a link between toxic waste and health (see Dolk *et al.*, 1998; Fielder *et al.*, 2000) have been challenged on methodological grounds. Nevertheless, critics have been unable to reassure communities situated close to toxic waste processing facilities, such as incinerators and landfill sites, of their safety.

Nuclear power has been perceived as a serious environmental threat, particularly with regard to the Chernobyl disaster of 1986, not to mention the chequered history of the British nuclear industry over the years. The main health concerns about nuclear power arise from the following: the catastrophic consequences of a nuclear disaster, the effects of smaller emissions and leaks, problems arising from the transportation of radioactive materials and waste, and problems associated with waste storage and disposal. The poor image of the nuclear industry in the 1980s and 90s led to declining confidence among both the public and politicians, despite the fact that its energy is 'clean' in terms of the greenhouse effect, discussed below. This climate of opinion, coupled with revelations about the high cost of decommissioning, led the UK government in 1994 to announce a moratorium on the building of new nuclear power stations in the public sector.

In recent years, air pollution has been perceived as one of the most serious environmental issues. Many chemical compounds including sulphur dioxide, which causes 'acid rain', damage air quality. Nitrogen oxides and hydrocarbons, associated with heavy traffic congestion, can create a cocktail of gases leading to the generation of low-level ozone and photochemical smog. These cause lung irritation and can trigger respiratory illness, even to the point of mortality. Although, as with most forms of pollution, it is difficult to measure the direct impact on health (see COMEAP, 1995; Anderson *et al.*, 1996), it has been estimated that in Britain at least 12,000 deaths, and over 14,000 hospital admissions annually are linked to air pollution (COMEAP, 1998).

The transport system has been identified as a key factor in air pollution. Road traffic produces a fifth of carbon dioxide, a third of airborne particulates and volatile organic compounds (such as benzene, a known carcinogen), half of all nitrogen oxides and almost all the carbon monoxide in the air (Godlee, 1992c; ONS, 1997b). Further evidence on the cost of pollution from road transport was provided by a study of three countries, France, Austria and Switzerland (WHO, 1999b), which estimated that an additional 21,000 deaths from respiratory and heart disease occurred each year in adults over 30 years of age as a result of long-term exposure to air pollution from cars. This figure was double the number of annual road accident deaths in the three countries. The study also estimated that air pollution from cars caused 300,000 extra cases of bronchitis in children and 15,000 hospital admissions for heart disease, as well as over half a million asthma attacks in adults and children. This implies that the increasing reliance of individuals on the motor car, and of business on road haulage, has wide consequences for environmental health, not only for pollution, but also for road safety, discussed later in this chapter. Furthermore, an increasing level of car use may have an additional health effect because car usage is associated with a lower level of exercise, which is in turn related to heart disease and other health problems (Transport and Health Study Group, 1991; BMA, 1997a).

Transport also has implications for noise pollution, about which there are 100,000 complaints every year (Godlee, 1992d; Crombie, 1995). Noise pollution is linked to sleep deprivation and stress, both in turn being associated with illness and poor quality of life (Noise Review Working Party, 1990). Other causes of noise pollution include industrial processes and neighbourhood noise. Complaints about the latter rocketed in the 1980s and 90s: between 1981 and 1994, there was more than a fourfold increase (ONS, 1997b, p. 188), prompting new legislation to combat antisocial behaviour.

Finally, the quality of drinking water has attracted criticism in recent years (Exhibit 7.1). Infectious organisms such as campylobacter and cryptosporidium have been linked to outbreaks of gastroenteritis. There has also been concern about the chemical contamination of water by industrial sites, including landfill waste sites (DoE, 1988; Kinnersley, 1994). The pollution of water courses and ground water by nitrate fertilisers is also recognised as a health hazard; nitrates are particularly harmful to infants under six months of age (WHO, 1992). There is less evidence on the impact of pesticide contamination on human health through the water supply, although complacency is not warranted (see BMA, 1990). Directives on water quality have been introduced by the European Union, and adopted by the UK in a effort to keep all potentially harmful chemicals at a low level. Even so, debate continues over the extent to which even a low level of contamination can harm human health.

## Global Warming

During the 1980s, much attention was paid to the 'greenhouse effect', which scientists suggested could lead to a permanent rise in temperature and associated climatic changes. The recorded rise in temperature, particularly over the past two decades, suggests that this process has already begun. Global warming is caused by an increased level of carbon dioxide and other gases arising from pollution – chiefly the burning of fossil fuels – along with deforestation.

According to the UK Climate Change Impacts Review Group (1996, p. 197) 'it is a prudent assumption that climate change would on balance constitute a serious long-term hazard to human health.' The consequences are both direct and indirect (Godlee, 1992a; Rodriguez, 1995; UK Climate Change Impacts Group, 1996, p. 197; McMichael and Haines, 1997). Direct effects include mortality and illness arising from heatwaves (Kalkstein, 1993, 1995). Extremely hot weather exacerbates chronic conditions such as heart and respiratory disease and could lead to thousands of additional deaths among

---

Exhibit 7.1

---

### Drinking water and health

The quality of drinking water has a major impact on health. In Victorian times the contamination of water supplies was a key factor in epidemics such as cholera and typhoid (see Chapter 3). In modern times the main focus of attention has been upon chemical contamination, in particular from pesticides, landfill sites and industrial pollution and also from organisms such as cryptosporidium. Access to drinking water is also major issue. A more aggressive approach to water disconnection by the privatised water companies in the 1990s was heavily criticised for its health implications by the BMA among others. Moreover, the introduction of water metering has been shown to affect the health of those on low incomes who by rationing the use of water expose themselves and their children to the risk of infection (Barnardo's, 1993).

Some argue that water supplies should be used to promote health and prevent disease. There is evidence that fluoridation improves the dental health of children, particularly among deprived communities (Jones *et al.*, 1997). Studies that demonstrated a link between fluoridation and cancer, highlighted by opponents, were subsequently discredited (Doll and Kinlen, 1977; Cook-Mozaffari, 1996) as was a suggested association with arthritis (see Ansell and Lawrence, 1966). Even so there are lingering doubts, particularly about the link between fluoridation and bone fractures (Hillier *et al.*, 1996). Critics also point out that other potentially effective strategies, such as tackling the marketing practices of the food, drink and confectionery industries, have been rejected by government (see Chapter 8).

Efforts to introduce fluoridation during the 1970s and 80s were undermined by opposition from pressure groups (see Brand, 1971). In 1985 the law was changed to encourage fluoridation and although around 60 health authorities began the process of introducing it, not one scheme was actually implemented. More recently, the Acheson Report on health inequalities (see Appendix 1) recommended fluoridation as a means of improving the dental health of children. This was endorsed by the subsequent White Paper *Saving Lives: Our Healthier Nation* (Cm 4386, 1999, p. 112) which gave a commitment to compel water authorities to introduce fluoridation where strong local support was evident, subject to a scientific review of the latest evidence.

---

the young, frail, ill and elderly by the middle of the next century if current trends continue (Crombie, 1995). These adverse effects would be to some extent offset in temperate countries by a fall in the number of winter deaths as the temperature rose. Other direct effects of global warming include increased death and injury arising from disasters induced by climatic change, such as droughts, floods, storms and forest fires.

Indirect effects include the spread of vector-borne diseases such as malaria. It is also likely that communicable diseases, particularly food-related or water-related infectious diseases, would be transmitted more easily in a warmer climate. Food production might be disrupted by extreme weather conditions, although farming in temperate regions may benefit from an improved yield. A rising sea level, another consequence of global warming, could have a severe effect on the health and welfare of populations in coastal and low-lying areas. Finally, global warming is likely to exacerbate respiratory problems related to air pollution by encouraging the formation of low-level ozone. In addition, warmer temperatures affect the production of pollen and spores, leading to an increase in allergic reactions.

Of course, such a gloomy scenario may not materialise. Even if the temperature rises, there may be some adaptation to the new climatic conditions. Measures proposed include an improved system of public health surveillance, an improvement in environmental management and technological advances to tackle the consequences of global warming (see Haines and McMichael, 1997). There is, moreover, plenty of scope for addressing the root causes of the problem through energy conservation, antipollution policies and sustainable development, discussed later in this chapter. Nevertheless, the challenge of climate change is enormous and may in some respects be greater than initially predicted (see UN Environment Programme, 1999).

## The Ozone Layer

Ozone depletion in the stratosphere is associated with the production of chloroflourocarbons (CFCs), a byproduct of industrial processes, refrigeration and aerosol sprays. It appears that the ozone layer has thinned considerably, not only in the polar regions where the problem was first identified. The thinning process exposes animal and plant life to a higher level of ultraviolet light, with adverse implications for health. It has, for example, been estimated that a 10 per cent drop in ozone level could lead to 300,000 extra cases of skin cancers worldwide (UN Environment Programme, 1992).

The immune system can also be damaged by ozone depletion. Ultraviolet B radiation has been shown to be associated with immunosuppression (Godlee, 1992b) and with increased susceptibility to infections such as herpes simplex. Cataracts have been linked to exposure to ultraviolet light, and this is likely to be compounded by an ageing population. In addition, the eyes and skin can be damaged in the short term by an overexposure to ultraviolet light, conditions such as erythema (inflammation of the skin) and keratitis (inflammation of the cornea) being likely to increase. Individuals can, of course, avoid an overexposure to sunlight by the use of sunblock creams, hats and sunlight-resistant fabrics; in some countries, such as Australia, much has been done to persuade people to protect themselves from the sun's rays. Efforts have also been made to combat the emission of substances damaging the ozone layer. An internat-

ional protocol in Montreal in 1987 and subsequent agreements have implemented plans to phase out the use of ozone-depleting gases. However, because
these compounds persist for a long period in the atmosphere, the benefits of
discontinuing their use will only realised in the longer term.

## Anti-pollution Policy

Until fairly recently, the policy response to environmental harm was to regulate specific pollutants and industrial processes in isolation. No attempt was
made to assess the cumulative impact of pollution and depletion, nor was
there any official acknowledgement of the social and economic systems that
underpinned those industrial processes causing the damage. Even this
modest antipollution policy was slow to develop during the twentieth
century. In 1956, a Clean Air Act was passed to combat the problem of urban
smog (see Elsom, 1987), but apart from this, little was done to combat pollution through primary legislation until the passage of the Control of Pollution
Act in 1974, which introduced a new requirement to provide more information on pollution to the public and gave individuals new powers to take legal
action against polluters.

The election of the Thatcher government in 1979, with its ideological
emphasis on entrepreneurialism, international competitiveness and economic
growth at all costs, did not bode well for the environment. Yet by the
late 1980s, environmental issues were high on the political agenda. This was
partly due to the growing strength of the Green lobby, but another factor was
the opportunism of Margaret Thatcher, who adopted environmental concerns
to reinforce her profile as an international stateswoman (McCormick, 1991). In
addition, the privatisation of the electricity and water industries in the late
1980s posed difficult environmental questions that the Thatcher government
could not ignore. As a result, new regulatory authorities were created and
environmental requirements included in the relevant legislation. A further
factor, to be examined in greater detail later in this chapter, was the development of environmental policies at the European and international level, which
placed pressure on the UK to implement stronger national policies.

In 1990, the Environmental Protection Act was passed, heralding a number
of significant policy changes. Her Majesty's Inspectorate of Pollution, created
in 1987 from an amalgamation of several inspectorates, was given the responsibility of implementing integrated pollution control, whereby all aspects of
pollution from a factory – in water, air and land – would be assessed together
(O'Riordan and Weale, 1989). Under this new regime, sites would now have to
obtain an authorisation from Her Majesty's Inspectorate of Pollution by
demonstrating that they were using the 'best available technology not using
excessive cost' (BATNEEC) rather than, as previously, adopting a policy of

'best practicable means' (BPM). In addition, where sites caused several different types of pollution, they would have to show that they had chosen the 'best practicable environmental option' (BPEO). Two further principles underpinned this policy. First was the precautionary principle, which in its most basic form meant that pollution hazards should be assessed in advance and steps taken to prevent or minimise harm (see O'Riordan and Cameron, 1994, for a further discussion). The second was the 'polluter pays' principle – the costs of environmental harm and associated regulatory costs should ultimately be met by the polluters.

## The Environment Agency and Other Developments

There was much criticism of the new arrangements. First, there was some confusion because several authorities continued to have a role in regulating pollution. For example, processes that caused only air pollution were regulated under a system of local air pollution control implemented by local authorities. Meanwhile, the National Rivers Authority was the main regulatory body for water quality standards and worked in conjunction with Her Majesty's Inspectorate of Pollution on discharges in this medium. Second, there was dissatisfaction about the operation of Her Majesty's Inspectorate of Pollution, arising largely from underfunding and poor morale among staff. As a result, many called for a new agency that could genuinely co-ordinate regulation in all aspects of environmental pollution. Eventually, in 1996, the Environment Agency (EA) was established as a non-departmental body responsible for all aspects of pollution control and incorporating the functions of the former Her Majesty's Inspectorate of Pollution, the National Rivers Authority and the waste regulatory authorities. The local air pollution control system implemented by local authorities, however, remained in place in England and Wales. Meanwhile in Scotland, a separate authority, the Scottish Environmental Protection Agency, was created and given responsibility for both integrated pollution control and local air pollution control.

## Towards an Environmental Health Policy?

In 1996, the Major government proposed new targets for environmental health in areas such as air quality, radon level, noise and drinking water to extend its *Health of the Nation* strategy set out four years previously (DoH/DoE, 1996). These targets were derived from the government's sustainable development strategy, discussed later in this chapter. The UK government also devised a national environmental health action plan, promoted by a Europe-wide initiative (Cm 3323, 1996). The plan, however, displayed the complacent tone of many previous official publications on environmental issues (for example, water quality, despite public concern, was rated as 'very high') and failed to break new ground. Nevertheless, it provided a useful summary of current policy, reiterating a commitment to the precautionary principle, restating targets for the reduction of pollutant levels in water and repeating the government's insistence that landfill waste disposal was a last resort (a landfill tax was introduced in 1994 to discourage this). At the time of writing, the UK national environmental health action plan is being revised to incorporate the policy changes introduced by the Blair government in this field.

Finally, the Major government published an air quality strategy (DoE, 1996a), which set new standards for the most dangerous pollutants and gave local councils new duties to monitor pollution. The strategy was, however, criticised by environmental campaigners for not taking a tougher approach to road traffic. In 1994, the Royal Commission on Environmental Pollution presented a controversial report that called for a trebling of the proportion of journeys undertaken by public transport by 2020, a doubling of the cost of petrol and diesel in real terms by 2005, powers to curb traffic when pollution levels were exceeded and large public subsidies for rail, public transport and cycle routes. It also set targets for the reduction of carbon dioxide (by 20 per cent by 2020) and maintained that the WHO air quality guidelines for pollutants produced by motor cars should be complied with by 2005 (Cm 2674, 1994).

## Traffic and Transport Policy

The Royal Commission presented the Major government with a seemingly intractable political problem. Private motoring and road haulage were actively promoted by the Conservative governments of the 1980s and early 1990s. This policy was consistent with party's ideological hostility to public transport and the longstanding 'pro-road' bias within the Department of Transport. A further problem was that the public's dependence on the motor car made any attempt to limit its use extremely controversial. Moreover, influential lobbies such as car manufacturers, road hauliers, road construction companies and the petroleum industry, all of which included contributors to the Conservative Party's funds, could not be ignored. Transport and environment ministers timidly called for a debate on the issue (Cm 3234, 1996). Schemes to encourage cycling and walking were endorsed, but without any real commitment to changing the transport infrastructure. However, the imposition of an above-inflation increase in petrol and diesel duty from 1995 onwards (a policy known as the fuel escalator) was acknowledged as a more positive step.

## *The Blair Government and Pollution*

The Blair government promised a stronger approach to pollution. In 1997, a new air quality information service was introduced, which included a reclassification of quality standards in order to publicise more effectively warnings of dangerous pollution levels. The new regime covered a wider range of pollutants, including diesel particulate and carbon monoxide levels (DoE, 1997). A review of the National Air Quality Strategy was also established at this time. It later recommended tougher objectives for reducing levels of five of the eight key airborne pollutants (DETR, 1999a). The Blair government subsequently introduced a revised strategy that adopted stricter targets for reducing benzene, carbon monoxide, butadiene, nitrogen dioxide and lead. The targets for ozone and sulphur dioxide remained the same. The target for particulates was, however, dropped because it was believed to be unattainable. This decision was criticised by environmentalists (Cm 4548, 2000).

Meanwhile, the Pollution Prevention and Control Act of 1999 heralded a further change in the British system of regulating pollution. The Act was introduced to meet the requirements of the 1996 European Directive on Integrated Pollution Prevention and Control, which is discussed more fully later in this chapter. The new Act gave the Secretary of State for the Environment wide powers to make regulations to extend integrated pollution control to more installations, while increasing the scope of intervention to cover other environmental risks and threats in addition to chemical pollution.

The Blair government also promised a more radical approach to transport policy than its predecessor. In 1998, it published a transport White Paper that set out a vision of integrated transport within the context of the need to reduce harm to the environment, improve economic efficiency and tackle social exclusion (Cm 3950, 1998). The document proposed a Commission for Integrated Transport to advise on improvements to the transport system, local transport plans to ensure priority for public transport, pedestrians and cyclists, quality partnerships to improve bus services, a Strategic Rail Authority to adopt a stronger approach to the regulation of the railways, and lower bus fares for elderly people.

However, the White Paper fell short of earlier policy statements in a number of respects (Hibbs, 1999). Controversial ideas, such as an additional charge for parking facilities at out-of-town leisure and retail sites, were not adopted. The strategy was also criticised for refusing to adopt road traffic reduction targets and for failing to invest sufficient capital resources in public transport (Harman, 1999; Knowles, 1999). A recommendation from the Urban Task Force – to devote 65 per cent of transport public expenditure to schemes that benefitted pedestrians, cyclists and public transport users – placed further pressure on government with regard to this issue (DETR, 1999b). Even so, the ministers did seem more concerned not to offend motorists and the roads lobby.

Other contentious proposals – charges for workplace parking and motorway use – were shelved, although it was later agreed that local authorities would be given powers to introduce congestion charging schemes (including charges for workplace parking and entering urban areas, as well as tolls on trunk roads, bridges and tunnels) and retain the funds generated to invest in local transport improvement schemes. It was, however, envisaged that these schemes would be subject to local approval and would be unlikely to begin until 2002 at the earliest. The Blair government also introduced a package of fiscal measures aimed at reducing pollution, energy use and global warming, which are discussed in the context of sustainable development policy in the following section.

# Sustainable Development

From the late 1980s onwards, discussion on specific environmental problems at national level became absorbed into a much broader global debate about the sustainability of economic development. The UK environment policy has consequently been strongly influenced by international agreements to combat problems such as global warming and ozone depletion (see Weale, 1992). These will be explored in a moment. First, however, another crucial influence on domestic policy must be examined: the UK's membership of the European Community (and subsequently the European Union).

## Europe and the Environment

The European Community actively pursued an environmental policy from the 1970s onwards (Haigh, 1992; Collier, 1997). The first European action programme on the environment was introduced 1972 and was followed by four further programmes. As Weale (1992) noted, an alternative legal basis had to be used because environmental policy was not covered by the original Treaty of Rome. Instead, powers to reduce barriers to trade through harmonising market rules and product standards were used to justify a range of environmental initiatives on issues such as the protection of species, water quality and acid rain. They also provided the means of incorporating environmental considerations into planning decisions, in the form of the 1985 Directive on Environmental Impact Assessment (Exhibit 7.2)

The competence of the European Community in environmental matters was extended by the Single European Act of 1987, which explicitly recognised

Exhibit 7.2
___

## Environmental Impact Assessment

Another tool for integrating environmental concerns is Environmental Impact Assessment (EIA) (see DoE, 1989; BMA, 1998; Bartlett and Kurian, 1999), which incorporates an analysis of the potential environmental effects of a policy or project within decision-making processes. Environmental assessment can be applied strategically within the policy and planning process (BMA, 1998; DETR, 1998a), but can take many different forms. In the UK, guidance has been issued on policy appraisal within central government (DoE, 1991a, 1994, 1995; DETR, 1998b) to promote environmental considerations across the whole range of government policies, but this is not as yet compulsory. Other countries, including Norway and Austria, have introduced formal systems of strategic EIA (BMA, 1998; DETR, 1998a). At the time of writing, a draft European directive is being considered to promote its use across the European Union (European Commission, 1996).

Environmental assessment for specific projects is well established within the European Union. Since 1988, following a European directive (*Official Journal of the European Communities*, 1985), local planning authorities have had to take EIAs into account when making decisions on certain projects, such as nuclear power stations. A second category of projects may be considered for EIA depending on various circumstances, such as the scale and location of the proposed development. A further directive of 1997 (*Official Journal of the European Communities*, 1997), which came into force in the UK in 1999, extended the scope of projects subject to mandatory environmental assessment to include, among others, the construction of dual carriageways over 10 km long, the construction of overhead power lines and the construction of facilities for the incineration of non-hazardous waste. Additions were also made to the category of projects that could be considered for EIA, including wind farms and theme parks. The new directive also introduced a number of procedural changes, including a requirement for planning authorities to give the main reasons for their decision and the major measures to avoid, reduce or offset the greatest adverse effects of a development.

One of the main criticisms of EIA has been that health is not given sufficient weight in the process. A review commissioned by the BMA revealed that potential health effects had received adequate coverage in fewer than 30 per cent of the environmental impact statements studied (see BMA, 1998). This has led to calls for a more integrated approach in which health is explicitly incorporated into EIA processes not only for specific projects, but also for strategic decision making at national, regional and local level (Scott-Samuel, 1996; Environmental Health Commission, 1997; Joffe and Sutcliffe, 1997). A major obstacle, however, is the lack of clear evidence linking environmental factors and ill health. Another is the difficulty of obtaining an accurate measure of the costs of environmental hazards and the benefits of reducing them. A review of this field, for example, found that estimates of the health benefit from a reduction in air pollution varied between £2600 and £1.4m per life saved (DoH, 1999c).

the environment as a matter of concern and set out basic principles of policy such as the prevention of harm and the 'polluter pays'. It also required that environmental protection be a component of all Community policies. This was followed in 1990 by the formation of the European Environment Agency to provide information and advice to Community decision makers. The Maastricht Treaty of 1992 further extended the competence of the Community (now the European Union), enabling the adoption of a range of measures to protect the environment, including those of a fiscal nature and further measures concerning planning, land use and the management of water resources. The Treaty also added a further policy objective of promoting international action to deal with environmental problems. Subsequently, in the Amsterdam Treaty of 1997, the powers of the European Union were further clarified. Sustainable development was enshrined as a key objective of the European Union. A requirement was introduced to integrate environmental protection in European Union policies. As a result, all key policy proposals must be evaluated for their potential impact on the environment. The European Union is also attempting to extend the use of Environmental Impact Assessment (EIA) at a strategic level within member states (Exhibit 7.2).

The European Union continues to intervene on environmental matters. For example, a landfill directive has been proposed, requiring a drastic cut in the amount of household waste at landfill sites (*Official Journal of the European Communities*, 1999). Moreover, the separate pollution control systems of each member state, including the UK, are due to be replaced by 2007 under the terms of a European directive on Integrated Pollution Prevention and Control (*Official Journal of the European Communities*, 1996). The directive aims to achieve a high level of environmental protection by creating a prior authorisation process specifying limits for emissions and other conditions. These permits are to be issued on the basis of 'best available techniques', for which benchmarks will be set by a European Integrated Pollution Prevention and Control Bureau, rather than on the BATNEEC principle, discussed earlier. The directive also aims to prevent damage to the environment in a wider sense, so non-chemical pollution – noise, light, heat and vibration – was therefore included in its remit. In addition, matters relating to waste management, energy efficiency, the consumption of raw materials and accidents are also included. The directive has sought to produce a greater integration of pollution control by focusing on entire installations rather than industrial processes, and to promote a more rational, comprehensive and consistent regulatory process. Moreover, it has extended integrated pollution control to more types of installation, notably food and drink factories, waste sites and large poultry and pig farms. As noted earlier, the UK has sought to comply with the directive by enacting the Pollution Prevention and Control Act of 1999.

Despite the growing powers of the European Union in the environmental sphere, some observers (Collier, 1997; Ward, 1997) argue that European Union environmental policy in recent years has lost momentum. Problems include a poor implementation of directives and long delays in adopting legislative proposals. The limits of European Union environmental policy were to some extent reflected by the Amsterdam Treaty of 1997, which was seen by observers as a consolidation of previous achievements rather than as breaking new ground (Jordan, 1998).

## Global Action

Over the past two decades, the WHO, and the European Regional Office, have sought to raise the profile of environmental health issues (WHO, 1986b). In 1989, the WHO Regional Office for Europe published a Charter on Environment and Health, Entitlements and Responsibilities (WHO Regional Office for Europe, 1990, p. 4), which set out the entitlement of individuals to 'an environment conducive to the highest attainable level of health and well-being; information and consultation on the state of the environment, and on plans, decisions and activities likely to affect both the environment and health'; and 'participation in the decision-making process'. The document maintained that 'every government and public authority has the responsibility to protect the environment and to promote human health within the area under its jurisdiction and to ensure that activities under its jurisdiction or control do not cause damage to human health in other states.' Other clauses called for public agencies to co-operate with each other to resolve the problems of the environment and health, and for every public and private body to assess its impact on the environment.

The profile of environmental health has also been raised by conferences, commissions and working parties under the auspices of the WHO. The Commission on Health and the Environment (WHO, 1992), for example, recommended that governments and international agencies should prioritise the development of a sustainable basis for the health of their populations and called for action to reduce overconsumption and waste. In addition, the Commission recommended new ways of promoting involvement in policy and planning, and called for institutional and regulatory structures to give a stronger emphasis to the prevention of pollution, intersectoral decision making and participation. This was followed by a European Environmental Health Action Plan, endorsed by a ministerial conference on health and the environment in 1994 (WHO Regional Office for Europe, 1994). As noted earlier, the UK was one of the first countries to pilot a national environmental health action plan.

The WHO's growing interest in environmental health coincided with international pressure to respond to global warming and the depletion of the ozone layer. In the 1980s, international efforts had been successful in reaching an agreement to limit CFC gases, identified as a threat to the ozone layer. The threat of global warming suggested that similar action would be needed to tackle the so-called 'greenhouse gases'. A further catalyst for action was the report of the World Commission on Environment and Development chaired by Gro Harlem Brundtland, which highlighted the importance of sustainable development, defined as 'development that meets the needs of the present without compromising the ability of future generations to meet their own needs '(1987, p.43).

The momentum continued with UN 'Earth Summit' in 1992 at Rio de Janeiro, which produced two separate international conventions – on biodiversity and climate change – signed by 150 countries (Grubb *et al.*, 1993). The Rio Summit also produced three further non-binding agreements: the Rio Declaration, comprising 27 principles for action; the forest principles, which arose out of a failed attempt to produce a convention on the protection and management of forests; and Agenda 21, a plan of action for achieving sustainable development.

The Agenda 21 document was particularly significant in view of its comprehensive coverage of environmental and related issues, including economic development, natural resources and fragile ecosystems, the participation of major groups in the strategy and the means of implementation. Although Agenda 21 was not above criticism, not least for stating the obvious, it acted as a set of guidelines and benchmarks against which national policies and programmes could be appraised. It has also been praised for stimulating and encouraging action by communities particularly through LA21, discussed later in this chapter. The major limitation of Agenda 21 is that it cannot be enforced, although a Commission on Sustainable Development exists to oversee implementation. Much depends on the willingness of individual states, business and other interests to comply with the spirit of the document and to co-operate in promoting sustainable development.

Previous international agreements, such as those relating to CFCs, demonstrate that it is politically possible for countries to join together in formulating global environmental strategies. But compromises are seemingly inevitable given the structural constraints of international decision making and the political and economic power of the world's biggest polluter, the USA (Paterson, 1996). The shortcomings of the decision-making process were further illustrated by the disappointment surrounding the outcome of the subsequent Kyoto convention on climate change in 1998. Agreement was reached among industrialised nations to reduce the emission of greenhouse gases by 5.2 per cent (from 1990 levels) by 2008–12. There was, however, criticism that the cut was insufficient to combat climate change, and a fear that some countries, notably the USA, would refuse to ratify the agreement, rendering it meaningless. There was also concern that the agreement allowed for an emissions trading system enabling richer countries to pay poorer countries for permission to continue emitting a high level of greenhouse gases, and that the agreement applied only to industrialised nations and therefore failed to address the problem of higher emission from the newly industrialising countries.

During the late 1990s, reports from the UN Environment Programme and the WHO indicated the scale of task ahead (WHO, 1997b; UN Environment Programme, 1999). Both noted some success, mainly in the establishment of structures for co-operation and intervention, the development of international agreements and protocols such as those already mentioned, and the raising of awareness about the necessity of controlling environmental pollution and depletion. They also, however, made it clear that the steps already taken had not gone far enough. The UN Environment Programme report observed that while some environmental problems, such as air pollution and ozone depletion, were showing signs of improvement, others, notably water shortage, the use of toxic chemicals and global warming, were deteriorating. It recommended urgent action in four areas: filling the gaps in knowledge about environmental problems and the impact of policies; tackling the root causes of environmental problems, including a shift from material consumption; taking an integrated approach whereby environmental issues were incorporated into mainstream decision making; and finally, mobilising action, by individuals, community groups and non-governmental bodies and industry, to protect and improve the environment. The WHO report made similar points, calling for wide-ranging reforms to deal with the assessment and management of risk within a framework of sustainable development, and highlighting the need to develop a multisectoral approach to the problems of the environment.

It is by no means certain that such recommendations will be heeded as there are powerful forces operating against environmental improvement strategies. It has been shown that large business corporations have opposed environmental policies that appear to constrain their profitability or limit their markets (see, for example, Leggett, 1999). Furthermore, the political influence of these corporations is institutionalised not only within national governments, but also within international bodies that have an impact on the environment. The World Trade Organisation (WTO), for example, which regulates international trade, has been accused of favouring commercial profitability and free trade over environmental and health considerations (Juniper, 1999). Its role is considered further in the context of food policy in the next chapter.

## Sustainable Development in the UK

In 1994, the Major government introduced a sustainable development strategy for the UK (Cm 2426, 1994), which was heavily criticised in several respects. It failed to relate environmental issues to other sectors of policy making, notably health. Although indicators were later identified to measure progress in tackling environmental problems (DoE, 1996b), these were regarded as too narrow, failing to reflect broader issues such as health, quality of life, the immediate environment and equity. Above all, the strategy failed to create procedures through which sustainable development could be prioritised within the all sectors of decision making. New advisory bodies, such as the Panel on Sustainable Development and the Round Table on Sustainable Development, were created, but in practice these had little influence over policy (Voisey and O'Riordan, 1997).

The Blair government made a number of significant changes that had a bearing on the strategy. Shortly after taking office, it created the Department of the Environment, Transport and Regions (DETR), in effect merging the Departments of Transport and Environment, on the grounds that this would improve the co-ordination of policy (although in 1999, this was partially reversed when day-to-day responsibility for transport was given to the transport minister, Lord Macdonald). A new Cabinet committee was also established to co-ordinate policies on the environment and sustainable development. The responsibilities of ministers for 'Green' issues in other government departments were clarified in an effort to strengthen interdepartmental action on the environment. Together they make up a committee under the chairmanship of the environment minister. A Sustainable Development Unit was also created within the DETR to offer advice on green issues across government departments. In addition, further guidance on environmental policy appraisal was issued (DETR, 1998b).

Following a period of consultation (DETR, 1998c), the Blair government put forward proposals to reform the sustainable development strategy (Cm 4345, 1999). Changes included broadening the strategy to take into account the quality of life and the immediate social, as well as physical, environment in which people lived. Indicators were proposed that reflected these factors, including healthy life expectancy, the quality of housing stock and crime rate, social exclusion and inequality. In addition, institutional changes were proposed. The two advisory bodies created under the previous government's strategy (the Round Table and the Panel) were subsumed within a new Sustainable Development Commission, to monitor progress in this field as well as seek to build consensus among stakeholders on future action.

The new strategy also proposed a change in the planning system. It was envisaged that the planning of economic development, regeneration and transport would be more closely integrated. At regional level, the new Regional Development Agencies established in England in 1998 were given responsibility for sustainable development as well as economic development and regeneration. These bodies would be expected to work alongside government regional offices, local authorities, business and other stakeholders to produce coherent plans within a framework that reflected sustainable development priorities. It was proposed that regional plans should in future be subject to EIA (see Exhibit 7.2 above). The strategy also emphasised the importance of local authorities. Guidance was issued to local authorities on how to build sustainable development into the planning process and local development plans (DETR, 1998d). In addition, the government continued to endorse local action within the context of LA21 (see below). In 1997, the DETR issued guidance on how to prepare an effective LA21 strategy (DETR, 1997a), and the Prime Minister set a target that all local authorities should have such a strategy by the year 2000.

Additionally, important areas of policy relevant to sustainable development, including transport and air quality, were reviewed, as already discussed in this chapter. Meanwhile, on the issue of global warming, the Blair government set a primary target of a 12.5 per cent reduction in carbon dioxide emission by 2010 (an earlier manifesto pledge having set a target of a 20 per cent reduction). The government was also prepared to express its Green credentials through fiscal policy. The 1999 Budget contained a raft of measures, including lower taxation for fuel-efficient cars, a change to the taxation of company cars to discourage high mileage and inefficient vehicles, tax relief for employers' transport schemes that reduced the number of car journeys (such as the provision of buses), and an increase in the fuel escalator, petrol and diesel duty being raised 6 per cent higher than the rate of inflation. Following protest from the road haulage industry and motoring organisations, however, the government announced the abandonment of the fuel escalator policy in late 1999. It was decided that, in future, above-inflation increases would be made on a discretionary basis, and any excess duty raised would be ploughed back into transport. In the year 2000 Budget, the government showed even more sympathy for this lobby by cutting road tax for lorries and not increasing fuel duty above inflation. It did, however, announce plans to link the taxation of company cars and new vehicles more closely to their effect on pollution. It also announced a cut in VAT on energy-saving materials to 5 per cent.

The landfill tax, introduced in 1996 by the Major government, was increased by the Blair government, although some commentators (see Pearce, 1998) noted that the current system encouraged the illegal tipping of waste and other undesirable practices (such as the relabelling of waste as inert to avoid paying a higher rate of tax). The Blair government also proposed a climate change levy, to be imposed on business users of energy from 2001. Following pressure from industry, the government announced a cut in the rate of tax and a higher discount rate to energy-intensive sectors that agreed to improve their efficiency. In addition, renewable energy sources and combined heat and power schemes were exempted from the levy, and investment allowances were proposed for companies moving towards environmentally friendly technologies. It should also be noted that the Blair government had earlier reduced VAT on domestic gas and electricity (imposed by the Major government) from 8 to 5 per cent and announced a shift in energy policy in favour of coal-fired power stations, both of which can be regarded as retrograde steps in terms of preventing global warming.

As a footnote to this, it should be noted that two further reports, appearing early in the year 2000, called for more action by government on sustainable development in a number of areas. The first, by the Environmental Audit Committee (2000) of the House of Commons, analysed the government's initiative on green issues across departments. It called for Green ministers to set out a strategic assessment mapping the environmental impacts of each department and to identify the priorities for environmental gains and avoiding adverse impacts. The Committee noted that only one department, the Department for Education and Employment, was explicitly committed to the environmental appraisal of all policy proposals. Furthermore, its report called for stronger leadership from the very top of government and in individual departments in order to stimulate cross-departmental initiatives on environmental issues. The second report, by the House of Commons' Environment, Transport and Regional Affairs Committee (2000b), focused on the climate change programme. It was critical of the confusion surrounding the government's targets to reduce greenhouse gases: the official target of 12.5 per cent and the Labour manifesto target of a 20 per cent cut in carbon dioxide emissions by 2010. Although noting that the UK government had done much to emphasise the former, the Committee was concerned that this was a short-term target. In particular, it believed that much progress had been achieved by 'one-off' measures rather than ongoing improvements. The Committee called for more effort to promote long-term improvements through behavioural change that would require a more sophisticated approach than simple advertising campaigns, for example.

## *The Local Environment: LA21*

LA21 is based on a belief that sustainable development and environmental improvement can be achieved through 'bottom-up' strategies formulated by local authorities and other stakeholders. In theory, as Littlewood and While (1997) have noted, LA21 could provide 'the impetus for new trajectories in local decision making based on principles of participation, inclusion and sustainability'. Ideally, LA21 encourages local authorities to think holistically about their activities, particularly about how different sectors such as transport, waste disposal and planning impact upon the environment. At the same time, there are parallels between LA21 and the public policy principles of *Health for All* and *Healthy Cities*, (see Chapter 4) notably the holistic and intersectoral approach to policy making and an emphasis on consulting local people and working with local organisations.

Many local authorities have demonstrated their support for LA21 (Tuxworth and Thomas, 1996). Some have taken steps to break down the barriers between sectors and have been active in developing new modes of participation, although it is too early to tell how influential these mechanisms might be (Young, 1996). Most local authorities have begun to produce LA21 action plans. According to the latest available figures, 36 per cent of local authorities have an LA21 strategy and a further 45 per cent expect to have one in place by the end of the year 2000 (Environmental Audit Committee, 2000). Leicester City Council, for example, in conjunction with local health bodies and the private and voluntary sectors, devised a plan in 1998. This outlined out a range of actions in fields such as crime, prevention, transport, economic development, housing, health, land use and planning, energy, the arts, culture and leisure, and waste management. Explicit targets have been set for, for example, crime reduction and improvement in health (Leicester City Council, 1998). Nonetheless LA21 has not yet become integrated within most local authority decision-making processes (Littlewood and While, 1997). Indeed, economic development, rather than health or the environment, remains the main priority. There are many reasons for this (Voisey *et al.*, 1996): a lack of resources for implementing LA21, the fact that it is not a statutory requirement, and the power of local economic interests opposed to the LA21 approach relative to environmental, health and community groups.

Health should be a key component of LA21. Local government planning functions impinge on health, and services such as housing and education have an important health dimension. In addition, local environmental health services provide a range of functions to protect and promote the health of local people, such as enforcing regulations in the field of food safety (see Chapter 8), air and noise pollution (see above), health and safety at work and road safety (see below), and housing (Audit Commission, 1991; McCarthy, 1996). Local government can set an example as a major employer and can improve standards through commissioning services. It is a large and significant player that has the ability to co-ordinate a range of other local stakeholders such as private business, other public bodies and the voluntary sector. Local authorities are also closer to the community than is central government and have great potential to improve public participation in decisions affecting environmental health.

The significance of local authorities in relation to health is increasingly being acknowledged. In 1999, a statutory responsibility was given to local authorities in England and Wales to co-operate with health authorities in order to advance the health and welfare of the population. A duty was imposed on local authorities to participate in devising and achieving health improvement plans for their communities. The Blair government placed upon local authorities statutory powers to promote the economic, social and environmental wellbeing of their areas (Cm 4014, 1998). Moreover, as noted in Chapter 5, more radical changes have been suggested, such as transferring the public health and health promotion roles of the NHS to local government.

Although it is too early to assess fully the impact of LA21, largely because its implementation has been uneven (Voisey *et al.*, 1996) and because it has coincided with other initiatives, it does appear to have promoted innovative ways of thinking about intersectoral approaches to the environment, with potential benefit to the health of local communities. But the future development of LA21 depends on a number of factors. Continued support from central government within a helpful planning and resources framework, is vital. So too is allowing local decision makers the discretionary power to improve the local environment. Consensus and co-operation at local level between the different authorities and organisations involved is also important. Finally, local authorities need to ensure that they have the public support to improve the local environment as well as the legitimacy to act as champions of the people (Wilson and Game, 1994).

In the remainder of this chapter, two other important aspects of environmental health are discussed: accident prevention and health and safety at work. These further illustrate the importance of multisectoral action to improve the environment in which people live.

# Accident Prevention

Accidents are responsible for a large proportion of illness, injury and death. Every year, around 12,000 people die in the UK as a result of accidents, and 9.7 million people require hospital treatment (RoSPa, personal correspondence). Accidental death is the most common cause of mortality in children aged 1–14 years, and accidents are a major cause of death and disability in both young and elderly people. Treatment for injuries costs the NHS £1.2 billion every year (Cm 3852, 1998). Notably, accidents are inversely correlated with social class (Quick, 1991): men in social class V are eight times more likely than those in social class I to die in a fire, five times more likely to die of suffocation, six times more likely to die from other non-traffic accidents and three times more likely to be killed in road traffic accidents. Accident and injury deaths in children also vary according to social class (see Chapter 10).

Accident prevention programmes have been running in the UK for many years, although it is only recently that specific goals have been set. *The Health of the Nation* strategy for England (Cm 1986, 1992) aimed, by 2005, to reduce the death rate from accidents among children under 15 by at least a third, among young people aged 15–24 by at least a quarter, and among elderly people aged over 65 by a third, using 1990 as a base year. This reflected targets set by the WHO in Europe (WHO Regional Office for Europe, 1985a, 1993a) to reduce the number of deaths from accidents by a quarter by the year 2000. Subsequently, two new targets – to reduce the overall rate of accidents by at least a fifth between 1996 and 2010 and that of serious accidental injury by a tenth – were set by the Blair government in its White Paper on public health (Cm 4386, 1999). The targets set by government in recent years appear to be tough, but they must be seen in the context of a long-term decline in accident mortality. The overall mortality rate from accidents in 1971 stood at 36 per 100,000 population; by 1995, this had fallen to 21 per 100,000. The death rate for persons under 15 fell even more sharply over this period, the rate in 1995 being only a quarter of that prevailing in 1971.

*The Health of the Nation* strategy sought to promote a holistic approach to accident prevention at local level by bringing agencies such as health authorities, the police, the fire brigade, ambulance trusts, schools and local authorities together to share information, produce joint initiatives and develop a co-ordinated strategy on accident prevention. A number of arrangements subsequently evolved, often based on existing schemes. In Liverpool, for example, an Accident Prevention Group was established, jointly funded by the health authority and the local authority, to co-ordinate policy in accidents, while in Gateshead, a Multi-agency Accident Prevention Group was established incorporating all local stakeholders (Hopkins, 1997). Although there are examples of local action, and some have been able to demonstrate benefits, there has been no systematic evaluation of their effectiveness (see DoH, 1993d). The Blair government subsequently sought to build on this collaborative approach by encouraging local partnerships to engage in activities such as audits of community safety, road safety measures and interventions to reduce accident-related illness, injury and death in the home.

## Accidents at Home and on the Roads

Accidents in the home cause the most deaths and injuries in the UK, resulting in over 4000 deaths and three million injuries requiring hospital treatment every year (DTI, 1998). This represents 40 per cent of all fatal accidents and a third of all accidental injuries needing hospital treatment. More attention is, however, focused on accidents in the workplace (see below) and road accidents. Road accidents account for around 3500 deaths in the UK every year, roughly a third of the total number of accidental deaths. The number and rate of road deaths have fallen in recent decades, being half the level that prevailed in the 1970s. The UK has a comparatively good record overall on road safety among European countries, only Sweden having a lower rate of death on the road, although the number of children and young people killed and injured on our roads is above the European average.

Successive UK governments have responded to the problem of road accidents through education and legislation. This initially took the form of isolated campaigns and legislative responses to particular problems, such as drink-driving, but gradually the approach became more strategic. In 1987, the Department of Transport set a target to reduce the number of road accident casualties in Great Britain by a third by the year 2000 (using an average of casualties in the period 1981–85 as a baseline). A separate initiative for child road safety was introduced in 1990, which led to the development of educational campaigns and environmental changes, such as traffic calming measures. This was later reiterated with the launch of a Child Pedestrian Strategy in 1996, which coincided with the publication of evidence that reducing speed is an effective way of reducing death and injury (Plowden and Hillman, 1996).

Education initiatives have focused on changing the behaviour of pedestrians, particularly children, and drivers. Child road safety campaigns have been running for many years (Thompson, 1991). One of the main campaigns was the Green Cross Code, established during the 1970s. More recently, there has been an effort to move the emphasis of road safety programmes towards community-based approaches that involve much more practical training in 'pedestrian skills'. Examples include the Kerbwise and Walk Wise schemes, in which children are encouraged to develop practical skills in real situations rather than simply be told about the dangers and how to avoid them. Education and training programmes are increasingly accompanied by guidance on good practice in an effort to improve standards of road safety education (DETR, 1998e). There has also been an attempt to integrate road safety training in schools with personal and social skills development in order to develop a more comprehensive approach to risk awareness.

Over the years, drivers have been told not to drink and drive, to 'kill their speed' and to 'clunk click every trip', and their passengers have been asked to 'belt up in the back'. There is less community-based education for motorists, although some probation schemes for motoring offenders now involve an education or retraining element. A large body of law governs driving standards and competence, including a licensing and disciplinary system. Legislation has been passed on specific issues such as speed limits, seat belts, motorcycle helmets and drinking and driving. Much of this has been contentious, raising issues of civil liberty. Nevertheless, most industrialised countries have legislated on these issues, and within a short period of time, much of the controversy has dissipated.

During the 1960s, for example, the UK government was cautious about introducing the breathalyser test and a specific legal limit for blood alcohol. Eventually, on the basis of evidence of a link between intoxication and accidents, the government was persuaded to legislate in spite of opposition from some lobby groups (notably motoring organisations and the licensed trade) and sections of the public. Following the passage of the Road Safety Act in 1967, public opinion, and many of the groups that opposed the breathalyser law, gradually came round to support the legislation. Drink-driving has become socially unacceptable as well as subject to legal constraints, but it nevertheless remains a significant cause of road accidents. Anti-drink-driving campaigners are, however, currently unhappy about the government's refusal to lower the legal limit for alcohol in the bloodstream (see Chapter 9). It should also be noted in this context that there has recently been an increase in awareness about the impact of other drugs, ranging from medicines to recreational drugs, on road safety (see DETR, 1997b).

The law has also been used to maintain and improve vehicle standards in an effort to make vehicles safer. The MOT test is one example. There is also legislation governing vehicle specification, an example being the law requiring vehicles to be fitted with seat belts. Regulations have often followed voluntary improvements to safety made by vehicle manufacturers, such as 'antiburst' door locks. Innovations generally become standard, and subsequently underpinned by legal provision, when the modification has been proved effective. However, the current controversy surrounding airbags illustrates that not all changes made by manufacturers are viewed as being unambiguously beneficial: there is evidence that children and smaller adults have been injured, in some cases fatally, by the inflation of airbags in minor accidents (Roberts and DiGuiseppi, 1997).

There have also been efforts to alter the environment in order to reduce the risk of accidents. This intervention takes the form of traffic management at accident blackspots, for example improved lighting and the introduction of pedestrian crossings or walkways, roundabouts or traffic lights. Traffic calming schemes have expanded rapidly of late, their uptake boosted by evidence that they are effective in reducing accidents. One study found that the frequency of accidents fell by 60 per cent (child pedestrian/child cyclist accidents by two-thirds) in schemes that adopted a 20 mph speed limit (Webster and Mackie, 1996). There is also evidence that speed cameras can reduce accidents; in a six-year study of cameras in West London, accident deaths fell threefold and serious injuries by a quarter following their introduction (Highways Agency, 1997).

In 2000, the Blair government introduced a new strategy to combat speeding, aiming to cut the annual death rate on the roads by 40 per cent, and that in children by half, by 2010 (DETR, 2000). The strategy proposed stricter law enforcement, including an increase in the use of speed cameras, as well as tougher sentences and fines for offenders. Road safety campaigners have, however, been disappointed by the government's failure to introduce a mandatory speed limit of 20 mph on urban and 50 mph on rural roads. It was widely believed that pressure from the road transport lobby, along with worries about the unpopularity of road safety measures among motorists was responsible for this.

It is often argued that road accidents are not taken seriously enough. Leichter (1991), for example, quotes the UK government's earlier review of road safety policy in 1987 as stating that 'the subject of road safety appears by and large not to be regarded within opinion forming circles... as a particularly interesting or important one' (Department of Transport, 1987, p. 19). There has been a strong element of fatalism in this field, reflecting perhaps an acceptance that accidents are a price that must be paid for our dependence on road transport. Although this is perhaps slightly less true today given the official commitment to accident reduction, road safety has yet to become a dominant principle of transport policy.

It has also been argued that road safety policy is misdirected. Much effort is aimed towards changing the behaviour of groups, such as children, the elderly and cyclists, who are the victims rather than the perpetrators of accidents. This is not only 'victim blaming' (Quick, 1991) but has wider health consequences. It is, for example, well known that children do not walk or cycle as much as in the past, particularly to and from school, partly because of worries about road safety. Yet, as DiGuiseppi *et al.* (1997) have shown, such a change in the travel patterns of children, although contributing to a fall in the number of accidental deaths, means they take less exercise, raising questions about serious health consequences in later life.

The Blair government attempted to tackle the problems of the 'school run' by encouraging school travel plans (DETR/DFEE/DoH, 1999), which involved the production of local plans as well as plans for individual schools. In 1999, a School Travel Advisory Group was established. This group later called for a reduction in the proportion of school journeys by car from 37 per cent to 20 per cent by 2010. It also recommended bringing schools' performance in cutting car use within the brief of OFSTED inspections, improved school courses in pedestrian and cyclist safety and standard fares for school buses (School Travel Advisory Group, 2000). Also relevant was the Safe and Sound initiative launched by the DoH, the Department of Environment, Transport and the Regions (DETR) and the Department for Education and Employment, which encourages the development of school-based schemes to encourage safer, healthier and environmentally friendly ways of travelling to school. Although these initiatives have been welcomed by safety groups, they are unlikely to be effective in the absence of measures that reduce unsafe driving behaviour.

Evidence supporting some road safety interventions has been challenged. It appears that certain strategies have been pursued with little evidence to support their effectiveness, in some cases even when there is evidence against employing such strategies. Quick (1991) states that the UK government has been formally committed to road safety measures that are largely ineffective. In at least one case – the introduction of compulsory seat belts – it has been alleged that the Department of Transport's own research was suppressed because it showed that the measure would not save lives. Adams (1995) discusses the same issue, arguing that states that had not passed seat belt laws by 1980 experienced a greater decrease in the number of accident deaths than those that had. This is of course not to say that all road safety interventions are useless. Instead, the lesson is that evidence must encompass the whole range of factors that impinge on accidents. In particular, 'risk compensation', in which behavioural change to some extent offsets the impact of intervention, must be taken into account (Adams, 1995). Indeed, it is often argued that safer motor vehicles encourage risky behaviour and that drivers find ways of circumventing environmental controls that increase the risk of injury to others and ultimately themselves.

A further criticism is that road safety interventions deal with the symptoms of the problem, the root cause being the heavy dependence we place on road transport, in particular private motoring. According to this perspective, the situation will be significantly improved only following the adoption of an integrated transport policy that explicitly recognises road safety (along with environmental pollution) as a primary objective (see Quick, 1991). Notably, alternative forms of transport, such as rail, have much better safety record than roads, although as the 1999 disaster at Paddington illustrated, much remains to be done to improve the safety of Britain's railways as well. Furthermore, cycling or walking is a fairly hazardous mode of transport – but would be much safer if the transport infrastructure was improved to give added protection to the pedestrian and the cyclist.

# Health and Safety at Work

Around 300 workers are killed each year in Great Britain, and a further hundred members of the public are killed in workplace-related accidents. These figures are small relative to the number of people killed on the roads and in other accidents, and it should also be noted that the number of workplace fatalities has declined considerably: in 1938, 2668 people died in industrial accidents, and as recently as 1961, the number of workplace fatalities totalled over one hundred a month. The reduction in work fatalities has been the result of two main factors (Quick, 1991): an improvement in safety and a decline in the most dangerous industries such as mining.

Concern about the level of workplace deaths has nevertheless persisted, fuelled by an occasional increase in the death rate, such as in 1997 when the number of fatalities rose by 20 per cent. Health and safety issues have been kept in the public eye by periodic scandals involving the exposure of workers or the public to dangerous substances. The classic case is asbestos contamination. Three thousand people a year now die from the asbestos-related disease, a figure that could rise to an estimated 10,000 by 2025 (*Independent on Sunday*, 1996). Furthermore, health and safety at work remains an important issue largely because of the wider impact of the workplace on illness and injury. It has been estimated that 2.2 million cases of work-related illness occur every year. The total annual cost of work-related injury has been estimated to be between 2 and 3 per cent of the gross domestic product (Davies and Teasdale, 1994). Indeed, occupation-related diseases such as dermatitis, asthma and deafness are a significant burden on the NHS, accounting for 7 per cent of GP consultations (McCormick *et al.*, 1995). There is now a greater awareness of disease and injury associated with working environments, such as shops and offices, previously thought to be relatively safe, repetitive strain injuries being one example. A further problem that has been recognised is work-related stress, which has been linked to a range of mental health problems (Jenkins, 1993). The stress level in the workplace is believed to have increased in recent years as a result of several factors: job insecurity, longer working hours and the acknowledgement of workplace 'bullying'.

Occupational health risks were evident in Greek and Roman times (Rosen, 1993), while modern efforts to combat ill health and injury in the workplace date back to the Factory Acts of the nineteenth century (see Chapters 2 and 3). The growth of this legislation engendered a patchwork quilt of regulation that lacked consistency. Criticism intensified during the 1960s, prompted mainly by the growing interests of trade unions in health and safety issues (Rhodes, 1981), coupled with high-profile regulatory failures, notably the Factory Inspectorate's inadequate response to the asbestos issue (Parliamentary Commissioner for Administration, 1976). This pressure led to a review of health and safety regulation (Cmnd 5054, 1972), culminating in the Health and Safety at Work Act 1974. The Act brought most other inspectorates under the control of a Health and Safety Executive (HSE) accountable in turn to a Health and Safety Commission, which was given overall responsibility to protect people at work and the public from hazards arising from industrial activity. This was not a one-off reform but instead created a process aimed at promoting a more efficient and workable system of regulation on the basis of consensus between workers, employers and regulators. The HSE is responsible for the regulation of workplaces employing the majority of the working population (Watterson, 1994b), while local authority environmental health departments are responsible for health and safety in offices, shops and smaller workshops.

Since 1974, the system of regulation has been increasingly influenced by developments in Europe (Murray, 1999). Particularly important was the 1989 European Framework Directive, which placed a responsibility on employers to safeguard the health and safety of their employees (*Official Journal of the European Communities*, 1989) and set out key principles on matters such as the prevention of occupational risks and the protection of health and safety. An important consequence of this directive was that employers had formally to assess and document the whole range of hazards and risks in the workplace. Formal assessment had previously only been required in respect of specific hazards, such as hazardous substances. The framework directive also set out measures regarding health surveillance, information and training. A number of other directives (known as 'daughter directives') were subsequently issued within the terms of this framework, covering issues such as protective equipment, pregnant workers, manual handling, display screen equipment, safety signs and the control of carcinogens and biological agents. Europe has also inspired other developments. There is now a European Agency for Safety and Health at Work, which was established in the mid-1990s. Its objective is to promote an improvement in the working environment by disseminating information about the threats to health and safety at work and good practice in this field, although, as Murray (1999) has noted, the agency is still in its infancy, and it remains to be seen how effective it will be.

Although there has been much activity in the field of health and safety at work policy, current arrangements are criticised on several grounds: that regulation is too soft on the employer, that health and safety is not a priority and that insufficient attention is paid to the role of the workplace as a means of health promotion. Beginning with this first point, it must be realised the system of regulation in the UK has never been tough or adversarial. The British tradition of regulation – in the field of health and safety and other areas such as pollution control and professional regulation – emphasises voluntarism, co-operation and persuasion (Rhodes, 1981; Vogel, 1986). Much emphasis has in the past been placed on voluntary agreements and codes of practice, although they have increasingly been underpinned by legal instruments. Adherence or otherwise to codes of practice can be used in evidence' when prosecution is taking place. Moreover, as noted above, employers' responsibilities have been outlined more clearly in recent years, opening up greater possibilities for prosecution and compensation claims.

Even so, it is claimed that the system of regulation is too friendly towards the employer. Critics point out the infrequency of inspection and prosecution. Enforcement notices and prosecutions are issued only as a last resort, their number having declined in recent years. In 1996/97, for example, only 1256 prosecutions occurred, a 30 per cent fall from the figure two years previously. The number of enforcement notices fell by a similar extent to 7333 in 1996/97. Only 115,726 planned inspections took place in 1996/97, meaning that sites are visited on average once every seven years. In practice the HSE inspects high- and medium-risk premises more frequently: the former expect an annual visit, the latter a visit every six years (*Health and Safety Bulletin*, 1998).

The low level of inspections and prosecutions has been justified in terms of the consensus philosophy adopted by the HSE since its inception. Others, however, have highlighted the cut in resources to the HSE during the 1980s and 90s (Watterson, 1994a). In the 1980s, the number of inspectors fell by over 10 per cent, and funding fell by about a fifth. As a result of periodic budget cuts, funding and staffing levels have hardly improved since. Moreover, the situation was made worse by the increased workload resulting from the extension of the HSE portfolio during the 1990s and the burden of enforcing new regulations. At the same time, local authority environmental health departments, which also have an important role in relation to health and safety at work, faced budgetary problems, staff shortage and overload due to the allocation of new responsibilities.

For many observers, these trends reflect the low priority given to health and safety over the past two decades. Throughout the 1980s and 90s, government policy was explicitly geared to deregulation, and, as a result, health and safety regulation was seen by those driving policy as a burden that needed to be lifted. Good employers and the trade unions resisted efforts to deregulate in this area but were unable to prevent decisions such as those which reduced the budget for health and safety law enforcement (Watterson, 1994a). Moreover, these policies were compounded by other factors, not least the growth of small businesses and the number of those self-employed – all of which tend to have a poorer health and safety record than large employers. Meanwhile, according to some, the tougher economic climate of the past two decades created a situation in which the quest for survival and short-term profit overrode the need to look after the health of employees, and even conscientious employers were forced to alter their priorities (Quick, 1991). It is even suggested that these economic circumstances also affected trade unions' priorities in this field: according to Quick (1991), the unions responded by concentrating on defending jobs, and health and safety became less of a priority in consequence. Others, however, disagreed that this was the case, pointing out the expansion of health and safety work within the trade union movement since the late 1970s (Dalton, 1992).

The third criticism of health and safety policy and practice is that it has not exploited the potential that exists for promoting the health of workers. The scope for improving health through well-planned workplace initiatives is well documented (see Dugdill and Springett, 1994). Possible interventions include health education – on nutrition, exercise, alcohol and smoking, for example. The workplace can also be used to screen for illness (although screening programmes themselves are open to criticism – see Chapter 6), and to provide counselling services for workers. *The Health of the Nation* strategy (Cm 1986, 1992) was important in identifying the workplace as a key setting in which health promotion could take place. This led to the establishment of a Task Force to examine the scope for improvement, which subsequently made a number of recommendations, including the creation of a steering committee to take the agenda forward (DoH Workplace Task Force, 1994). Subsequently, in 1996, the Workplace Health Advisory Team was formed to encourage the formation of alliances between smaller and medium-sized businesses to undertake health promotion activities.

Finally in this section, it should be noted that the Blair government has introduced a number of initiatives relevant to health and safety at work. Some have arisen from European directives, such as the working time directive that places a limit on the hours of work for most employees. The government also signed up to the European Social Chapter of the Maastricht Treaty, opening up the UK to further European initiatives on employee health and welfare. The Blair government launched a Healthy Workplace initiative in 1999, aimed at giving health and safety much higher priority in business, fostering partnerships and networks, and extending good practice. Healthy workplaces were emphasised in the White Paper on public health as a focus for health promotion. Both these initiatives relied on employers perceiving that 'improving health is everybody's business' (DoH, 1999e, p. 1) and voluntarily participating in various schemes. More significantly perhaps, the HSE began a review of occupational health, and the DETR meanwhile launched its own strategic appraisal of health and safety; both of these raised the possibility of further initiatives in this field in the future. The HSE also announced a new policy of increasing publicity for firms convicted of health and safety offences and proposed a target of increasing the investigation of reported injuries at work by 3 per cent. This, however, fell short of what some believed was needed. For example, in a critical report, the House of Commons' Environment, Transport and Regional Affairs Committee (2000a), cast doubt on the ability of the HSE to increase investigations in the absence of increased resources. The report also called for improvements in the reporting system for industrial injuries and an increase in the fines imposed on those breaching health and safety regulations, and urged that a new offence of corporate killing be introduced.[1]

# Conclusion

Although the environmental health agenda is diverse, many of the problems are related (Crombie, 1995). Noise and air pollution, global warming and accidents are all, for example, linked to an increasing level of road traffic. By attempting to solve one problem, another is sometimes created, a current example being the need to reduce landfill waste, which implies the use of other forms of waste disposal (notably incineration) that also have implications for environmental health. It is therefore important that problems are not considered in isolation. A cross-sectoral strategy is therefore required, one in which government and planning authorities fully evaluate the implications of their decisions. This obviously requires an improved level of co-ordination between different parts of government at all levels (Environmental Health Commission, 1997; BMA, 1998). It also depends on the development of a philosophy incorporating environmental health, public health and sustainable development in its widest sense. There have been several important steps in this direction, as reflected in the Blair government's plans for transport, local planning, public health, pollution control and sustainable development. The political obstacles to change are, however, formidable, and it remains to be seen what will actually be achieved in terms of genuine cross-sector working.

Second, there is great scope for improvement in the collection and dissemination of information on environmental health. The under-recording of environment health problems is common. A further problem is that information is often collected for one purpose but is not shared with other agencies that might make good use of it. Related to this is a need to improve the quality of evidence on the impact of environment on health (BMA, 1998). This is particularly difficult given the multiple factors often implicated in environmental health problems, their interaction with each other and, in many cases, their long-term effects. As a result of limited evidence, there is often disagreement between scientists on the scale of risk (see contributions in Bate, 1999, which seek to show that many environmental fears are exaggerated), adding to the confusion and raising the prospect of errors of commission or omission on the part of policy makers. In the absence of such evidence, it is much more difficult to promote intervention to deal with perceived problems (although recent cases such as the BSE crisis – see Chapter 8 – seem to have made policy makers more inclined to err on the side of caution, at least for the time being). Environmental and health impact assessment is being promoted and may well contribute to an improvement in decision making at all levels. As noted, however, there is a case for health factors to feature more strongly in such assessments, and much better-quality evidence of potential health impacts is therefore needed.

Third, environmental health should not focus purely on creating an ideal physical environment as conceived by planners and experts. The social environment is just as important in enhancing health in a positive sense, as reflected in the Blair government's revised sustainable development strategy. Moreover, environmental health strategy should allow the public to participate in decisions about the environment, giving people an opportunity to influence physical and social conditions and giving them appropriate and timely information to enable them to make such decisions. The principles of public participation in the field of environmental health have been endorsed by the WHO (1997b) and the UN Environment Programme (1999). Furthermore, a broad legal framework for participation in environment and health matters, including a minimum requirement for public involvement, information and access to justice was enshrined in the Aarhus Convention of 1998, signed by 39 nations and the European Community (Convention on Access to Information, Public Participation in Decision-making and Access to Justice in Environmental Matters, 1998). It remains to be seen how and to what extent this framework will be translated into practical arrangements within the policy-making process (WHO Regional Office for Europe, 1999). However, as the Environmental Health Commission (1997) and the Royal Commission on Environmental Pollution (Cm 4053, 1998) have both noted, there is an urgent need to improve civic participation and engagement in environmental health, because this enables initiatives to be built from the bottom up rather than imposing top-down solutions with little legitimacy or popular support.

# Note

1. As this book went to press, the Blair Government in June 2000 published a ten-year strategic document *Revitalising Health and Safety* (DETR, 2000b). The document proposed removing Crown immunity from government organisations currently exempt from health and safety legislation. New targets were set, including a 10 per cent reduction of deaths and major injuries in the workplace by 2010. The Government also proposed the appointment of company safety directors, which it believed would make it easier to prosecute firms for serious accidents. Higher fines and other penalties for breaches of health and safety regulations were also proposed. It should also be noted that in May 2000 the Home Office published a consultation document that proposed the introduction of a new offence of 'corporate killing'.

# 8

# Food, Diet and Health

No one would seriously argue with the contention that 'sufficient, safe, nutritious food is an essential ingredient for good health' (Tansey and Worsley, 1995, p. 49). An inadequate supply of food generally reduces resistance to disease, while specific diseases such as beri-beri and rickets are directly associated with the absence of particular nutrients. Although such deficiencies are most commonly found in developing countries where poverty and hunger are more widespread, developed countries are not free from undernutrition. Indeed, they harbour significant deprived communities where food supply is inadequate (Strugnell, 1996; Caraher *et al.*, 1998). Furthermore, even the affluent can suffer from nutrition-related disease if they fail to consume a balanced diet.

A significant proportion of illness and mortality has been linked to dietary factors, such as a low intake of fresh fruit and dietary fibre, and an excessive consumption of fats and sugars. Furthermore, obesity has been identified as a risk factor for a range of diseases including diabetes, heart disease and some cancers. Moreover, the safety of food products has obvious implications for health. For example, bacterial agents such as salmonella and *Escherichia coli* have posed a serious threat to health in recent years. More generally, there has been much anxiety about the impact of modern production and distribution methods on food safety with regard to bacterial infection and other potentially harmful agents, such as veterinary medicines, pesticide residues, food additives and, more recently, genetically modified (GM) ingredients.

In view of the importance of food and diet in the promotion of good health, it might be expected that policy in this field would be strongly influenced by health considerations. As will become clear, this has not been so, although recent developments indicate that health matters carry greater weight now than was previously the case. This chapter explores how this has transpired by investigating the problems highlighted in recent years and by analysing the main policy responses.

# Diet and Health

## Food Supply and Availability

Food policy in the UK has been overwhelmingly focused upon 'food security' – the need to protect the state from the political and military implications of an inadequate food supply – rather than by a desire to improve diet and nutrition (see Centre for Agricultural Strategy, 1979; Mills, 1992). Threats to national security have, however, highlighted problems with nutrition as well as food security, thereby presenting at least some opportunity to improve the national diet. As noted in Chapter 3, for example, military failures during the Boer War raised questions about the physical fitness of recruits and the efficiency of the armed forces, and led to measures to improve the nutritional standards of vulnerable groups such as children. Subsequently, during the First World War, the UK government introduced food planning on an unprecedented scale: a Ministry of Food was established to regulate food production and supply, and rationing was introduced. But although there was a nutritional input to decisions about food supplies, this was not the primary consideration, and such advice was often ignored (Mills, 1992).

These controls were dismantled after the war, only to be restored when hostilities broke out again in 1939 (Hammond, 1951). The resurrection of the Ministry of Food and a rationing system was regarded as being highly successful in ensuring that all individuals received an adequate supply of food. Indeed, the system of wartime rationing in some respects made a major contribution to improved nutrition, along with initiatives such as the National Milk Scheme, which ensured that milk supplies reached priority cases such as pregnant women and children. According to the official historian of wartime food policy, 'the diet theoretically available to the British civilian was not only maintained but actually improved during the war' (Hammond, 1951, p. 369). During the 1930s, a number of studies had identified hunger and malnutrition among poor and unemployed people. A survey by Boyd Orr (1936), for example, found that many people could not afford an adequate diet. A third of the population were found to have a deficient diet in terms of proteins and fats, while a tenth had a deficiency in all nutritional aspects. In the Second World War, as in the Great War, nutritionists were incorporated into the decision-making process. Although much was achieved, particularly in terms of improving the diet of the poor, food policy remained largely determined by strategic and technical factors (Hammond, 1951).

## The Post-war Period

After the Second World War, the Ministry of Agriculture Fisheries and Food (MAFF), which took over the responsibilities of the Ministry of Food and the Agriculture Ministry in 1956, sought to ensure an adequate supply of food through a stable market that maintained farming income. This policy was implemented by a complex regime of subsidies and guaranteed prices underpinned by a close working relationship between farmers' representatives, in the form of the National Farmers' Union, and MAFF (Self and Storing, 1962; Body, 1991; Smith, 1993). Consequently, the interests of producers – the farming and food industry – prevailed in the food policy arena, and those of others, such as doctors and nutritionists, were marginalised. Indeed, medical advice was located in the Ministry of Health and was at arm's length from key decisions on food policy.

By the 1970s, health and nutrition policies were divorced from those concerning food and agriculture (Centre for Agricultural Strategy, 1979). Worse still, relationships between the Health Departments and MAFF were such that health considerations had little impact on policy except in extreme circumstances, such as serious outbreaks of food poisoning. These interdepartmental relations were, however, to become even more strained in the years ahead, as concerns about healthy diet and food safety intensified.

## The Western Diet

From the 1970s onwards, evidence became available suggesting that a large proportion of illness and mortality was attributable to the so-called 'Western diet', one rich in fats, sugars and proteins. A link between fat consumption, blood cholesterol level and coronary heart disease was identified (Keys, 1980). Excessive salt consumption was associated with high blood pressure, a known risk factor for heart disease and stroke (WHO, 1982; Intersalt Co-operative Research Group, 1988). In addition, sugar consumption was linked directly to dental caries and related oral diseases (Rugg-Gunn and Edgar, 1984). It was estimated that diet was responsible for around 40 per cent of cancer, perhaps more (Doll and Peto, 1981; Austoker, 1994b): the consumption of pickled and smoked food and a low fibre intake were identified as risk factors. High-fat diets were associated with certain cancers, including those of the bowel (Royal College of Physicians, 1981) and prostate (WHO, 1990). Finally, a range of gastrointestinal conditions including gallstones, appendicitis, haemorrhoids and constipation were linked with dietary factors, particularly a low intake of dietary fibre (WHO, 1990).

## Obesity

In addition to evidence linking ill health to specific aspects of the diet, it was also revealed that overnutrition, in the form of obesity, had an adverse implication for health. Obesity is defined in relation to body mass index (BMI), which is calculated on the basis of a weight–height ratio (the body mass in kg being divided by the square of the individual's height in metres). Anyone whose weight–height ratio exceeds a certain level (that is, a BMI of over 30 in England and Wales) is classified as obese. Such individuals have been found to have an increased risk of high blood pressure (and thereby coronary heart disease and other circulatory diseases), respiratory diseases, diabetes mellitus and gastrointestinal conditions such as gallstones (see Royal College of Physicians, 1983b; Garrow, 1988, 1991; Office of Health Economics, 1994; Wilding, 1997; WHO, 1998c). Obese women have been found to have an increased risk of cancer of the gallbladder, breast and uterus, while men have a greater risk of prostate cancer (WHO, 1990, p. 71).

## Food and Nutrition Policies in the 1970s and 80s

The UK government was relatively sluggish in responding to the evidence on health and nutrition that emerged during the 1970s and 80s (see Cannon, 1987; Calnan, 1991; Mills, 1992). Other countries, for example the USA and Norway, were more active in pursuing dietary goals in this period (WHO, 1988, 1990; Mills, 1992). It was not until 1992 that the Major government set targets for dietary risk factors and the reduction of obesity, and even then it refused to adopt policies that had been proposed as an effective way of promoting dietary change.

This cautious approach was reflected in the initial response of UK governments to the available evidence regarding diet and health. The Committee on the Medical Aspects of Food Policy (COMA), an official advisory committee located within the DoH, first investigated the link between diet and heart disease in the early 1970s. Although COMA advocated a lower intake of fat and recommended that sugar and salt consumption should not rise (COMA, 1974), it did not set explicit guidelines or targets. Two years after the publication of the COMA report, the Royal College of Physicians (RCP) produced dietary guidelines aimed at preventing coronary heart disease (RCP/British Cardiac Society, 1976), but these lacked official support and did little to raise public consciousness.

Some doctors and nutritionists, worried by this failure of government to encourage dietary change, pressed for a national strategy. An opportunity was presented in 1979 with the appointment of NACNE (National Advisory

Committee on Nutrition Education) to devise a strategy for nutrition education. A NACNE subcommittee was also established to compile a statement of
consensus on nutritional issues. Its draft reports were, however, rejected
because they stated dietary guidelines rather than, as the government had
requested, producing a consensus statement on nutrition and health. Ministers and civil servants were furious with the subcommittee for seeking to
commit government to a population-based strategy aimed at changing the
eating habits of the whole population (see Cannon, 1987).

When the NACNE report was finally published (NACNE, 1983), it set out
guidelines on nutrition and made a series of recommendations about how
these goals should be met. It recommended a long-term reduction in salt and
sugar intake of 50 per cent, and a 50 per cent increase in fibre intake. A cut in
alcohol consumption of 33 per cent was also proposed (interesting in the light
of later research demonstrating health benefits for moderate drinkers – see
below), as well as a reduction of total fat intake by 25 per cent, with a 50 per
cent cut in saturated fat intake. The report also recommended an improvement in food labelling and called on government departments to plan food
supply to incorporate these recommended changes in diet.

The government not only refused to endorse the report, but promptly abolished NACNE. Another committee, the Joint Advisory Committee on Nutrition Education was then appointed to undertake the task of producing a
leaflet giving nutritional advice on how to avoid heart disease. But there was
further controversy when the chairperson of the new committee threatened to
resign over alleged interference from government departments (see Mills,
1992). The leaflet was eventually published, only to be criticised by nutrition
experts for oversimplifying the issues.

Meanwhile, a panel established by COMA re-examined the relationship
between diet and cardiovascular disease. Its report (COMA, 1984) was seen
by some as a means of distracting attention away from the NACNE report
while further narrowing the terms of the nutrition debate (see Mills, 1992).
The COMA report did, however, set a target for the reduction of fat consumption (to 35 per cent of calorie intake) and recommended that sugar and salt
intake should not rise, that consideration should be given to reducing salt
consumption, and that dietary fibre intake should increase. The report also
endorsed clearer food labelling and made a number of recommendations
about food supply, including joint government–industry initiatives to reduce
the fat content of food products.

These recommendations, welcomed by nutritionists and consumer groups,
were hardly radical, yet even these limited steps were impeded by government departments, the food and farming industries and the constraints
imposed by the Common Agricultural Policy and other international agreements, discussed later in this chapter. The farmers and food producers
believed that profitability would fall if the public chose products that had

lower fat, sugar and salt content. The biggest opponents of change were the cattle, sheep and dairy farmers, as well as the manufacturers of dairy products, soft drinks and snack foods. The views of the food and farming industry were represented within government by MAFF and also through the Department of Trade and Industry. These interests were also strongly represented in Parliament and within the Conservative Party, which was in government throughout the 1980s and most of the 1990s. Furthermore, these commercial interests exerted a high degree of influence over decisions of international bodies, including European Community institutions. It should be noted in this context that, as Mills (1992) has shown, the Common Agricultural Policy inhibited a change in eating habits by subsidising products with a high fat content and encouraging the destruction of surpluses of healthy food such as fruit (see also Calnan, 1991; Lobstein, 1998). Recent failed attempts to reform the Common Agricultural Policy to give greater weight to environmental and health factors provide a further example of the power of entrenched economic interests (Lobstein, 1999).

The farming and food industries were effective in opposing a restriction on marketing their products. They opposed full nutritional labelling in the belief that high fat, sugar and salt content would deter consumers. When nutrition labelling was introduced in the 1980s, it was on a voluntary basis, and only details of saturated fats had to be revealed. New regulations were subsequently introduced in 1993 but did not compel manufacturers to include comprehensive nutritional information on labels. The labelling regulations were based on minimum standards and actually prevented the development of user-friendly nutritional labelling schemes that were being developed by some British retailers. Plans by the European Commission to introduce compulsory nutritional labelling were shelved following pressure from food manufacturers and from some member governments, including that of the UK. However, following a change of policy in the UK and other member states, and a more positive attitude towards nutritional labelling in sections of the food industry, these plans have now been revived, and at the time of writing the European Commission is reviewing its policy.

Shifting attitudes within the food industry, on both nutritional labelling and other issues such as food safety, have occurred mainly for commercial reasons. Retailers and manufacturers, perceiving a heightened awareness among the public with regard to healthy eating, have successfully incorporated health messages into their marketing strategies. Because most nutritional claims are not defined in law, the public can, however, easily be misled – particularly with regard to claims about low fat and sugar content. There have consequently been calls for further regulation in this area from consumer groups and from sections of the food industry who are making genuine claims (see Dibb, 1998).

*Further Pressure*

Changes in public preference regarding diet in the 1980s and 90s, coupled with growing fears about food safety, discussed later in this chapter, placed the UK government under pressure to promote healthier and safer food. This was reinforced by the activities of a range of voluntary organisations that called for improved food standards. There was also increased activity at an international level, the WHO taking a greater interest in food and health issues. The WHO European Region set out a strategy for preventing nutrition-related disease (WHO Regional Office for Europe, 1988), and a WHO Study Group recommended concerted action by governments to prevent chronic diseases related to diet (WHO, 1990). In 1992, the International Declaration on Nutrition set out nine strategies, one of which was to promote appropriate diets and healthier lifestyles. The setting of objectives and targets at the international level, while having no legal status, nevertheless required member states to devise action plans and placed their policies under much greater scrutiny. Subsequently, in 1993, six priorities were identified by the WHO Nutrition Programme, one of which was to tackle obesity and diet-related disease. Targets were set, including a reduction of the energy derived from fat to 30 per cent of the total energy intake (as recommended by WHO, 1990), and a task force on obesity was established (WHO, 1998c). It should be noted that the WHO has since been active through its regional offices in monitoring member states' policies on food and nutrition (see WHO Regional Office for Europe, 1998b).

## The Health of the Nation *Strategy*

The pressure on government to adopt a more health-oriented food policy, and the countervailing pressure to avoid policies that threatened the short-term profitability of the food and farming industries, was evident in the development of the Major government's health strategy (Cm 1986, 1992). Several of the main targets identified in the strategy specified a reduction in mortality from diseases related to nutrition, including cancer, heart disease and stroke. Furthermore, dietary risk factor targets were set (to be achieved by 2005): a reduction in high levels of alcohol consumption (defined at the time as over 21 units of alcohol per week in men and over 14 in women) by 30 per cent; a reduction in the proportion of obese men aged 16–64 by 25 per cent and of such women by a third; a reduction in the amount of energy derived from saturated fat intake by at least 35 per cent; and a reduction in the average percentage derived from total fat by 12 per cent. Another target relevant to diet was a reduction in the mean systolic blood pressure in the adult population by at least 5 mmHg by 2005.

This policy was taken up by a Nutrition Task Force (NTF) comprising the various interests in the field, including the food industry, consumer groups, the NHS, scientists and relevant government departments (DoH/NTF, 1994). The NTF made a number of recommendations, including improved nutritional labelling, a review of advertising codes of practice, product development by the food industry to increase the availability of healthier products, a reduction of fat in the food chain and a high-profile media campaign to promote a healthier diet (DoH/NTF 1996a).

These proposals had already been diluted by representatives of the food industry and their allies serving on the panels set up by the NTF to consider specific issues. Further opposition to the recommendations of the NTF was mobilised by these interests. The food industry opposed a reduction in the fat content of food where this conflicted with commercial priorities and refused to develop new, healthier products in the absence of explicit consumer demand. Initial plans to set targets for product development within the food industry were dropped in the light of this opposition. Sections of the food industry were also opposed to NTF's idea for more extensive nutritional labelling. A joint working group was established between NTF and the Food Advisory Committee of MAFF, which was dominated by food industry representatives. Consequently, NTF accepted the industry's position that supplementary labelling should be confined to one or two nutrients, specifically fats. The proposal for a large-scale media campaign to promote healthy eating was dismissed by the food industry and the government, which balked at the cost, estimated to be over £3m a year.

There was a more positive response to the NTF's recommendation that the advertising codes governing food should be reviewed. Some minor changes to the broadcasters' advertising codes were introduced in 1995 in an effort to discourage advertising that disparaged healthy eating or condoned overindulgence. However, the Advertising Standards Authority, whose code of practice governs advertising in the non-broadcast media, declined to impose similar restrictions on food products, although it did introduce some additional controls on food advertising aimed at children in its 1995 Code of Practice. Critics, however, believed that these changes did not go far enough, noting evidence that children tended to avoid healthy foods when given a choice (Hackett *et al.*, 1997). It is possible that advertising shapes and reinforces these preferences (see Jeffrey *et al.*, 1982; Taras *et al.*, 1989). Indeed, some countries, including Sweden and Norway, prohibit all advertising aimed at the under-12s. Reviews of research in relation to food advertising and children's choices suggest, however, that the link is complex and that other variables such as parental supervision and behaviour, and the prevailing patterns of diet, are also important (see, for example, the MAFF-funded review by Young and Hetherington, 1996).

The NTF was involved in further political controversy when one of its panels, examining the diet of low-income groups, was criticised by the government for exceeding its brief when it called for a comprehensive strategy to improve the nutritional level of the poor (DoH/NTF, 1996b). Meanwhile, a joint report drafted by the NTF and the Physical Activity Task Force, another body established under *The Health of the Nation* initiative, courted controversy by suggesting a large reduction in the fat content of foods. The final report was delayed while industry representatives protested about its content and it was eventually published in a diluted form (DoH/NTF/PTF, 1995). Furthermore, by urging better standards for hospital and school meals, the NTF again sailed close to the wind. Indeed, this appeared to contradict government policy, reflected in the earlier abolition of nutritional standards for school meals, to create market opportunities for private contractors in this field. These recommendations were nevertheless accepted, and new guidelines were introduced for both hospital catering, in 1995, and school meals, in 1997. The latter are likely to be strengthened by new proposals to ensure that school caterers offer alternative carbohydrates and a minimum level of vegetables, meat and fish (DFEE, 1998).

Despite its efforts to accommodate all the interested parties, the NTF unavoidably made recommendations that were unwelcome to commercial interests and to government departments closely linked to these interests. It was hardly surprising when, in 1996, the Major government decided to abolish the organisation. Other official bodies, however, continued to cause annoyance to the food industry. A further report on diet and heart disease by COMA (1994) recommended a reduction in salt intake and in the consumption of full-fat products, as well as a 50 per cent increase in the consumption of fruit, vegetables, bread and potatoes. Again, the food industry lobbied strongly to ensure that these recommendations were not translated into official policy. They sought to mobilise public opinion by portraying the report as interfering with individual dietary choice. The government consequently distanced itself from a number of the report's recommendations, including the reduction of salt content.

A further strand of government policy in this period was to promote healthy eating through local health alliances (see Chapter 4). These depended very much on an effective partnership between health and local authorities and the voluntary sector. There was little in the way of central prescription or guidance, but examples of good practice could nevertheless be found (see DoH, 1994b; Scriven, 1998): in some areas, such as Bradford, the local council and health authorities developed local nutrition policies for various population subgroups. Elsewhere, such as in Avon, steps were taken to improve the training of primary care professionals in nutritional issues. Alliances increasingly broadened their outlook and began to undertake project work in several different but related areas of nutrition. The South Humber Health Authority's heart disease prevention programme, for example, aimed to promote diet and other lifestyle changes over a range of settings, including schools, sports centres and community events (see Holmes and Ward, 1996).

Given the reluctance of government to take on commercial interests and its failure to fund local initiatives, it came as no surprise to discover that key dietary targets were not being met. The percentage of women drinking more than 14 units of alcohol a week actually rose from 11 to 13 per cent in the first half of the 1990s (NAO, 1996a) and has continued to rise since. Obesity also increased. By the late 1990s, 17 per cent of adult men and almost 20 per cent of adult women in the UK were classified as obese, compared with 7 per cent of men and 12 per cent of women in 1986.

## *The Blair Government's Approach*

The Blair government initially set out a much tougher policy on food and health compared with its Conservative predecessor. This was reflected in its decision to set up a Food Standards Agency, discussed below, responsible for some aspects of nutrition as well as food safety. In other respects, however, the government's approach appeared less radical. The previous government's risk factors targets, including those on blood pressure, obesity and alcohol consumption, were discontinued. Some believed that this would make it easier for the government to evade responsibility for tackling dietary causes of illness. Official sources denied this, claiming that food and dietary policies would be part of an integrated strategy to reduce heart disease and cancer, two of the main national targets areas identified by the Blair government's health strategy (see Chapter 4).

Notwithstanding the change of government, the food industry remained powerful and lobbied strongly against any strategy that involved a substantial change in eating habits. This was illustrated by the response to a report on diet and cancer from COMA (renamed the Committee on the Medical Aspects of Food and Nutrition Policy and now destined to be replaced by a Scientific Advisory Committee on Nutrition). COMA (1997) recommended that people maintain a healthy body weight throughout their lives and increase (by 50 per cent for the population as a whole) their fruit and vegetable intake. Its report also advised those consuming an above-average level of red meat (90 g a day) to consider reducing their consumption and those who ate a high level (over 140 g a day) to reduce their intake. Following an objection from some members of COMA, as well as from MAFF and the meat industry, this advice was changed to recommend merely that those with an above-average intake should consider reducing their consumption of meat. Health ministers denied that they had been unduly influenced by colleagues in other departments or by the meat industry, although the suspicion remained that this had occurred.

## Further Controversies

A problem facing those advocating a change in diet has been the lack of conclusive evidence on the impact of such a change on health. In recent years, new evidence has come to light regarding the relationship between diet and health, some of which has confirmed or clarified earlier findings. Other studies have, however, raised doubts about the validity of previous research, and this has had considerable implications for policy.

The role of vegetables in preventing cancer has been confirmed by other studies (see COMA, 1997), although doubt has been cast on the role of fibre as a protective agent against cancer. One large-scale study (Fuchs *et al.*, 1999) was not able to find a link between individual fibre intake and the risk of colorectal cancer in women. A study of US males, however, revealed a reduction in bowel cancer related to an increased intake of fruit (Platz *et al.*, 1997), while a controlled trial of men in seven countries found a 10 g increase in fibre to be associated with a 33 per cent lower risk of bowel cancer over 25 years (see Jansen *et al.*, 1999). These contradictory findings are confusing, and, as Schenker (1999) has observed, the doubts over the impact of fibre on cancer will only become clear with the advent of highly controlled intervention studies relating dietary change to a declining cancer rate.

Researchers have highlighted further nutrition-related cancer risks. There is an association between a higher energy intake in childhood and cancer in later life (Frankel *et al.*, 1998). In a further study, a significant association was found between height (viewed as an indicator of early nutrition) and cancer, tall men (those over 6 ft) facing more than a 30 per cent greater risk of cancer, other than that related to smoking (Davey Smith *et al.*, 1998b). Another research project discovered that the number of non-tobacco-related cancer deaths was linked to leg length (Gunnell *et al.*, 1998), which is regarded by some as a more nutritionally sensitive measure of energy intake in early life (Albanes, 1998).

There have also been new findings on the relationship between diet and heart disease. One large-scale study (Key *et al.*, 1996), for example, found a significantly reduced mortality from heart disease in vegetarians and health-conscious people. A link between the intake of fibre and a reduced risk of coronary heart disease in women was confirmed by Wolk *et al.* (1999). The same research team had earlier found that the frequent consumption of nuts appeared to give some protection against coronary heart disease (Hu *et al.*, 1998). The danger of an excessive level of salt in the diet has been further highlighted (Elliott *et al.*, 1996). Meanwhile, several studies have contradicted earlier findings on the relationship between alcohol and heart disease. In the 1990s, researchers revealed that alcohol consumed in moderation is associated with a lower risk of dying from heart disease and other causes. This finding does not, however, justify an increase in average alcohol consumption because of the wider health and social problems this could produce. This issue is discussed further in Chapter 9.

The orthodoxy that heart disease is closely and directly linked to the consumption of fats, particularly saturated fats, has also been challenged (see Atrens, 1994; Skrabanek, 1994). It has been pointed out that a high fat consumption can be associated with a low rate of heart disease, such as in South West France (Atrens, 1994). Critics also maintain that a change in fat intake within countries has not been mirrored by a corresponding change in mortality from heart disease (see Atrens, 1994; Le Fanu, 1994b). In addition, a number of studies have not found a positive relationship between the intake of animal fats and a higher risk of certain types of heart and circulatory disease. Ischaemic heart disease was not found to be associated with animal fat intake in the Caerphilly study (Fehily *et al.*, 1993), for example. Furthermore, an American study found that a higher fat intake (including saturated fats) was associated with a reduced risk of ischaemic stroke (Gillman *et al.*, 1997).

The relationship between cholesterol level and heart disease is also more complex than has been portrayed. In the past, coronary heart disease was believed to be linked simply to a high level of cholesterol in the blood, but it now appears that low-density lipoprotein is the main culprit. Consequently, efforts have been made to reduce the level of low-density lipoprotein by dietary change, a drug regime or some combination of both. Meanwhile, high-density lipoprotein has been shown to be inversely related to the build-up of cholesterol in the arteries – one of the signs of coronary heart disease (Tall, 1990). Researchers have also identified cell receptors for high-density lipoprotein, opening up the prospect of manipulating the high-density lipoprotein level in the body in an effort to prevent coronary heart disease (see Acton *et al.*, 1996).

Others go further, arguing that cholesterol is something of a 'red herring' in the epidemiology of heart disease (see Ramsay *et al.*, 1994; *Men's Health*, 1996). According to this view, targeting cholesterol, rather than other risk factors such as high blood pressure, obesity or smoking, is an ineffective way of tackling the problem. Although cholesterol level is related to coronary heart disease mortality across different cultures, there is nevertheless a wide range in the mortality rate at each given cholesterol level, indicating the importance of these other factors (Verschuren *et al.*, 1995). Some even believe that reducing cholesterol is misguided because of harmful side effects, such as depression and an increased risk of suicide (see Jacobs *et al.*, 1992; Dunnigan, 1993; Gallerani *et al.*, 1995) although this has been challenged by others (Law *et al.*, 1994a, 1994b; Wannamethee *et al.*, 1995). Moreover, it should be noted that the theoretical possibility of an increased risk of cancer has been identified in relation to some cholesterol-lowering drugs (Newman and Hulley, 1996).

Research into the causes of obesity has also generated new findings. The majority of experts believe that obesity is as much the result of a lack of physical activity as overeating (Prentice and Jebb, 1995; Weinser *et al.*, 1998). In Britain, for example, an increasing obesity level has corresponded with a falling nutrient intake, providing the basis for recommendations to increase physical activity (Exhibit 8.1). A difference in body metabolism has also been suggested as a possible cause of obesity. However, problems with the collection of data on diet (as obese people have a tendency to under-report nutrient intake – see Lichtman *et al.*, 1992) and evidence that obese people do not necessarily expend less energy (Prentice *et al.*, 1986) have undermined this approach.

Research has nevertheless continued to focus on metabolism through a genetic predisposition to obesity (Roberts and Greenberg, 1996). Several genes have been linked to the disproportionate storage of fat in the body (see Trayhurn, 1997; Cormuzie and Allison, 1998). Related to this are investigations into nutrient intake and energy storage, as well as into the specific role of a protein, leptin in these processes. Research on rodents has revealed that leptin sends signals the brain to reduce food intake while increasing energy expenditure, thereby affecting body weight (Baskin *et al.*, 1998). Not surprisingly, leptin has been highlighted as a potential key to a more effective drug therapy for obesity in humans, even though its role in humans is more complex than in rodents and is apparently less amenable to manipulation (see Trayhurn, 1997; Hirsch, 1998). The only drugs currently available are appetite suppressants, now regarded as relatively ineffective, and pancreatic lipase inhibitors (orlistat), which reduce the absorption of fat up to 30 per cent and can be effective in reducing obesity in conjunction with dieting (see Siddall, 1998).

Other researchers, meanwhile, have revealed a link between the availability of food in the environment and the amount of leptin produced (Wang *et al.*, 1999). In laboratory experiments, rats exposed to an abundant diet had a reduced level of leptin and maximised their consumption. The group that faced a restricted diet, however, had a raised level of leptin and a lower appetite. The implication therefore is that the more plentiful the food supply, the greater the tendency to increase food intake and store energy. This also suggests that at an ecological approach to obesity (Egger and Swinburn, 1997; Hill and Peters, 1998), which regards obesity as a response to an abnormal environment and which proposes interventions to improve this environment in ways conducive to health, may be more fruitful than concentrating purely on treating obese individuals.

This is not to say that genetic factors are unimportant, nor that improved therapies should not be sought. Indeed, experiments on mice have led to the cloning of a gene that appears to suppress diet-induced obesity (Nagle *et al.*, 1999). Mice with the mutated 'mahogony' gene did not significantly gain weight when placed on a high-fat diet compared with a normal diet. In contrast, those with the normal gene showed a significant gain in weight

Exhibit 8.1

## Physical exercise and health

The decline in the level of physical activity has been identified as one of the factors involved in obesity (Prentice and Jebb, 1995). Physical exercise is also recognised as a way of preventing obesity and specific illnesses such as heart disease, diabetes and depression (Powell *et al.*, 1987; Royal College of Physicians, 1991; Fentem, 1994). Researchers have also indicated that it may improve mental and physical agility among elderly people (Kramer *et al.*, 1999). Yet surveys of physical activity show that one in four of the population in England is sedentary, classified as not indulging in at least one session per week of moderate-intensity activity (such as gardening, house-work or cycling) lasting at least 30 minutes (ONS/HEA, 1997).

In an effort to improve the level of physical fitness in the population, the Major govern-ment established a Physical Activity Task Force. This set out three aims (DoH/PATF, 1995; DoH/NTF/PATF, 1995): to encourage sedentary people to indulge in at least one session of moderate-intensity activity a week; to encourage those undertaking moderate-intensity activity to do this at least five days a week; and to encourage those already taking some vigorous activity to undertake three sessions a week of at least 20 minutes.

The Task Force recognised that physical activity was not simply a matter of individual choice. Its recommendations included planning for safe cycle routes and footpaths, and improving access to leisure facilities. Schools were identified as a key area for intervention, recommendations including more time for PE and schemes to encourage walking and cycling to school. Some of these recommendations were taken up at local level, as were others, such the prescription of exercise by GPs, but many proposals went against the grain of government policy, both directly, in the form of the national curriculum, which restricted the time available for games and PE, and indirectly, in the sale of school playing fields, which resulted from government funding policies. Further-more, transport policy (see Chapter 7), which was focused on motoring, allowed few opportunities to increase walking and cycling.

The Major government took a limited step at national level to improve the level of exer-cise, including the availability of National Lottery Funds for sport and leisure facilities. In 1994, planning guidance was issued on transport and land use that included better provision for cyclists and pedestrians. In 1996, a national cycling strategy was launched, with aim of doubling the number of cycle journeys between 1996 and 2002 (and with a further target of again doubling the number of journeys by 2012). The effect of these particular strategies is as yet unknown. It should, however, be noted that the impact of short-term interventions to promote exercise has been shown to be limited, and it is therefore important that activities to promote exercise are sustained over a longer period (Harland *et al.*, 1999).

The Blair government introduced a number of initiatives that may bring change in the medium to long term. Healthy Living Centres (see Chapter 5) may offer a greater

---

Exhibit 8.1 *(cont'd)*

---

opportunity to improve fitness and levels of physical activity. The new transport strategy heralds a greater role for cycling and walking, but again much depends on implementation (see Chapter 7). The Healthy Schools initiative could facilitate efforts to improve physical activity among children (guidance notably being issued in 1999 setting a minimum requirement of two hours a week physical exercise for secondary school children). Finally, a Sports Strategy was introduced in 2000. Although the plan included an expansion of sports facilities, most critics agreed that it did little to encourage fitness among the majority of young people.

---

when placed on the high-fat diet. The mahogony gene produces a protein, found in various body tissues, including the hypothalamus, which has an important role in relation to appetite and the control of body weight. It is similar to the human protein attractin, so this discovery therefore implies the possibility of a similar process in humans and improves the future prospect of new therapies in this field.

In summary, research into obesity has confirmed that it results from a complex interaction of genetic, environmental and behavioural factors. The lesson to be drawn is that the promotion of healthy eating is one of a number of possible interventions, alongside encouraging physical activity, altering other environmental factors that shape dietary habits, and developing therapies based on our increasing knowledge of genetic and biochemical factors.

## Is Obesity the Problem?

An alternative view, however, is that the emphasis on tackling obesity is misplaced. This is associated, albeit not exclusively, with the feminist standpoint (see Chernin, 1983; Orbach, 1978), which identifies the obsession with weight and weight loss as a form of suppression and exploitation. These writers point out that the pressure on women to attain an 'ideal' (and for many unreasonable) body weight is a major cause of ill health, leading to eating disorders as well as psychological and other physical health problems (Cataldo, 1985). It has also been pointed out that while severe obesity is linked to a higher risk of certain diseases, definitions of obesity are imprecise and result in people (both men and women) being wrongly labelled as 'unhealthy' or 'at risk'. Noppa *et al.* (1980) found that only marked obesity was correlated with heart attacks and angina. Others have argued that 'overweight' people are often physically fit (Gaesser, 1996, cited in Bennett and DiLorenzo, 1999, p. 32). Researchers have found that being obese yet physically fit is less risky to health than being lean and unfit (Lee *et al.*, 1999), suggesting that promoting exercise rather than tackling obesity should be the primary aim.

From this perspective, doctors, nutritionists and health campaigners are seen as part of a labelling process leading to the oppression of particular groups such as those on a low income, some ethnic minority groups and women, who tend to have a higher level of obesity. Notably, doctors in some countries are less likely than those in others to diagnose obesity (see Payer, 1989), illustrating that the deviation of body weight from the norm is related to cultural values and expectations. Moreover, as the 'ideal' body weight plummets, particularly for women, the burden of psychosocial and physical problems associated with striving towards this ideal is likely to grow (see Lawrence, 1987). Evidence that a variation in weight over time is bad for one's health (Blair *et al.*, 1993) and that the benefit of leanness is limited to those who are also physically fit (Lee *et al.*, 1999) similarly suggests a more careful approach to the problems of obesity.

Others go further and argue that antiobesity strategies represent an attack on individual liberty and private choice. This view has been developed in controversial style by Bennett and DiLorenzo (1999) in the USA, who contend that, based on poor evidence, 'the food and drink police', nannies, busybodies and petty tyrants are waging a moral war against the pleasures of ordinary folk. The main aim of these bureaucrats, professionals and campaigners is, according to Bennett and DiLorenzo, to achieve social control rather than an improvement in public health.

Such controversies serve to confuse further a public already faced with contradictory media messages about diet and health. Furthermore, people are increasingly uncertain about other aspects of food and health, in particular the safety of food products and processes. The remainder of this chapter focuses on some of the main concerns regarding food safety and examines how these have led to pressure on government and the food industry to strengthen regulation in this field.

## Food Safety

Public anxiety about food safety is not new. There was, for example, great public agitation in the Victorian period following revelations that products such as bread, tea, milk, pepper and wine were deliberately adulterated with harmful substances (Smith, 1979). Yet even by historical standards, food safety is a major issue today. A succession of serious problems over the past two decades – including salmonella in eggs, listeria contamination, new variant Creutzfeldt–Jakob disease (CJD), and *Escherichia coli* 0157 infection –

have created enormous media interest and public panic. In addition, there have been fears about the safety of food, relating to chemical additives, pesticides and antibiotics, as well as GM foods.

## Chemical Additives in Food

An enormous range of chemicals are added to food, including colourings, preservatives, flavourings and other substances incorporated to improve the efficiency of the food production process, such as enzymes and solvents (see Millstone, 1986; Wheelock, 1986). Some, including the colouring tartrazine, are associated with allergic reactions, while others, including the sweetener, saccharin, have been associated with cancers in laboratory experiments. (Channel 4 Television, 1992; Maga and Tu, 1994). Food colourings have also been associated with hyperactivity in children (Maga and Tu, 1994). Particular criticism has been levelled at the excessive use of colourings and flavourings used merely to increase consumer appeal. However, preservatives, which arguably have a more useful role, have not escaped criticism when they are employed primarily as a means of increasing shelf-life rather than to protect the consumer's health.

Campaigners have called for a greater restriction on additives. Some manufacturers, often under pressure from retailers, have responded by removing colourings, particularly from food eaten by vulnerable groups such as babies and small children. In addition, there have been a number of changes to the regulation of additives, stemming largely from European Union initiatives. In an effort to harmonise food additive rules throughout Europe, member states approved a common list of permitted additives, but instead of restricting their use, this move actually increased the number of additives that could be used in the UK. Bizarrely, this permitted additives previously banned in the UK, such as sodium cyclamate, an artificial sweetener used in soft drinks, which has been linked to testicular atrophy (shrinking of the testicles) in animal experiments (*Food Magazine*, 1997). It is also believed in some quarters that commercial pressure, notably as a result of the free trade agreements discussed later, will make it more difficult to prohibit the use of potentially harmful additives.

Another criticism is that the labelling requirement for additives is too lax. Most additives are currently identified on food labels, although the details are rarely presented in a form comprehensible to the consumer (see Dibb, 1998). Furthermore, some foods, including most dairy products, eggs, alcoholic drinks and takeaway food, are exempt from these rules. As a result, consumers are denied information about additives and cannot make the choice to avoid them. This situation again looks unlikely to improve in the presence of pressure to reduce barriers to trade.

Other forms of chemical contamination include pesticide residues, which have a potentially serious implication for health (BMA, 1990). There are specific fears about long-term exposure to pesticides associated with cancer (Agriculture Committee, 1987), such as lindane, which has been linked to breast cancer (see Chapter 6). In all, over 1 per cent of food samples tested in 1998 contained a level of pesticide residues higher than the maximum permitted. A further 26 per cent of samples contained traces of pesticide below this level (MAFF/HSE, 1999). These revelations have led to a demand that the most potentially harmful pesticides be banned. While this may in the long term reduce the level of food contamination, it must be remembered that pesticide residues persist in the environment for many years. Indeed, traces of DDT – a pesticide banned in the UK for over a decade – can still be found in food samples.

Chemicals can also enter the food chain in the form of veterinary medicines and growth-promoting drugs. In recent years, there has been much controversy about bovine somatotropin, a growth hormone that increases milk yield in cattle (see Hansen, 1998; Kingsnorth, 1998). The drug has a number of side effects in cattle, including increasing the incidence of mastitis (inflammation of the udder). The resulting treatment with antibiotics could have an implication for microbial resistance, discussed below. Furthermore, there are worries that the hormone could raise the level of another hormone, insulin-like growth factor I, in milk supplies to a level that would pose a cancer risk to humans (see Challacombe and Wheeler, 1994; Mepham *et al.*, 1994; Chan *et al.*, 1998; Hankinson *et al.*, 1998). Bovine somatotropin is currently banned within the European Union, although recent trade agreements, discussed below, could permit its future use despite the surplus of milk here and notwithstanding the arguments of those who predict dire consequences for animal and human health.

Antibiotics are also seen as threat to health because of their routine use in promoting growth and productivity in farm animals. Although antibiotics may in the short term help to maintain health, their indiscriminate use is damaging in the long term, not only for animals, but for humans too. The main problem here is antibiotic resistance (see Exhibit 2.1). As bacteria in animals become exposed to antibiotics, they can develop resistance, which could be transmitted to humans. This compounds the problem of antibiotic overuse in humans, which is already recognised as a source of bacterial resistance (House of Lords Science and Technology Select Committee, 1998a). A ban on the routine use of antibiotics in animals has been proposed (see Agriculture Committee, 1998). There are precedents here – Sweden imposed a ban on antibiotics in animal feed in 1986. Furthermore, in 1999, the European Commission proposed a ban on four antibiotics used in animal feed. At the time of writing, these proposals are being challenged by the producers of veterinary medicines who have threatened legal action over the loss of sales arising from such a ban.

## New Technologies

The dangers of antibiotic resistance and pesticide residues raise wider questions about potential threats to human health posed by modern farming practices and food production processes, as well as food irradiation, novel foods and GM foods. Food irradiation, legalised in the 1990s after being banned three decades earlier, extends the shelf-life of products and is often extolled by the food industry as a means of protecting public health because it kills harmful bacteria. It has, however, been argued that the process destroys vitamins while leaving toxins unharmed and could compound the harmful effects of pesticide residues and other chemicals in food (see House of Lords Select Committee on European Communities, 1990; Webb and Lang, 1990). In the absence of evidence on the longer-term effect of irradiation, some states, including Australia, have banned the practice. Irradiated food is permitted in the UK providing it is correctly labelled, and under current rules, irradiated ingredients must be labelled if they make up a quarter or more of the ingredients of a product. Studies have, however, shown that this is flouted not only in the UK but throughout Europe (*Food Magazine*, 1995).

Novel foods have also provoked alarm. It is now possible to create synthetic products that can be used to replace natural nutrients. One example is the fat substitute Olestra, which is already used in a range of foods in the USA (*Food Magazine*, 1998). The main worry about such products is that they may have unforeseen side effects on human health and the environment. These foods lack nutritional value, a feature promoted by sections of the food industry, which argue that consumers welcome products that are calorie-free, but beyond this there are environmental health concerns: synthetic products do not biodegrade as quickly as their natural counterparts. It has been argued, for example, that synthetic fat substitutes could lead to a widespread blockage of drains, toilets and sewage systems, with obvious implications for the environment and public health. At the time of writing, plans to introduce Olestra in the UK have been shelved.

There has also been much anxiety about GM foods in recent years. Most scientists appear to believe that fears surrounding this technology are exaggerated and point out that genetic manipulation is hardly new as both crops and animals have for generations been subject to selective breeding. As Burke (1998) has pointed out, the novelty lies in the transfer of genes from one species to another. Defenders of genetic modification argue that there are clear advantages in producing crops that do not rot quickly or are more resistant to insects or disease. Genetic manipulation may also offer the opportunity to produce healthier food, such as lower-fat animal carcasses or herbicide-resistant crops containing a lower level of pesticide residue.

Critics have a number of legitimate concerns (see Mendelson, 1998; Nottingham, 1998). They are worried about the long-term impact of new genetic variants on the environment, arguing that it could damage wildlife and undermine biodiversity. Organic farmers are particularly worried about cross-pollination arising from proximity to GM crops, which they believe will ruin their livelihood and reduce consumer choice. There is anxiety too about the impact on human health. Unplanned hybrids could lead to the development of further resistance to antibiotics and pesticides. Another possibility is that GM foods could have a direct effect on the human body, causing gastrointestinal conditions for example.

Such dangers are theoretical. As a report from the UK government's Chief Medical Officer and Chief Scientific Officer observed, 'there is no *current* evidence to suggest that the GM technologies used to produce food are inherently harmful' (emphasis added) (Donaldson and May, 1999, p. 2). There is no evidence that significant harm will result – but then again there is no guarantee that it will not. Indeed, even if GM food did create a health problem it would be years before any evidence would emerge, and even then other factors could easily be blamed. Extreme caution should be exercised when deciding to use this technology, but, unfortunately, this has not been the case. Powerful multinational corporations, bolstered by 'the free trade at any costs' ethos of international trade agreements and governments keen to exploit the economic benefits of the biotechnology industry, have been able to experiment with and introduce GM foods within weak regulatory systems where health considerations appear to have been a low priority.

Regulation within the European Union, for example, in the form of that on the labelling of GM foods in 1998, has been criticised (Emmott, 1998; Sadler, 1998). The European Union labelling requirements originally applied to only two products – maize and soya. Subsequently, these have been changed, but products containing less than 1 per cent GM products are now exempt from the regulations. Some European countries have gone further, such as Austria and Luxembourg, which have banned the import, marketing and use of GM food, although such prohibitions face being overturned as a restraint of trade. In the UK meanwhile, controls on the labelling of GM foods were introduced in 1999 amid intense media coverage, public concern, lobbying from environmental pressure groups and agencies, and direct action by some campaigners. Most UK supermarkets (and some food manufacturers, including Nestlé and Unilever) announced plans to withdraw GM ingredients from their own-label products. The Blair government continued to defend GM foods, although it did make a concession by proposing a reform of the structure and composition of advisory bodies on genetic technology in order to increase the participation of lay people, environmentalists, consumer representatives and health professionals. Subsequently, it also stated that there would be no general unrestricted cultivation of GM crops until farm trial evaluations had been completed, based on a voluntary agreement with the biotechnology and farming industries. It should be noted, however, that this move did not address the concerns about the impact of GM food on human health. Nor did it prevent the accidental sowing of GM oilseed rape that had not been cleared for commercial planting, which came to light in May 2000 (*Independent*, 2000c).

## International Regulation

The anxiety expressed about GM foods, food irradiation, antibiotic resistance and pesticide contamination reflect a deeper concern with the methods of the farming and food industries. As Body (1991) has noted, there has been an incentive for many years to encourage food output at whatever cost. Farmers and food manufacturers were slow to appreciate that other considerations, such as compassion to animals, human health and the protection of the wider environment, should carry more weight. Meanwhile, the framework of governance and regulation, dominated by commercial interests, has continued to emphasise profit as the main priority, as reflected in the weak approach to food regulation hitherto adopted.

Commercial interests have exerted a great deal of influence over international agreements on food standards and the bodies that implement these agreements. In the Uruguay round of the General Agreement on Tariffs and Trade (GATT) talks, for example, agreement was reached on the harmonisation of regulations on technical barriers to trade and health standards in order to encourage trade in agriculture and food products. Despite the implications for public health, these moves were, however, determined primarily by commercial factors. Similarly, the WTO, established in 1995 to monitor and enforce international trade agreements, has lacked a public health perspective (Correa, 1999; Drager, 1999). It has been argued this must be remedied by a 'health presence' at future world trade talks (see Labonte, 1998a). Notably, the WHO was invited to attend the 1999 WTO ministerial conference in Seattle, which broke up without agreement following protests from environmentalists and trade unionists among others.

Nonetheless, the WTO's interpretation of whether countries have a legitimate case to protect the standard of health by restricting trade in food depends heavily on another body. This is the Codex Alimentarius Commission (known as Codex), established in 1963 under the auspices of the WHO and the Food and Agriculture Organisation, which develops international standards for food products. Trade agreements give Codex a central role in standard-setting for the labelling and composition of food, additives, pesticide and veterinary drug residues. Commercial interests are strongly represented on the Codex committees. In contrast, consumers and health interests are under-represented (Avery *et al.*, 1993; Tansey and Worsley, 1995), although a number of international consumer agencies, including the International Association of Consumer Food Organisations, have been granted 'observer status'.

The prospect is of health standards being lowered: unless domestic standards can be clearly justified on health grounds, they will be interpreted as a restraint on trade, and the WTO will penalise such nations. Governments setting higher health standards will be forced to open their markets to imports, which will at the very least prevent improvement in health protection and may jeopardise current standards. The row over bovine somatotropin, mentioned earlier, is a case in point. The European ban on the use of bovine somatotropin was challenged by the USA, and the WTO ordered the European Union to lift its ban on beef from hormone-treated cattle. Moreover, when in 1999 the European Union banned all imports of US beef on health grounds after hormone residues were found in supposedly 'hormone-free' imports, the WTO again sided with the USA.

It is, however, possible that competitive pressure may work in the direction of better standards, for although markets may be opened up, consumers may decide not to buy. In the UK, competition between food retailers has led to an increased emphasis on the quality of food products as well as on price. At the same time, the concentration of food retailing in large supermarket chains has given them greater influence over farmers and food manufacturers, not to mention an ability to shape consumer choice (Wrigley, 1998). This has enabled them to launch initiatives to improve the quality and range of food products (and to respond quickly to consumer fears). Recent actions include removing certain additives and GM ingredients from own-branded products and setting out guidelines for clearer nutritional labelling. In addition, they have developed their own systems of regulation, which go beyond food safety and hygiene legislation (Marsden and Flynn, 1997; Flynn *et al.*, 1999).

Much therefore depends on changing consumer preference and concerns about food standards, and on how these are communicated to food businesses and regulators. Periodic crises with regard to the chemical safety of food, against a background of growing public concern about food production processes in general, have led to a greater sensitivity among some sections of the food industry and within governments and regulatory bodies. Other concerns have also fed this process, notably worries about microbiological contamination and the transmission of pathogens from animals to man.

## Mad Cow Disease

Perhaps the most significant of these food safety crises was the furore over BSE, known as 'mad cow disease' (Baggott, 1998; Hodgett, 1998; Ratzan, 1998). Although this principally affected the UK beef industry, and cost the UK government £3.4 billion (NAO, 1998b), it eventually had a wider implication for food regulation throughout the European Union. The controversy surrounded the transmission of a degenerative brain disease between species.

The manifestation of such a disease in sheep, known as scrapie, was well documented, but evidence of a similar disease in cattle – BSE – raised the possibility that an infective agent 'had crossed the species barrier and could do so again, this time to humans. Suspicion alighted on cattle feed, which included proteins derived from rendering sheep carcasses and waste products. It was pointed out that deregulation, coupled with technological changes in the early 1980s, had led to a lax approach to the processing of materials used in feed, and that it was possible that infective agents had not been destroyed. Other theories were also advanced, for example that infection was caused by damage to the immune system of cattle inflicted by pesticides (Purdey, 1996), although there was little evidence to support this thesis.

The UK government's reaction was initially to play down the link between scrapie and BSE. Any association with a similar disease in humans – CJD – was also denied. CJD affected a small number of mainly elderly people in the UK every year. Nevertheless, a scientific committee established by the government in the late 1980s did recommend a series of precautionary measures, including a ruminant feed ban, cattle, sheep and deer not being allowed protein derived from other animals, a ban on specified bovine offal (cattle brains, spinal cord, thymus, spleen, intestines and tonsils) in human food, and a limited compensation scheme that gave farmers with BSE-infected cattle half the market price for keeping them out of the food chain.

The government's proposals were widely criticised. In particular, it was argued that the specified bovine offal ban should apply to all cattle rather than just those aged six months and over. The compensation scheme was attacked – even by the DoH's own medical advisors – for not giving enough incentive to farmers to keep sick animals out of the food chain. The calls for a computerised tracking system to identify the movement of healthy and unhealthy animals was rejected (although a scheme was introduced in Northern Ireland and has since been extended across the UK). There were also worries about the cross-infection of feed for cattle and sheep from that given to pigs and poultry which contained protein derived from animals. Further criticism was levelled at the Agriculture Ministry's control of the research process, which ruled out projects that might reveal the true extent of BSE infection in the British cattle herd or that might shed light on the transmission process. Proposals to survey cattle brains randomly at slaughter were rejected, while research into the transmission of BSE to dogs was actually stopped by the ministry when preliminary findings suggested a link between BSE and CJD. But the issue would not go away, as other countries became worried about the safety of British beef. There were also revelations about the failure of abattoirs and feed mills to implement the BSE regulations, and about the illegal use of banned animal feed.

Eventually, in March 1996, the UK government admitted that a new variant of CJD had been identified affecting younger people. The European Union immediately banned the export of British beef. The industry would have collapsed completely had it not been for the introduction of a slaughter scheme aimed at restoring public confidence in beef. Not until July 1999 was this ban fully lifted, by which time over 40 people had died from the new form of CJD. Evidence given to a public inquiry into the handling of the BSE crisis illustrated the breathtaking complacency of ministers and officials (*The BSE Inquiry*, 2000).

It was clear from the evidence given to the inquiry that commercial considerations took priority over public health, even though the beef industry would have been less severely damaged had earlier steps been taken to confront the problem. Relationships between the DoH and the Ministry of Agriculture were poor, and the latter department was shown to be introspective and secretive in its handling of the crisis. Other inquiries displayed the European Commission in a poor light. Although it had often been cast in the role of the defender of public health with regard to this particular issue, it transpired that the Commission had itself mishandled the crisis by thwarting research into the BSE–CJD link, yielding to pressure from the UK Ministry of Agriculture and generally downplaying the health risk to avoid any disruption of the beef market (European Parliament, 1997).

The European Commission subsequently reorganised its responsibilities for health, renaming the relevant directorate as Consumer Policy and Health Protection and bringing scientific committees on issues such as pesticides, veterinary matters and food under a new body within this directorate. At the same time, the Office of Inspection and Veterinary and Phytosanitary Controls, which examined the implementation of food hygiene standards, was transferred to the Consumer Policy and Health Protection Directorate. Following a restructuring of the Commission in 1999, a new portfolio, Health and Consumer Protection, was formed, with the aim of integrating departments concerned with consumer policy, food and veterinary matters, animal and plant health and public health (see Chapter 4). Later in the same year, the President of the Commission endorsed the idea of an independent European Food Authority and announced that policy proposals and an action plan would be published in due course.

## Food Safety Regulation in the UK

The BSE crisis also added momentum to campaigns for more effective food regulation in the UK. Earlier food crises, such as the salmonella in eggs issue of the 1980s, had caused political problems for the government and widespread public distrust (see Agriculture Committee, 1989; Doig, 1990). This crisis, along with others during this period – for example concerns about listeria in cheese and pâté – led to the Food Safety Act of 1990, which established a new committee to monitor the microbiological safety of food (although ironically, only a few years earlier in 1983, the government had abolished its Food Hygiene Advisory Committee in an effort to reduce regulation in this area). The 1990 Act also gave new powers to EHOs in this field, including the immediate closure of outlets on public health grounds. In addition, the maximum fine for breaking food safety laws was increased. Other measures included the registration of food outlets and compulsory training for food-handlers.

The legislation was, however, criticised by food campaigners, who argued that the legal provision provided no real deterrence and that the policing of the Act depended on under-resourced environmental health departments. Indeed, an Audit Commission (1990) report at the time revealed the scale of their task: it found that one in eight premises inspected by EHOs posed a risk to health. Furthermore, there was a belief that food outlet registration lacked clear criteria and that a more rigorous licensing system to prevent those with poor standards from trading was needed. Finally, the Act was criticised for giving ministers the power to regulate food technology, making it easier to legalise controversial processes such as food irradiation without adequate public scrutiny and debate.

In addition to these legislative provisions, MAFF was reorganised, with the creation of a Food Safety Directorate advised by a consumer advisory panel. This did not, however, satisfy critics, who pointed out that the directorate operated within MAFF and that the advisory panel excluded those consumer groups and food campaigners which had in the past been most critical of the ministry's policies on food safety. Other measures were subsequently introduced, arising mainly from the European Commission directives, notably the Red Meat Directive of 1991, the 1993 Directive on Food Hygiene and a further Directive of 1994 covering minced meat and meat preparations.

The Red Meat Directive prompted changes in the regulation of slaughterhouses, culminating in the creation of a national Meat Hygiene Service in 1995, which took over the local authority's role in meat inspection and the implementation of hygiene and welfare standards in slaughterhouses. Meanwhile, the Meat Products (Hygiene) regulations of 1994 required the approval of premises producing meat products and set out specific conditions relating to layout, construction, facilities, hygiene and the handling of food products. This was followed by the Food Hygiene (General Food Hygiene) regulations of 1995, which required food businesses to assess potential hazards and control them. In addition, member states were encouraged to develop specific codes of practice on hygiene for each part of the food industry.

Food businesses were encouraged to use a system known as Hazard Analysis Critical Control Point (HACCP). This involves the identification of hazards associated with each stage of the food production and handling process, the assessment of risks, the identification of the stages at which controls are critical to safety, the listing of preventive measures that can be taken to tackle each hazard, and the maintenance of effective monitoring, recording and verification procedures. HACCP was endorsed by the Codex Alimentarius Commission, the WHO and the European Community as a means of preventing foodborne disease (Codex Alimentarius, 1992; WHO, 1993; *Official Journal of the European Communities*, 1993) Even so, the implementation of HACCP has been slow (see, for example, Scottish Office, 1997; Agriculture Committee, 1998). This is because its adoption has not been mandatory. Implementation has also been affected by a lack of resources and a limited awareness of the system among those expected to implement it (Ehiri *et al.*, 1997; Ehiri and Morris, 1998).

In spite of these developments, the pressure on government to improve food safety regulation continued. Between 1987 and 1997, the number of cases of food poisoning reported rose from 58.3 to 179.6 per 100,000 people (Agriculture Committee, 1998). Although partly the result of an increased willingness to report such infection, these figures were seen as an indicator of deteriorating food standards. In addition a number of serious outbreaks of infectious disease attracted particular concern. Much attention in the late 1990s focused on incidents involving *Escherichia coli* 0157, a bacterium that can have a devastating impact, particularly upon weak, ill or elderly people and young children. Those who succumb suffer dreadful symptoms that can include haemorrhagic colitis (bloody diarrhoea), kidney failure and death. The most serious outbreak so far occurred in central Scotland in 1996 and was traced to a local butcher. Five hundred people were affected, of whom 20 subsequently died. The inquiry into the incident, chaired by Professor Hugh Pennington, called for more research into the disease and recommended better surveillance and reporting systems for food poisoning, improved co-ordination plans between health and local authorities on the issue, and tougher controls on premises handling meat products, including a licensing system for butchers' shops (Scottish Office, 1997).

# A Food Standards Agency

The cumulative pressure for tougher regulation was by now irresistible. The Major government, in spite of its commitment to deregulation, eventually agreed that a new regulatory body would be necessary to restore public confidence in the safety of food. The proposal, however, fell short of a new and independent food agency, which many campaigners now called for and which was endorsed by the Labour Party, then in opposition. The Labour leadership invited Professor Philip James to develop proposals for such an agency. His report argued that the new agency should put the public interest first and be removed from political pressure and interference from vested interests; that it should be a statutory non-departmental body with executive powers, accountable to Parliament; that it should be open and transparent in its work; that it should have a remit that covered the whole food chain, 'from the plough to the plate' (James, 1997, p. 5); and that its responsibility should cover not only microbiological and chemical safety, but also the nutritional quality of diets, GM foods, novel foods and processes, aspects of animal health affecting food, food labelling and public education on food matters. James recommended that a new agency should be to some extent modelled on the Health and Safety Commission, albeit with more scope for public involvement and direct Parliamentary accountability, and should take over all those aspects of MAFF and the DoH that dealt with food standards and safety.

Following Labour's victory in the 1997 General Election, James' interim proposals had a much greater chance of becoming a reality. Once in office, however, the Labour leadership was pressured by farmers, food manufacturers and retailers, as well as civil servants within MAFF, the DoH and other relevant government agencies, to move away from James' proposals. The food industry was particularly worried about giving the new agency responsibility for nutrition and labelling. The Royal Society also advised that nutritional advice should be located elsewhere. Meanwhile, civil servants argued that the removal of food responsibility from government departments to an independent agency would actually undermine accountability because that body was not headed by a minister. They also argued that the change would produce a serious dislocation in the short term as new responsibilities were reallocated.

In the meantime, the Blair government introduced a number of interim initiatives, including a commitment to greater openness on food issues within MAFF. This was accompanied by an increase in the lay membership of MAFF's advisory committees. In addition, a joint food and safety standards group was established to co-ordinate the work of MAFF and the DoH, along with a joint Risk Communication Unit. Also, the Chief Medical Officer was given a higher profile in relation to the co-ordination of food and health policy. In the event, and after some delay, the Blair government establish a Food Standards Agency (FSA) with powers relating to all aspects of food, including nutritional information and labelling (Cm 3830, 1998). Criticism, however, persisted. Some believed that the independence of the new agency could be compromised by being accountable to Parliament via the Secretary of State for Health and by the granting of reserve ministerial powers to restrict the FSA. Also, the DoH retained responsibility for nutritional advice and other public health aspects of nutrition policy. This confusing allocation of responsibility for nutrition was criticised by, among others, the House of Commons Agriculture Committee (1998). MAFF kept its responsibilities for farming and animal husbandry, including pesticide regulation and veterinary medicine, although the control of animal feed became a joint responsibility between the Ministry and the new agency. The government also maintained that the FSA would be able to intervene in farming matters where MAFF was evidently not exercising its responsibility effectively.

The Food Standards Act, which created the statutory basis for the FSA, eventually became law in 1999. One of the main reasons for this delay was the controversy over the funding of the agency. MAFF argued that the tax-payer should contribute to the running costs of the agency, whereas the Treasury believed its costs should be fully funded by the food industry. The draft legislation contained proposals to impose a flat rate levy on all food businesses. However, following a lobbying campaign by the industry, supported by food safety campaigners who believed that the independence of the agency would be compromised if it were industry funded, the government decided that the agency would be financed out of general taxation.

Interestingly, the delay in establishing the FSA bore some similarity to the problem experienced with the implementation of the earlier Pennington Report, which, although relating primarily to Scotland, had implications for the rest of the UK (Scottish Office, 1997). One of Pennington's key recommendations – the licensing of butchers not covered by the Meat Products (Hygiene) Regulations 1994 – was not immediately implemented (although a revised scheme will come into effect in the year 2000). Little progress was made with regard to other important recommendations, such as those relating to education about handling and cooking food and the separation of raw meat and other food products. Some additional funding was given to encourage the implementation of hazard analysis, but this was widely regarded as insufficient given the scale of the task. One explanation for the limited response to the Pennington Report is that because it related primarily to a Scottish food poisoning outbreak, it was easier for the authorities in England and Wales to play down its findings and recommendations. Another possible reason is that the report was overtaken by the creation of the new FSA and that the full implementation of Pennington's recommendations could not be taken forward until this was in place. A further likely explanation for the delay was, however, the opposition from farming industry and meat trade to the imposition of heavier and more costly regulation of their businesses.

# Conclusion

Pressure for change has been evident in the field of food safety and nutrition, manifested not only in a call for better health education, but also in the demands for greater regulation of commercial activities in relation to food. As we have seen, sections of the food industry have responded unilaterally to this pressure by taking steps to improve food standards, often to the extent of going beyond minimum legislative requirements. Meanwhile, political pressure on UK government, and within supranational bodies such as the European Commission and the WHO, has initiated new efforts to promote a healthier diet and safer food.

However, there are powerful counter-pressures that have limited the impact of these initiatives. Harmonisation in Europe, while masquerading as improved regulation, has often worked in the opposite direction, for example inhibiting initiatives to improve nutritional labelling and extending the legitimate range of food additives. Meanwhile, the Common Agricultural Policy continues to undermine public health by encouraging a high-fat diet. Moreover, international free trade agreements have created a regime that has given rise to additional competitive pressures to reduce rather than raise food standards. Another countervailing factor is the power of the agriculture and food industries, which remain well placed to lobby against policy initiatives that they perceive as being against their commercial interests.

Policy development in this field has been and will continue to be shaped by other factors too. First is the traditional separation of food/farming policy from health policy within government, which has in the past often inhibited effective policies on food and health. It is clear that an integrated approach is required in order to ensure that food policy is consistent with and conducive to the achievement of health priorities. In the British context, it remains to be seen whether or not the FSA will be able to challenge the dominant policy paradigm that emphasises food security and commercial profitability. Second, the role of scientific evidence in the development of policy is crucial. Yet in spite of the volume of research findings on nutrition and health, and on chemical and microbiological threats to health within the food chain, the evidence base remains in many respects underdeveloped. This means that many policies are based on shaky empirical foundations and that, as we saw in relation to nutrition policies, the legitimacy of policies can be undermined. Clear evidence often does not emerge until after intervention has taken place. Worries about GM food, bovine somatotropin, and food irradiation may be difficult to prove, but given the potentially catastrophic implications should things go wrong, theoretical risks must be taken very seriously. This was certainly the central lesson of the BSE crisis.

This leads on to a final point: food scandals and crises have exerted an enormous impact on food policy in recent years, but they are not an efficient way of identifying risks or developing effective strategies. All stakeholders in the food and health debate – including the food and farming industries – would benefit from a more considered approach that *prevented* such food crises, that elevated health considerations to the same importance as commercial considerations, and that sought to encourage a more open and informative dialogue with consumers about risk, rather than leaving them to the mercy of media sensationalism.

# 9

# Alcohol, Tobacco and Drugs

The recreational use of drugs is linked to a range of health problems as well as social problems such as crime and violence, which can in turn affect health. This chapter examines the public health implications of legal and illegal addictions, the range of possible interventions and the reasons why particular policies have been pursued and others rejected.

## Tobacco and Health

Tobacco has gone in and out of fashion since it was first introduced into Britain in the sixteenth century. Its popularity increased sharply in the early part of the twentieth century, reaching a peak in the 1950s, when over three-quarters of the male population in the UK smoked tobacco. Although smoking declined in the second half of the century – to less than 30 per cent of the adult population in the 1990s – it remained popular among specific population subgroups: in 1996 around 15 per cent of girls aged 11–15 admitted to smoking regularly compared with 11 per cent in 1982 (ONS, 1997c).

### The Health Risks of Smoking

The dangers of tobacco smoking are well documented. Over 110 000 deaths annually in the UK (HEA, 1991) can be attributed to the habit. Smoking is associated with 24 different causes of death, including cancer, for example that of the lung, mouth and larynx, respiratory disease, such as chronic obstructive pulmonary disease, and circulatory disease, including stroke and coronary heart disease (Doll *et al.*, 1994a). Around one in six deaths are smoking related (HEA, 1991), and it is estimated that half of all regular smokers will die from the habit (Doll *et al.*, 1994a). Smoking is also a major cause of morbidity, responsible for over 225,000 hospital admissions each year (HEA, 1991). In total, the social cost of smoking in England and Wales –

including the cost to the NHS, social security payments to those incapaci-
tated by smoking-related diseases, and the cost of fires caused by smokers –
has been estimated at £1.2 billion per year (Back and Godfrey, 1997).

People have been aware of the health consequences of smoking for almost
as long as the habit has been practised. In the seventeenth century, enthusiasm among the medical profession for tobacco as a panacea gave way to
concern about its adverse effects. Evidence was provided by autopsies
performed on smokers who had died prematurely:

> One Jackson, who frequented Little Britain Street, has died suddenly, and being
> opened, it was judged by the surgeons that it was from the smoke of tobacco, which
> he took insatiably. (Calendar of State Papers, 29 December 1601, quoted by
> Harrison, 1986, p. 554).

Medical opinion hardened further against the recreational use of tobacco
following King James I's *Counterblaste to Tobacco* (King James I, 1616). This
monarch-inspired anti-smoking campaign was accompanied by a higher tax
on tobacco and the licensing of tobacco retail outlets (see Harrison, 1986). Yet
it was far less draconian than some approaches adopted elsewhere, notably
in Russia, China and the Ottoman Empire, where smokers were subjected to
severe and humiliating punishments if caught indulging in the habit. In
seventeenth-century Russia, for example, people caught smoking were muti-
lated, and purveyors of tobacco were often flogged to death (see Corti, 1931;
Skrabanek, 1994). Despite such measures, tobacco smoking flourished, and
governments soon found themselves highly dependent on the trade. Tobacco
raised vital tax revenues, and provided other economic benefits such as
export revenue, jobs and profits. So although its harmful effects were already
known, the trade was rarely challenged. Indeed, when new epidemiological
evidence on the health impact of smoking tobacco was presented in the
second half of the twentieth century, it took a massive political campaign
over several decades to persuade policy makers to tackle the problem (see
Pollock, 1999).

During the 1950s, the British government privately acknowledged new
evidence linking tobacco smoking to lung cancer (Doll and Hill, 1950) and
other diseases (Doll and Hill, 1956). An official committee chaired by the
government actuary in 1954 concluded that there was a causal association
between smoking and cancer of the lung. But concerns about tax revenue led
the government to adopt a much more cautious position in public and ministers denied that there was any firm evidence of an association, calling instead
for more research. Despite pressure from some backbench MPs, the government refused to intervene, although by 1956 it had publicly acknowledged an
association between smoking and lung cancer. The tension within govern-

ment was, however, evident when the Chancellor of the Exchequer let it slip at a private meeting that 'we at the Treasury do not want too many people to stop smoking' (*Hansard*, 1957) Following the publication of a Medical Research Council report in 1957, calls for a substantial health education campaign and a ban on advertising were rejected. Pressure increased, however, during the early 1960s, following a report from the Royal College of Physicians (RCP, 1962) that summarised the compelling evidence on smoking and health. In response, a small health education campaign was launched, and, following a change of government, a ban on the television advertising of cigarettes was imposed in 1965. Efforts by backbench MPs to extend this ban to all forms of tobacco advertising were blocked by government and the tobacco industry.

A turning point came in early 1971 with the publication of a second report from the RCP on the dangers of smoking and the formation of Action on Smoking and Health (ASH). Unlike the RCP, whose influence operated chiefly through élite medicopolitical networks, ASH was a high-profile, media-oriented campaigning organisation (Popham, 1981). It quickly established good Parliamentary and media links, and was regarded as being extremely effective in promoting the antismoking message. But the tobacco industry proved stronger. Despite overwhelming evidence linking smoking and disease, the UK government would not adopt policies – such as higher taxation, a comprehensive advertising ban, and a ban on smoking in public places – advocated by the antismoking lobby. Throughout the 1970s, attempts by backbench MPs to legislate were frustrated by the lobbying efforts of the tobacco industry.

Meanwhile within government, the Treasury and the Trade, Industry and Employment departments opposed tougher policies on smoking (Taylor, 1984). Instead of legislation, the government introduced a series of voluntary agreements on issues such as tobacco advertising and sponsorship, health warnings and tar levels. From time to time, these agreements were renegotiated, usually in response to some new revelation about the health risks of tobacco (see RCP, 1977; Calnan, 1984). The voluntary agreements were heavily criticised by antismoking campaigners, who saw them as a means by which the tobacco industry could buy time and safeguard its financial future by diversifying into other non-tobacco product areas (including, ironically, life insurance), producing low-tar tobacco products and marketing their products more aggressively to Third World countries. Consequently, the smoking rate in developing countries rose, and currently around one in three tobacco-related deaths is in the developing world. According to Richard Peto, Professor of Medical Statistics at Oxford University, 70 per cent of the then 10 million deaths attributable to tobacco by 2025 will be in the Third World (*Independent*, 1997).

## Smoking Policy in the 1980s and 90s

During the 1980s, the antismoking campaign was reinforced by the BMA, which launched a high-profile attack on government policy and the tobacco industry (BMA, 1986a). The publication of a further report from the RCP (1983a) also strengthened the hand of the antismoking lobby. The anti-interventionist approach of the Thatcher government, however, created obstacles for health campaigners; in particular, the prospects of a tobacco advertising ban nose-dived in the context of this government's endorsement of commercial freedom. Even so, the Thatcher government did raise tobacco duty – which helped to reduce consumption through higher price – and increased resources for antismoking education programmes. Subsequently, the Major government adopted explicit targets for reducing smoking in its *Health of the Nation* strategy (Cm 1986, 1992). The strategy aimed to cut the death rate from lung cancer by at least 30 per cent in men under 75 and 15 per cent in women under 75 by the year 2010 (using 1990 as a baseline); to reduce the prevalence of cigarette smoking in men and women aged 16 or over to no more than 20 per cent by the year 2000; to reduce the consumption of cigarettes by 40 per cent by the year 2000; to ensure that at least one third of women smokers stopped smoking at the start of their pregnancy; and to reduce the prevalence of smoking among 11–15-year-olds by at least a third by 1994.

As already noted in Chapter 4, these targets proved difficult to achieve, and in the case of smoking among teenage girls, the trend actually moved in the opposite direction. The Major government did commit £12m to an anti-smoking advertising campaign and pledged to increase the tobacco tax by 3 per cent above the rate of inflation each year. Antismoking campaigners, however, believed that stronger policies were necessary, particularly with regard to the promotion of tobacco products. The UK policy on tobacco promotion appeared weak compared with the approach adopted by some other countries. In Norway, a comprehensive advertising ban was imposed in 1975 (see Baggott, 1988), and others, such as France, Canada, Australia and New Zealand, later followed suit. Research into the effects of tobacco advertising on children (see, for example, Goddard, 1990; Hastings *et al.*, 1994; While *et al.*, 1996) created pressure for a similar policy in the UK. Even the DoH's own review of advertising bans showed that they were effective in reducing smoking (see DoH, 1992; Health Committee, 1993).

Encouraged by this, MPs introduced a Tobacco Advertising Bill in 1993, although they were again frustrated by the tobacco lobby. Instead of legislation, another set of voluntary agreements was negotiated, which included a cut in shopfront advertising, tougher health warnings on adverts and a ban on advertisement in teenage magazines. By now, however, the industry was facing a more serious attack from the European Union. In 1989, the British government had to concede to European standards on tobacco labelling, which included the introduction of stronger and larger health warnings on tobacco products. A draft directive aimed at banning advertising and sponsorship ensued, which was strongly opposed by the industry and by some member states, including the UK. Eventually, the European Union agreed to ban all forms of tobacco promotion by 2006 and in the meantime, the UK introduced its own plans to ban tobacco advertising (see below).

This is unlikely to be the end of the story. At the time of writing, the tobacco industry is challenging the legality of both the UK and European bans (see Sheldon, 1998). It should be noted that the ban was invoked under Article 100A of the 1987 Single European Act and that the Union has no powers to harmonise health legislation (although it has since acquired new competences in this area – see Chapter 4). Alternatively, cases could be brought on grounds of freedom of speech (to the European Court of Human Rights) or on grounds of unfair restraint of trade (under the auspices of the WTO). Moreover, despite the European Union's efforts to combat smoking, it is often found facing both ways, as reflected in the subsidies granted to European Union tobacco producers (Joosens and Raw, 1995). Efforts to harmonise the tobacco tax across the European Union have been criticised for inhibiting countries from implementing a higher rate of taxation on tobacco products, while the relaxation of border controls within the European Union has encouraged cross-border purchasing and the illegal smuggling of tobacco (and alcohol), leading to a lower price and the avoidance and evasion of tax.

The European Union is not alone in facing internal tension on the tobacco issue. The Blair government, which came to office with a strong antismoking policy, was soon accused of bowing to pressure from the industry and its allies. There was controversy over funds donated to the Labour Party by the businessman Bernie Ecclestone, the Vice President of Formula One motor-racing's governing body, which some saw as an attempt to influence the government's position on tobacco sponsorship in motor racing. This was strenuously denied by Ecclestone, his organisation, the Labour Party and government ministers, and the donation was returned. When the European directive on tobacco promotion was finally agreed, however, sports and events organised at an international level (a category that included Formula One motor racing) had been granted an extra three-year period (2003–6) to comply.

## Passive Smoking

The Blair government was also criticised for diluting its policy on passive smoking following lobbying from industrial interests. As Chapman and colleagues have noted (1990), the tobacco industry fears the passive smoking issue because it legitimises smoking as a social rather than simply an individual health problem, opens up the possibility of widespread litigation (and the introduction of 'defensive' bans by employers, encouraged by their insurers) and directly reduces the opportunity to smoke (see also Berridge, 1999). All this is very bad news for the industry and explains its ferocious response. When in 1988 the Independent Scientific Committee on Smoking and Health claimed that several hundred people a year were dying from lung cancer as a result of exposure to other people's smoke (DHSS, 1988), the industry and its allies launched a massive counter-attack on its findings. The subsequent publication of the US Environmental Protection Agency (1992) report on involuntary smoking and other findings (see below) received a similar response.

Conclusive evidence on passive smoking is difficult to obtain as people encounter tobacco smoke in a wide range of settings. Moreover, the presence of other carcinogens, such as radon, in the environment, complicates the calculation of harm resulting from exposure to other people's tobacco smoke (see Flew, 1994; Nilsson, 1999). Yet there is a growing body of circumstantial evidence that passive smoking can contribute to a range of diseases including lung cancer, heart disease, respiratory disease and ear infection, children and pregnant women being particularly at risk. The UK Scientific Committee on Tobacco and Health (1998) found that living with a smoker raised the risk of developing lung cancer and heart disease by around a quarter (see also Hackshaw *et al.*, 1997; Law *et al.*, 1997). It also estimated that one in five cot deaths was attributable to the mother smoking, and that where both parents smoked, the child had at least a 50 per cent greater risk of asthma. In a further report, the WHO found an increase in the risk of lung cancer among those who breathed in other people's tobacco smoke (WHO, 1998b), while other researchers found that passive smoking could increase the risk of heart disease by around a quarter (He *et al.*, 1999).

The Major government had previously set a target that 80 per cent of public places should have an antismoking policy. This policy was taken forward by a voluntary code of practice on smoking in public places (DoE, 1991b) and guidance on how to tackle the problem of passive smoking in the workplace (Health and Safety Executive, 1992). Although a smoking ban had been voluntarily introduced by many employers, antismoking campaigners in the UK argued that a legislative ban, already adopted by such countries as Australia and Belgium, was now necessary. The Blair government initially appeared willing to consider banning smoking in all public places, including pubs and restaurants. After discussions with these businesses, however, it adopted an approach not dissimilar to that of its predecessor. A Charter was introduced to encourage establishments to introduce their own measures to improve indoor air quality, including for example the use of more efficient ventilation systems. Meanwhile, a Code of Practice was considered as a means of improving the environment for non-smokers at work.

## The White Paper on Smoking

The Blair government set out its policy in a White Paper (Cm 4177, 1998). The main targets were to reduce smoking among schoolchildren from 13 per cent to 9 per cent or less by 2010, with a fall to 11 per cent to be achieved by 2005; to cut adult smoking in all social classes from 28 to 24 per cent, and in the interim to 26 per cent by 2005; and to reduce the percentage of women smoking during pregnancy from 23 to 15 per cent by the year 2010, with a fall to 18 per cent by 2005. New commitments included a plan to raise tobacco tax above the rate of inflation (subsequently in 1999 a further commitment was made to earmark tobacco tax increases for preventing and treating smoking-related diseases), a closer surveillance of tobacconists to combat sales to children and a £60m fund to encourage health authorities and professionals to persuade adults to give up the habit. A further £50m health education campaign against smoking was also proposed. Finally, the government announced the supply of nicotine patches to those who could not afford them, to help them to quit smoking. It also agreed to implement the European Union ban on tobacco promotion and proposed a ban on tobacco advertising in the UK from December 1999.

But would the White Paper be fully implemented? Antismoking campaigners were concerned that the Blair government was backsliding when it later extended the time given to the tobacco industry to comply with aspects of the UK advertising ban. Their fears were also raised when plans to increase the tobacco tax were scaled down during 1999. Meanwhile, doubts remained about the probable impact of the government's policy on smoke-free areas. In addition, some believe that the strategy fails to take into account the circumstances of those on low incomes, who are disproportionately represented among smokers. As Graham (1993a) and Dorsett and Marsh (1998) have shown, those in poverty, particularly lone parents and single mothers, find it more difficult to stop smoking. Indeed, Marsh and McKay (1994) argued that raising the price of cigarettes may increase the hardship of poor people because they do not respond to the price disincentive and end up spending more of their income on tobacco. This has, however, been contested by others, who argue that lower socio-economic groups are more responsive to a change in price and that tax increases are therefore a vital part of a package to reduce smoking across the board (Townsend *et al.*, 1994). A further criticism is that tobacco companies will discover a way to circumvent the advertising ban (through a 'cross-branding' of consumer goods, for example) or will be able to overturn it in the courts.

However, the courts may well decide against the industry, as they have done in recent years, particularly in the USA. The tobacco industry has faced litigation from smokers with smoking-related diseases. Most cases have centred on allegations that the industry knowingly sold a product injurious to health and conspired to conceal the facts about smoking. Others cases have been brought against employers for illnesses caused or exacerbated by passive smoking. For antismoking campaigners, litigation has brought two main benefits. It has hit tobacco companies financially: in the USA, the industry has been forced to pay billions of dollars in compensation to lung cancer victims. Meanwhile, passive smoking cases have encouraged the development of no-smoking areas, which have implications for the industry's sales and profitability. An added bonus for campaigners has been revelations about the tobacco industry's resistance to government intervention. In several legal cases in the USA, internal documents have been obtained that reveal how the industry sought to buy the influence of scientists, opinion formers and politicians over the years (see Glantz *et al.*, 1996). These revelations not only provide a powerful incentive for governments to regulate the industry further, but, by exposing the methods used to block government intervention in the past, could also undermine the industry's future efforts at resistance.

Finally, it is increasingly recognised that action on a global scale is needed to limit tobacco consumption because the industry operates at a global level and can undermine national efforts to control it. The European Union ban on advertising is one example of how nations can come together to tackle the industry. In addition, the WHO introduced strategies and action plans on tobacco (see WHO Regional Office for Europe, 1993b; WHO, 1996, 1997c), although until recently these posed no real threat to the tobacco trade. The WHO initiative on tobacco control was not well resourced and relied mainly on persuading member states to adopt a stronger policy. But it does now seem that tobacco has a much higher priority. In 1998, WHO launched its Tobacco Free Initiative, which seeks to introduce more effective global controls, including the development of an international framework convention on tobacco. However, the extent to which this new global initiative will be able to succeed in the face of opposition from the powerful tobacco industry and its allies remains to be seen.

## Alcohol Policy

Alcohol is also a popular and legally available drug, although it differs from tobacco in a number of important ways. The adverse consequences of alcohol are more diverse, raising issues relating to law and order, for example. It is more popular than tobacco, indulged in by the vast majority (in the UK around 90 per cent) of the adult population. Unlike tobacco, if consumed in moderation and in certain appropriate environments, alcohol can be at worst harmless and at best a considerable benefit to health and social wellbeing.

The adverse consequences of alcohol have been documented by several authoritative reports over the past 20 years or so (see, for example, Royal College of Psychiatrists, 1979, 1986; Royal College of General Practitioners, 1986; RCP, 1987; Faculty of Public Health Medicine/RCP, 1991; All Party Group on Alcohol Misuse, 1995). These include 28,000 premature deaths in England and Wales annually (from a range of causes including suicide, murder, death from fire, accidents and drownings; Anderson, 1988). In addition, over a quarter of male hospital admissions are alcohol related, including those relating to treatment for injuries sustained in accidents and violent incidents, and longer-term physical and mental illness due to alcohol abuse (Luke, 1998). There appears to be an association between the amount of alcohol consumed by society as a whole and the level of problems experienced by that society. Hence the rising toll of alcohol-related problems in the second half of the twentieth century was associated with a doubling of consumption between 1950 and 1980 (although total consumption has levelled off since this time). Studies have revealed an association between overall per capita consumption and the level of alcohol-related problems (see Colhoun *et al.*, 1997; Her and Rehm, 1998).

Although the overall level of consumption is problematic, this has tended to be obscured by other more specific concerns. Almost two million people, more than 6 per cent of men and 2 per cent of women, consume more than what is regarded as a safe level of alcohol – 50 units of alcohol a week in the case of men and 35 units for women (a unit being approximately equivalent to half a pint of beer or lager or a 125 ml glass of wine). Meanwhile, much anxiety has been expressed about alcohol consumption by children and young people (BMA, 1999a). There is no clear evidence to suggest that more children are drinking alcohol – surveys consistently find that the majority of those aged 16 have tried alcoholic drinks (Lister Sharp, 1994) – and there has been a fairly small increase (from 13 to 17 per cent between 1988 and 1994) in the percentage of 11–16-year-olds reporting that they consume alcohol on a weekly basis (Goddard, 1996). There are, however, some indications that young drinkers are consuming a larger quantity. (Newcombe *et al.*, 1995; OPCS, 1996) and are more likely to experience alcohol problems (British Paediatric Association/RCP, 1995). Finally, drink-driving has been regarded for many years as a particularly serious social problem. Despite the introduction of roadside breath testing in the 1960s, drink-driving is held responsible for over 500 deaths in Great Britain every year (see Chapter 7).

## Tackling Alcohol Problems

Alcohol problems have a long history. The first law restricting the sale of alcohol in England was passed in the fifteenth century amid concerns about public disorder. In the eighteenth century, there was much anxiety about gin drinking, as famously illustrated in Hogarth's etching *Gin Lane*. Later, in the Victorian age, the consumption of alcohol was high by modern standards, drunkenness was widespread, and there was an enormous toll of alcohol-related disease and mortality (see Chapter 2). The tightening of regulations on alcohol sale and consumption in the first three decades of the twentieth century played a vital role in reducing the scale of the alcohol problem. War, economic depression and alternative leisure pursuits such as the cinema all played a part in weaning the population away from abusing its favourite drug. Consequently, by the 1950s, alcohol abuse was seen as a specific problem of a small minority of the population, who required treatment and rehabilitation.

An awareness of a growth in alcohol consumption and problems associated with drinking resurfaced during the 1960s and early 1970s and revived interest in population-based prevention initiatives (Baggott, 1990). Policies such as an improved regulation of the availability, price and promotion of alcohol products were supported by a range of interest groups. Most vociferous were the organisations that had survived since the heyday of the Victorian and Edwardian campaigns against alcohol – the temperance societies. Although much reduced in status and influence, these organisations remained active in publicising the dangers of alcohol and calling for greater regulation. Their concern was echoed by voluntary organisations that had emerged to provide counselling, advice and support to those suffering from alcohol problems. But these groups were under-resourced and carried little political weight. More significant were the views of professional organisations whose members dealt with problems related to alcohol abuse. These included health professionals (particularly psychiatrists, GPs and those working in accident and emergency departments), social workers, probation officers, magistrates and the police, all of whom began to raise the issue within their representative organisations and professional bodies, and through their membership of expert advisory bodies (Thom, 1999).

Alcohol problems began to attract the attention of the media during the 1970s. Although the image of the 'down and out' alcoholic persisted, there was an increasing challenge to the stereotype. Media coverage of alcohol-related problems, such as drink-driving, violence and disorder, and the specific problems of under-age drinking, served to raise a much broader public awareness about alcohol problems. The drinks industry, traditionally a very powerful lobby, was worried by what it saw as a fresh attempt to demonise alcohol. Although the modern anti-alcohol campaign lacked the overtly moralist tones of the Victorian era, it was potentially more dangerous. The risks of alcohol were now convincingly presented by professionals in scientific terms and highlighted by the media in the context of increasing health consciousness among the public. The drinks industry searched for ways of deflating what was developing into a broad campaign against alcohol, raising the prospect of further legal restrictions on consumption, higher tax and greater control of marketing and promotion.

## The Alcohol Industry Strikes Back

The industry's response was two-pronged. First, it did not seek to ignore the consequences of alcohol abuse but acknowledged that there were problems that urgently needed to be addressed. It established its own research network and supported particular strategies that did not undermine its profitability. Central to this was the construction of alcohol problems as primarily individual rather than social in origin. This shifted the focus away from population-based intervention, which aimed to reduce the level of consumption or to promote a change in the drinking culture and environment, towards strategies geared to educating the individual about the risks of alcohol abuse. At the same time, the industry sought to minimise the criticism of its practices by attempting to self-regulate its more controversial activities. This included the production of codes of good practice and training programmes for the licensed trade on issues such as under-age drinking. In 1989, these initiatives were consolidated. The Portman Group, created by the largest drink companies, developed prevention initiatives in relation to drink-driving, young people and alcohol, and violence on licensed premises. It worked with the police and the voluntary sector, commissioned research and published its own reports on how to deal with specific alcohol problems. The Portman Group also acquired a self-regulatory role, particularly with regard to marketing and retail issues, and in connection with this implemented a special code of practice on alcoholic drinks advertising.

Self-regulation was used to deflect criticism and pre-empt direct regulation. At the same time, the industry used its political leverage to crush any attempt to introduce policies that threatened its profitability while also seeking to persuade government to relax some aspects of its alcohol policy (see Baggott, 1990). The industry has always maintained a strong Parliamentary presence, including MPs with relevant constituency interests as well as those employed as advisors and consultants. Although the rules on the disclosure of MPs' interests have been tightened and a ban on paid advocacy imposed, the industry still has powerful friends in Parliament.

The industry is well represented in Whitehall, having good contacts with most departments, ranging from the Home Office and the DoH to the Department of Trade and Industry, the Treasury and the Ministry of Agriculture. It has been able to put its case at the highest level of government, including the Prime Minister's office when necessary. In the late 1970s, when a government think-tank undertook a review of the problem of alcohol abuse, its report was suppressed largely as a result of industry pressure, although a leaked copy was later published in Stockholm (Central Policy Review Staff, 1982). The UK government rejected the report's strong recommendations (which included maintaining the real price of alcohol and a cross-departmental strategy to combat alcohol problems), producing instead a rather anodyne report that painstakingly avoided making any serious policy commitment (DHSS, 1981). An even more disturbing sequence of events occurred in the early 1980s, when a junior minister at the DHSS adopted a tougher approach to the drinks and tobacco industries. After senior figures in both industries had expressed their disapproval at the highest level, he was replaced by an MP who had previously been a consultant to the licensed trade.

The industry has not been content with blocking proposals but has actively sought the deregulation of alcohol. It has often criticised the licensing laws for being outdated. But while it is true that our present system owes much to legislation introduced in the first two decades of the twentieth century, which were primarily a means of enhancing Britain's military effort in the First World War, it should not be forgotten that they were successful in countering a high level of alcohol abuse, which is why they were retained. Moreover, the lesson of history is that relaxing the legal control on alcohol has often produced an increase both in consumption and alcohol-related problems (see Baggott, 1986).

The drinks industry has long campaigned for a more flexible approach to alcohol licensing and has been able to count on a number of allies, in particular the tourist and leisure industries, who see greater alcohol availability as a key to greater profitability. These interests have been rewarded with extended hours and the abolition of afternoon breaks for pubs, clubs and restaurants. Other measures have included permission to allow children into licensed premises. The supporters of these changes argue that no harm has resulted, although the evidence is not clear cut (see, for example, Tether and Godfrey, 1990), but this uncertainty did not stop calls for further liberalisation, a policy endorsed by the government's Better Regulation Task Force in 1998.

In the year 2000, the Blair government introduced plans to alter the licensing laws, proposing a dramatic relaxation in those provisions covering hours of sale in England and Wales (Scotland has had a more liberal system since the mid-1970s). The law, however, may become more restrictive in other respects. For example, the police powers to close premises affected by disorder are to be increased. Furthermore, the law governing under-age drinkers may be tightened, although the rules on young people buying alcohol with a meal and allowing children in pubs are to be relaxed. It is also likely that licensees may face stricter conditions when applying for and seeking to renew licences. Local authorities will become responsible for alcohol licensing matters (as is currently the case in Scotland) and may be able to use their powers to influence the level of alcohol problems. In this context, they should perhaps take note of research undertaken in other countries suggesting that both the concentration of outlets in a particular area (Gruenewald *et al.*, 1993) and the prevalence of certain types of outlet (Stockwell *et al.*, 1992) have an adverse effect on the level of alcohol problems.

The drinks industry's influence has been seen in other areas of policy too. Evidence linking moderate alcohol consumption to a reduction in heart disease in certain population subgroups (in particular middle-aged men and postmenopausal women) came to light from the early 1990s (see Jackson *et al.*, 1991; Razay *et al.*, 1992; Doll *et al.*, 1994b; Gronback *et al.*, 1995; Rimm *et al.*, 1996). Bodies such as such as the RCP, the Royal College of Psychiatrists, the Royal College of General Practitioners, the BMA and the WHO were concerned that this should not obscure the fact that alcohol abuse remained a serious problem and that most people would benefit from reducing rather than increasing their consumption (see RCP, 1995). They recommended that the safe drinking limit (as opposed to the heavy drinking level referred to earlier), set at 21 units a week for men and 14 units for women, should remain in force. Other researchers have subsequently cast doubt on the protective effect of alcohol (Hart *et al.*, 1999; Law and Wald, 1999).

The drinks industry argued that the safe limit should be raised. The government was also predisposed to raise the limits as they related to a policy target that was not being met. *The Health of the Nation* strategy aimed to reduce the proportion of men drinking over 21 units of alcohol from 28 per cent in 1990 to 18 per cent by 2005 and to reduce the proportion of women drinking more than 14 units from 11 per cent to 7 per cent. By 1994, the government was not on course for achieving these targets, as 27 per cent of men and 13 per cent of women were drinking beyond the maximum recommended levels.

An interdepartmental committee was established to review the position (DoH, 1995c), the membership of which included representatives from departments with an interest in promoting the drink industry's economic performance. The committee approved a change in the limits, and the DoH subsequently decided to increase the safe limit to 2–3 units per day for women and 3–4 units per day for men, implying an increase in the weekly recommended limit.

Those concerned about the scale of the alcohol problem were critical of the way in which the evidence on moderate drinking had been manipulated, but this was nothing compared with the furore surrounding the treatment of an authoritative report *Alcohol Policy and the Public Good* in 1994 (Edwards *et al.*, 1994). This was produced by a committee of experts to provide a scientific basis for the WHO Regional Office's European action plan on alcohol (WHO Regional Office for Europe, 1993c, 1996). The action plan itself followed earlier initiatives: reducing alcohol consumption was already part of the European *Health for All* strategy and a specific target of reducing alcohol consumption by 25 per cent by the year 2000 had been set (WHO Regional Office for Europe, 1985b). The findings of the *Alcohol Policy and the Public Good* were unacceptable to the drinks industry, largely because they were based upon a philosophy that overall consumption was related to the level of the alcohol problem in society and that reducing consumption was therefore a legitimate policy aim. The report also endorsed specific policies that the industry disliked, such as the use of taxation to control the price of alcohol and legal restrictions on its availability, while claiming that some of the policies endorsed by the industry, such as school-based education and mass public education campaigns, were relatively ineffective. The industry responded by paying a number of academics to submit critical reviews of the report in an effort to undermine its credibility (see *Independent on Sunday*, 1994).

Then along came the 'alcopops' issue. During the mid-1990s, there was much controversy surrounding the marketing of fruit-flavoured alcoholic drinks, which some feared were deliberately targeted at children and young people. The industry denied this, even though the Portman Group itself was openly critical of some of the marketing practices being used. Researchers found that these drinks appealed to young people and that consumption was associated with less-controlled drinking environments, drunkenness and heavy drinking (McKeganey *et al.*, 1996; Hughes *et al.*, 1997). Fearing a public backlash, the industry responded by renaming some of these brands and withdrawing plans for some new products. The Major government was reluctant to intervene, although it did increase excise duty on them in the 1996 Budget, aligning them with other alcoholic drinks. The Blair government initially took a tougher line and examined the case for a ban on alcopop advertisements. The Portman Group responded with a revised code of practice, including a ban on generic soft drink names such as cola or lemonade. Some retailers voluntarily ceased stocking the products while others continued to stock the products but banned in-store promotions.

While the industry managed to avoid a complete ban on alcopops, it now faced an attack on another front. Although the number of deaths and injuries resulting from drink-driving incidents had fallen since the introduction of the breathalyser in the 1960s, there was a widespread feeling among police and road safety pressure groups that more could be done. In particular, the anti-drink-driving lobby began to press for a lower alcohol limit. Other European countries such as France, Belgium and Germany had set a lower limit than the UK (whose limit remained at 80 mg alcohol/100 ml blood), and there was pressure from the European Commission to introduce a standard limit. The Blair government initially appeared keen to respond to these demands. In 1998, it proposed a two-tier limit by which motorists would be guilty of a lesser offence if found to have more than 50 mg/100 ml of alcohol in their bloodstream, with a tougher penalty for those over the current 80 mg/100 ml limit. This, however, produced an angry response from the licensed trade, particularly in rural areas, where pubs and restaurants claimed that they would lose custom if the legal limit were lowered. Pressure from the industry and from the wider rural lobby persuaded the government to reconsider, and as a result, no commitment to lower the limit was forthcoming.

At the time of writing, the Blair government is still considering its alcohol policy (see Raistrick *et al.*, 1999). A commitment to developing a national alcohol strategy was mentioned in the Green Paper *Our Healthier Nation* in 1998. It is expected that the government's proposals will emerge during the year 2000, although if previous interdepartmental battles on this issue are any guide, a further delay can be expected.

# Illicit Drugs

## *The Extent of the Problem*

In most contemporary Western societies, a sharp distinction is drawn between legal addictions such as those to alcohol and tobacco, and those to illicit drugs such as heroin, cocaine, cannabis and ecstasy. Yet to a nineteenth-century observer, this distinction would seem strange. What would be regarded today as illicit drugs – opium, for example – were widely available in Victorian times (Berridge and Edwards, 1981; Stimson and Oppenheimer, 1982). There was concern about the misuse of opium and other drugs, which led to increased regulation during the nineteenth century, but this was balanced by a widespread recognition of the beneficial effects of these drugs, in contrast to alcohol, which was seen by many Victorians as unmitigated social evil.

The development of drug policy in the UK will be explored further in a moment, but one first needs to ask why opiates and other drugs are today seen as a greater social problem than alcohol and tobacco. For in terms of mortality, alcohol and tobacco kill a far greater number of people. In 1998, over 2100 deaths were attributed to drug misuse, a fraction of those dying from alcohol- and tobacco-related disease and injury (ONS, 1999). The picture is more complicated when one looks at drug-related morbidity (see BMA, 1997b). Official statistics record only the number of people seeking help for drug addiction problems. In 1996, over 43,000 people in the UK did so. But this is a poor measure of the scale of addiction, reflecting the availability of services and the willingness of people to seek help rather than the extent of the problem. Official estimates suggest that between 100,000 and 200,000 people are addicted to drugs (Cm 3945, 1998).

It should not be assumed that all will suffer long-term health problems as a result, as some may give up their habit, but for those who do not, the longer-term consequences are serious. Studies of heroin users have found that those who continue their habit have poorer health compared with those who abstain (Tobutt *et al.*, 1996). Furthermore, chronic health problems are not confined to so-called hard drugs, cannabis, for example, being linked to psychoses, memory impairment, cancer and lung disease (Caplan and Brigham, 1990; WHO, 1997d; *New Scientist*, 1998). Another specific area of morbidity linked to drug use is fetal damage (ISDD, 1995). While the effects of maternal cannabis use on the fetus do not appear to be serious, there is evidence that women who take heroin and cocaine while pregnant risk damage to their baby. It should be noted that tobacco and excessive alcohol consumption by pregnant women can also adversely affect the fetus.

Many health problems associated with drug abuse result not just from the absorption of a drug, but from the way in which it is administered. Cannabis, for example, is usually smoked with tobacco, which is itself harmful. Heroin and amphetamines are often injected, leading to severe damage to veins and to infection with hepatitis and HIV/AIDS as a result of needle-sharing. It has been estimated that 4 per cent of AIDS cases in the UK became contaminated as result of injecting drugs (Wood, 1998) and that 60 per cent of drug users contacting the health services are infected with hepatitis C (Waller and Holmes, 1995). The realisation that much damage results from the way in which people use illicit drugs has led to an increased emphasis on harm reduction rather than outright prohibition, as we shall see later.

Solely in terms of harm to health, illicit drugs appear to be less of a threat than is commonly supposed. Certainly, when one compares the health impli- cations of alcohol and tobacco, the UK's illicit drug problem looks compara- tively small. The rationale for taking action is, however, not based merely on the current level of harm but on the predicted future trend. Also, the principal justification for such action lies in the wider social consequences of illicit drug abuse, such as crime, violence and disorder associated with the drug lifestyle and the drugs trade, which have important implications for public health.

Because drug abuse is an illegal activity, there are obvious difficulties in obtaining good evidence about individual habits. Social surveys fail to reach precisely those people who use drugs the most. Furthermore, those surveyed may not wish to admit to drug taking (or, conversely, may falsely admit to drug use). Nevertheless, most surveys show a fairly consistent picture of drug-taking trends. Around a third of the adult population have taken illegal drugs at some time in their lives, a tenth in the previous year and 5 per cent in the previous month. The most popular are so-called soft drugs such as cannabis; fewer than 1 per cent of the population admit to using cocaine or heroin. The vast majority of illegal drug users are under 35 years of age, and the percentage admitting to previous and regular drug use is increasing (see Leitner *et al.*, 1993; HEA, 1996; Ramsay and Spiller, 1997), although interest- ingly the reported rate of illegal drug use among teenagers (14–15-year-olds) appears to be declining (*Independent*, 2000a).

The use of illegal drugs among the young is perceived as being particularly serious, in terms of both individual health and social wellbeing in a broader sense. Surveys indicate that between 40 and 50 per cent of 16-year-olds have tried illegal drugs (Parker *et al.*, 1995; Miller and Plant, 1996; Balding, 1998). The most commonly-used drugs are cannabis and 'dance drugs' such as ecstasy and amphetamines. Any complacency is dismissed by those who argue that soft drugs are merely 'gateways' to the harder drugs. However, there is no evidence to support a simplistic thesis that people move in a linear fashion from soft to hard drugs. In reality, the choices made by children and young people are far more complex (see Measham *et al.*, 1998; Parker *et al.*, 1998) and involve legal as well as illicit drugs.

One must also consider the broader costs of illicit drug misuse and its impact on social welfare and public health. The total cost of illicit drug misuse in the UK has been officially estimated at £4 billion (Cm 3945, 1998). This includes the costs of policing, the criminal justice system and the health services. Other costs are less tangible and measurable but are nevertheless important. These include the cost of family breakdown and child neglect associated with drug abuse. Given the important role of the family in maintaining health, preventing illness and nurturing children, this has obvious implications for the health of the community as a whole. One must, however, be aware that illicit drug abuse can itself result from trauma within the family, so the relationship between the two is not at all straightforward (BMA, 1997b).

Another social cost is imposed by drug-related crime. When such crime becomes endemic within a community, it compounds the health and social problems and can therefore be regarded as a public health problem. There is disagreement over how much crime is attributable to the drug habit. Obviously, by definition, people are committing a crime by supplying or possessing drugs. However, the link with other crime is complex. Prostitution, robbery, assault and theft are believed to be associated with illicit drug habits, while assaults, homicides and fraud are linked to the trade. It should also be noted that organised crime is believed to be heavily involved in alcohol and tobacco smuggling and distribution. According to a study by Bennett (1998), 61 per cent of those arrested had taken more than one illegal drug; just under half those arrested had taken cannabis, 18 per cent opiates and 10 per cent cocaine or crack. A quarter had taken alcohol. Around half said that drug use was connected with offending. Although these figures have been used to highlight the link between drugs and crime, it has been suggested the sampling was not representative and that the results could not be generalised (Stimson *et al.*, 1998).

Another study found that a sample of 1100 drug addicts committed over 70,000 crimes over a two-year period at a cost of £34m (DoH, 1996c). Others have shown that although the level of crime committed by drug addicts is high in absolute terms (Dorn *et al.*, 1994), users often have other legitimate sources of income (Hammersley *et al.*, 1989). Those who need a large income to maintain their habit – chiefly heroin and cocaine users – are in the minority, and their contribution to overall crime is, as a result, relatively small (perhaps as little as 1 per cent of property crime according to Dorn *et al.*, 1994). Moreover, the link between drugs and crime is complicated by the observation that drug users may commit a crime for reasons to do more with their personality, lifestyle and social situation than with drug taking (Bennett, 1998).

## Drug Policies

The first three decades of the twentieth century saw the introduction of international agreements to control the drug trade and the development of control policies in individual countries. In Britain, responsibility for control was given to doctors, who could prescribe addictive drugs if they believed that this would enable the patient to live an otherwise normal life. The problem of drug addiction was thus medicalised and to some extent removed from controversy. By the late 1950s, however, the so-called 'British system' was under strain (Strang and Gossop, 1994). In the face of widespread public concern, highlighted by the media, about drug taking among young people, the government established an interdepartmental committee to investigate the problem. This committee, under the chairmanship of Sir Russell Brain, reported that no fundamental change in the law was necessary (Interdepartmental Committee on Drug Addiction, 1961). However, when the number of known addicts rose significantly, the Brain Committee was reconvened and this time decided that some doctors were overprescribing drugs and that regulation should be tightened (Interdepartmental Committee on Drug Addiction, 1965).

Following the second Brain Report, government introduced a system of central registration for drug addicts. It also decided to encourage the development of a more specialised drug service, which limited the role of the GP and expanded that of specialist drug dependence units. This was to prove a mistake as drug taking spread beyond its urban/inner city base and became more diverse, highlighting the need to involve, not exclude, primary care professionals. By the mid-1980s, following an influential report form the Advisory Committee on the Misuse of Drugs, this policy was to some extent reversed (ACMD, 1982). The importance of a community-based approach to drug misuse, emphasising prevention as well as treatment, has since been reflected in a number of initiatives including the establishment of Community Drug Teams in most health districts during the 1980s, the Drugs Prevention Initiative of 1990, which aimed to evaluate and promote community-based approaches to prevention, and the development of Drug Action Teams in the 1990s.

According to Stimson (1987), drugs policy in the 1980s moved from a narrow medical response to a more extensive and diffuse approach that incorporated a broader range of ideas and agencies. Others challenged the notion of this paradigm shift, arguing that the response to drug addiction has long been based on the twin concepts of the addict as a sick person and a threat to public health in a wider sense (see Smart, 1984). It is, however, certainly true that non-medical initiatives, including law enforcement became more prominent. Enforcement powers were increased in 1967 following the second Brain Report, and the law was consolidated in the form of the 1971 Misuse of Drugs Act, which remains in force. The 1971 Act controls drugs in three classes (A, B and C), offences relating to Class A drugs (such as heroin) attracting greater penalties than those relating to Class B and C drugs. In 1985, the Misuse of Drugs Regulations increased penalties and reclassified some drugs, while the 1986 Drug Trafficking Offences Act (since replaced by the Drug Trafficking Act of 1994) facilitated the confiscation of a drug trafficker's assets.

There was also an expansion of health education about drugs in this period. In 1985, a high-profile £2m anti-heroin campaign aimed at young people and parents was launched. This was subsequently shown to have had little impact on attitudes of young people, although it did appear to raise awareness among parents (Research Bureau Ltd, 1986). Other expensive media campaigns have followed despite evidence that they are of limited effectiveness. School-based drugs education received increased funding in the 1980s with the provision of central government grants to enable local education authorities to employ drug and health education co-ordinators. Further grants were subsequently made available to facilitate the training of teachers in drug education and for other school-based (and other community-based) education projects. According to OFSTED (1997), four-fifths of schools had drug policies, and this was expected to increase in the future. Drug education at primary school level was, however, relatively slow to develop despite research suggesting that it might be effective in giving children the knowledge and ability to resist peer pressure to take drugs (McGurk and Hurry, 1995, 1997).

Another feature of drug policy during the 1980s was the increasing emphasis placed on harm minimisation, in which 'the task is to limit the potential injury associated with drug use' (Bayer, 1993, p. 15; see also Caulkins and Reuter, 1997). This was not, however, a completely new philosophy, as treatment regimes have always been intended to avoid such consequences as premature death and to cut crime. These aims were behind the introduction of methadone maintenance schemes introduced to treat opiate addiction (see Farrell *et al.*, 1994), even though some schemes have been associated with an increased number of deaths (Newcombe, 1996).

Harm minimisation became an increasingly important aspect of the policy response, largely due to the emergence of HIV and AIDS (Stimson, 1995; Berridge, 1998; Wood, 1998). Wider public health considerations about the transmission of the disease through unhygienic drug-taking practices such as needle-sharing led government and local agencies to promote safer drug habits (and less risky sexual practices) among drug users. This was reflected in the establishment of needle-exchange schemes, health promotion campaigns based on harm minimisation rather than total abstinence from drugs, and 'safe-sex' campaigns aimed specifically at drug-using populations (notably drug-using prostitutes). Worries about HIV and AIDS helped to promote a more enlightened approach towards the health of drug users, an approach that was credited with minimising infection among drug addicts. The harm reduction philosophy was also evident in other areas of drug use unconnected with HIV/AIDS. In some cities, for example, health promoters focused on minimising the harm from dance drugs such as ecstasy by giving advice on how to avoid adverse side effects rather than by promoting total abstention.

By the 1990s, a more enlightened drugs policy began to emerge. In 1995, the Major government published a strategy document, *Tackling Drugs Together: A Strategy for England*, which sought to address some of the flaws evident in earlier policy initiatives (Cm 2846, 1995). For example, in an effort to tackle the problem of a poor co-ordination of policies at local level, Drug Action Teams (DATs) were established throughout England incorporating senior representatives from health authorities, local authorities, the police and the probation service. Similar bodies were established in Scotland and in Wales (where these bodies also had responsibility for alcohol problems in the community). At the same time, the document promised improved interdepartmental co-ordination at the national level and an increase in funding earmarked for drug initiatives. The level of funding – £20m – was criticised by many as inadequate and did indeed seem to limit the effectiveness of the DATs (Newburn and Elliott, 1998).

## Recent Developments

In 1997, the Blair government appointed Keith Hellawell, the former Chief Constable of West Yorkshire, as its Anti-drugs Coordinator (better known as the 'Drugs Czar'). In the following year, the strategic document, *Tackling Drugs To Build a Better Britain* (Cm 3945, 1998), set out a longer-term approach and suggested an even greater effort to co-ordinate action at a local level. It envisaged moving beyond local co-ordination to create partnerships to combat drug abuse alongside other social problems such as crime, poor education, ill health and deprivation. The strategy also proposed a system of performance assessment that involved setting targets for DATs and monitoring their activities more closely. It also outlined ways in which DATs could become more accountable to the populations they served and hence more responsive to the needs of the community. The thrust of *Tackling Drugs To Build a Better Britain*, like that of the previous strategy, was very much on preventing drug misuse. It was, however, pointed out a prevention-oriented strategy would be difficult to achieve given that existing resources were tied up in counselling, treatment and rehabilitation of those who already had a drug problem. The only solution would be to increase resources substantially. A further £200m was allocated to the strategy, and the government announced that additional resources would be released by the seizure of drug dealers' assets.

The strategy was later revised (Cabinet Office, 1999), a greater emphasis being placed on tackling heroin and cocaine, and providing treatment facilities. In addition, several key performance targets were set. These included: increasing the number of people in treatment programmes (by two-thirds by 2005 and by 100 per cent by 2008); reducing the proportion of young people under 25 using heroin and cocaine (by a quarter by 2005 and by half by 2005); reducing repeat offending by drug misusers (by a quarter by 2005 and by half by 2008); and reducing access to heroin and cocaine by a quarter (by 2005 and by half by 2008).

The strategies of the 1990s demonstrated a commitment to prevention and treatment and a desire to formulate policy on the basis of research, evaluation and experience. Government policy, however, remained opposed to the decriminalisation of drug use, which had been identified as a possible solution in view of experience elsewhere (see below). Campaigners disagreed with the government's position, particularly in relation to cannabis, which had been identified in the treatment of multiple sclerosis and chronic pain (see BMA, 1997c; House of Lords Science and Technology Select Committee, 1998b). Permission was, however, granted to allow research that would enable cannabis to be considered at some stage under drug licensing procedures, raising the possibility that it might in future be legalised.

A further development occurred in the year 2000 with the publication of a controversial inquiry into drug legislation established by the Police Foundation, a charitable research organisation (Independent Inquiry into the Misuse of Drugs Act 1971, 2000). The inquiry concluded that Britain's drug laws were outdated and ineffective. It proposed a change in the system of drugs classification based on the relative harm caused. This would mean, if implemented, that cannabis would become a class C drug, and that ecstasy and LSD would fall into the class B category. Heroin and cocaine would remain as class A drugs according to the new criteria, but there would be reduced penalties for possession. This was in line with the Inquiry's view that the UK regime was too severe on those found guilty of possessing drugs and that resources should be allocated to help treat and educate drug users, while adopting a tougher approach to traffickers and dealers. Despite its reasoned tone, the report received a hostile response from government, which argued that it sent out the wrong signals and that any relaxation of the regime might encourage illicit drug use.

## International Responses

One should not look at the British case in isolation. Other countries have pursued contrasting policies on drugs, and important lessons can be drawn from their experiences. Furthermore, one should be aware that international agencies and institutions have also shaped national responses to drug problems.

National responses to drug abuse have three main components: a legal framework and an enforcement system to inhibit the supply of drugs, policies to inform people about drug risks, and a system of care and rehabilitation for those who need help as a result of their drug-taking habits. But the importance of these components varies. Some countries emphasise control and enforcement, in effect declaring a war on drugs. This takes the form of high penalties for drug trafficking, dealing and possession, offences involving hard and soft drugs being treated with similar severity. This tough approach feeds through to information policies that communicate horrific messages about the dangers of drug use and emphasise total abstinence. The dominant philosophy also has an effect on care and treatment policies, which tend to be less compassionate towards addicts sacrificing their health needs to the priority of drug control.

The above describes the kind of approach pursued by the USA over recent decades (see Epstein, 1977; Wisotsky, 1986). During the 1970s, although some states did adopt a more liberal policy (Maine, for example, decriminalising cannabis), the federal government led by President Nixon adopted a hard-line approach declaring a 'War on Drugs'. This policy was reiterated under President Reagan in the early and mid-1980s, supplemented with prohibitionist educational campaigns promoting a 'Just Say No' message. A move towards a more treatment- and health-oriented approach in the late 1980s was reversed in 1989 with the appointment of William Bennett, the US 'Drugs Czar',who explicitly favoured supply-side control policies.

The problems of the prohibitionist approach are well documented (see Mishan, 1990). It criminalises those who are merely experimenting with drugs, perhaps increasing the likelihood that they will become marginalised and willing to try harder drugs. It makes the drugs trade very profitable. Short supply raises prices; it also provides a greater incentive for dealers to adulterate drugs, creating further health problems. The fact that drug sales occur 'underground' also means that quality control is poor, allowing further opportunity for adulteration. Prohibition creates a greater role for organised crime, which in turn has wider social consequences in terms of gang warfare and links with other 'rackets' such as prostitution. The war on drugs is also expensive, the USA spending at least £4 billion combating the drugs trade. A further problem is that, by concentrating on supply, factors affecting demand are ignored. The underlying causes of drug use are complex, particularly among the young (Measham *et al.*, 1998). However, a lack of social and economic opportunities for young people is certainly relevant and needs to be tackled as part of a comprehensive strategy on drugs.

The prohibitionist approach is authoritarian, giving law enforcers power to interfere, often unnecessarily, in the lives of others. For politicians, it provides a convenient rallying point, an issue on which they win votes by stoking up public fears. For example, in the US, it has provided them with a rationale for centralising and controlling the sprawling federal government bureaucracy. Indeed, according to Wisotsky (1986) the US drug wars have been borne out of political expediency above all else.

This is not to say that drugs should be freely imported, bought and sold, but some countries have pursued a more liberal policy aimed not so much at eliminating drug use, but minimising harm. The Netherlands is the classic example (see Lemmens and Garretson, 1998; Spruit, 1998), although there are others (see Fischer's 1995 account of recent developments in German policy). In the mid-1970s, the Dutch government adopted a policy that distinguished sharply between hard and soft drugs. A policy of discretion developed so that while legal penalties remained, suppliers and users of cannabis were not prosecuted providing they obeyed certain guidelines. Hence coffee shops were allowed to sell cannabis providing they did not supply hard drugs, refused to sell to young people (that is, those under 18), sold only small quantities (initially 30 g per customer) and did not cause a public nuisance. Meanwhile, harder drugs such as heroin faced a stricter regime in terms of penalties and law enforcement, although even here the emphasis was very much on harm reduction. For example, drug addicts who were repeatedly arrested were offered treatment options as an alternative to long prison sentences.

Dutch policy became more restrictive during the second half of the 1990s, when measures were introduced to limit the number of coffee houses and to reduce the amount of cannabis (to 5 mg) that could be sold to each customer. This resulted from both internal and external pressure. Within Holland, there was more concern about the nuisance caused by coffee houses and more generally by drug tourism: the liberality of the Dutch drug laws was believed by some residents to attract problem drug users from other countries. More significant, however, was the pressure on the Dutch government from other countries, particularly European Union member states, who were concerned about the implications for the proposed abolition of border controls. They believed that if the Dutch did not impose further restrictions, they would be unable to prevent drugs being freely imported into their own countries.

Domestic drug policies do not operate in a vacuum but are influenced by other countries' experiences. Hence some of the language of the 'War on Drugs' in the USA has been imported into the UK over the past few decades. The appointment of a 'Drugs Czar' is but one example. At the same time, however, the Dutch experience and experiments with other liberal policies elsewhere have fuelled campaigns in the UK to relax the regulation of soft drugs, notably cannabis, and to treat hard drug users more humanely.

In addition, domestic policies operate in the context of international institutions and processes. In the post-war period, the UN, along with the WHO, has been the main source of global initiatives in this field. The UN Commission on Narcotic Drugs was established in 1946 to develop proposals to combat drug abuse. This body is responsible for implementing the various conventions that have been introduced by the UN, such as the Single Convention on Narcotic Drugs (1961), the 1972 Protocol that amended this convention, the Convention on Psychotropic Substances (1971) and the Convention Against the Illicit Traffic in Narcotic Drugs and Psychotropic Substances (1988). Another organisation – the International Narcotics Control Board – is responsible for promoting compliance with international agreements and has a brief to point out weaknesses in current arrangements.

In 1990, dissatisfaction with the existing drug control system led to the creation of a single UN Drug Control Programme (UNDCP). In addition, a global action programme was launched in the same year with the aim of reducing drug use and harm, the UN declaring the 1990s the Decade Against Drug Abuse. UN initiatives have also been developed in conjunction with the WHO (the Global Initiative on Primary Prevention of Substance Abuse is a joint WHO/UNDCP initiative). In addition, the WHO has an advisory role in relation to the UNDCP and runs its own programme that seeks to promote health by preventing or reducing the adverse consequences of substance use. The common themes of both the UN and WHO initiatives in this field are to promote global co-operation on drug issues, to promote partnership at all levels and to mobilise communities against the consequences of drug abuse. Recently, however, there has been further criticism of the international efforts to tackle drug abuse. A review of the UNDCP found evidence of poor co-ordination between UN agencies, a need for greater co-operation between the UNDCP and International Narcotics Control Board, confusion surrounding the role of the Commission on Narcotic Drugs, and inadequate funding for the drug control programme (UN Commission for Narcotic Drugs, 1999). These issues are currently being addressed by the UN.

The European Community took a much greater interest in drug abuse during the 1990s (see European Commission, 1997). In 1990, the first European plan on drugs was devised, being shortly followed by initiatives to combat money laundering by drug traders. In 1993, the European Monitoring Centre for Drugs and Drug Addiction was established in an effort to produce good-quality information to decision makers within the European Union on the drug problem. The Maastricht Treaty, which established the European Union in 1992, explicitly referred to the problem of drug addiction and was followed by a further action plan in 1994. Two years later, a plan of action to prevent drug dependence was introduced. This set out a five-year programme to encourage co-operation between organisations in member states, to encourage research and the dissemination of information about drugs and to improve health education and training in this field. In the same year, member states agreed to approximate their laws on drug control laws and co-operate more closely to combat drug trafficking. The European Union's commitment to action on drugs was reiterated by the Amsterdam Treaty of 1997, which specifically referred to the need to complement member states' action to reduce drug-related damage. Finally, it should be mentioned that the European Union works with other international bodies on drug strategy and policy, such as the UNDCP, mentioned earlier, and regional institutions such as the Association of South East Asian Nations and the Pompidou group (the Cooperation Group to Combat Drug Abuse and Illicit Trafficking in Drugs, which operates under the auspices of the Council of Europe and includes both European Union and non-European Union European countries).

## Conclusion

In one sense, the problem of drugs (including legal drugs such as alcohol and tobacco) is insoluble. As Gossop (1996) has observed, every society has its own drugs, and campaigns to rid society of drugs are therefore futile. He argues that we have to learn to live with drugs, seeking to minimise their harmful effects rather than merely prohibiting them. This chapter has shown that policies in the UK have shifted towards a harm minimisation approach, although not as much as in some other countries, notably the Netherlands. It has also shown that policies on alcohol, tobacco and drugs do not operate in a domestic vacuum. These issues require a global response, and the European Union, the WHO and the UN have all been active in this field in recent years.

What more could be done to tackle these problems? Policies certainly need to be more closely aligned to the needs of young people, who are the most vulnerable to the adoption of drug habits and to the consequences of legal and illegal drug misuse. All too often in the past, drug policies have been devised without consulting young people or seeking to understand their attitudes to risk (see Denscombe and Drucquer, 1999), so it is hardly surprising that they have been ineffective. Another problem is that drug policies have been based on myths rather than evidence (see Edwards *et al.*, 1993). The knee-jerk reaction to drug misuse is not the best response, and the motives of politicians have often been questionable.

Policy must bring together all aspects of drugs use. Alcohol and tobacco raise major public health issues, but for too long they have been given a much lower priority than illicit drugs (Goldstein and Kalant, 1993). It has been estimated that in terms of their consequences for society, alcohol- and tobacco-related harm rivals that associated with some controlled drugs (Independent Inquiry into the Misuse of Drugs Act 1971, 2000). It is also apparent that legal drugs can be as addictive as illegal ones. A report from the RCP (2000), for example, stated that nicotine was as addictive as hard drugs, such as heroin. Comprehensive policies and integrated strategies across the range of addictions are required in spite of the political obstacles such as those noted by Lawton (1989, p. 31):

> the government may not wish to link the three areas of smoking, drinking and drug misuse because such a combined campaign might reveal the inconsistencies of spending several million pounds on drug prevention publicity, while at the same time allowing hundreds of millions to be spent promoting the two drugs alcohol and tobacco, whose abuse costs the nation so much more dearly.

There are signs of an increased willingness to look at the problems of alcohol and tobacco in the broader context of drug abuse. For example, education programmes have addressed legal as well as illegal drugs. But, strategically speaking, alcohol, tobacco and drugs are treated differently and separately. Although some international programmes relate to legal as well as illegal addictions, there is no global umbrella regulating alcohol and tobacco problems (see Fischer *et al.*, 1997). For example, unlike those covering illegal drugs, international agreements relating to alcohol and tobacco do not reflect public health considerations (although, as noted above, this may change in the future with regard to tobacco). It seems sensible that drug policies should incorporate a balanced assessment of the risks and benefits of the different types of drug used. These policies should also be realistic and should prioritise harm minimisation. Furthermore, they must be based on a clearer understanding of why individuals and societies use and misuse drugs and should therefore be linked to broader policies aimed at improving individual and social welfare.

# 10

# The Social and Economic Context of Public Health

In previous chapters, it has been argued that individual choices about healthy lifestyle are influenced by a range of social and economic factors. Significant improvements in public health are unlikely to occur unless policies fully acknowledge this. This chapter explores further the socio-economic context of public health and discusses policies that have been proposed as a means of improving health through wider social and economic reform.

## Inequalities and Inequities

Debates about the impact of social and economic factors have tended to focus on health inequalities, but the concepts of inequality and inequity (and by the same token 'equality' and 'equity') require explanation. For although inequality and inequity are often used interchangeably, they have a different meaning (see King's Fund, 1999). Inequalities are empirical constructions – they are intrinsically neither 'good' nor 'bad' – while inequities are inequalities perceived as being unfair or unjust. Not all inequalities are necessarily inequitable: for example, that younger people tend to enjoy better health than elderly people is not regarded as inequitable. In contrast, the relatively poorer health of working-class people relative to the middle classes is viewed by many as inequitable. Concepts of equity and inequity are therefore rooted in beliefs about 'what should be'. They are thus contestable, and there is consequently much controversy about whether certain inequalities are actually inequitable.

### Concepts of Equity

In an attempt to clarify this further, Pereira (1993) outlined six basic concepts of equity: egality, entitlement, decent minimum, utilitarianism, Rawlsian

221

maximin and envy-free allocations. *Egality* means equalising individual net benefit or, if this is not possible, equalising the opportunities to achieve such benefit. The problem with this concept is that it fails to establish why equalisation should take place. When applied crudely to health, it implies that everyone should have an equal health status or at least to have the resources to achieve this end, even though this is plainly unrealistic and fails to take into account factors such as age and genetic predisposition to disease. Distribution according to *entitlement* implies that equity is achieved when individuals acquire their status justly. The application of this principle tends, however, to produce a large inequality of outcome that appears unjust to most people – such as a systematic inequality in health status between people of a similar age but a different socio-economic background. The *decent minimum* is presented as a way of ameliorating the harsh consequences of applying the entitlement principle. The main problem here, however, lies in establishing the level below which no one should fall. This is particularly difficult to achieve in health, where there are many different dimensions to consider and where expectations vary considerably between individuals.

The *utilitarian* approach, which seeks to maximise aggregate benefit in society, implies considerable inequalities in health status. Resources will be allocated on the basis of an individual's capacity to benefit from social interventions, and this is likely to disadvantage people whose baseline health status may be regarded as low (such as very elderly, chronically sick and disabled people). In contrast, the *Rawlsian* position seeks to maximise the position of the least well off in society rather than simply maximising overall social utility. According to this, inequalities in health can be justified only if these people gain benefit. There are, however, a number of theoretical problems with this approach. For example, it leads to the rejection of interventions that might benefit the majority but leave the least well-off unaffected. There are also practical difficulties in distinguishing between inequalities that benefit the least well-off and those which do not. The concept of *envy-free allocations* judges people's relative advantage in terms of their preferences for others' situations. Here, an equitable distribution occurs where all individuals do not prefer each other's situation to their own. This is a more subjective approach than those previously discussed and has strengths that derive from being rooted in individual perceptions of the situation of others. Its main shortcoming, however, lies in excluding any collective sense of what is just and fair, which is regarded by many as extremely relevant when allocating resources at the community level.

Pereira also discusses alternative equity formulations, notably that developed by Le Grand (1987). According to Le Grand, an inequitable situation arises when health inequalities result from factors outside the control of individuals. This approach seems attractive because it considers how particular outcomes emerge while seeking to incorporate consumers' own preferences.

There are, however, problems in interpreting health choices: it is well known that consumers have limited knowledge, competence and information when making such decisions. Another alternative is the health maximisation principle, which states that a distribution is equitable only if it serves to maximise the health of the whole community. This at first appears an attractive notion, emphasising the barriers that inequity places on efforts to maximise the health of the population. Nevertheless, as Pereira (1993) notes, it has attracted criticism for placing too much emphasis on efficiency, treating distributional matters as secondary to the achievement of aggregate levels of health benefit, and opening it up to allegations of crude utilitarianism. Another alternative is the 'basic capabilities' approach of Sen (1985), which, according to Pereira, provides a clarification of the debate over whether resources or welfare should be the aim of an equitable policy. Sen argues that basic human capabilities are essential in transforming resources into welfare outcomes. An individual's health is shaped not only by resources, personal characteristics and environmental factors, but also by that individual's capacity to derive benefit. Therefore, according to Sen, the guiding principle of equity should be *equality of basic capabilities*, which implies that interventions should promote equal opportunities to enjoy good health.

The importance of equality of opportunity is also reflected in a definition proposed by Whitehead (1992, p. 433), in the context of *Health for All* (WHO, 1981), which states that 'equity in health implies that ideally everyone should have a *fair opportunity* to attain their full health potential and, more pragmatically, that none should be disadvantaged from achieving this potential, if it can be avoided.' The implication is that equity is primarily concerned with creating equal opportunity for health and reducing the health differential to the lowest possible level. Whitehead also sets out several relevant principles to guide policy in this field. First, equity policy should be concerned with living and working conditions, in order to prevent inequality and to enhance equality of opportunity. Second, it should be directed towards enabling a healthier lifestyle and should acknowledge that some social groups are more restricted than others in their ability to make lifestyle choices. Third, equity policy requires a commitment to decentralisation and participation, giving ordinary people a voice in decision making. Fourth, there is a need to look holistically at the causes of inequity across a range of sectors and to devise co-ordinated multisectoral policies. Finally, equity is not merely about unjust differences within countries, but concerns those which exist between nations as well. Policies must therefore accept that improvements in health standards in some countries should not be at the expense of other nations.

Whitehead outlined two further principles: that equity in health care should be based on the principle of making high-quality health care available to all; and that equity policies should be based on an active search for information on the extent of the problem and how best to tackle it. She also argued that equity policies should be properly monitored to assess their effectiveness and in order to detect any possible adverse consequences. In this chapter, the extent to which policies adopted in the UK have reflected these principles will be explored. First, however, it is important to assess the nature of health inequalities in the UK, beginning with an examination of the relationship between socio-economic background and difference in health status before moving on to explore specific issues such as unemployment and job insecurity, inadequate housing, gender and ethnic health.

# Health Inequalities in the UK

## Socio-economic Status and Health

There is a considerable difference in mortality between social classes (see Townsend *et al.*, 1992; Whitehead and Drever, 1997; Shaw *et al.*, 1999). In the period 1991–93, the standardised mortality rate for males aged 20–64 in England and Wales was almost three times higher for social class V (unskilled manual) than social class I (professional and managerial). As many as 62 out of the 66 major causes of death in men are more common in social classes IV and V (unskilled and semi-skilled manual workers) than other social classes. In women, 64 out of the 70 major causes of death are more common among women married to men from social classes IV and V. In the case of coronary heart disease, there is a large difference in the male mortality rate (see National Heart Forum, 1998), the rate in men in social class V being three times that of social class I. There is also an association between socio-economic status and survival from a heart attack (Greenwood *et al.*, 1995; Morrison *et al.*, 1997). The survival rates for most cancers are also superior for higher-income categories and socio-economic groups (Kogevinas, 1990; Thames Cancer Registry, 1994). For patients diagnosed with cancer between 1986–90, the most affluent were between 5 and 16 per cent more likely than deprived patients to survive over a five-year period (ONS/Cancer Research Campaign/London School of Hygiene and Tropical Medicine, 1999).

Life expectancy also varies between social classes: on average, men in social classes I and II live five years longer than those in social classes IV and V (Hattersley, 1997). There is some evidence of inequality in morbidity too. In 1996, 17 per cent of professional men aged 45–64 compared with 48 per cent of unskilled men in the same age group reported long-standing illness (ONS, 1998). A study by Borooah (1999) has shown that 25 per cent of inequality in long-term limited illness in men (and 20 per cent in women) resulted from a difference in occupational class. Obesity and high blood pressure (Colhoun and Prescott-Clarke, 1996), as well as poor mental health (Meltzer *et al.*, 1995), are more common among women in social classes IV and V than I and II.

Further evidence of inequality in health and illness was provided by a study of civil servants (Marmot *et al.*, 1991), which found that employment grade and salary was strongly related to both objectively measured and self-reported health status.

Health inequality can be found among infants and children (Exhibit 10.1). In England and Wales, the infant mortality rate for social classes I and II was 4.5 per 1000 in the period 1993–95 compared with 7.7 per 1000 for social classes IV and V, while the mortality rate for children aged under 14 years of age was almost two-and-a-half times greater in social class V compared with social class I in the period 1991–3 (Botting, 1997). Accident and injury rates for children also vary considerably by social class. In the early 1990s, death rates from injury and poisoning for children in social class V were five times higher than in social class I (Roberts and Norton, 1996). At the other end of the age range, one finds that the inequality persists into later life. Research by Marmot and Shipley (1996) found that socio-economic status was associated with health inequality among the elderly, although occupational grade had less impact after retirement than did other factors such as car ownership.

---

Exhibit 10.1

---

### Child poverty and child health

Health inequalities among children and young people are associated with socio-economic factors (see BMA, 1999b). Children born to fathers in social classes IV and V have suffered consistently worse health than those born to fathers in higher social classes, and these differentials have persisted in recent years (see Botting, 1997); in some respects, notably the child injury death rate, they have actually widened (Roberts and Power, 1996). In addition, there is now considerable evidence to suggest that socio-economic factors in childhood have an impact not only on the health of children, but also upon their subsequent health status as adults (see the review by Lundberg, 1993; Roberts, 1997; Davey Smith *et al.*, 1998a, Dike van de Mheen *et al.*, 1998). In particular, social disadvantage seems to operate on a number of levels, having both a direct effect on the health of children and young people, and an indirect effect through lower birth-weight for example (see Bartley *et al.*, 1994). This is illustrated by the impact of poverty on nutrition. The diet of poor families contains well below the recommended level for the intake of nutrients such as fibre, vitamin C, iron, zinc, folate and calcium (James *et al.*, 1997; MAFF, 1998b), with implications for health at all stages of child development from birth to adolescence, into adulthood and through to future generations.

The link between material deprivation in childhood and health inequality is viewed as being particularly worrying in the light of the growth in child poverty in the 1980s and 90s (Hewlett, 1993; Wilkinson, 1994; Spencer, 1996; Dennehy *et al.*, 1997). A quarter

Exhibit 10.1 *(cont'd)*

of children live in poverty (defined as living in a household with below half-average income before housing costs are taken into account), but when housing costs are taken into account, this rises to one in three. In view of these figures, it is hardly surprising that practitioners have found a re-emergence of diseases in children associated with poverty, such as rickets and tuberculosis (Health Visitors' Association, 1996).

Much can be done to alleviate the problem of child health inequality (see Arblaster *et al.*, 1997; Independent Inquiry into Inequalities in Health, 1998). At one level, better income support for poor families can be effective (see Kehner and Wolin, 1979), but other forms of social support, such as support programmes for parents, are also important (Barker *et al.*, 1994). Other specific interventions of proven effectiveness include providing free school milk, targeting effective interventions to reduce the number of accidents, and providing smoking cessation programmes to pregnant women (Arblaster *et al.*, 1997).

In 1991, the Blair government stated its intention to end child poverty within 20 years. It was claimed that welfare reforms such as the Working Families' Tax Credit, the minimum wage and child benefit increases, as well as 'New Deals' for lone parents and unemployed people, would help to raise the incomes of poorer families. Several other programmes were also introduced with the aim of addressing the particular needs of children in deprived areas. These included the continuing emphasis on school-based health promotion, Education Action Zones, and the Sure Start programme which seeks to improve the emotional, physical, intellectual and social development of pre-school children through the provision of additional, improved and integrated services. Another relevant programme, announced in the 2000 Budget, was the creation of regional and local funds for voluntary sector projects aimed at meeting children's needs.

## Explaining Health Inequalities

As already discussed, the statistical evidence of health inequality does not necessarily mean that this should be looked upon as inequity. Indeed, there are several possible explanations for health inequality, each of which has different implications for policy (see Carr-Hill, 1987; Townsend, 1990; Klein, 1991; BMA, 1995). One explanation suggests that health inequality is artificially inflated by the use of occupation as a proxy for social class (Illsley, 1986). It is believed that because the mortality rate is calculated on the basis of the occupation of the deceased taken from the death certificate, previous occupations that might place the individual in a higher social category are ignored. Furthermore, changes in the sizes of social classes could be responsible for exaggerating the inequality. Between 1931 and 1981, social class V shrank by 55 per cent while social class I grew by 217 per cent. Although health inequality could reflect a high mortality within a declining section of society, a number of studies have found that such inequality remains significant even when a change in the size of social classes is taken into account (see Pamuk, 1985; Goldblatt, 1989; Fox *et al.*, 1990; Davey Smith *et al.*, 1994).

Another explanation is that social class differences in health arise from a process of social selection (Stern, 1983; Illsley, 1986). According to this view, health inequality is partly caused by healthy people being upwardly mobile, while less healthy people accumulate in social classes IV and V. In other words, health inequality produces social inequality rather than the other way round. There is some evidence that health status influences job selection, particularly in manual occupations, and this should be acknowledged when undertaking a comparison of mortality rates between specific occupations (Carpenter, 1987; Goldblatt *et al.*, 1990). Social mobility nevertheless appears to have a minor impact on health inequality (Goldblatt, 1989; Fox *et al.*, 1990; Blane *et al.*, 1993; Power *et al.*, 1996; Bartley and Plewis, 1997; Hart *et al.*, 1998).

A third explanation focuses on the behaviour of individuals within social classes. Variations in health status have been associated with differences in lifestyle between social classes. Hence excessive drinking, smoking and obesity are more common in social classes IV and V than in classes I and II. While this cannot be denied, it must be recognised that individual choice is only one of several factors shaping lifestyle. As has been shown in previous chapters, the social and economic environment within which individuals are located is also relevant (see also Backett and Davison, 1995). Such factors are important in explaining why certain subgroups continue to pursue a lifestyle that carries health risks, such as smoking for example and poor nutrition (see Dobson *et al.*, 1994; James *et al.*, 1997; MAFF, 1998). Moreover, studies of health inequality have found that class gradients in health status persist even after adjusting for behavioural risk factors (Marmot *et al.*, 1984).

The other remaining explanation is that factors associated with social class are an underlying cause of health inequality. Some authors argue that occupational class is a useful proxy for a range of socio-economic variables and can provide a powerful explanation of health inequality (see Townsend *et al.*, 1992). Others, however, have focused on the specific factors that produce social class inequality, such as inequality in health between geographical areas, deprivation, unemployment, a shortage of good quality, low-cost housing and income inequalities.

## Health and Place... and Deprivation

One way of exploring the impact of socio-economic factors on health is to look at the inequality between geographical areas. In the UK, this has been depicted in very crude way as a 'North–South' divide. Although in the North (as well as in Wales, Northern Ireland and Scotland) there are more areas with a relatively poor level of health compared with the South (Britton, 1990), the real situation is more complex. There is often a considerable variation in health status between districts of the same city, particularly in large cities such as London (Bardsley, 1998). According to Charlton (1996), rural and prosperous areas are the most healthy while urban areas, especially inner city estates and deprived industrial estates, are the least healthy. This is reflected in self-reported health (DoH, 1999a) and in life expectancy (Soni Raleigh and Kiri, 1997). Further research has shown that people living in the worst tenth of areas in Britain are 42 per cent more likely to die before 65 years of age than is the average person (Shaw *et al.*, 1998). This study argued that such geographical inequality was not simply a passive reflection of social inequality but reflected other 'contextual' factors. Similarly, others have recognised the impact of the local social and physical environment upon health, suggesting that public health may be to some extent improved by focusing on places as well as people (MacIntyre *et al.*, 1993).

Nevertheless, the main factor behind regional and local variations in health status appears to be deprivation (Sloggett and Joshi, 1994): the most economically deprived areas tend to be the least healthy (Carstairs and Morris, 1989; Drever and Whitehead, 1995; Eames *et al.*, 1993). Deprivation is difficult to measure but can be revealed by statistics that reflect material and social factors such as car ownership, employment and housing status, and social class. Although there is a high concentration of deprived areas in urban areas, explaining the kinds of difference in health status described above, it should be acknowledged that poverty is also a feature of rural societies (Cox, 1998). There is growing evidence to suggest that poverty in rural areas is a significant problem (Cloke *et al.*, 1994; Joseph Rowntree Foundation, 1994), which, coupled with the isolation of some communities, has serious implications for health. There is indeed perhaps a greater polarisation in the countryside, the rural poor living cheek by jowl with relatively wealthy people, such as landowners, entrepreneurs and commuters. It is not surprising therefore that researchers have identified a substantial health inequality in rural areas (Phillimore and Reading, 1992).

## Unemployment

It has been known for some time that unemployment has a deleterious effect on the health of most people (WHO Regional Office for Europe, 1985a). Unemployed people have worse health than the employed population (Bethune, 1996), and the loss of employment is associated with an increased mortality (Fox and Shrewry, 1988). One study (Morris *et al.*, 1994) estimated that, even after adjustment for variables such as social class, health status and lifestyle, the relative risk of mortality after five years for middle-aged men who lost employment was almost twice that of those who remained continuously employed. In relation to mental health, unemployed people experience twice the level of neurotic symptoms of those in employment (Meltzer *et al.*, 1995). The difference between employed and unemployed people cannot be explained wholly in terms of previous health or pre-existing circumstances (Moser *et al.*, 1990), although men in manual occupations with limiting longstanding illness are more likely to be unemployed than are those with a similar illness in a higher socio-economic group (Bartley and Owen, 1996). Notably, the threat of unemployment and job insecurity also carries significant adverse health consequences (Ferrie *et al.*, 1995; Bartley *et al.*, 1996).

## Housing

Another important indicator of deprivation is the housing standard, also closely associated with health. As Arblaster and Hawtin (1993, p. 5) have observed, 'living in poor housing or being homeless are not just housing problems. They have profound implications for the health of people and of society.' Parts of the nation's housing stock is in a parlous state, one in thirteen homes being unfit for human habitation and one in six needing substantial urgent repairs (National Housing Forum, 1994; Forrester, 1994). There is a general acknowledgement that 'housing and health are strongly related' (Conway, 1995, p. 141). This is supported by various studies (Burridge and Ormandy, 1993; Standing Conference on Public Health, 1994; Hunt, 1997; Marsh *et al.*, 1999). In addition, there are specific links between illness and poor housing, for example overcrowding and psychological stress in women (Gabe and Williams, 1993), and injury from fires and accidents (Lowry, 1991); furthermore, cold and damp housing conditions have been linked to respiratory problems such as asthma and other allergies and infections, particularly among children (Platt *et al.*, 1989)

It is perhaps more appropriate to focus on the effect that housing has on the community and environment within which individuals live rather than its direct impact on specific conditions and illnesses. This was supported by a longitudinal study of the impact of poor housing, which indicated that greater housing deprivation led to a higher probability of ill health in general and that this impact was likely to be greater among those affected earlier in life (Marsh *et al.*, 1999). In addition, the absence of a home undoubtedly has an effect on health status, as revealed by surveys of the health of homeless people (Conway, 1988; Child Accident Prevention Trust, 1991; Shanks and Smith, 1992; Fisher and Collins, 1993; Bines, 1994).

The relationship between health and housing, and their 'triangular relationship' with deprivation (see Goodchild, 1998), requires closer scrutiny. In particular, more needs to be known about the impact of housing and antipoverty strategies on health, raising the prospect of evidence-based interventions across the field of social welfare (see Conway, 1995; Smith and Mallinson, 1997), a point that will be returned towards the end of this chapter.

## Income Inequality and Health

Few informed observers now doubt that health status is affected to some extent by social class, deprivation, unemployment and poor housing. More controversially, it has been argued that health inequality is related to the income differential within a society rather than to any absolute level of deprivation. This *relative income thesis* is closely associated with the work of Richard Wilkinson (1992, 1996, 1997) and others (see Lynch and Kaplan, 1997). According to these researchers, the more equal the income distribution of a particular country, the better its average level of health will be, as reflected in measures such as life expectancy and mortality rate.

Three types of evidence are cited in support of this. First, within developed countries, the income differential is closely correlated with the difference in mortality and life expectancy, while a change in the overall material standard appears to have little impact on the standard of health in these countries. Second, mortality tends to be lower in societies where the income differential is smaller, even after controlling for average income level, absolute poverty level and other socio-economic factors. This has also been found at subnational level in a comparative analysis of US states (Kennedy *et al.*, 1996; Wolfson *et al.*, 1999) and in studies of English local authorities and districts (Ben-Shlomo *et al.*, 1996; Stanistreet *et al.*, 1999). Third, as countries become wealthier and the population ages, the increase in life expectancy gets smaller and relative economic positions become more important in determining health. One reason suggested for this is that chronic disease, which tends to increase as a proportion of the illness burden as countries industrialise, disproportionately affects poorer people.

Although the precise causal link between income distribution and health is unclear, a number of potential causes have been suggested. Material inequality may affect psychosocial health through the perception of social injustice. This could be associated with a higher level of stress-related illness, although the link is difficult to measure because of the presence of many other factors affecting health. Notably, the study by Kunst *et al.* (1998) found that the strength of the link between mortality and social class varied according to the cause of death both within and between countries, casting doubts on a direct relationship between stress and vulnerability to disease. Another explanation, for which there is more support, is that inequality affects social cohesion. Wilkinson (1997), for example, cites research identifying social trust (as indicated by membership of voluntary groups and the level of trust in the community) as a factor linking income distribution and health (Kawachi *et al.*, 1997; Kawachi and Kennedy, 1997). Meanwhile, a study by Kaplan *et al.* (1996) found that variations in health outcomes and social indicators were paralleled by the scale of investment in human and social capital.

Critics have attacked the relative income thesis on several grounds. It has been argued that the link between income inequality and overall health standards is tenuous and that health inequality is more closely related to specific factors, such as absolute poverty and unemployment. It has also been pointed out that there is limited evidence available on the supposed relationship between unfairness, trust or social capital, and health. Furthermore, it has been claimed that the relationship between income inequality and general level of heath is largely a statistical artefact. This requires further explanation. One argument centres on what is known as 'the ecological fallacy': relationships between variables at an aggregate level being wrongly interpreted as applying at the individual level (Robinson, 1950; MacRae, 1994). According to Gravelle (1998), the use of aggregated data exaggerates the importance of the relative income hypothesis. This is because the effect of increased income on individual risk of mortality is smaller at a higher income than a lower income (that is, there is a non-linear relationship between income and mortality). This means that societies with a more equal distribution of income will tend to have lower mortality anyway, even where there is no underlying relationship between the distribution of income and an individual's risk of mortality. Although he does not deny that a relationship may exist between income distribution and mortality, Gravelle makes it clear that its impact can be measured accurately only by data relating to individuals, even though income inequality is by its very nature an aggregate variable (Kaplan *et al.*, 1996).

Other critics include Judge (1995), who has argued that the relative income hypothesis is based on flawed measures of income distribution, such as family income rather than individual income, and has criticised the quality of aggregate data used in these studies. Interestingly, Judge's own analysis failed to find a significant relationship between income distribution and life expectancy. Wilkinson (1995) countered with a criticism of Judge's measures on inequality and mortality, while vigorously defending his own methodology. Further research into comparative health inequality has, however, cast further doubt on Wilkinson's hypothesis. Mackenbach *et al.* (1997) did not find that health inequality was smaller in countries where egalitarian principles exerted more influence over social and economic policies. Further criticism of Wilkinson's approach has focused on its limited explanatory power. Muntaner and Lynch (1999) argue that this model plays down class relations as well as the underlying processes of class domination and exploitation. They also point out that an emphasis on social cohesion can be used to blame 'communities' rather than specific social processes and relationships for health inequities.

What are we to make of this controversy? The relative income hypothesis certainly stands on softer ground than the absolute income hypothesis (for which there are 'individualised' data; see Sloggett and Joshi, 1994). But, given the problems of the data available – in particular those relating to cross-national comparisons (see Mackenbach *et al.*, 1997; Kunst *et al.*, 1998) – this is hardly surprising. It seems sensible therefore that the hypothesis should not be rejected until better-quality research findings are available by which to judge it.

# Other Inequalities

## Race and Ethnicity

Some ethnic groups have a higher mortality rate and poorer health than the rest of the population (see Balarajan and Soni Raleigh, 1995; Smaje, 1995; Harding and Maxwell, 1997; Nazroo, 1997a, 1997b; Wild and McKeigue, 1997). For example, people from African, Afro-Caribbean and Indian communities have a higher than average rate of limiting longstanding illness (Charlton *et al.*, 1994; Smaje and Le Grand, 1997a). Standardised mortality ratios for all ethnic groups, except Afro-Caribbean people and South Asian women, are higher than average (Wild and McKeigue, 1997). The neonatal death rate is generally higher for ethnic groups than for the general population (with the exception of the Bangladeshi community); the post-neonatal death rate is lower than average among people of Indian, African and Bangladeshi origin, but above average for Afro-Caribbean and Pakistani communities (OPCS, 1992; see also Botting, 1997). In addition, Scottish and Irish migrants living in England have worse than average health (Wild and McKeigue, 1997).

The Asian community has a much higher mortality rate from coronary heart disease than the general population (Wild and McKeigue, 1997). It is also more at risk of other circulatory diseases, as are people born in the Caribbean and in Africa. Certain cancers, such as liver cancer, are more common in ethnic groups, although cancer mortality as a whole is lower than in the general population. People originating from the Indian subcontinent have a much higher than average rate of tuberculosis infection, and there is a disproportionately high incidence of diabetes in West Indian and Asian communities. In addition, a small number of diseases are wholly or mainly confined to ethnic populations, including rickets (predominantly affecting people of Asian origin) and sickle-cell anaemia and thalassaemia (affecting people originating from Africa, Asia, the Middle East and the Mediterranean). Finally, there are apparent variations in mental health, as reflected in above-average reported rates of mental illness and admission to mental hospitals among the Caribbean community (Cochrane and Bal, 1989; Cope, 1989; Nazroo, 1997b).

One can find several explanations for these variations, each carrying different policy implications (see Ahmad, 1993a; Smaje, 1995; Nazroo, 1998). Some variation may be caused by certain biases arising from inadequate research methods. Criticism has centred on the higher reported rates of mental illness and admission for Caribbean people, mentioned above, which has been attributed to misdiagnosis and racial stereotyping (see Sashidaran and Francis, 1993). More generally, the methods used to categorise people can produce misleading conclusions. In mortality studies, ethnic status is based on country of birth, which is a very crude indicator of ethnicity. Indeed, Nazroo (1997a) found that when a more detailed approach to ethnic classification was adopted, certain subgroups did not actually have a higher rate of mortality. In the case of coronary heart disease, for example, it was found that Pakistani and Bangladeshi people were responsible for the higher rate of Asian mortality, while the Indian community had a similar rate to that of whites. Furthermore, within the Indian community, Hindus and Sikhs had a low rate of coronary heart disease mortality, while Muslims had a relatively high rate.

Although there are undoubtedly major methodological problems in measuring the relative health status of ethnic groups, no one seriously believes that the observed variations are entirely artefactual. Indeed, ethnic differences may also be due to cultural or genetic factors. Cultural factors include a variation in healthy lifestyle between different ethnic groups, for which there is some evidence (HEA, 1997; Nazroo, 1997a). Indian, Pakistani and Bangladeshi men, for example, report a lower level of physical exercise than the general population, while Afro-Caribbean and Bangladeshi men report a higher rate of smoking. Genetic factors also play a part in health inequality. As already noted, some ethnic groups are known to be vulnerable to a number of diseases, and it is possible that genetic scientists may well discover others in the future.

Material explanations relate excess mortality and ill health among ethnic groups to socio-economic disadvantage. There is evidence to suggest that socio-economic class difference is relevant to some ethnic groups: Afro-Caribbean people and the Pakistani and Bangladeshi communities (but not the Indian community) are significantly over-represented in social classes IIIm, IV and V, and in lower-income groups (Nazroo, 1998). Two-thirds of Pakistani and Bangladeshi households fall into the bottom fifth of the income distribution compared with 19 per cent of white households (ONS, 1998). Some argue that social class is an inadequate explanation of the difference in mortality between ethnic groups and the general population (Harding and Maxwell, 1997). Others have commented that conventional measures of social class fail to capture the material circumstances of ethnic groups relative to others (see

Nazroo, 1997a, 1998). Indeed, when alternative measures of socio-economic disadvantage (such as car ownership) are used, such factors do correspond to an inequality in health between various ethnic groups. Moreover, other forms of disadvantage, including social exclusion and the ecological effects of living in a particularly unhealthy locality, might affect ethnic health (Nazroo, 1998). This in turn raises questions about the impact of racism on health. It is possible that overt and implicit racism has an effect on mental and physical health (Williams *et al.*, 1994). Similarly institutional race discrimination and insensitivity in service provision (see Kelleher and Hillier, 1996) may affect the mortality rate if people from ethnic backgrounds receive inadequate or inappropriate health care (see Lear *et al.*, 1994; Nazroo, 1997a; Smaje and Le Grand, 1997) or face difficulty accessing services (see Smaje and Le Grand, 1997 for a recent analysis of ethnicity and the equitable use of health services).

## Gender

Important differences in health status exist between men and women (for a more detailed discussion see Miles, 1991; Doyal, 1995). Women live on average five years longer than men, and the death rate is lower for women than men in every age group. Older women, however, describe a higher rate of self-reported longstanding illness compared with men in the same age group, and women of all ages are more likely than men to use GP and outpatient health services (OPCS, 1996). Men and women differ in their susceptibility to different kinds of morbidity. For example, disorders and diseases of the reproductive system are more commonly found in women, and women report a higher level of psychiatric morbidity (Meltzer *et al.*, 1995). Men, however, are more prone to injury and accidental death compared with women in the same age group.

Aside from obvious anatomical differences between the sexes, a range of factors explain the variation in health status. Socio-economic factors have a differential impact on male and female health: the class gradient for mortality and life expectancy is steeper for men than women (MacIntyre and Hunt, 1996; Soni Raleigh and Kiri, 1997). This is not to say that women are invulnerable to the health effects of socio-economic disadvantage. Indeed, a strong socio-economic gradient exists for psychosocial health: disadvantaged women, in particular single mothers, have a poor level of psychosocial health (Macran *et al.*, 1996). This may be partly explained by the difficulties faced by women performing the caring role in the context of financial hardship (Graham, 1993b).

The changing role of women in society is also extremely relevant when considering gender differences in health. Increased female participation in the labour market – often in casual, part-time and relatively low-paid jobs –

has ambivalent health implications. Although paid work brings in extra income, which may improve the quality of life, it can also bring added stress, particularly when coupled with family responsibilities (Doyal, 1995). Paid employment has been associated with more illness for working-class women with children but less illness for middle-class women with the same family responsibilities (Blaxter, 1990). Much seems to depend on the aspect of health under consideration and the kind of work undertaken. The association between paid work and better health is less apparent for physical than mental health, and applies less to women in full-time work and those in professional and managerial posts (Bartley *et al.*, 1992). Interestingly, this study found no relationship between employment status and domestic conditions, suggesting that the impact of paid work in terms of improved income may offset the negative effects of combining a high domestic work-load with employment.

Womens' role in society has changed in other ways relevant to health. Many women have greater financial independence and more freedom of choice than they did a generation ago. They now participate more in further and higher education, in the professions and in other institutions that were almost exclusively male less than half a century ago. At the same time, women's lifestyles have changed, and this too has implications for health. Women are more likely than men to diet, and they are more prone to eating disorders (Lawrence, 1987). At the same time, women are becoming more similar to men in other aspects of health behaviour. Alcohol consumption is increasing in young women, and this has been paralleled by an increase in drink-related problems (Ettore, 1997). Around a third of women under 50, the same proportion as men, are smokers. Among teenage schoolchildren, more girls than boys now smoke, raising the prospect that female lung cancer sufferers could outnumber men in the future. When examining the health variations associated with gender, one should be aware that these interact with cultural and ethnic differences. Many of the changes in female work and lifestyle have not occurred uniformly, and there is in some ethnic groups a greater cultural resistance to these trends. In view of this, one must take into account the interaction between ethnic background, gender and social class when evaluating the impact of social change on health of women.

## Inequities and Inequalities: The Policy Response

Having now explored the main dimensions of health inequality in some depth, the remainder of this chapter is devoted to an analysis of the policy response. This section begins by examining the approach of the Conservative governments of the 1980s and 90s, before moving on to consider the Blair government's initiatives in this field.

## The Conservatives' Record

In their study of inequality in the UK, Goodman *et al.* (1997, p. 274) comment that 'one thing that can be stated without fear of contradiction is that the income distribution has grown wider.' According to an inquiry by the Joseph Rowntree Foundation (1995), income inequality grew rapidly from the late 1970s up to the early 1990s, reaching a level not seen since 1945. Between 1979 and 1992, the top tenth of the income distribution enjoyed a more than 60 per cent increase in income (after housing cost was taken into account), while the income in the bottom 10 per cent fell by 17 per cent. The deprivation level also increased in the 1980s and the early 1990s. By 1996, one quarter of all households were living on below half the average income (after deducting housing costs) compared with 9 per cent in 1979 (Department of Social Security, 1998). These inequalities persisted throughout the 1990s. By 1995, the richest fifth of the population received 40 per cent of total household disposable income (up from 36 per cent in 1979) while the share of the poorest fifth fell from 9.4 per cent to 7.9 per cent.

It has, however, been suggested that the rise in income inequality had begun to slow down during the middle of the 1990s (see Goodman *et al.*, 1997). It is also the case that the welfare state continued to redistribute towards the poor, particularly with regard to benefits in kind, as reflected in the provision of public services (Hills, 1997). The average original income of the top fifth of households in 1995–96, for example, was 16 times that of the bottom fifth before adjusting for taxes and benefits in kind, but only three-and-a-half times greater after these were taken into account (ONS, 1998).

Furthermore, one should mention that other measures of inequality – based on expenditure rather than income – indicate a less dramatic increase in inequality since the 1970s (see Goodman *et al.*, 1997). Also, the composition of the poorest group is not fixed: just over half of the poorest 20 per cent of the population in 1991 were still in the same category in 1995 (ONS, 1998). So inequalities may be exaggerated by the temporary circumstances of people who will later be found in a higher income group (such as students before graduation or people who are temporarily unemployed). Nevertheless, income inequality certainly increased. This was due to broader social and economic changes, such as the decline in long-term, full-time employment and the growth of low-paid, casual work, early retirement, the rise of dual-income families and the growth of single parenting. These trends were compounded by government policies. The Thatcher and Major governments' main priorities were to restrict inflation and reduce public expenditure and taxation while improving the incentive to work and enterprise, while other objectives, such as full employment and income redistribution, were disregarded. Policies were introduced that reduced the burden of taxation for those on a high income, cut entitlements to welfare benefits and abandoned low-wage regulation.

These policies were heavily criticised for undermining economic performance and creating unnecessary social divisions (Commission for Social Justice, 1994). The economic and social trends of the 1980s and 90s were characterised by Hutton (1996) as the '40:30:30 society', 40 per cent of the population having secure permanent jobs and a good material standard of living; 30 per cent having insecure and casual employment and living a fairly precarious existence; and 30 per cent being marginalised, unemployed or living on poverty wages. These divisions were not unique to the UK. In the USA, Galbraith (1992) identified a similar phenomenon, 'the culture of contentment', in which the experience of a contented majority contrasted sharply with that of a deprived underclass.

Widening social and economic inequalities were also associated with greater health inequalities. During the 1980s, the overall mortality rate increased and life expectancy improved for all social classes, but the improvement was greater for the higher social classes than for social classes III, IV and V (Drever and Bunting, 1997; Hattersley, 1997), leading to increased inequality. Indeed, the mortality rate for social class V was actually higher in the period 1991–93 than 20 years before (Drever *et al.*, 1996). As a consequence, the differential in mortality rate between social classes V and I rose from almost twofold to almost threefold in this period (Drever and Bunting, 1997). Other studies found a similar trend. Blane *et al.* (1990) identified a widening of social class differential in terms of years of life lost through premature death. Phillimore *et al.* (1994) found an increasing mortality differential between affluent and deprived areas in northern England, while McLoone and Boddy (1994), in a study of affluent and deprived areas in Scotland, identified a greater difference in mortality rate for heart disease and lung cancer in 1990–92 than a decade earlier. Later, Soni Raleigh and Kiri (1997) found a growing gap in life expectancy between affluent and deprived areas in England, while Shaw *et al.* (1998) revealed a polarisation in the life expectancy rate within Britain as a whole. Further research, including data up to 1996, found an even wider gap in mortality, with an almost 10-year difference in male life expectancy between social classes I and V (Shaw *et al.*, 1999).

Throughout the 1980s, the Thatcher government denied that health inequality was caused by material factors, instead attributing it to statistical artefact, social mobility or, more often than not, individual behaviour (see above). This was reflected in the rejection of the Black Report of 1980, which argued for policies to improve material conditions for the poor (DHSS, 1980; Townsend *et al.*, 1992). The Thatcher government also denied that health inequality was widening as a result of its policies, but when the Health Education Council commissioned a study to update the finding of the Black Report, further evidence emerged to challenge these denials. It was shown that health inequality was growing in line with social and economic inequalities (Whitehead, 1987; Townsend *et al.*, 1992). In particular, the report noted the growing threat to health posed by homelessness, unemployment and child poverty, and criticised the government's failure to tackle these problems.

## The Major Government

The Major government accepted the need for a national health strategy but refused to incorporate equity as a key objective. Subsequently, the *Health of the Nation* strategy (Cm 1986, 1992), discussed at length in Chapter 4, was heavily criticised for not seeking to reduce health inequality. A reference to the WHO European regional target for inequalities (see below) was made in the Appendix to the Green Paper outlining the strategy (Cm 1523, 1991), but only to make the point that it would probably not be achieved. Neither the Green nor the White Paper explicitly discussed the link between poverty and ill health, although both acknowledged that there were 'variations' in health status between different socio-economic groups and attributed these to 'a complex interplay of genetic, biological, social, environmental, cultural and behavioural factors' (Cm 1986, 1992, p. 122). A controversial section on housing and ill health did appear in an earlier draft of the Green Paper but was deleted before publication (Moore, 1991). The White Paper stated that the government would 'continue to promote choice and quality in housing, having regard to health and other benefits' (Cm 1986, 1992, p. 28), and identified 'healthy housing' as a setting for health promotion.

As the Major government sought to implement its health strategy, it became increasingly difficult to ignore the mounting evidence on the impact of social inequality on health (see Benzeval *et al.*, 1995). Indeed, the government's own health targets were being undermined by a variation in health status between socio-economic groups. Consequently, following pressure to examine the issue further, particularly from those professionals encountering adverse socio-economic conditions in everyday practice (see BMA, 1995, 1999; Health Visitors' Association, 1996), the DoH established a review of 'health variations' (chosen in preference to the more politically charged term 'inequalities'). The review was confined to making recommendations about what the DoH and the NHS could do about the problem; it did not cover other government departments and agencies. Unsurprisingly, its report was a rather cautious document, the main recommendations concerning the use of the commissioning process at local level to identify and reduce health variations. It also called for more evidence in this field, which prompted an increase in funding for research into 'health variations' (DoH, 1995a).

The failure fully to acknowledge health inequality related to socio-economic class was based on political reasoning. Those who were disadvantaged in terms of material welfare, and who had the worst health, tended not to vote for the Conservative Party. Studies by Davey Smith and Dorling (1996, 1997) showed a strong negative association between voting Conservative and mortality rate (and, correspondingly, a strong positive association between voting Labour and mortality rate) at the general elections of 1983, 1987, 1992 and 1997. It appears that the Conservative governments recognised that there were too few votes in tackling socio-economic inequality.

In contrast, the Conservative governments were much more wary of the women's vote and took steps to ensure that policies reflected at least some of the concerns expressed by women's organisations. Hence the expansion of screening services for breast and cervical cancer was a key priority from the mid-1980s (see Chapter 6). Practitioners were also encouraged to develop services that were more closely geared to women's needs in areas such as maternity services and general practice, but beyond this, there was no comprehensive strategy aimed at improving womens' health during the 1980s and 90s, nor was there a programme to improve the health of disadvantaged women. Notably, there was an absence of social policies that reflected women's changing role in society, such as improved child care provision. Furthermore, some women, particularly those towards the bottom of the income distribution, such as single mothers, were disadvantaged by government reforms (particularly in the field of social security), with adverse implications for their health and the health of their children.

The Thatcher and Major governments responded to some extent to the issue of ethnic health inequality, not wishing to alienate ethnic voters unnecessarily. Hence a few measures specifically geared to this were introduced in the 1980s. These included the Stop Rickets Campaign and the Asian Mother and Baby Campaign, but such initiatives were regarded as piecemeal (Smaje, 1995; Johnson, 1993). In the early 1990s, policy began to focus more on the health needs of ethnic groups, and there was an increase in the amount of research in this field. In addition, new rules were introduced to try to improve the representation of ethnic groups within the NHS. Although these initiatives were welcomed, they did not equate to the comprehensive and co-ordinated strategy to improve the health of ethnic minorities that was called for (Ahmad, 1993a, 1993b; Smaje, 1995; Jamdagni, 1996).

## International Developments

Health inequality is not confined to the UK, other countries also having had a poor record in this field (see Fox, 1989; Power, 1994; Mackenbach *et al.*, 1997; Kunst *et al.*, 1998). Even so, the refusal of the Thatcher government (and later the Major government too) to acknowledge the impact of material inequalities on health was increasingly out of step with developments elsewhere. The fact that the UK had become one of the most unequal among industrialised countries (UN Development Programme, 1996) was ignored. In contrast, some nations viewed material inequality as problematic and adopted policies to tackle health-related inequality (see Dahlgren and Whitehead, 1992). Moreover, these policies operated within an international framework: *Declaration of Alma Ata. Report of the International Conference on Primary Health Care* (WHO, 1978) emphasised the attainment of the highest possible level of health for all people. These sentiments were reiterated throughout the 1980s at international conferences organised by the WHO and others, such as the First International Conference on Health Promotion (WHO, 1986a),which generated the Ottawa Charter on Health Promotion. This document identified equity as a key goal of health promotion and stated that 'health promotion focuses on achieving equity in health. Health promotion action aims at reducing differences in current health status and ensuring equal opportunities and resources to enable all people to achieve their fullest health potential'. Subsequently, the Adelaide Recommendations, produced by the Second International Conference on Health Promotion (WHO, 1988) continued this theme by stating that 'inequalities in health are rooted in inequities in society' and that, in order to close the gap between advantaged and disadvantaged people, policies would be required to 'improve access to health-enhancing goods and services and create supportive environments'.

Equity was a key feature of the WHO's *Health for All* strategy (WHO, 1981). In 1985, specific targets were set for the European region that included a reduction of at least 25 per cent in the difference in health status between groups and countries by improving the health of disadvantaged groups (WHO Regional Office for Europe, 1985b). Another target was that 'by the year 2000 all the people of the region should have a better opportunity of living in houses and settlements that provide a healthy and safe environment' (WHO, 1985b, p. 89). Meanwhile, at the local level in the UK, an effort was made to improve the health of poorer people through various social interventions in areas such as housing, transport, community facilities and economic regeneration (see Betts, 1993; King's Fund, 1999). This occurred in a number of cities across the UK, some of which were involved in the original WHO *Healthy Cities* initiative (Davies and Kelly, 1992) and others that were not (see Chapter 4). Yet, in the absence of a national strategy, these efforts were unlikely to achieve their full potential. Moreover, central government policy was in many respects inimical to these local projects, particularly in areas such as housing and transport where local authorities' powers were limited.

## The Blair Government

When the Blair government came to office in 1997, most observers believed that equity in health would have a higher priority than over the previous two decades. In opposition, the Labour Party had frequently criticised the Conservative government's refusal to acknowledge the relationship between health inequity and material inequality. Furthermore, Labour was traditionally closer to organisations such as trade unions and welfare organisations that had campaigned vigorously for action in this area.

Meanwhile, activities at an international level continued to emphasise the need to reduce health inequality. The WHO, which had begun to reformulate its *Health for All Strategy*, placed even greater emphasis on equity in health (see WHO, 1998a). The European regional targets were updated, the equity target now stating that 'by the year 2020 the health gap between socio-economic groups within countries should be reduced by one fourth in all member states, by substantially improving the health of disadvantaged groups' (WHO Regional Office for Europe, 1998a, p. 180). Another relevant target (updating the housing target mentioned earlier in this chapter) was that 'by the year 2015 people in the region should have greater opportunities to live in healthy physical and social environments at home, at school, at the workplace and in the local community' (p. 193). In particular, it was specified that 'the safety and the quality of the home environment should be improved, through increased personal and family skills for health promotion and protection, and the health risks from the physical home environment should be reduced' (p. 193). Meanwhile, the importance of equity in health had been emphasised by subsequent international conferences on health promotion organised by WHO. The Jakarta Declaration, the product of the Fourth International Conference on Health Promotion (WHO, 1997a), called among other things for the inclusion of 'equity-focused health impact assessments as an integral part of policy development'.

Partly in response to these international developments, a number of countries, including Finland, Sweden and Spain, established an official inquiry into health inequality. In the UK, an independent inquiry into inequality was appointed, under the chairmanship of Sir Donald Acheson, a former Chief Medical Officer. The Acheson inquiry made 39 key recommendations (Appendix 1). These included: incorporating inequality within HIA (see Exhibit 7.2); giving a high priority to policies aimed at improving health and reducing inequality among women of childbearing age, expectant mothers and young children; and endorsing policies to reduce inequality of income and improve living standards for those receiving social security benefits (Independent Inquiry into Inequalities in Health, 1998). The inquiry also recommended additional resources for schools in deprived areas, as well as policies to increase work opportunities, to improve the quality of housing and public transport and to tackle ethnic and gender inequalities in health.

Despite earlier commitments, the Blair government was ambivalent about health inequality. Although one of the key aims of its public health strategy set out in a Green Paper during 1998 was 'to improve the health of the worst off in society and to narrow the health gap' (Cm 3852, 1998, p. 5), the government cautioned that it would not seek to narrow the health gap between the worst off and better off in society 'by slowing the drive for further progress in improved health among the many' (Cm 3852, 1998, p. 56). Narrowing health inequality was to be regarded as a longer-term policy that would inform strategy in the main target areas (in England, mental health, cancer, heart disease, accidents and stroke) rather than be identified as a target itself.

Responsibility was placed on local health authorities to establish HImPs, which included targeting and tackling health inequality. In so doing, health authorities were expected to work with other stakeholders, including local authorities (see Chapter 4). The emphasis was very much on encouraging local decision makers to set their own targets and devise appropriate strategies. This, however, proved to be easier said than done. A report from the Kings' Fund (Kendall, 1999) noted that many different types of target existed but that there was little consensus about which should be used. It identified *symbolic targets*, which are mainly intended to motivate and inspire, their main value lying in their articulation of long-term goals and values. The main disadvantage is that they are of little practical use and can demotivate if unattainable in the short term.

A second type of target is based on *risk factors associated with ill health*, such as the smoking or unemployment rate. Such targets are more concrete than symbolic targets but could again fail to inspire if too ambitious. A third approach focuses on *health outcomes*, such as infant mortality. The advantage of this type of target is that it is very clearly understood by the public and health professionals; the main disadvantage is that less quantifiable outcomes (for example, an improvement in the quality of life) may not be detected by such an approach. The fourth approach defines targets in terms of *groups or areas at particular risk*, such as the health of children in deprived areas. This may be advantageous because it takes into account several different dimensions of the problem group or area, but an over-reliance on this approach may neglect those with pressing needs who fall outside these categories, such as poor people living in relatively affluent rural areas. As the King's Fund report observed, an eclectic approach to target setting is most appropriate and is commonly adopted in practice by those with most experience of tackling health inequality.

When the Blair government published its White Paper on Public Health (Cm 4386, 1999), no further commitments on health equity were given. The DoH (1999d) did issue an 'action report' to the Acheson Report in which it described policies already adopted across government to address the issue of health inequality (DoH, 1999d). Both the White Paper and the action report placed a great emphasis on cross-governmental (or in the modern parlance 'joined-up government') solutions to health problems, including inequality. A commitment made in the earlier Green Paper to apply HIA to key policies was reiterated, specifically mentioning impact on health inequality (the reforms to the Single Regeneration Budget, discussed below, for example having already been subjected to HIA).

## Social Expenditure

The Blair government declared its aim of tackling the underlying causes of poor health. A number of programmes were introduced, aimed specifically at improving children's health and social needs, particularly in deprived areas (see Exhibit 10.1). In addition, £3.6 billion was allocated to local authorities to renovate their housing stock, although this fell short of the estimated £10 billion needed to meet the cost of repairs (Malpass, 1999). A programme of welfare reform was set in motion, which included 'New Deals' for unemployed people, for communities and, more controversially, for lone parents and disabled people (Cm 3805, 1998). Although these programmes were applauded by some for providing a greater opportunity for those on welfare, they were more cynically viewed as a way of limiting the welfare budget. It was suspected by some, notably claimants' organisations and welfare pressure groups, that this motive was stronger than the need to alleviate poverty, a concern echoed among Labour MPs, some of whom rebelled against their leadership on this issue.

Other social and economic policies also attracted criticism. The Blair government accepted the need for a minimum wage and imposed a rate of £3.60 an hour in April 1998, but this level was criticised for being too low and for not applying in full to younger workers. The government was also attacked by some for not redistributing income. The conclusion drawn by the Institute for Fiscal Studies, however, was that the Blair government's early budgets were mildly redistributive, taking some resources from the high-income groups and redistributing them to those in the middle and bottom of the income distribution. The cumulative impact of the 1997–2000 Budgets was that the poorest tenth of the population gained by 9.2 per cent. The second, third and fourth deciles gained by 8.5, 5 and 3 per cent respectively, while the top two deciles in the income distribution lost out slightly. (Reed, 2000). Another factor potentially contributing to decreased inequality was the increase in spending for services such as education and health, which represent important 'benefits in kind'. It remains to be seen, however, whether these budgetary decisions will actually reduce the inequity between rich and poorer members of the community. A report in 1999, found that income and health inequalities increased in the period 1995–98 (Howarth *et al.*, 1999). The latest available figures indicate that income inequality is increasing further, the top fifth of earners in 1998–99 taking 45 per cent of income after adjusting for tax and benefits, while the share of the poorest fifth fell to only 6 per cent (*Independent*, 2000b).

## Social Exclusion and Regeneration

The broader structural factors underlying health inequality and other social problems were examined by the Blair government. A Social Exclusion Unit was established within the Cabinet Office in 1997 and was given the task of formulating policies aimed at tackling multiple deprivation in England. (Other parts of the UK, though expected to draw on the work of the Social Exclusion Unit, had responsibility for their own particular strategies.) It published a report, *Bringing Britain Together* (Cm 4045, 1998), which was both a diagnosis of the problem and a prescription of what needed to be done. Building on new and existing regeneration programmes discussed below, the strategy set out by the Social Exclusion Unit aimed to introduce a multisectoral effort to improve the welfare of communities. This would require collaboration between various stakeholders at local level and improved co-ordination between relevant government departments. The Social Exclusion Unit was given the responsibility for co-ordinating government departments, 18 action teams being established to tackle specific aspects of social exclusion. The work was organised under five themes: getting people to work, improving community support systems and networks, building a future for young people, improving access to services such as shops and banks (somewhat ironic in the light of the banks' attitudes to branch closures), and improving the way in which government at all levels tackles social exclusion.

It was envisaged that this strategy would be closely associated with regeneration programmes, such as New Deal for Communities, which allocated £800m over 10 years to address multiple deprivation in particular neighbourhoods. This complemented programmes established by the Conservative governments in the 1980s and 90s, such as the Single Regeneration Budget, which was introduced in 1994 as a result of an amalgamation of various existing schemes. Although at the time this rationalisation was welcomed, criticism of government policy in this area remained, focusing on the lack of strategic purpose, poor accountability, the lack of involvement of stakeholders and the lack of genuine assessment of the relative needs of the regions and localities (see Regional Policy Commission, 1996). The Blair government retained the Single Regeneration Budget but initiated a number of changes with a view to relating the allocation of resources more closely to needs, promoting greater involvement on the part of communities and stakeholders and providing a more strategic overview at regional level through new Regional Development Agencies. It also intended that these new arrangements would integrate regeneration programmes with broader environmental strategies: the Regional Development Agencies' remit includes the promotion of sustainable economic development as well as social and physical regeneration.

A further aim of the Blair government was to improve the link between regeneration programmes and other programmes such as housing, health and education. After taking office in 1997, the Blair government announced a series of action zones, in education, employment and health, where needs were particularly great. These were expected to dovetail with the broader regeneration programmes described above. Another development was the report of the Urban Task Force in 1999 under the chairmanship of Lord Rogers, which identified a grim picture of Britain's cities and set out a vision for revitalising urban areas (DETR, 1999b). It proposed concentrating housing development within urban areas, incentives to encourage people to live in inner city areas and for builders to renovate properties, disincentives for countryside developers, a £500m renaissance fund for local groups to improve their own neighbourhoods, and transport schemes to encourage pedestrianisation, cycling and public transport (see Chapter 7).

As a footnote to this, the Social Exclusion Unit produced a national strategy for neighbourhood renewal (Cabinet Office, 2000a) which set a framework for consultation in this field. It proposed a 10-year strategy to improve the most deprived neighbourhoods, which included a cross-cutting unit to drive forward the strategy in Whitehall, incentives for local partnerships involving public, private, community and voluntary sector organisations, services to have explicit performance targets and resources to deliver improvements and to build up these communities using 30 'key ideas'. These included community finance initiatives to provide funding for small businesses, increasing use of neighbourhood wardens to patrol estates, 'job squads' based on estates and neighbourhood learning centres to improve adult skills. None of the ideas put forward was particularly original, although by bringing them together in one comprehensive strategy, the Social Exclusion Unit at least emphasised that disjointed, piecemeal and reactive interventions were no longer appropriate. However, the extent to which this agenda would be embraced and resourced by government and other stakeholders remained to be seen.

## Will Regeneration Work?

The scope of these initiatives is potentially wide, and they provide an opportunity to improve the health status of deprived people and communities. Although health has been increasingly recognised as an important part of the regeneration agenda (see HEA, 1998; DoE, 1996c), it is, however, only one of many competing considerations. It is also relatively easy to overlook, particularly when health priorities conflict with economic priorities. To put it another way, economic regeneration must incorporate a philosophy of health promotion, and this has been rather slow to develop. Moreover, the regeneration strategy says little about geographical areas that are arguably 'overdeveloped' or individuals whose wealth and income are extremely high. Yet these factors contribute much to social exclusion and inequity. Moreover, it can be argued that social exclusion policies that tend to concentrate on the poor and deprived areas and the people living in them tend towards victim blaming (Scott-Samuel, 1998). Notwithstanding the budgetary changes mentioned earlier, the Blair government appeared reluctant to seriously challenge the existing distribution of income and wealth in Britain.

## Conclusion

Nonetheless, the prospects of a greater equity in health in the future look better than they have done for two decades. There does appear to be a greater commitment to the kind of equity principles outlined by Whitehead (1992) and discussed in the early part of this chapter. Moreover, domestic policies are operating in a favourable international context, as reflected by the revised WHO targets for Europe (and also the London declaration of 1995, which calls on health professionals to lobby for policies to reduce poverty and improve the health of the population; see Action in International Medicine, 1995). There are of course powerful countervailing pressures: global capitalism generates huge inequality not only between, but also within countries. As a result, the ever-changing social and economic structure continues to set  new patterns of inequality that are not amenable to simple redistributive solutions.

There is nevertheless much evidence to suggest that intervention can make a difference. Whitehead (1995) identified four different levels of policy intervention: (1) strengthening individuals, (2) strengthening communities, (3) improving access to essential facilities and services, and (4) encouraging macroeconomic and cultural change. Interventions at policy levels (1) and (2) have tended to treat symptoms of the problem rather than the underlying causes, and because they have tended to be relatively small scale, their overall impact has been minimal. Policy interventions (3) and (4) tend to involve the whole population rather than a specific subgroup. These tend to confer substantial health benefits, particularly among the most vulnerable groups. Hence Whitehead concludes that an effective policy must include income maintenance policies, education and training policies and equitable fiscal and income distribution policies.

This is not to say that targeted and smaller-scale interventions are irrelevant; instead, they should be introduced within a broader framework. While specific measures can be effective (Arblaster *et al.*, 1997), one has to look at impact of the package of measures as a whole. There is above all a need for co-ordination between the various sectors of decision making that impinge on disadvantage and deprivation, such as economic regeneration (HEA, 1998), housing (see Standing Conference on Public Health, 1994; Conway, 1995) and education (Benzeval *et al.*, 1995; Dennehy *et al.*, 1997).

Despite the volume of research that has been generated in recent years, better-quality evidence on the causes of health inequality is still required. The relationship between individuals and their social context must also be more fully understood. This requires not only a better understanding from a lay perspective of how inequalities arise (Popay *et al.*, 1998), but also a more complete analysis of the complex interaction between such variables as ethnicity, gender, place and socio-economic inequality (MacIntyre *et al.*, 1993; MacIntyre and Hunt, 1997; Nazroo, 1998). The relationship between relative income inequality and health inequality merits further inquiry in view of the controversies outlined earlier in this chapter. Furthermore, in view of the growing support for a lifecourse perspective on inequality (see Blane *et al.*, 1998; Dike van de Mheen *et al.*, 1998), more must be known about the impact of cumulative disadvantage on health, in particular about the critical periods when disadvantage appears to contribute most to inequality in health status.

# 11

# Conclusions

In Chapter 1, three broad approaches were outlined as a framework for analysing public health policy: ideological perspectives, models of the policy process and theories of expertise and risk. Having explored public health issues in some detail in the intervening chapters, it is now possible to draw some general conclusions within the context of this framework.

## Ideological Perspectives

The revival of interest in public health since the 1970s can be explained by support from a range of ideological perspectives. Socialists, predisposed to collective solutions to health problems, communitarians, seeking to integrate collectivist solutions with greater individual responsibility, and Greens, favouring ecological and holistic approaches, espoused principles consistent with the new public health agenda. Although these ideological perspectives were in many ways incongruous with the Conservative government's agenda during the 1980s and 90s, they did exert an indirect influence upon decision makers in this period. Underlying public support for Green principles, combined with pressure from the international community on issues such as global warming, did lead to a limited 'greening' of government in the UK.

Meanwhile, the public's continued attachment to collective solutions to welfare problems, particularly in the field of health, made it difficult for government to reform policies and programmes according to neo-liberal principles. Moreover, those promoting neo-liberalism, although hostile to the 'nanny state', endorsed many public health initiatives because they believed this would lead to increased individual responsibility for health and reduce the burden on the state as people became healthier. In reality, however, this created further pressure on government to introduce a more interventionist strategy in this field. There is an interesting parallel here with the public health interventions of the Victorian era, including improvements in sanitation, which were initially justified on the basis of individualist ideas and aimed to reduce the burden on the state imposed by the sick poor. But this eventually led to an expansion of state involvement and responsibility, leading to policies that addressed the underlying social and economic roots of illness, which were firmly rooted in collectivist principles.

It is also possible to comment on the ideological forces that have shaped the Blair government's policies on public health. There has in principle been a commitment to communitarian ideals – combining individual rights with responsibilities and invoking state authority when necessary to uphold the common good. The White Paper on Public Health for England (Cm 4386, 1999) reflected these themes, setting out contracts for health in which government, other agencies and individuals all had a part to play. Prevention, through social and environmental interventions, as well as health service restructuring and reforms of health promotion and screening services, was identified as the key to health improvement. One must be careful to distinguish rhetoric from reality as health promotion and disease prevention still account for a relatively small proportion of the health budget. Indeed, whether or not health consider-ations will be increasingly reflected across the range of government policies remains to be seen. Nonetheless, it is important in this context to note that the rhetoric of prevention is itself politically significant, enabling governments to manage pressing problems of health policy, in particular by reorienting profes-sional activity, extending government competence in health policy making and asserting individual responsibility (Freeman, 1992, 1995).

Although collectivist and Green ideas have done much to place and main-tain public health on the agenda, the liberal/individualist perspective has remained extremely influential with regard to the nature of the interventions adopted. This to some degree confirms the conclusion of Mills and Saward (1993) that the British state has tended to favour negative liberty, the freedom of the individual from interference, rather than positive liberty, which implies constraint on some activities in order to enable individuals to flourish. This explains in part the reluctance of both Labour and Conservative governments in the past to adopt tougher regulatory policies to improve public health in fields such as transport, the environment, alcohol and tobacco, and food. In addition, there has been ideological opposition to radical income redistribu-tion policies aimed at minimising health inequity. The persistence of these neo-liberal ideologies both in society and among governing élites helps us to understand the difficulties faced by the Blair government in seeking to formulate and implement policies in these areas, notably transport policy, and its tentative approach hitherto on redistribution.

Opposition to public health intervention on libertarian grounds is not new. Campaigns for the freedom to eat beef on the bone and to drink unpasteurised milk or unfluoridated water have antecedents in the actions of the Victorian campaigners against vaccination and the Contagious Diseases Acts. It is often said that liberal democratic governments ignore the popular will at their peril. In reality, it is possible for them to ignore and even oppress significant minorities and continue to govern for many years, as the experience of the Thatcher government clearly illustrated. A more serious problem for government occurs when powerful commercial interests are threatened. These can influence the media and mobilise public opinion under the banner of individual liberty, as has occurred for example on alcohol- and tobacco-related issues over the years.

This is not to say that the demon of the nanny state is without foundation. There are genuine fears about intolerance shown towards people with particular lifestyles or specific eating and drug-taking habits (Bennett and DiLorenzo, 1999). To attempt to force these individuals down a particular path is not only illiberal; it may also be counterproductive, leading to hostile opposition or passive alienation. This is particularly important to note given that an unhealthy lifestyle may be seen by some, particularly disaffected young people, as a way of rejecting authority. Public health policies may need to coerce individuals in the interests of the broader community and in some cases for their own personal welfare, but this must be done in such a way that recognises the cultural context in which people are located and that respects their rights as an individual, otherwise such interventions are likely to fail. This implies a more participatory approach to public health than has been countenanced hitherto, a point that will be returned to shortly in the context of risk identification and communication.

Public participation and involvement must take place in conjunction with approaches that combine effectiveness with a least objectionable approach to improving public health. Weale's (1983) discussion of the 'liberal paternalist' perspective is particularly relevant here. This perspective combines a respect for individual liberty (in a negative sense) with an acknowledgement that intervention is necessary to protect public health. From the point of view of a liberal paternalist, intervention is justified where health hazards are identified beyond reasonable doubt, and that such hazards have been established by experimental or quasi-experimental means. Liberal paternalists also prefer that the least coercive measures (such as taxation and the provision of information) should be chosen when seeking to change people's behaviour in order to improve personal and public health. Coercive measures, such as direct regulation, may, however, be warranted if there is clear evidence of harm and providing the impact of such measures is monitored.

# The Policy Process

What conclusions can be drawn about the public health policy process? The first and most obvious point, as others have noted, is that there is an increasingly important international dimension to public health (Beaglehole and Bonita, 1997). Although this book has focused mainly on the UK (and, more specifically, on England), the influence of international factors has been evident throughout. International agreements on pollution and drug control have created new frameworks within which national policies have developed. WHO strategies, such as *Health for All* (WHO, 1981) and other initiatives across a range of public health issues, from environment and health through to nutrition, have also provided useful guidance, although some countries, including the UK, have ignored key targets. The European Union has also developed a greater public health role and has influenced domestic policies in areas such as health and safety, the environment, drugs control, tobacco regulation and food policy.

Several factors have inhibited public health policy at the international level. Within Europe, commercial and national interests have prevented important reforms that might improve health. It has, for example, proved difficult to reform Common Agricultural Policy in such a way as to reflect health and environmental considerations. Moreover, the European Union harmonisation process has not necessarily improved health standards. There are instances (for example, the food additive and GM labelling regulations discussed in Chapter 8) when harmonisation has apparently weakened domestic regulation. Meanwhile, at a global level, agreements on world trade and the associated mechanisms for ensuring free and fair trade have failed to place sufficient weight on the health dimension. In addition, global industries, such as the tobacco, alcohol, food and chemical industries, have frustrated international efforts to counter specific public health problems and have even intimidated individual countries and trading blocs attempting to take independent action.

The influence of commercial interests over public health policy operates at the domestic level as well. The preceding text is littered with examples of how they have successfully opposed and limited policies that threaten their profitability. As a result, potentially effective policies on alcohol abuse, tobacco, food, health and safety, and the environment have not been adopted or not fully implemented. Commercial interests have economic leverage, are politically well resourced, liaise closely with government on health-related issues, and are represented on key advisory committees, particularly in the areas of transport, the environment and food. They also have significant Parliamentary influence as well as effective links with the media.

As has been shown, however, commercial interests do not always and everywhere operate against public health. In Chapter 8, for example, it was observed that some enterprises, notably in the food retail sector, have shown greater sensitivity to public opinion than others. The increasing economic leverage of the large supermarket chains has produced some positive results from a public health perspective, although a great deal depends on the public awareness of health issues. Hence the supermarkets have been responsive on high-profile issues such as GM foods but less sensitive on issues such as the environmental impact of retail distribution, which have yet to penetrate public consciousness.

The media has played an important role in raising the profile of public health, largely through its coverage of health scares. It has also given tacit, in some cases overt, support to pressure-group campaigns in the field of public health. But the oxygen of publicity is not necessarily distributed according to the degree of health risk. The media are interested in health risks that are newsworthy. Anything to do with food safety, for example, is good copy because it potentially affects us all. Minority health issues, however, are less important to the media, particularly when the minority in question is relatively weak as a political force. This perhaps explains the limited media coverage given to the specific health problems facing the poor, such as bad housing conditions. Moreover, the media often adopt a simplistic view of public health that can impede the development of effective policies. The portrayal of GM technologies as 'Frankenstein foods', while attracting public attention, does not help a rational and constructive debate on the issue. In relation to cancer screening, the media overwhelmingly focus on the technology of clinical prevention, which is portrayed as unambiguously beneficial. Failures in screening services are attributed to managerial or professional factors, such as flawed management systems, poor training and professional incompetence, while the true cost effectiveness of screening programmes and the search for the underlying cause of such cancers attract very little attention, except perhaps for genetic factors, which are also related to the development of therapies rather than primary prevention.

Furthermore, sections of the media could be described as 'anti-public health' in that they are critical of efforts to improve health by promoting a change in lifestyle. The tabloid press in particular are aware that there is popularity to be gained by opposing certain interventions. Attempts to raise taxes on alcohol and tobacco, limit the use of the motor car and reduce the consumption of foods with a high fat and sugar content are hardly popular to begin with. The tabloids find it easy (and presumably, in terms of newspaper sales, commercially beneficial) to pillory public health campaigners on such issues as interfering busybodies who want to remove all traces of pleasure from the life of ordinary people irrespective of the merits of the policy in question.

Pressure groups campaigning for an improvement in public health are gaining in strength but remain relatively weak in comparison to the commercial lobbies. Attempts to create a single lobby group in this field have only recently come to fruition – with the formation of the UK Public Health Alliance in 1999 – and it remains to be seen how effective this new body will be. The public health lobby is by its very nature fragmented into a host of single-issue groups, environmental pressure groups and professional organisations. It is at its most effective when these groups pull more or less in the same direction, as occurred in the case of GM foods (see Chapter 8). There is much scope for joint campaigning. Outsider groups, which are not regularly consulted by government, can nevertheless mobilise public and parliamentary opinion and, in some cases, launch direct action. Their efforts can be complemented by professional bodies and associations, which have tended to have greater status and more opportunities to comment on government proposals at an early stage through the consultation process.

It should be noted in this context that doctors, and other experts in fields such as environmental health, transport, food, addictions and social welfare, have not acted as neutral agents, but have operated within the policy process, advocating policies that they believe are effective in promoting health and opposing those they believe to be harmful. The medical profession's arguments for a tobacco advertising ban, for example, has been advocated by doctors' organisations such as the BMA and through channels of medical advice within government.

Nonetheless, there has been concern that public health is still dominated too much by the medical profession, in particular by doctors concerned more with care and cure than prevention. Even those who do take a greater interest in public health issues tend to favour clinical prevention. Moreover, as Chapter 5 showed, public health medicine remains a fairly low-status speciality within medicine, and its practitioners seem to have lurched from one crisis to the next. It was also shown that, despite efforts to create a more multidisciplinary approach, doctors still dominate the public health function and the public health aspects of primary care. The same to some extent applies to public health campaigns, for according to Beaglehole and Bonita (1997), public health movements are heading down a narrow, disease-focused route that is consistent with an orthodox medical approach. But, as noted in earlier chapters, this approach is flawed, and the lesson appears to be that public health campaigns must be as inclusive as possible and incorporate an awareness of the broader social, economic and environmental context of health if they are to maximise their impact on policy.

A related point is that the policy networks that determine public health policy remain relatively closed. Expert advisory committees seem to have played an important role in the development of public health policies in areas such as HIV/AIDS, food safety, alcohol and tobacco use, drug abuse and cancer screening, to name but a few examples. A problem when assessing their influence, however, is that many advisory committees are often shrouded in secrecy. There has recently been a limited attempt to open up some of these committees by publishing more details of their composition and activities. In the light of criticism that they contain members with close connections to commercial interests, committees have published details about their members' interests. The number of lay appointments has also been increased. This has not, however, dispelled criticism that these are token gestures to stave off pressure for even greater public accountability and involvement.

Another problem is that because public health is so fragmented, policies develop in different networks. Food and agriculture policies have tended to be dominated by farming and food industry interests, transport by the roads lobby and so on. Efforts have been made to integrate health (and environmental) considerations in other areas of policy making, but this remains underdeveloped. The greater use of strategic EIA, incorporating health impact assessment, may enhance this process of integration, but it would be more effective if policy networks in areas relevant to public health were further integrated by improved communication, the sharing of information, greater openness and wider and more inclusive consultation processes to enable those representing public health interests to engage more effectively with decision makers in these policy sectors.

Within central government, public health policy has too often been seen as the responsibility of the health departments. This has had led to a rather narrow view of public health, dominated by medical concepts and interests and downplaying socio-economic or environmental factors. As a result, the NHS has been identified as the main vehicle for improving public health, even though it cannot achieve this alone. It is now recognised that the whole of government has a role in promoting health improvement. The Blair government's approach to 'joined-up government' is a welcome development from this perspective, but much more needs to be done in co-ordinating and integrating decision making if this is to become a reality, not just at local and regional level, but in central government too (see Cabinet Office, 2000b). Indeed, there have been suggestions that overall responsibility for public health should be located within the Cabinet Office in order to improve the integration of health considerations across the whole range of government policies, and that Government Offices of the regions should co-ordinate public health at the subnational level.

Other political institutions outside central government have had an impact on public health policy. Parliament, which in the UK has been dominated by central government for most of the post-war period, has nevertheless to some extent shaped policy, largely through its scrutiny function. For example, a number of select committees have reported on public health matters such as AIDS, food safety, cancer screening, heart disease prevention and the government's health strategy. Parliament rarely has an overt direct impact on policy: its influence lies in provoking government to respond to issues of concern or to reconsider specific aspects of its policy and legislation.

Local government is also weak relative to central government. Nevertheless, public health initiatives have been launched by local authorities, often in conjunction with other agencies such as the voluntary sector and health authorities (see Chapter 4). *Health for All* (WHO, 1998a), *Healthy Cities* (Davies and Kelly, 1992) and LA21 have encouraged local authorities in this area. But the lack of central government guidance accompanying these international initiatives has been unhelpful to say the least. Signs of a more positive lead from the centre have, however, emerged in recent years. The Blair government proposed that local authorities should have powers to promote the economic, social and environmental wellbeing of their areas and imposed a requirement to collaborate with the NHS on HImPs. Also, sustainable development issues related to health have been highlighted as an important aspect of economic and transport planning, and regeneration.

Finally in this section, has policy-oriented learning, discussed in Chapter 1, been evident in the development of public health policies? There are a few examples that deserve mention here. The Major government adopted a health strategy after a decade during which the Conservatives had rejected such an approach. This government also discounted health inequality as a policy problem but was later forced to recognise 'health variations', partly because of the impact these had on the attainment of health targets. Finally, for many years, British government refused even to consider policies that would reduce traffic congestion and pollution, but the 'advocacy coalition' supporting integrated and sustainable transport policies grew in strength to the extent that the predominant pro-road advocacy coalition became vulnerable, raising the prospect of such measures being implemented in the future. Subsequent developments, however, indicated that the battle would be a long-term one, as the pro-road lobby won concessions from government (see Chapter 7).

Policy-oriented learning can occur between as well as within political systems. Indeed, there is further evidence to support Leichter's (1991) view that public health policy ideas flow between countries. The UK has certainly adopted policy ideas – such as the precautionary principle in environmental policy – that have arisen in other countries. Other reforms, including the FSA, an integrated transport policy and EIA, have been to some extent influenced by experiences elsewhere. However, as Leichter noted, policy convergence is not always the outcome of policy learning, as countries may avoid introducing certain reforms because they perceive them as failing elsewhere. For example, New Zealand's experience of an independent public health commission was widely perceived as a failure, undermining the case to adopt a similar approach in the UK (see Chapter 5).

## Experts, Trust and Risk

As noted in the introductory chapter, there is much controversy surrounding the concept of risk in modern societies. According to some, modern society is host to an array of high-consequence risks. Others argue that these risks are exaggerated by processes of social construction. What light does this study shed on this debate? As has been shown, ill health has been associated with an exposure to pollution, drugs, chemicals, diet and social circumstances.

Individuals in modern societies therefore face many health risks, although whether these risks are greater than those of earlier historical periods is difficult to substantiate. Nonetheless, modern health risks do appear to arise from a more complex combination of environmental, social and individual factors than in the past. Furthermore, they are manifested at various, interdependent levels: international, national and local. The international level is particularly important as decisions or events here can have a wide impact, as illustrated by the ramifications of world trade agreements, discussed in Chapter 8. Even so, global risks to health are not entirely new: in the past, both plague and war have created public health crises across international boundaries. Moreover, the modern development of international initiatives offers the opportunity to regulate such risks by setting common standards and targeting the main threats to health at the global level.

The perception of the range of health risks certainly appears to be greater than in the past, but our understanding of the cause of illness is impeded by a weak empirical basis for decision making in some areas and contradictory findings in others. Indeed, some argue that epidemiology has been misused (Beaver, 1997; Feinstein, 1999) in such a way that health risks have been exaggerated. On the other hand, it can be argued that some health problems are virtually impossible to detect through conventional epidemiological methods because of the complex interaction of various risk factors. It is, for example, extremely difficult to establish links between food additives and chronic diseases because of long time lags and the variety of other possible factors involved. In other words, an over-reliance on conventional epidemiology – measuring what is easily quantified – may distract us from important underlying causes of ill health, leading to a neglect of economic, social and environmental factors. Certainly, one of themes of this book has been the lack of high-quality empirical research into the impact of such factors on health.

There is also disagreement about the role of scientists and other experts in the identification of risk in modern societies. According to some, such as Furedi (1997), Lupton (1995) and Castel (1991) among others, experts employ risk concepts as a means of control. It is true that public health interventions can lead to a loss of individual liberty. Some interventions, notably screening, involve surveillance and control. Others, such as antismoking and anti-obesity policies, have been criticised for compounding the process of social exclusion. Paradoxically, however, while experts exert considerable influence over risk identification and policy, the public appear to be ambivalent towards them. According to some writers, notably Beck (1992) and Giddens (1991), trust in experts is declining, although, as Wynne (1996) observed, this thesis is difficult to prove (see Chapter 1).

What is clear, in the field of public health at least, is that the public are confused, and this has led to a certain amount of scepticism about expert advice (see, for example, Travis, 1999, who reported a considerable public distrust of scientific advice on food safety and other scientific issues). There are a number of reasons for this. There are legitimate public concerns about the probity of scientists and other experts and their proximity to commercial interests, which has led many people to doubt the reassurances of scientists on subjects such as GM food (see Chapter 8). It should be acknowledged, however, that there is no simple formula for bringing science into policy decisions and that scientific advisors can never limit themselves to purely scientific issues (Jasanoff, 1990). Conflicting research findings on health issues are common. The controversy over the health impact of alcohol consumption (see Chapter 9) is but one example. The way in which findings are reported to the public through the media often adds to confusion and misunderstanding. It is widely acknowledged that a much more effective system of communicating information about health risks to the public is required. This is, however, unlikely to be effective if confined to information about healthy lifestyle. An information strategy must include all potential health risks, even to the point of giving the public greater access to official information on public health matters. But the UK government is reluctant to do this. Freedom of Information campaigners have been highly critical of 'open' government legislation, arguing that it imposes too many restrictions on the right to know about significant risks to public health and safety.

What else can be done to improve the public's faith in experts and its comprehension of public health risks, while at the same time strengthening the legitimacy of public health interventions? First of all, the independence of scientific experts and advisors needs to be protected as much as possible. The creation of separate regulatory agencies such as the FSA and the Environment Agency, with a commitment to openness and probity, is seen as a step in the right direction. The public health function also requires a certain amount of independence and should be open to public scrutiny. As shown in Chapter 5, there is a range of possible measures that could be implemented to strengthen the independence of public health doctors and other professionals working in this field. It was, however, also noted that some of these options, such as the creation of an independent public health commission or the transfer of public health functions to local government, while superficially attractive, have problems of their own.

Independence is not enough to guarantee good decision making, nor will it ensure that such decisions have legitimacy. In order to achieve this, an improvement in public participation is needed (Mills, 1993; Williams *et al.*, 1995; Beaglehole and Bonita, 1997). Public participation means more than getting people actively engaged in health promotion campaigns by stopping smoking, exercising or eating a healthier diet. Public health experts and governments must consult with people in order to understand their concerns and priorities. As some of the preceding chapters have shown (see, for example, Chapters 5 and 7), lay participation is lacking and needs to be encouraged. Moreover, communicating risk must not be a one-way process but should seek to involve the public and the organisations that represent them and understand their perspectives (Irwin and Wynne, 1996; DoH, 1998d).

It is important that lay knowledge and experiences are fully integrated into both the research process and the policy process. Some have emphasised the importance of lay epidemiology (Davison *et al.*, 1991; Popay and Williams, 1994; Watterson, 1994c). Such an approach is sensitive to the concerns of those potentially at risk from factors that may harm health. Rather than merely studying the health of populations, those with relevant expertise can be used by communities to gather relevant information, to develop skills and knowledge among lay people, and even to enhance their participation at all stages of the policy process. Such an approach can also identify contextual and subjective factors that impinge on health and could improve the knowledge base and thereby the effectiveness of future policies. It is also possible to devise deliberative systems that incorporate the views and experiences of ordinary people, increasing both participation and legitimacy in this field of policy making (Labonte, 1998b). Increased participation re-emphasises the collective and inclusive nature of public health. It also adds further impetus to broadening the horizons of public health in order to incorporate a greater awareness of environmental, social and economic factors in ways that can enhance the effectiveness of health strategies. In short, public health has much to gain by bringing in the people.

# Appendix

## The Acheson Report on Health Inequalities: key recommendations

1. As part of health impact assessment, all policies likely to have a direct or indirect effect on health should be evaluated in terms of their impact on health inequalities, and should be formulated in such a way that by favouring the less well off they will, wherever possible, reduce such inequalities.

2. A high priority should be given to policies aimed at improving health and reducing health inequalities in women of childbearing age, expectant mothers and young children.

3. Policies to further reduce income inequalities, and improve the living standards of households in receipt of social security benefits.

4. The provision of additional resources for schools serving children from less well off groups to enhance their educational achievement.

5. Further development of high quality pre-school education so that it meets the needs of disadvantaged families.

6. The further development of 'health promoting schools', initially focused on, but not limited to, disadvantaged communities.

7. Further measures to improve nutrition provided at school, including: the promotion of school food policies; the development of budgeting and cooking skills; the preservation of free school meals entitlement; the provision of free school fruit; and the restriction of less healthy food.

8. Policies which improve the opportunities for work and which ameliorate the health consequences of unemployment.

9. Policies to improve the quality of jobs, and reduce psychosocial work hazards.

10. Policies which improve the availability of social housing for the less well off within a framework of environmental improvement, planning and design which takes into account social networks, and access to goods and services.

11. Policies which improve housing provision and access to health care for both officially and unofficially homeless people.

12. Policies which aim to improve the quality of housing (including policies to improve insulation and heating systems to reduce further the prevalence of fuel poverty).

13. The development of policies to reduce the fear of crime and violence, and to create a safe environment for people to live in.

14. The further development of a high quality public transport system which is integrated with other forms of transport and is affordable to the user.

15. Further measures to encourage walking and cycling as forms of transport and to ensure the safe separation of pedestrians and cyclists from motor vehicles.

16. Further steps to reduce the usage of motor cars to cut the mortality and morbidity associated with motor vehicle emissions.

17. Further measures to reduce traffic speed, by environmental design and modification of roads, lower speed limits in built up areas, and stricter enforcement of speed limits.

18. Concessionary fares should be available to pensioners and disadvantaged groups throughout the country, and local schemes should emulate high quality schemes, such as those of London and the West Midlands.

19. A comprehensive review of the Common Agricultural Policy (CAP)'s impact on health and inequalities in health and a strengthening of the CAP Surplus Food Scheme to improve the nutritional position of the less well off.

20. Policies which will increase the availability and accessibility of foodstuffs to supply an adequate and affordable diet (including the further development of policies which will ensure adequate retail provision of food to those who are disadvantaged).

21. Policies which reduce poverty in families with children by promoting the material support of parents; by removing barriers to work for parents who wish to combine work with parenting; and by enabling those who wish to devote full-time to parenting to do so.

22. Policies which improve the health and nutrition of women of child-bearing age and their children with priority given to the elimination of food poverty and the prevention and reduction of obesity (including policies which increase the prevalence of breastfeeding; fluoridation of the water supply; further development of programmes to help women to give up smoking before or during pregnancy, and which are focused on the less well off).

23. Policies that promote the social and emotional support for parents and children (including the further development of the role and capacity of health visitors to provide social and emotional support to expectant parents, and parents with young children).

24. Measures to prevent suicide among young people, especially among young men and seriously mentally ill people.

25. Policies which promote sexual health in young people and reduce unwanted teenage pregnancy, including access to appropriate contraceptive services.

26. Policies which promote the adoption of healthier lifestyles, particularly in respect of factors which show a strong social gradient in prevalence or consequences. Specifically: policies which promote moderate intensity exercise including: further provision of cycling and walking routes to school, and other environmental modifications aimed at the safe separation of pedestrians and cyclists from motor vehicles; and safer opportunities for leisure. Also policies to reduce tobacco smoking including: restricting smoking in public places; abolishing tobacco advertising and promotion; and community, mass media and educational initiatives and increases in the real price of tobacco in tandem with policies to improve the living standards of low income households and polices to help smokers in these households become and remain ex-smokers including making nicotine replacement therapy available prescription. Also, policies which reduce alcohol-related ill health, accidents and violence, including measures which at least maintain the real cost of alcohol.

27. Policies which will promote the material well being of older people including uprating of benefits and pensions according to principles which protect and, where possible, improve the standard of living of those who depend on them and which narrow the gap between their standard of living and average living standards.

28. The quality of homes in which older people live should be improved.

29. Policies which will promote the maintenance of mobility, independence, and social contacts of older people.

30. The further development of health and social services for older people, so that these services are accessible and distributed according to need.

31. The needs of minority ethnic groups should be specifically considered in the development and implementation of policies aimed at reducing socioeconomic inequalities.

32. Further development of services which are sensitive to the needs of minority ethnic people and which promote greater awareness of their health risks.

33. The needs of minority ethnic groups should be specifically considered in needs assessment, resource allocation, health care planning and provision.

34. Policies which reduce the excess mortality from accidents and suicide in young men.

35. Policies which reduce psychosocial ill health in young women in disadvantaged circumstances, particularly those caring for young children.

36. Policies which reduce disability and ameliorate its consequences in older women, particularly those living alone.

37. Providing equitable access to effective care in relation to need should be a governing principle of all policies in the NHS. Priority should be given to services at every level of the NHS specifically health authorities, working with Primary Care Groups and providers on local clinical governance, agree priorities and objectives for reducing inequities in access to effective care. These should form part of the Health Improvement Programme.

38. Priority should be given to the achievement of a more equitable allocation of NHS resources. Specifically it is recommended that the principle of needs-based weighting be extended to non-cash limited General Medical Services resources. In addition the size and effectiveness of deprivation payments in meeting the needs and improving the health outcomes amongst the most disadvantaged populations, including ethnic minorities should be assessed. It is also recommended that the size and effectiveness of the Hospital and Community Health Service formula and deprivation payments in influencing the health care outcomes of the most disadvantaged populations, should be reviewed and alternative methods of focusing resources for health promotion and public health care to reduce health inequalities should be considered. Furthermore, a review should be undertaken of the relationship of private practice to the NHS with particular reference to access to effective treatments, resource allocation and availability of staff.

39. Directors of Public Health should produce an equity profile for the population they serve, and undertake a triennial audit of progress towards achieving objectives to reduce inequalities in health. There should be a duty of partnership between the NHS Executive and regional government to ensure that effective local partnerships are established between health, local authorities and other agencies and that joint programmes to address health inequality are in place and monitored.

*Sources*: Independent Inquiry into Inequalities in Health (Acheson Report) (1998), London, Stationery Office

# Postscript

## Policy Update

*(see also www.palgrave.com/nursinghealth/policyupdates)*

There is always a danger that any book which attempts to cover contemporary policy issues will quickly be overtaken by events. This is perhaps increasingly the case given today's fast-moving political agenda and the seemingly limitless capacity of government to produce wave after wave of policy initiatives and reforms. As I was writing *Public Health: Policy and Politics* I was very mindful of this. Despite being permitted to make some changes at proof stage, it was impossible to take into account the NHS Plan which emerged only a month before publication.[1] I am therefore grateful for the opportunity to add a postscript, the main aim of which is to outline the Plan's proposals relating to public health, as well as the relevant proposals made by the respective strategic plans for Scotland and Wales. I shall also refer to a number of other important developments that have occurred since publication of *Public Health: Policy and Politics* as much has happened.

## NHS Plan

The NHS Plan arose out of the Blair government's attempt to deal with yet another political crisis surrounding the service. In January 2000, media criticism of the government's handling of the NHS intensified, highlighting serious shortcomings in the service and raising questions about the level of funding. This was coupled with dissension from within the ranks of the Labour Party itself, with Labour peer and high-profile medic, Lord Winston, openly criticising government policy. Given the sensitivity of the health issue, with probably only a year before the next general election, the government had to respond. There followed a commitment to increase NHS funding in order to bring UK health spending more into line with the EU average. But the Treasury exacted a price for its rare generosity: various aspects of the service were reviewed in order to identify areas for improvement. Modernisation Action Teams (MATs) were established to advise on a national plan, each covering specific areas of NHS activity: Prevention and Inequalities; Partnership; Performance; Professions and Workforce; Patient Care (speed of access) and Patient

Care (empowerment). These teams contained ministers, civil servants, NHS managers, academics, health professionals and patients' representatives.

Public health issues fell within the remit of the Prevention and Inequalities MAT. Its deliberations fed into what became Chapter 13 of the NHS Plan, which made a number of commitments on public health and inequality:

- The introduction of national health inequalities targets (see Chapter 10 of *Public Health: Policy and Politics*).

- Measures to distribute NHS resources and services more equitably (including a new funding formula aimed at reducing inequalities and new Personal Medical Services pilots – see Chapter 5 – to improve access to primary care in disadvantaged areas).

- Local NHS action on inequalities and equitable access to health care to be measured and monitored through the NHS performance framework.

- An expansion of the Sure Start scheme, to cover a third of children under four living in poverty (see Chapter 10).

- Creation of a Children's Fund.

- Reform of the Welfare Foods Programme so as to promote effective use of resources, to ensure children in poverty have a healthy diet and to increase support for breastfeeding and parenting.

- Implementation of a teenage-pregnancy strategy (see Chapter 3).

- A new sexual health and HIV strategy (including new screening programmes).

- Effective and appropriate screening programmes for women and children (including a new screening programme for haemoglobinopathy and sickle-cell disease).

- An expansion of smoking cessation initiatives, including making nicotine-replacement therapy available on prescription from GPs and providing access to specialist smoking cessation clinics.

- A national school fruit scheme to give a free piece of fruit daily to schoolchildren aged six and under and to children at nursery. This to be part of a national campaign to improve children's diet.

- A programme to increase the consumption of fruit and vegetables (to five portions a day).

- Work with industry to improve access to fruit and vegetables; where necessary to set up local food co-operatives, and to improve the overall balance of diet.

- Local action to combat obesity and physical inactivity.

- A hospital nutrition policy to improve the outcomes of care for patients.

- Strengthening treatment services for drug misusers by establishing a national treatment agency.

- A forthcoming strategy for alcohol misuse.

- The development of local strategic partnerships for neighbourhood renewal, involving the NHS. (It was envisaged that in the medium term these would integrate the various action zones, including Health Action Zones discussed in Chapter 5, as well as Employment and Education Action Zones.)

- The introduction of integrated public health groups across NHS regional offices and government offices of the regions (these to be accountable through the Regional Director of Public Health to the NHS Regional Director and the Director of the Government Office of the Regions).

- A 'Healthy Communities' collaborative to disseminate best practice. This would operate under the Modernisation Agency (a new body established by the NHS Plan to promote improvement in services) based on evidence from the Health Development Agency.

- A leadership programme for community nurses and health visitors to help them to work more effectively with local community representatives in an effort to improve health.

Elsewhere in the Plan the government announced an expansion of prevention services, such as the identification of disease management registers for those at risk of developing heart disease, and an extension of cancer screening programmes (breast cancer screening extended to 65–70 age group, introducing new screening technologies for cervical cancer and, subject to evidence of cost effectiveness and acceptability, new screening programmes for colorectal and prostate cancer).

Some of these commitments were not entirely new, having been trailed in earlier policy documents. For example, the announcement of a forthcoming alcohol strategy had appeared in the 1998 Green Paper on Public Health. However, there were some surprises, notably the national inequalities targets which the government had not previously endorsed. In early 2001 the Department of Health set two targets – reducing the gap in infant mortality between the bottom social class and the national average by at least ten per cent over the next ten years and at least ten per cent reduction in the life-expectancy gap between the bottom fifth of health authorities and the English average. Other 'commitments' were less clear, and some extremely vague, such as the discussions with the food industry on dietary issues.

More broadly, there was concern that the NHS Plan downgraded public health by focusing mainly on service developments. Public health was addressed towards the end of the document and there were few explicit links with other key elements in the Plan. It was also noted that the relationship between the public health commitments in the Plan with the earlier policy document, the White Paper *Saving Lives* (1999), was not discussed in any detail. Indeed, even taking into account its service orientation, the NHS Plan appeared to take a different approach to the priorities set out by the earlier White Paper. For example, one of the target areas identified in *Saving Lives*, accident prevention, was not mentioned in the plan. The health promotion aspects of another target area, mental health, referred to in *Saving Lives* and in the National Service Framework for Mental Health, was largely ignored in the NHS Plan. Critics also pointed out that the NHS Plan had little to say on some crucial issues such as joint working on public health between health services, the voluntary sector and local government.

The government's plans for public health were scrutinised by a House of Commons Health Committee inquiry.[2] Its report was published in the spring of 2001 and made a number of recommendations including:

- That health policy should not be targeted on the most deprived but on the least well off on a sliding scale.

- The development of intermediate targets for each 'headline' inequality target.

- That every government department should agree to conduct health audits and inequality targets. (The committee also suggested that a Parliamentary Health Audit Committee should be considered to monitor this.)

- Efforts should be made to integrate initiatives aimed at reducing health inequalities. The committee also recommended that the Chief Medical Officer's final report on the public health function (see Chapter 5 and below) should be published without delay. (Curiously, this much-delayed report suddenly appeared on the same day as the Health Committee's own report.)

- The lack of co-ordination on public health issues between government departments, statutory agencies, elected authorities and the voluntary sector was noted by the committee.

- The committee also noted that there was a general lack of involvement of lay individuals in programmes aimed at improving the health of their communities (including Health Action Zones and Health Improvement Plans – see Chapter 5).

- There was concern about the Health Development Agency not being properly resourced and the committee recommended that its funding be ring fenced and kept apart from mainstream funding so as to preserve its independence.

- The committee wanted the DoH to assess whether primary care actually had the capacity to take on a public health role. It also stated that if GPs were to be more involved in public health work they should be given time and sufficient incentives within a career and pay structure to enable them to do this.

- It recommended that the government should ensure through performance management that Primary Care Groups and Trusts (PCGs/Ts) take up their public health responsibilities and that relevant training and support be made available to help them to do this. Also, the committee stated that PCGs/Ts should have an additional designated officer from the local authority and should be given more information about how local government works.

- The committee recommended a review of the role of the health visitors, arguing that this should develop into a more holistic, public health function and saw health visitors as the key public health resource for all community health care professionals. It also recommended that the contribution of school nurses to public health could be improved by rationalising their employment structures.

- Another area of concern was the mismatch between the Health Improvement Plan, which tended to be disease dominated, and the local authority's community plan. The committee recommended that health should be a key element in the community plan. The committee also urged that health be at the heart of neighbourhood renewal strategies.

- The committee was concerned about the lack of priority given to population health at annual health authority meetings and recommended that this be a mandatory agenda item. It was unimpressed with the role of Directors of Public Health, and argued that they did not generally provide the necessary leadership. Joint health/local authority appointments were viewed in a positive light but were not the only way forward. Coterminosity of health and local authorities was seen as important as were new accountability structures for public health directors and their respective authorities.

- The committee endorsed population-based funding for public health programmes which took into account factors which affected need, including deprivation. It was critical of the 'bidding culture' with regard to public health funding initiatives and called on government to review this.

- It also called for greater central government co-ordination on public health especially on issues such as health and regeneration, and sport and health.

- The committee was concerned that service issues dominated health policy and that new high level indicators should be developed around public health to monitor performance.

- It recommended that the DETR and DoH develop a shared Public Service Agreement based on the need to narrow health inequalities.

- The committee did not support moving responsibility for public health from the DoH but believed that the case for relocation would be strengthened in the absence of evidence that public health was a priority for the department.

- The committee believed that the regional tier had much to contribute to 'joined-up' policy and that the NHS Regional Offices could do more to develop public health strategy. They agreed with the commitment in the NHS Plan to develop joint accountability for public health at regional level, but urged that there should also be coterminosity between Regional Development Agencies and DoH regions.

## Scottish and Welsh Strategies

The focus of the Health Committee's inquiry was upon public health in England. But, as noted in Chapter 4 (see especially Exhibit 4.2), different parts of the UK have adopted their own strategies to improve public health in the context of devolution. In Scotland, the emphasis on tackling the social and economic roots of ill health has continued, and indeed was a strong theme in the Scottish version of the NHS Plan.[3] The Scottish Executive allocated Scotland's share of the earmarked tobacco tax – £100m over a three-year period – to a new Health Improvement Fund. In 2001, a further £1.5m over three years was set aside for the NHS and local government in Scotland to develop joint strategies to improve health. Local authorities and health boards were expected to match this funding with their own resources. New initiatives to improve child health emerged: a Health Promoting Schools Unit was proposed, to begin work in 2001 (England and Wales have their own schemes to promote healthy schools.) A Diet Action Plan was also devised, along with a National Diet Action Co-ordinator, to help implement improvements in dietary lifestyles. A Physical Activity Task Force was also proposed, to begin work in 2001. An earlier commitment, to establish a Public Health Institute for Scotland to focus and co-ordinate efforts to improve public health, was implemented in 2001. This was recommended by a review of public health functions in Scotland[4] which in turn arose out of the Scottish White Paper on Public Health (Cm 4269, 1999). A review of the nursing contribution to public health was undertaken in Scotland and this led to some important new initiatives, including further investment in school-nurse and health-visitor training, aimed at encouraging their health promotion activities and, in the longer term, removing the barriers between these professionals, giving them a common title of 'public health nurse'. A further development was the creation of a 'public health practitioner' role.[5] These new posts, which will be filled mainly by nurses and health visitors, are to be based in local health care co-operatives (which bring together general practices in Scotland) and are expected to promote links with the community and enhance collaboration between the various agencies involved in public health at this level.

So in Scotland the focus on health promotion has remained strong. The differences in emphasis between England and Scotland were perhaps reflected in the titles of the strategic national plans. The title of the Scottish Plan specifically refers to health (*Our National Health: a Plan for Action, a Plan for Change*) whereas the NHS Plan does not. Moreover, in the Scottish Plan 'improving health' featured in Chapter two, while in the NHS Plan the corresponding text appeared towards the end of the document (Chapter 13).

Since devolution, the National Assembly for Wales has also produced several health policy documents, including a health promotion strategy[6] and a plan for health and the NHS.[7] As in Scotland, these place great emphasis on the social, economic and environmental roots of ill health, the need to tackle health inequalities, and the need to forge strong partnerships in order to promote the health and wellbeing of the whole population. Central to these plans is the development of lifelong investment in health and the reorientation of the NHS as a health, rather than a sickness, service. The Welsh Plan is being overseen by a Health and Wellbeing Council (chaired by the Minister of Health and Social Services and involving representatives of key stakeholders including patients, managers, staff, local government and the voluntary sector). A number of actions have been identified to take the strategy forward. They include, a healthy schools initiative, a strategy to improve health in the workplace, more emphasis on community health development work, a nutrition strategy, a task force to address the impact of healthy and active lifestyles on health, additional funding to help reduce health inequalities, and an expansion of health impact assessment. In addition, efforts have been made to improve working relationships between different agencies at the local level in order to sharpen the focus on the promotion of health and wellbeing. Local health alliances, led by local authorities, have been further encouraged. Local strategic partnerships on health and wellbeing are also being created, involving health and local government in joint working across a whole range of services focusing in particular on primary and community care. Other important developments in Wales include a review of the public health function. The Welsh Health Plan also proposed the abolition of health authorities, which is expected to lead to a greater role for Local Health Groups (the Welsh counterpart to English Primary Care Groups) in commissioning health services, co-ordinating health and social care, tackling health inequalities, and improving public health and wellbeing. The Welsh Assembly has also decided to extend free prescriptions to all under 25 years of age, implement free dental checks to those under 25 and over 60 years of age, and plans to introduce a new free eye-care service.

## Chief Medical Officer's Report

The delayed publication of the Chief Medical Officer's review of the public health function in England[8] was seen by some as further evidence that public health was perhaps less of a priority in England than north of the border. More cynically, it was suggested that its publication, which as noted earlier coincided with the House of Commons report on public health, was designed to counter criticism by the latter. The CMO's report sets out a large number of recommendations, and claims that these have been, or are being, implemented. It is true that some are being addressed by current initiatives, including proposals set out in the NHS Plan for England, such as the integration of public health in decision-making at regional level for example. However, many of the recommendations in the CMO's report are quite vague, representing no more than broad aspirations, or relate to further reviews of specific public health functions, rather than actual initiatives.

## Phillips Inquiry on the BSE/CJD Crisis

Since publication, many other developments have taken place across the broad range of issues covered by this book. It is possible to cover only the main highlights here. In October 2000 the long awaited report of the Phillips Inquiry[9] on the BSE/CJD crisis was published. The Inquiry identified intensive farming methods (recycling animal protein in ruminant feed) as the cause of the problem. The report was less critical of government, and of individual ministers and civil servants, than many believed it would be. It states that the measures introduced were sensible but 'not always timely nor adequately implemented or enforced'. It did not find that government had deliberately lied in an attempt to cover up the problem. The main criticism was that those in government had not given due weight to the potential risks to human health. They were preoccupied with preventing an alarmist reaction, considering that such risks were remote. The Phillips report concluded that 'It is now clear that this campaign of reassurance was a mistake'. The culture of secrecy in government was criticised in the report. Another area of criticism was the lack of co-ordination between departments, and in particular the failure of the Ministry of Agriculture Fisheries and Food to consult with the Department of Health and the Chief Medical Officer about implications of BSE for human health. The Phillips report had wider implications for public health that went beyond the issue of BSE/CJD. It argued that there was a need for transparency in government with a policy of openness with regard to risk and recommended that scientific committees should not water down their assessments of risk to avoid causing alarm. It also recommended that there should be an emphasis on reasonable precautionary measures even where health risks are remote.

In the early months of 2001 the emphasis on food aspects of health continued, with the appointment of a new advisory committee on nutrition. This began work in the context of heightened concerns about obesity,[10] particularly among children, and continuing public anxiety about GM foods, pesticides, additives and food poisoning. A major outbreak of foot-and-mouth disease in February 2001 raised further questions about cross-infection arising from methods of intensive farming and the systems of transport and slaughter of animals. As the crisis went on there were added concerns about threats to public health, in particular pollution of water supplies from rotting carcasses and air pollution from the burning of dead animals.

## Public Health Policy in the European Union

Turning to the European dimension, we must note the continuing development of public health policy in the European Union.[11] In June 2000 the European Commission proposed a new programme of action in the field of public health. The overall aim of this programme is 'to make a contribution to the attainment of a high level of health protection by directing action towards improving public health, preventing human illness and diseases and obviating sources of danger to health'. It was planned to begin in January 2001 and end on 31 December 2006, but was delayed by the need to secure agreement between the Council of Ministers and the European Parliament on the proposal. Although there seems to be a consensus on the principle of greater European co-operation on public health, some states, notably the UK, are concerned that the proposal might lead to an extension of Community 'competencies' in this field. The three main aspects of the proposed programme are: improving health information (by developing and operating health monitoring systems and by developing and using mechanisms for analysis, advice, reporting, information and consultation, on health issues); responding rapidly to health threats (by enhancing the capacity to tackle communicable disease and strengthening the capacity to tackle other health threats); and addressing health determinants (by developing strategies and measures on lifestyle-related health determinants, socio-economic health determinants; and health determinants related to the environment). It is proposed that the following measures may be used to implement these actions: support for the preparation of Community legislative instruments and for co-operation on the position of the Community and member states in fora where health-related issues are discussed; support for statistical reports on health; support for the development of information and consultation systems at Community level for the mobilisation of resources to combat health threats and through the sharing and exchange of information between the Community and member states; the promotion and provision of inform-ation by the Community and member states to professions and the public; and support for the development and implementation of disease prevention and health promotion activities involving non-governmental bodies as appropriate. However, the proposal states that public health does not fall within the exclusive competence of the European Community and action should only be taken if it could be better achieved by the Community rather than by individual states. Furthermore, it was emphasised that the programme would be implemented with the close co-operation of member states.

Other European public health issues of note include new initiatives on health and nutrition. More generally, the European Union is taking a much closer interest in food and health and a European Food Authority has been proposed. On the tobacco issue, the EU is introducing new directives on tobacco labelling. However, a European Court of Justice decision overturned an earlier Commission proposal for a ban on tobacco advertising on the grounds that the legal basis was insufficient to support such action. The Commission intends to bring forward a new directive in the light of the ECJ judgement. Meanwhile the UK is pressing ahead with its own legislation in this area.

Finally, on the international scene, the implications of global warming have continued to arouse concern. In the autumn of 2000 great anxiety was created by the heaviest rain and consequential flooding in Britain in living memory, which some attributed to climate change. A more systematic appraisal on the likely impact of global warming came from a United Nations report in February 2001 which detailed the threat of malaria, tainted water supplies, and coastal erosion over this century.[12] But efforts to limit the likely damage of climate change were thwarted. In November 2000, at the Hague Summit, attempts by European countries to drastically cut carbon emissions were opposed by the USA, which is responsible for around a quarter of such emis-sions. Even more ominously, in the spring of 2001, the new US President, George W. Bush, announced that the US would abandon the Kyoto protocol (see Chapter 7) which had aimed to cut greenhouse gases, in an attempt to protect the US economy.

So since the publication of *Public Health: Policy and Politics* much has happened. Yet none of these developments leads me to depart from the main themes set out in the book, nor contradicts its central arguments and conclusions. Readers should also note that I intend to update this postscript when time permits. Updates will appear on the Palgrave website at (www.palgrave. com/nursinghealth/policyupdates). Additional information of relevance to public health may also appear from time to time on the De Montfort Health Policy Research Unit website (www.dmu.ac.uk/ln/hpru).

# Notes

1. Department of Health (2000) *The NHS Plan: A Plan for Investment, A Plan for Reform* (London, The Stationery Office).
2. House of Commons Health Committee (2001) *Public Health* Second Report 2000/2001 (London, The Stationery Office). HC 30.
3. Scottish Executive (2000) *Our National Health: a Plan for Action, a Plan for Change* (Edinburgh, Scottish Executive).
4. Scottish Executive (1999) *Review of the Public Health Function* (Edinburgh, Scottish Executive).
5. Scottish Executive (2001) *Nursing for Health: A Review of the Contribution of Nurses, Midwives and Health Visitors to Improving the Public's Health in Scotland* (Edinburgh, Scottish Executive).
6. National Assembly for Wales (2001) *Promoting Health and Well Being: Implementing the National Health Promotion Strategy* (Cardiff, National Assembly for Wales).
7. National Assembly for Wales (2001) *Improving Health in Wales: A Plan for the NHS With its Partners* (Cardiff, National Assembly for Wales).
8. Department of Health (2001) *The Report of the Chief Medical Officer's Project to Strengthen the Public Health Function* (London, Department of Health).
9. The BSE Inquiry (2000) *The BSE Inquiry Report* (London, The Stationery Office).
10. National Audit Office (2001) *Tackling Obesity in England* (London, The Stationery Office) Session 2000/1, HC 220; P. Bundred, D. Kitchener and I. Buchan (2001) 'Prevalence of Overweight and Obese Children between 1989 and 1998; Population-based Series of Cross-sectional Studies', *British Medical Journal* **322**, 326.
11. Proposal for a decision of the European Parliament and of the Council adopting a programme of community action in the field of public health (2001–6) *Official Journal of the European Communities* C 337 E/122 28 November 2000 (2000/C 337 E 16).
12. United Nations Environmental Programme (2001) *Climate Change 2001: Impacts, Adaptation and Vulnerability: Report of Working Group II of the Inter Governmental Panel on Climate Change* (Geneva, UNEP).

# Bibliography

ACMD (Advisory Council on the Misuse of Drugs) (1982) *Treatment and Rehabilitation* (London, HMSO).

Abel-Smith, B. (1964) *The Hospitals 1800–1948* (London, Heinemann).

Action in International Medicine (1995) 'London Declaration', *Bulletin*, Winter, 1–8.

Acton, S., Rigotti, A., Landschulz, K., Xu, S., Hobbs, H. and Krieger, M. (1996) 'Identification of Scavenger Receptor SR-BI as a High Density Lipoprotein Receptor', *Science*, **271**, 518–20.

Adams, I. (1993) *Political Ideology Today* (Manchester, Manchester University Press).

Adams, J. (1995) *Risk* (London, UCL Press).

Adams, L. (1989) 'Healthy Cities, Healthy Participation', *Health Education Journal*, **48** (4), 179–82.

Adler, M. (1997) 'Sexual Health: A Health of the Nation Failure', *British Medical Journal*, **314**, 1743–7.

Age Concern (1996) *Not At My Age* (London, Age Concern).

Agriculture Committee (1987) *The Effect of Pesticides on Human Health*, 2nd Report 1986/87, HC 379 (London, HMSO).

Agriculture Committee (1989) *Salmonella in Eggs*, 1st Report 1988/89, HC 108 (London, HMSO).

Agriculture Committee (1990) *BSE*, 5th Report 1989/90, HC 449 (London, HMSO).

Agriculture Committee (1998) *Food Safety*, 4th Report 1997/98, HC 331 (London, HMSO).

Ahmad, W. (1993a) 'Promoting Equitable Health and Health Care: A Case for Action'. In Ahmad, W. (ed.) *Race and Health in Contemporary Britain* (Buckingham, Open University Press), pp. 201–14.

Ahmad, W. (ed.) (1993b) *Race and Health in Contemporary Britain* (Buckingham, Open University Press).

Akehurst, R., Godfrey, C., Hutton, J. and Robertson, E. (1991) *Health of the Nation: An Economic Perspective on Target Setting* (University of York, Centre for Health Economics).

Albanes, D. (1998) 'Height, Early Energy Intake and Cancer', *British Medical Journal*, **317**, 1331–2.

Alexander, F.E., Anderson, T.J., Brown, H.K. *et al.* (1999) '14 Years of Follow Up from the Edinburgh Randomised Trial of Breast Cancer Screening', *Lancet*, **353**, 1903–8.

All Party Group on Alcohol Misuse (1995) *Alcohol and Crime: Breaking the Link* (London, Alcohol Concern).

Allsop, J. (1990) 'Does Socialism Necessarily Mean the Public Provision of Health Care?' In Carrier, J. and Kendall, I. (eds) *Socialism and the NHS: Fabian Essays in Health Care* (Aldershot, Avebury), pp. 31–41.

Alm, J., Swartz, J., Lilja, G., Scheynius, A. and Pershagen, G. (1999) 'Atopy in Children of Families with an Anthroposophic Lifestyle', *Lancet*, **353** (9163), 1485–8.

Anderson, E.D.C., Muir, B.B., Walsh J.S. *et al.* (1994) 'The Efficacy of Double Reading Mammograms in Breast Screening', *Clinical Radiology*, **49**, 248–51.

Anderson, H.R., Ponce de Leon, A., Bland, J.M., Blower, J.S. and Strachan, D.P. (1996) 'Air Pollution and Daily Mortality in London 1987–92', *British Medical Journal*, **312**, 665–9.

Anderson, P. (1988) 'Excess Mortality Associated with Alcohol Consumption', *British Medical Journal*, **297**, 824–6.

Andersson, I., Aspergen, K., Janzon, L., Larberg, T. Lindholm, K. and Linell, F. (1988) 'Mammographic Screening and Mortality from Breast Cancer: the Malmo Mammographic Screening Programme', *British Medical Journal*, **297**, 943–50.

Ansell, B.M. and Lawrence, J.S. (1966) 'Flouridation and the Rheumatic Diseases: A Comparison of Rheumatism in Watford and Leigh', *Annals of the Rheumatic Diseases*, **25** (1), 67–75.

Appleyard, B. (1994) 'Healthism is a Vile Habit', *Independent*, 21 September, p. 19.

Arblaster, L. and Hawtin, M. (1993) *Health, Housing and Social Policy* (London, Socialist Health Association).

Arblaster, L., Entwhistle, V., Fullerton, D., Forster, M., Lambers, M. and Sheldon, T. (1997) *Review of the Effectiveness of Health Promotion Interventions Aimed at Reducing Inequalities in Health* (York, NHS Centre for Review and Dissemination).

Armitage, L., Birt, C. and Davis, H. (1998) *Future Proposals for Public Health, Local Health and Health Authority Collaboration* (Brimingham, INLOGOV/HSMC).

Armstrong, D. (1993) 'Public Health Spaces and the Fabrication of Identity', *Sociology*, **27** (3), 393–410.

Arnold, S.F., Klotz, D.M., Collins, B.M., Vonier, P.M., Guillette, L.J. and McLachlan, J.A. (1996) 'Synergestic Activation of Estrogen Receptor with Combinations of Environmental Chemicals', *Science*, **272**, 1489–92.

Asbury, D., Boggis, C., Threlfall, A. and Woodman, C. (1996) 'NHS Breast Screening Program. Is the High Incidence of Interval Cancers Inevitable?', *British Medical Journal*, **313**, 1369–70.

Ashton, J. (1990) 'Public Health and Primary Care: Towards a Common Agenda', *Public Health*, **104** (6), 387–98.

Ashton, J. (1992) 'The Origin of Healthy Cities'. In Ashton, J. (ed.) *Healthy Cities* (Milton Keynes, Open University), pp. 1–12.

Atrens, D. (1994) 'The Questionable Wisdom of a Low Fat Diet and Cholesterol Reduction', *Social Science and Medicine*, **39** (3), 433–7.

Audit Commission (1990) *Environmental Heath Survey of Food Premises*, Information Paper 2 (London, HMSO).

Audit Commission (1991) *Towards a Healthier Environment* (London, HMSO).

Audit Commission (1993) *Practices Makes Perfect: The Role of the FHSA* (London, HMSO).

Audit Commission (1994) *Seen But Not Heard: Coordinating Community Child Health and Social Services for Children in Need* (London, HMSO).

Audit Commission (1996) *What the Doctor Ordered: A Study of GP Fundholders in England and Wales* (London, HMSO).

Audit Commission (1999) *First Assessment: A Review of District Nursing Services in England and Wales* (London, HMSO).

Austoker, J. (1994a) 'Screening for Cervical Cancer', *British Medical Journal*, **309**, 241–8.

Austoker, J. (1994b) 'Diet and Cancer', *British Medical Journal*, **308**, 1611–14.

Avery, N., Drake, M. and Lang, T. (1993) *Cracking the Codex: An Analysis of Who Sets World Food Standards* (London, National Food Alliance).

Back, D. and Godfrey, C. (1997) *Helping Smokers to Give Up: Guidance for Purchasers on Cost Effectiveness* (London, Health Education Authority).

Backett, K.C. and Davison, C., (1995) 'Lifecourse and Lifestyle – The Social and Cultural Location of Health Behaviours', *Social Science and Medicine*, **40** (5), 629–30.

Baeza, J. and Calnan, M. (1998) 'Beating the Bands', *Health Service Journal*, 24 September, 26–7.

Baggott, R. (1986) *The Politics of Alcohol: Two Periods Compared* (London, Institute for Alcohol Studies).

Baggott, R. (1988) 'Health v Wealth: The Politics of Smoking in Norway and the UK', *Strathclyde Papers on Government and Politics* (Glasgow, University of Strathclyde), p. 57.

Baggott, R. (1990) *Alcohol, Politics and Social Policy* (Aldershot, Avebury).

Baggott, R. (1995) *Pressure Groups Today* (Manchester, Manchester University Press).

Baggott, R. (1998) 'The BSE Crisis: Public Health and the Risk Society'. In Gray, P. and t'Hart, P. (eds) *Public Policy Disasters in Western Europe* (London, Routledge), pp. 61–78.

Balarajan, R. and Soni Raleigh, V. (1995) *Ethnicity and Health in England* (London, HMSO).

Balding, I. (1998) *Young People in 1997* (Exeter, Exeter University).

Bardsley, M. (ed.) (1998) *The Health of Londoners: A Public Health Report for London* (London, King's Fund).

Barker, A. and Peters, B.G. (1993a) 'Science, Policy and Government'. In Barker, A. and Peters, B.G. (eds) *The Politics of Expert Advice* (Edinburgh, Edinburgh University Press), pp. 1–6.

Barker, A. and Peters, B.G. (eds) (1993b) *The Politics of Expert Advice* (Edinburgh, Edinburgh University Press).

Barker, W.E., Anderson, R.M. and Chalmers, C. (1994) *Child Protection: The Impact of the Child Development Programme* (Bristol, Early Development Unit, Department of Social Work).

Barnardo's (1993) *Liquid Gold* (Ilford, Barnardo's).

Bartlett, R.V. and Kurian, P. (1999) 'The Theory of Environmental Impact Assessment: Implicit Models of Policymaking', *Policy and Politics*, **24** (4), 415–34.

Bartley, M. and Owen, C. (1996) 'Relation Between Socioeconomic Status, Employment and Health During Economic Change 1979–93', *British Medical Journal*, **313**, 445–9.

Bartley, M. and Plewis, I. (1997) 'Does Health-selective Mobility Account for Socio-economic Differences in Health?: Evidence from England and Wales 1971–1991', *Journal of Health and Social Behaviour*, **38**, 376–86.

Bartley, M., Montgomery, S., Cook, D. and Wadsworth, M. (1996) 'Health and Work Insecurity in Young Men'. In Blane, D., Brunner, E. and Wilkinson, R. (eds), *Health and Social Organization* (London, Routledge), pp. 255–71.

Bartley, M., Popay, J. and Plewis, I. (1992) 'Domestic Conditions, Paid Employment and Women's Experience of Ill Health', *Sociology of Health and Illness*, **14** (3), 313–45.

Bartley, M., Power, C., Blane, D., Davey Smith, G. and Shipley, M. (1994) 'Birth Weight and Later Socioeconomic Disadvantage from the 1958 British Cohort Study', *British Medical Journal*, **309**, 1475–9.

Bartrip, P. (1996) *Themselves Writ Large: The BMA 1832–1966* (London, BMJ Publishing Group).

Baskin, D.G., Seeley, R.J., Kuijper, J.L. *et al.* (1998) 'Increased Expression of mRNA for the Long Form of the Leptin Receptor in the Hypothalmus is Associated with Leptin Hypersensitivity and Fasting', *Diabetes*, **47** (4) 538–43.

Bate, R. (ed.) (1999) *What Risk?: Science, Politics and Public Health* (London, Butterworth Heinemann).

Bates, T. and Evans, R. (1995) *Report of the Independent Review Commissioned by the Royal College of Radiologists into Bronchial Plexus Neuropathy Following Radiotherapy for Breast Carcinoma* (London, Royal College of Radiologists).

Batt, S. (1994) *Patient No More: The Politics of Breast Cancer* (London, Scarlett Press).

Baum, M. (1999) 'Money May Be Better Spent on Symptomatic Women', *British Medical Journal*, **318**, 398.

Baumgartner, F. and Jones, B. (1993) *Agendas and Instability in American Politics* (Chicago, University of Chicago Press).

Bayer, R. (1993) 'The Great Drug Policy Debate: What Means This Thing Called Decriminalisation'. In Bayer R. and Oppenheimer G. (eds) *Confronting Drugs Policy: Illicit Drugs in a Free Society* (Cambridge, Cambridge University Press), pp. 1–23.

Beaglehole, R. and Bonita, R. (1997) *Public Health at the Crossroads: Achievements and Prospects* (Cambridge, Cambridge University Press).

Beauchamp, D. (1988) *The Health of the Republic. Epidemics, Medicine and Moralism as Challenges to Democracy* (Philadelphia, Temple University Press).

Beaver, M. (1997) 'Misuse of Epidemiology', *Public Health*, **111**, 63–6.

Beck, U. (1992) *The Risk Society* (London, Sage).

Ben-Shlomo, Y., White, I.R. and Marmot, M. (1996) 'Does the Variation in the Socioeconomic Characteristics of an Area Affect Mortality?', *British Medical Journal*, **312**, 1013–14.

Bennett, J. and DiLorenzo, F. (1999) *The Food and Drink Police: America's Nannies, Busybodies and Petty Tyrants* (New York, Transaction).

Bennett, T. (1998) *Drugs and Crime: The Results of Research on Drug Testing and Interviewing Arrestees*, Home Office Research Study 183 (London, Home Office).

Benzeval, M., Judge, D. and Whitehead, M. (1995) 'Unfinished Business'. In Benzeval, M., Judge, D. and Whitehead, M. (eds) *Tackling Inequalities in Health: An Agenda for Action* (London, King's Fund), pp. 122–40.

Beral, V., Hermon, C., Kay, C., Hannaford, P., Darby, S. and Reeves, G. (1999) 'Mortality Associated with Oral Contraceptive Use: 25 Year Follow Up of a Cohort of 46,000 Women', *British Medical Journal*, **318**, 96–100.

Beral, V., Hermon, C., Reeves, G. and Peto, R. (1995) 'Sudden Fall in Breast Cancer Death Rates in England and Wales', *Lancet*, **345**, 1642–3.

Berger, P. (ed.) (1991) *Health, Lifestyle and Environment: Counteracting the Panic* (London, Social Affairs Unit).

Berki, R. (1975) *Socialism* (London, Dent).

Berlin, I. (1969) *Four Essays on Liberty* (Oxford, Oxford University Press).

Berridge, V. (1996) *AIDS in the UK: The Making of Policy 1981–1994* (Oxford, Oxford University Press).

Berridge, V. (1998) 'AIDS and British Drug Policy a Post War Situation'. In Bloor, M. and Wood, F. (eds) *Addiction and Problem Drug Use: Issues in Behaviour, Policy and Practice* (London, Jessica Kingsley), pp. 85–108.

Berridge, V. (1999) 'Passive Smoking and its Prehistory in Britain. Policy Speaks to Science?', *Social Science and Medicine*, **49**, 1183–95.

Berridge, V. and Edwards, G. (1981) *Opium and the People* (London, Allen Lane).

Bethune, A. (1996) 'Economic Activity and Mortality of the 1981 Census Cohort in the OPCS Longitudinal Study', *Population Trends*, **83**, 37–41.

Betts, G. (1993) *Local Government and Inequalities in Health* (London, Avebury).

Bhatti, N., Law, M.R., Morris, J.K., Halliday, R. and Moore-Gillon, J. (1995) 'Increasing Incidence of Tuberculosis in England and Wales: A Study of Likely Causes, *British Medical Journal*, **310**, 967–9.

Billingham, K. (1991) 'Public Health and the Community', *Health Visitor*, **64**, 40–3.

Billingham, K. and Perkins, E. (1997) 'A Public Health Approach to Nursing in the Community', *Nursing Standard*, **11** (35), 43–6.

Bines, W. (1994) *The Health of Single Homeless People*, Discussion Paper 9 (York, Centre for Housing Policy, University of York).

Blair, S., Shaten, J., Brownell, K., Collins, G. and Lissner, L. (1993) 'Body Weight Change, All Cause Mortality in the Multiple Risk Factor Intervention Trial', *Annals of Internal Medicine*, **119** (2), 49–57.

Blane, D, Davey Smith, G. and Bartley, M. (1993) 'Social Selection: What Does It Contribute to Social Class Difference in Health?', *Sociology of Health and Illness*, **15**, 1–15.

Blane, D., Bartley, M. and Davey Smith, G. (1998) 'Making Sense of Socio-economic Health Inequalities'. In Field, M. and Taylor, S. (eds) *Sociological Perspectives on Health, Illness and Health Care* (Oxford, Blackwell), pp. 79–96.

Blane, D., Davey Smith, G. and Bartley, M. (1990) 'Social Class Difference in Years of Potential Life Lost: Size, Trends and Principal Causes', *British Medical Journal*, **301**, 429–32.

Blaxter, M. (1990) *Health and Lifestyles* (London, Tavistock/Routledge).

BMA (British Medical Association) (1986a) *Smoking Out the Barons: The Campaign Against the Tobacco Industry*, Report of the BMA Public Affairs Division (Chichester, John Wiley & Sons).

BMA (British Medical Association) (1986b) *Cervical Screening in Great Britain*, Board of Science and Education (London, BMA).

BMA (British Medical Association) (1989) *Hazardous Waste and Human Health* (Oxford, Waste Regulation Authority).

BMA (British Medical Association) (1990) *Pesticides, Chemicals and Health* (London, BMA).

BMA (British Medical Association) (1995) *Inequalities in Health*, Board of Science and Education Occasional Paper (London, BMA).

BMA (British Medical Association) (1997a) *Road Transport and Health* (London, BMA).

BMA (British Medical Association) (1997b) *The Misuse of Drugs* (Amsterdam, Harwood).

BMA (British Medical Association) (1997c) *Therapeutic Uses of Cannabis* (London, BMA).

BMA (British Medical Association) (1998) *Health and Environmental Impact Assessment – An Integrated Approach* (London, Earthscan).

BMA (British Medical Association) (1999a) *Alcohol and Young People* (London, BMA).

BMA (British Medical Association) (1999b) *Growing Up in Britain* (London, BMA).

Bodner, C., Godden, D. and Seaton, A. (1998) 'Family Size, Childhood Infections and Atopic Diseases. The Aberdeen WHEASE Group', *Thorax*, **53** (1), 28–32.

Body, R. (1991) *Our Food: Our Land* (London, Random Century).

Booker, C. and North, R. (1994) *The Mad Officials* (London, Constable).

Borooah, V.K. (1999) 'Occupational Class and the Probability of Long-term Limiting Illness', *Social Science and Medicine*, **49**, 253–66.

Bosanquet, N. and Hockley, T. (1998) *New Dynamics in Public Health Policy* (London, Social Market Foundation).

Botting, B. (1997) 'Mortality in Childhood'. In Drever, F. and Whitehead, M. (eds) *Health Inequalities: Decennial Supplement* (London, Stationery Office), pp. 83–95.

Bracht, N. (ed.) (1999) *Health Promotion at the Community Level: New Advances* (London, Sage).

Brand, J.A. (1971) 'The Politics of Flouridation: A Community Conflict', *Political Studies*, **19** (4), 430–9.

Brett, J., Austoker, J. and Ong, G. (1998) 'Do Women who Undergo Further Investigation for Breast Screening Suffer Adverse Psychological Consequences?', *Journal of Public Health Medicine*, **20** (4), 396–403.

Briggs, A. (1959) *The Age of Improvement*, (London, Longman).

Brinton, L.A. and Fraumeni, J.F. (1986) 'Epidemiology of Uterine Cervical Cancer', *Journal of Chronic Diseases*, **39** (12), 1051–65.

Brinton, L.A., Huggins, G.R., Lehman, H.F. *et al.* (1986b) 'Long Term Use of Oral Contraceptives and Risk of Invasive Cervical Cancer', *International Journal of Cancer*, **38** (3), 339–44.

Brinton, L.A., Reeves, W., Brenes, M.M. *et al.* (1989) 'The Male Factor in the Etiology of Cervical Cancer among Sexually Monogamous Women', *International Journal of Cancer*, **44** (2), 199–203.

Brinton, L.A., Schairer, C., Haenszel, W. *et al.* (1986a) 'Cigarette Smoking and Invasive Cervical Cancer', *Journal of the American Medical Association*, **255**, 3265–9.

British Paediatric Association/Royal College of Physicians (1995) *Alcohol and the Young* (London, Royal College of Physicians).

Britton, M. (1990) *Mortality and Geography* (London, HMSO).

Brown, J., Bryan, S. and Warren, R. (1996) 'Mammography Screening: An Incremental Cost Effectiveness Analysis of Double Versus Single Reading of Mammograms', *British Medical Journal*, **312**, 809–12.

Bruce, M. (1968) *The Coming of the Welfare State*, 4th edn (London, Batsford).

Bruyinckx, E., Mortelmans, D., Van Goethen, M. and Van Hove, E. (1999) 'Risk Factors of Pain in Mammographic Screening', *Social Science and Medicine*, **49**, 933–41.

Buckley, J.D., Harris, R.W., Doll, R., Vessey, M. and Williams, P.T. (1981) 'Case Control Study of the Husbands of Women with Dyplasia or Carcinoma of the Cervix Uteri', *Lancet*, **ii**, 1010–15.

Bunker, J., Frazier, H. and Mostelle, F. (1994) 'Improving Health: Measuring Effects of Medical Care', *Milbank Quarterly*, **72** (2), 225–58.

Burke, D. (1998) 'Why all the Fuss about Genetically Modified Food' *British Medical Journal*, **316**, 1845–6.

Burkitt, D. (1973) 'Some Disease Characteristics of Modern Western Civilisations', *British Medical Journal*, **1**, 274–8.

Burridge, R. and Ormandy, D. (eds) (1993) *Unhealthy Housing: Research, Remedies and Reform* (London, E. and F.N. Spon).

Bynum, W. (1994) *Science and the Practice of Medicine in the Nineteenth Century* (Cambridge, Cambridge University Press).

C 281 (1871) *Report of the Royal Commission on the Sanitary Laws*, House of Commons Sessional Papers, Vol. 35, 1.

Cd 1507 (1903) *Report of the Royal Commission on Physical Training (Scotland)* (London, HMSO).

Cd 2175 (1904) *Report of the Inter-departmental Committee on Physical Deterioration* (London, HMSO).

Cd 4499 (1909) *Royal Commission on the Poor Laws and Relief of Distress*, Majority and Minority Report (London, HMSO).

Cmd 693 (1920) *Interim Report on the Future Provision of Medical and Allied Services* (London, HMSO).

Cmnd 3569 (1968) *Report of the Royal Commission on Medical Education* (London, HMSO).

Cmnd 3703 (1968) *Committee on Local Authority and Allied Personal Services* (London, HMSO).

Cmnd 5054 (1972) *Safety and Health at Work*, Report of the Committee of Inquiry (London, HMSO).

Cmnd 7047 (1977) *Prevention and Health* (London, HMSO).

Cmnd 7615 (1979) *Report of the Royal Commission on the National Health Service* (London, HMSO).

Cmnd 9716 (1986) *Report of the Committee of Inquiry into an Outbreak of Food Poisoning at Stanley Royal Hospital, Wakefield* (London, HMSO).

Cmnd 9771 (1986) *Primary Health Care: An Agenda for Discussion* (London, HMSO).

Cmnd 9772 (1986) *First Report of the Committee of Inquiry into the Outbreak of Legionnaire's Disease in Stafford, April 1985* (London, HMSO).

Cm 249 (1987) *Promoting Better Health* (London, HMSO).

Cm 289 (1988) *Public Health in England* (Acheson Report) (London, HMSO).

Cm 1523 (1991) *The Health of the Nation: A Consultative Document for Health in England* (London, HMSO).

Cm 1986 (1992) *The Health of the Nation: A Strategy for Health in England* (London, HMSO).

Cm 2426 (1994) *Sustainable Development: The UK Strategy* (London, HMSO).

Cm 2674 (1994) *18th Report of the Royal Commission on Environmental Pollution: Transport and the Environment* (London, HMSO).

Cm 2846 (1995) *Tackling Drugs Together: A Strategy for England* (London, HMSO).

Cm 3234 (1996) *Transport: The Way Forward* (London, HMSO).

Cm 3323 (1996) *UK Environmental Health Action Plan* (London, HMSO).

Cm 3807 (1997) *The New NHS: Modern, Dependable* (London, Stationery Office).

Cm 3805 (1998) *New Ambitions for Our Country: A New Contract for Welfare* (London, Stationery Office).

Cm 3830 (1998) *The Food Standards Agency: A Force for Change* (London, Stationery Office).

Cm 3852 (1998) *Our Healthier Nation* (London, HMSO).

Cm 3854 (1998) *Working Together for a Healthier Scotland: A Consultation Document* (London, Stationery Office).

Cm 3922 (1998) *Better Health; Better Wales, Consultation Document* (London, Stationery Office).

Cm 3945 (1998) *Tackling Drugs To Build a Better Britain* (London, Stationery Office).

Cm 3950 (1998) *A New Deal for Transport* (London, HMSO).

Cm 4014 (1998) *Modern Local Government in Touch with the People* (London, Stationery Office).

Cm 4045 (1998) *Bringing Britain Together: A National Strategy for Neighbourhood Renewal*, Social Exclusion Unit (London, Stationery Office).

Cm 4053 (1998) *Setting Environmental Standards: 21st Report of the Royal Commission on Environmental Pollution* (London, Stationery Office).

Cm 4177 (1998) *Smoking Kills* (London, Stationery Office).

Cm 4269 (1999) *Towards a Healthier Scotland*, Scottish White Paper (London, Stationery Office).

Cm 4345 (1999) *A Better Quality of Life: A Strategy for Sustainable Development for the UK* (London, Stationery Office).

Cm 4386 (1999) *Saving Lives: Our Healthier Nation* (London, Stationery Office).

Cm 4548 (2000) *The Air Quality Strategy for England, Scotland, Wales and Northern Ireland* (London, Stationery Office).

Cabinet Office (1999) *Tackling Drugs To Build a Better Britain. UK Anti-drugs Coordinator's Annual Report 1998/99* (London, The Stationery Office).

Cabinet Office (2000a) *National Strategy for Neighbourhood Renewal: A Framework for Consultation. Report by the Second Exclusion Unit* (London, Cabinet Office).

Cabinet Office (2000b) *Reaching Out: The Role of Central Government at Regional and Local Level: A Performance and Innovation Unit Report* (London, Cabinet Office).

Cairns, J. (1995) 'The Costs of Prevention', *British Medical Journal*, **311**, 1520.

Calnan, M. (1984) 'The Politics of Health: The Case of Smoking Control', *Journal of Social Policy*, **13** (3), 279–96.

Calnan, M. (1991) *Preventing Coronary Heart Disease: Prospects, Policies and Politics* (London, Routledge).

Cannon, G. (1987) *The Politics of Food* (London, Century Hutchinson).

Caplan, G.A. and Brigham, G.A. (1990) 'Marijuana Smoking and Carcinoma of the Tongue: Is there an Association?', *Cancer*, **66** (5), 1005–6.

Caraher, M., Dixon, P., Lang, T. and Carr-Hill, R. (1998) 'Access to Healthy Foods: Part 1. Barriers to Accessing Healthy Foods: Differentials by Gender, Social Class, Income and Mode of Transport', *Health Education Journal*, **57**, 191–201.

Carpenter, L. (1987) 'Some Observations on the Healthy Worker Effect', *British Journal of Industrial Medicine*, **44**, 289–91.

Carr-Hill, R. (1987) 'The Inequalities in Health Debate: A Critical Review of the Literature', *Journal of Social Policy*, **16** (4), 509–42.

Carstairs, V. and Morris, R. (1989) 'Deprivation: Explaining Differences in Mortality Between Scotland and England and Wales', *British Medical Journal*, **299**, 886–9.

Castel, R. (1991) 'From Dangerousness to Risk'. In Burchell, G., Gordon, G. and Miller, P. (eds) *The Foucault Effect: Studies in Governmentality* (Hemel Hempstead, Harvester Wheatsheaf), pp. 281–98.

Cataldo, J.K. (1985) 'Obesity: A New Perspective on an Old Problem', *Health Education Journal*, **44** (4), 213–16.

Caulkins, J.P. and Reuter, P. (1997) 'Setting Goals for Drug Policy: Harm Reduction or Use Reduction?', *Addiction*, **92** (9), 1143–50.

Central Policy Review Staff (1982) *Alcohol Policies in the UK: The Report of the Central Policy Review Staff* (Stockholm, Sociologiska Institutionen).

Centre for Agricultural Strategy (1979) *National Food Policy in the UK* (Reading, Centre for Agricultural Strategy).

Cervical Screening Action Team (1998*) Cervical Screening Action Team – The Report* (London, DoH).

Chadda, D. (1996) 'The Narked Civil Servants', *Health Service Journal*, 21 March, 11.

Chadwick, E. (1842) *Report on the Sanitary Condition of the Labouring Population of Great Britain* (London, Poor Law Commission).

Challacombe, D.N. and Wheeler, E.E. (1994) 'Safety of Milk from Cows Treated with BST', *Lancet*, **344**, 1815.

Chamberlain, J. (1984) 'Which Prescriptive Screening Programmes are Worthwhile?', *Journal of Epidemiology and Community Health*, **38**, 270–7.

Chamberlain, J., Melia, J., Moss, S. and Brown, J. (1996) *The Diagnosis, Management, Treatment and Cost of Prostate Cancer in England and Wales* (Sutton, Cancer Screening Evaluation Unit, Institute of Cancer of Research).

Chan, J.M., Stampfer, M., Gionvannucci, E. *et al.* (1998) 'Plasma-like Insulin Growth Factor I and Prostate Cancer Risk: A Prospective Study', *Science*, **279**, 563–6.

Channel 4 Television (1992) *Food Additives: 'Look Before You Eat', A Shoppers Guide* (London, Broadcasting Support Services).

Chapman, S., Borland, R., Hill, D., Owen, N. and Woodward, S. (1990) 'Why the Tobacco Industry Fears the Passive Smoking Issue', *International Journal of Health Services*, **20** (3), 417–27.

Charatan, F.B. (1998) 'Prostate Cancer Screening Reduces Death', *British Medical Journal*, **316**, 1626.

Charlton, J. (1996) 'Which Areas Are the Healthiest?', *Population Trends*, **83**, 17–24.

Charlton, J., Wallace, M. and White, M. (1994) 'Long-term Illness: Results from the 1991 Census', *Population Trends*, **75**, 18–25.

Charny, M. (1994) 'The Costs of Screening'. In Le Fanu, J. (ed.) *Preventionitis*, (London, Social Affairs Unit), pp. 106–17.

Chave, S. (1974) 'The Medical Officer of Health 1847–74', *Proceedings of the Royal Society of Medicine*, **67**, 1243–7.

Chen, C.C., David, A.S., Nunnerly, H. *et al.* (1995) 'Adverse Life-events and Breast Cancer: Case-control Study', *British Medical Journal*, **311**, 1527–30.

Chernin, K. (1983) *Womansize: the Tyranny of Slenderness* (London, Women's Press).

Child Accident Prevention Trust (1991) *Safe As Houses: Guidelines for the Safety of Children in Temporary Accommodation* (London, CAPT).

Clarke, A. (1995) 'Population Screening for Genetic Susceptibility to Disease', *British Medical Journal*, **311**, 35–8.

Clarke, M.L. (1997) 'Working Together for Children', unpublished PhD thesis, University of London Institute of Education.

Clarke, P.R. and Fraser, N.M. (1991) *Economic Analysis of Screening for Breast Cancer* (Edinburgh, Scottish Home and Health Department).

Cloke, P., Milbourne, P. and Thomas, C. (1994) *Lifestyles in Rural England* (Salisbury, Rural Development Commission).

Cochrane, A. (1971) *Effectiveness and Efficiency: Random Reflections on Health Services* (London, Nuffield Provincial Hospitals Trust).

Cochrane, R. and Bal, S. (1989) 'Mental Hospital Admission Rates of Immigrants to England: A Comparison of 1971 and 1981', *Social Psychiatry and Psychiatric Epidemiology*, **24**, 2–11.

Codex Alimentarius (1992) *Guidelines for the Application of Hazard Analysis Critical Control Point System* (Rome, FAO).

Coley, C.M., Barry, M.J., Fleming, C., Fahs, M.C. and Mulley, A.G. (1997) 'Early Detection of Prostate Cancer: Part 2. Estimating the Risks, Benefits and Costs', *Annals of Internal Medicine*, **126**, (6), 468–79.

Colhoun, H. and Prescott-Clarke, P. (1996) *Health Survey for England 1994* (London, HMSO).

Colhoun, H., Ben-Schlomo, Y., Dong, W., Bost, L. and Marmot, M. (1997) 'Ecological Analysis of Collectivity of Alcohol Consumption in England. Importance of the Average Drinker', *British Medical Journal*, **314**, 1164–8.

Colin-Thome, P. (1999) 'Primary Care Perspectives'. In Jenkins, S. and Hunter, D. (eds) *Perspectives in Public Health* (Oxford, Radcliffe Medical Press), pp. 179–91.

Collaborative Group on Hormonal Factors in Breast Cancer (1996) 'Breast Cancer and Hormonal Contraception', *Lancet*, **347**, 1713–27.

Collaborative Group on Hormonal Factors in Breast Cancer (1997) 'Breast Cancer and HRT: Collaborative Reanalysis of Data from 51 Epidemiological Studies of 52,705 Women with Breast Cancer and 108,411 Without Breast Cancer', *Lancet*, **350**, 1047–59.

Collier, U (1997) 'Sustainability, Subsidiary and Deregulation: New Directions in EU Environmental Policy', *Environmental Politics*, **6** (2), 1–23.

Collingridge, D. and Reeve, C. (1986) *Science Speaks to Power: The Role of Experts in Policy Making* (London, Pinter).

Commission for Social Justice (1994) *Social Justice: Strategies for Social Renewal* (London, Verso).

Committee on Carcinogenicity of Chemicals in Food, Consumer Products and the Environment (2000) *COC Statement on Breast Cancer Risk and Exposure to Organochlorine Insecticides*: Consideration of the Epidemiology Data on Dieldrin, DDT and Certain Hexachlorocyclohexane Isomers (London, DoH).

Committee on Medical Aspects of Food Policy (1974) *Diet and Coronary Heart Disease* (London, DHSS).

Committee on Medical Aspects of Food Policy (1984) *Diet and Cardiovascular Disease* (London, HMSO).

Committee on Medical Aspects of Food Policy (1994) *Nutritional Aspects of Cardiovascular Disease* (London, HMSO).

Committee on Medical Aspects of Food Policy (1997) *Nutritional Aspects of the Development of Cancer* (London, HMSO).

Committee on the Medical Effects of Air Pollutants (1995) *Asthma and Outdoor Air Pollution* (London, HMSO).

Committee on the Medical Effects of Air Pollutants (1998) *The Quantification of the Effects of Air Pollution on Health in the UK* (London, HMSO).

*Convention on Access to Information, Public Participation in Decision-making and Access to Justice in Environmental Matters* (1998) Aarhus, Denmark, 25 June (http://www.mem.dk/aarhus-conference/index.htm).

Conway, J. (ed.) (1988) *Prescription for Poor Health: The Crisis for Homeless Families* (London, London Food Commission/Maternity Alliance/SHAC/Shelter).

Conway, J. (1995) 'Housing as an Instrument of Health Care', *Health and Social Care in the Community*, **3**, 141–50.

Cook-Mozaffari, P. (1996) 'Cancer and Flouridation', *Community Dental Health*, **13** (Supplement 2), 56–62.

Cooper, L., Coote, A., Davies, A. and Jackson, C. (1995) *Voices off: Tackling the Democratic Deficit in Health* (London, Institute for Public Policy Research).

Cope, R. (1989) 'The Compulsory Detention of Afro Caribbeans Under the Mental Health Act', *New Community*, **15** (3), 343–56.

Cormuzie, A.G. and Allison, D.B. (1998) 'The Search for Human Obesity Genes', *Science*, **280**, 1374–7.

Cornell, S.J. (1996) 'Do Environmental Health Officers Practice Public Health?', *Public Health*, (110), 73–5.

Cornell, S.J. (1999) 'Public Health and Primary Care Collaboration: A Case Study', *Journal of Public Health Medicine*, **21** (2), 199–204.

Cornish, Y., Russell-Hodgson, C., Fani-Kayode, S. *et al.* (1997) *Review of Health of the Nation in North Thames* (London, South East Institute of Public Health).

Correa, C. (1999) *Public Health and Multilateral Trade Agreements* (Geneva, WHO).

Corti, E.C. (1931) *A History of Smoking* (London, Harrap).

Costongs, C. and Springett, J. (1997) 'Joint Working and the Production of a City Health Plan: The Liverpool Experience', *Health Promotion International*, **12** (1), 9–19.

Council of the European Communities/Commission of the European Communities (1992) *Treaty on the European Union* (Luxembourg, Office for Official Publications of the European Communities), p. 49.

Cox, J. (1998) 'Poverty in Rural Areas', *British Medical Journal*, **316**, 722.

Creighton, C. (1965) *A History of Epidemics*, Vol. 2 (London, Frank Cass).

Crick, B. (1987) *Socialism* (Milton Keynes, Open University Press).

Crombie, H. (1995 ) *Sustainable Development and Health* (Birmingham, Public Health Alliance).

Crown, J. (1999) 'The Practice of Public Health Medicine: Past, Present and Future'. In Jenkins, S. and Hunter, D. (eds) *Perspectives on Public Health* (Oxford, Radcliffe Medical Press), pp. 214–71.

Cuckburn, J., Staples, M., Hurley, S. and de Suise, T. (1994) 'Psychological Costs of Screening Mammography?', *Journal of Medical Screening*, **1**, 7–12.

Cuckle, H. and Wald, N. (1984) 'Principles of Screening Antenatal and Neonatal Screening'. In Wald, N.J. (ed.) *Antenatal and Neonatal Screening* (Oxford University Press), pp. 1–22.

Currie, E. (1989) *Lifelines: Politics and Health* (London, Pan).

Curtice, C. (1992) 'Strategies and Values: Research and the WHO Healthy Cities Project in Europe'. In Davies, J. and Kelly, M. (eds) *Healthy Cities* (Buckingham, Open University Press), pp. 34–54.

Dahlgren, G. and Whitehead, M. (1992) *Policies and Strategies to Promote Social Equity in Health* (Copenhagen, WHO).

Dalton, A.J.P. (1992) 'Lessons from the UK: Fightback on Workplace Hazards 1979–92', *International Journal of Health Services*, **22** (3), 489–95.

Davey Smith, G. and Dorling, D. (1996) 'I'm Alright John: Voting Pattern and Mortality in England and Wales 1981–92', *British Medical Journal*, **313**, 1573–7.

Davey Smith, G. and Dorling, D. (1997) 'Associations Between Voting Patterns and Mortality Remain', *British Medical Journal*, **315**, 430–1.

Davey Smith, G., Blane, D. and Bartley, M. (1994) 'Explanations for Socio-economic Differentials in Mortality', *European Journal of Public Health*, **4**, 131–44.

Davey Smith, G., Hart, C., Blane, D. and Hole, D. (1998b) 'Adverse Socioeconomic Conditions in Childhood and Case Specific Adult Mortality: Prospective Observational Study', *British Medical Journal*, **316**, 1631–5.

Davey Smith, G., Shipley, M. and Leon, D.A. (1998a) 'Height and Mortality from Cancer among Men: Prospective Observational Study', *British Medical Journal*, **317**, 1351–2.

Davies, A. (1997) *Reporting the Public Health* (London, Institute of Public Policy Research).

Davies, J. and Kelly, M. (eds) (1992) *Healthy Cities: Policy and Practice* (London, Routledge).

Davies, N.V. and Teasdale, P. (1994) *The Costs to the British Economy of Work Accidents and Work Related Ill-health* (London, Health and Safety Executive).

Davison, C., Davey Smith, G. and Frankel, S. (1991) 'Lay Epidemiology and the Prevention Paradox: the Implications of Coronary Candidacy for Health Promotion', *Sociology of Health and Illness*, **13** (1), 1–19.

Davison, C., MacIntyre, S. and Davey Smith, G. (1994) 'The Potential Impact of Predictive Genetic Testing for Susceptibility to Common Chronic Diseases: A Review and Proposed Research Agenda', *Sociology of Health and Illness*, **16** (3), 340–71.

Day, P. and Klein, R. (1989) 'Interpreting the Unexpected: The Case of AIDS Policy Making in Britain', *Journal of Public Policy*, **9** (3), 337–53.

de Vet, H.C. and Sturmans, F. (1994) 'Risk Factors for Cervical Dysplasia: Implications for Prevention', *Public Health*, **108** (4), 241–9.

de Vet, H.C., Knipschild, P.G. and Sturmans, F. (1993) 'The Role of Sexual Factors in the Aetiology of Cervical Dysplasia', *International Journal of Epidemiology*, **22** (5), 798–803.

De Witt, R. and Carnell, J. (1999) 'Public Health Nursing'. In Jenkins, S. and Hunter, D. (eds) *Perspectives in Public Health* (Oxford, Radcliffe Medical Press), pp. 235–49.

Delaney, F. (1994) 'Making Connections: Research into Intersectoral Collaboration', *Health Education Journal*, **53**, 474–85.

Dennehy, A., Smith, L., Harker, P., Davey Smith, G. and Ben-Shlomo, Y. (1997) *Not To Be Ignored: Young People, Poverty and Health* (London, Child Poverty Action Group).

Denscombe, M. and Drucquer, N. (1999) 'Critical Incidents and Invulnerability To Risk: Young People's Experience of Serious Health Related Incidents and Their Willingness To Take Risks', *Health Risk and Society*, **1** (2) 195–213.

Dent, M. (1999) 'Our Time Has Come', *Health Service Journal*, 27 May, 27.

DETR (Department of Environment, Transport and the Regions) (1997a) *Sustainable Local Communities for the 21st Century* (London, Local Government Management Board/DETR/Local Government Association).

DETR (Department of Environment, Transport and the Regions) (1997b) *Incidence of Alcohol and Drugs in Road Accident Fatalities* Press Release 149/27 June (London, DETR).

DETR (Department of Environment, Transport and the Regions) (1998a) *Strategic Environmental Appraisal: Report of the International Seminar at Lincoln 27–9 May* (London, DETR).

DETR (Department of Environment, Transport and the Regions) (1998b) *Policy Appraisal and the Environment* (London, DETR).

DETR (Department of Environment, Transport and the Regions) (1998c) *Sustainable Development, Opportunities for Change: Consultation Paper on Revised UK Strategy* (London, DETR).

DETR (Department of Environment, Transport and the Regions) (1998d) *Planning for Sustainable Development: Towards Better Practice* (London, DETR).

DETR (Department of Environment, Transport and the Regions) (1998e) *Road Safety in Schools: Good Practice Guide* (London, DETR).

DETR (Department of Environment, Transport and the Regions) (1999a) *Report of the National Air Quality Strategy: Proposals to Amend the Strategy* (London, DETR).

DETR (Department of Environment, Transport and the Regions) (1999b) *Towards an Urban Renaissance: The Report of the Urban Task Force chaired by Lord Rogers of Riverside* (London, Urban Task Force).

DETR (Department of the Environment, Transport and the Regions) (2000) *Tomorrow's Roads: Safer for Everyone. The Government's Road Safety Strategy and Casualty Reduction Targets* (London, DETR).

DETR (Department of the Environment, Transport and the Regions) (2000b) *Revitalising Health and Safety: Strategy Statement* (London, DETR)

DETR/DFEE/DoH (Department of Environment, Transport and the Regions/Department for Education and Employment/Department of Health (1999) *School Travel* (London, DETR).

DFEE (Department for Education and Employment) (1998) *Ingredients for Success* (London, DFEE).

DHSS (Department of Health and Social Security) (1972) *Report of the Working Party on Medical Administrators* (London, HMSO).

DHSS (Department of Health and Social Security) (1976) *Prevention and Health: Everybody's Business* (London, DHSS).

DHSS (Department of Health and Social Security) (1980) *Inequalities in Health: Report of a Research Working Party* (London, DHSS).

DHSS (Department of Health and Social Security) (1981) *Drinking Sensibly* (London, DHSS).

DHSS (Department of Health and Social Security) (1986) *Neighbourhood Nursing: A Focus for Care. Report of the Community Nursing Review* (London, HMSO).

DHSS (Department of Health and Social Security) (1988) *Passive Smoking.* First Report of the Independent Scientific Committee on Smoking and Health (London, DHSS).

Di Guiseppi, C., Roberts, I. and Li, L. (1997) 'Influence of Changing Travel Patterns on Child Death Rates from Injury: Trend Analysis', *British Medical Journal,* **314**, 710–13.

Dibb, S. (1998) *What the Label Doesn't Tell You* (London, Thorsons).

Dike van de Mheen, H., Stronks, K. and Mackenbach, J. (1988) 'A Lifecourse Perspective on Socioeconomic Inequalities in Health: The Influence of Childhood Socioeconomic Conditions on Selection Processes', *Sociology of Health and Illness,* **20** (5), 754–777.

Dingle, A. (1980) *The Campaign for Prohibition in Victorian England* (London, Croom Helm).

Disken, S. (1990) 'Health for All and All for One', *Health Service Journal,* 10 May, 691.

Dix, A. (1997) 'Doing Their Own Thing', *Health Service Journal,* 15 May, 345.

Dobson, A. (1990) *Green Political Thought: An Introduction* (London, Unwin Hyman).

Dobson, B., Beardsworth, A., Keil, T. and Walker, R. (1994) *Diet, Choice and Poverty* (London, Family Policy Studies Centre).

DoE (Department of the Environment) (1988) *Assessment of Ground Water Quality in England and Wales* (London, HMSO).

DoE (Department of the Environment) (1989) *Environmental Impact Assessment: A Guide to the Procedures* (London, HMSO).

DoE (Department of the Environment) (1991a) *Policy Appraisal and the Environment: A Guide for Government Departments* (London, HMSO).

DoE (Department of the Environment) (1991b) *Code of Practice on Smoking in Public Places* (London, HMSO).

DoE (Department of the Environment) (1994) *Environmental Appraisal in Government Departments* (London, DoE).

DoE (Department of the Environment) (1995) *A Guide to Risk Assessment and Risk Management for Environmental Protection* (London, HMSO).

DoE (Department of the Environment) (1996a) *National Air Quality Strategy* (London, HMSO).

DoE (Department of the Environment) (1996b) *Indicators of Sustainable Development for the UK* (London, HMSO).

DoE (Department of the Environment) (1996c) *Health and Regeneration* (London, HMSO).

DoE (Department of the Environment) (1997) *The UK National Air Quality Strategy* (London, Stationery Office).

DoH (Department of Health) (1991) *Breast Cancer Screening: Guidance and Experience Since the Forrest Report*, Report of the Department of Health Advisory Committee (London, DoH).

DoH (Department of Health) (1992) *Effect of Tobacco Advertisements on Tobacco Consumption: A Discussion Document Reviewing the Evidence* (London, DoH).

DoH (Department of Health) (1993a) *Working Together for Better Health* (London, DoH).

DoH (Department of Health) (1993b) *Public Health Responsibilities of the NHS and Others* (London, DoH).

DoH (Department of Health) (1993c) *Population Based Health Outcome Indicators for the NHS in England* (London, DoH).

DoH (Department of Health) (1993d) *Key Area Handbook: Accidents* (London, DoH).

DoH (Department of Health) (1994a) *Public Health in England: Roles and Responsibilities of the DoH and the NHS in England* (London, DoH).

DoH (Department of Health) (1994b) *Nutrition and Health* (London, DoH).

DoH (Department of Health) (1995a) *Variations in Health: What Can the Department of Health and the NHS Do?* (London, DoH).

DoH (Department of Health) (1995b) *Fit for the Future: Second Progress Report on the Health of the Nation* (London, DoH).

DoH (Department of Health) (1995c) *Sensible Drinking: The Report of the Interdepartmental Working Group* (London, DoH).

DoH (Department of Health) (1996a) *Population-based Health Outcome Indicators for the NHS* (Guildford, University of Surrey).

DoH (Department of Health) (1996b) *Child Health in the Community* (London, DoH).

DoH (Department of Health) (1996c) *The Task Force to Review Services for Drug Misusers,* Report of An Independent Review of Drug Treatment Services in England (London, DoH).

DoH (Department of Health) (1997a) *Breast Cancer Services in Exeter and Quality Assurance for Breast Screening: Report to the Secretary of State* (London, DoH).

DoH (Department of Health) (1997b) *Improving Outcomes in Colorectal Cancer* (London, DoH).

DoH (Department of Health) (1998a) *Chief Medical Officer's Project To Strengthen the Public Health Function in England: A Report of Emerging Findings* (London, DoH).

DoH (Department of Health) (1998b) *The Health of the Nation: A Policy Assessed* (London, Stationery Office).

DoH (Department of Health) (1998c) *Modernising Health and Social Services National Priorities Guidance 1999/00–2001/2* (London, DoH).

DoH (Department of Health) (1998d) *Communicating about Risks to Public Health, Pointers to Good Practice* (London, Stationery Office).

DoH (Department of Health) (1998e) *Modernising Mental Health Services* (London, DoH).

DoH (Department of Health) (1999a) *Health Survey for England: Geographical Variations in Health Indicators by Health Authority 1994–6* (London, DoH).

DoH (Department of Health) (1999b) *The NHS Performance Assessment Framework* (London, DoH).

DoH (Department of Health) (1999c) *Economic Appraisal of the Health Effects of Air Pollution* (London, Stationery Office).

DoH (Department of Health) (1999d) *Reducing Health Inequalities: An Action Report* (London, DoH).

DoH (Department of Health) (1999e) *Tessa Jowell Launches the Healthy Workplace Initiative,* Press Release 1999/0133, 9 March

DoH (Department of Health) and UK Advisory Committee on the Microbiological Safety of Food (1999) *Microbial Antibiotic Resistance in Relation to Food Safety* (London, Stationery Office).

DoH (Department of Health) and Welsh Office (1995) *A Policy Framework for Commissioning Cancer Services: Report of an Expert Advisory Group* (London, DoH/Welsh Office).

DoH (Department of Health) Workplace Task Force (1994) *Report* (London, DoH).

DoH/DoE (Department of Health/Department of the Environment) (1996) *The Environment and Health: A Consultation Document* (London, DoH).

DoH/NHSE (Department of Health/National Health Service Executive) (1999) *Resistance to Antibiotics and other Antimicrobial Agents* (London, NHSE).

DoH/NTF (Department of Health/Nutrition Task Force) (1994) *Eat Well* (London, DoH).

DoH/NTF (Department of Health/Nutrition Task Force) (1996a) *Eat Well II* (London, DoH).

DoH/NTF (Department of Health/Nutrition Task Force) (1996b) Low Income Project *Team Low Income, Food Nutrition and Health: Strategies for Improvement* (London, DoH).

DoH/NTF/PATF (Department of Health/Nutrition Task Force/Physical Activity Task Force) (1995) *Obesity: Reversing the Increasing Problem of Obesity in England* (London, DoH).

DoH/PATF (Department of Health/Physical Activity Task Force) (1995) *More People, More Active, More Often* (London, DoH).

DoH/SMAC (Department of Health/Standing Medical Advisory Committee) (1998) *The Path of Least Resistance* (London, DoH).

DoH/SNMAC (Department of Health/Standing Nursing and Midwifery Advisory Committee) (1995) *Making it Happen: Public Health: The Contribution, Role and Development of Nurses, Midwives and Health Visitors* (London, DoH).

Doig, A. (1990) 'Routine Crisis and Muddle: Mishandling the Egg Crisis', *Teaching Public Administration*, **10** (1), 15–26.

Dolk, H., Vrijhend, M., Armstrong, B. *et al.* (1998) 'Risk of Congenital Anomalies Near Hazardous-waste Landfill Sites in Europe', *Lancet*, **352**, 423–7.

Doll, R. and Hill, A. (1950) 'Smoking and Carcinoma of the Lung', *British Medical Journal*, **2**, 739–48.

Doll, R. and Hill, A. (1956) 'Lung Cancer and Other Causes of Death in Relation to Smoking', *British Medical Journal*, **2**, 1071–81.

Doll, R. and Kinlen, L. (1977) 'Flouridation of Water and Cancer Mortality', *Lancet*, **1**, 1300–2.

Doll, R. and Peto, R. (1981) 'The Causes of Cancer', *Journal of the National Cancer Institute*, **66**, 1191–308.

Doll, R., Peto, R., Hall, E., Wheatley, R. and Gray, R. (1994b) 'Mortality in Relation to Consumption of Alcohol: 13 Years Observations on Male British Doctors', *British Medical Journal*, **309**, 911–18.

Doll, R., Peto, R., Wheatley, R., Gray, R. and Sutherland, I. (1994a) 'Mortality in Relation to Smoking: 40 Years Observation on Male British Doctors', *British Medical Journal*, **309**, 901–11.

Donaldson, L. and May, R. (1999) *Health Implications of Genetically Modified Foods* (London, DoH).

Donnelly, L. (1998) 'Split Heirs', *Health Service Journal*, 3 December, 14–15.

Dorn, N., Baker, O. and Seddon, T. (1994) *Paying for Heroin: Estimating the Financial Costs of Acquisitive Crime by Dependent Heroin Users in England and Wales* (London, Institution of Drug Dependence).

Dorsett, R. and Marsh, A. (1998) *Poverty, Smoking and Lone Parenthood* (London, Policy Studies Institute).

DoT (Department of Transport) (1987) *Interdepartmental Review of Road Safety* (London, HMSO).

Douglas, M. and Wildavsky, A. (1982) *Risk and Culture* (Los Angeles, University of California).

Dowding, K. (1995) 'Model or Metaphor? A Critical Review of the Policy Network Approach', *Political Studies*, **43**, 13–58.

Dowling, B. (1997) 'Effect of Fundholding on Waiting Times: A Database Study', *British Medical Journal*, **315**, 290–2.

Doyal, L. (1979) *The Political Economy of Health* (London, Pluto).

Doyal, L. (1995) *What Makes Women Sick? Gender and the Political Economy of Health* (London, Macmillan).

Drager, N. (1999) 'Making Trade Work for Public Health', *British Medical Journal*, **319**, 1214.

Draper, P. (ed.) (1991) *Health Through Public Policy: The Greening of Public Health* (London, Green Print).

Drever, F. and Bunting, J. (1997) 'Patterns and Trends in Male Mortality'. In Drever, F. and Whitehead, M. (eds) *Health Inequalities: Decennial Supplement* (London, Stationery Office), pp. 95–107.

Drever, F. and Whitehead, M. (1995) 'Mortality in Regions and Local Authority Districts in the 1990s: Exploring the Relationship with Deprivation', *Population Trends*, **82**, 19–27.

Drever, F., Whitehead, M. and Roden, M. (1996) 'Current Patterns and Trends in Male Mortality by Social Class (Based on Occupation)', *Population Trends*, **86**, 15–20.

DSS (Department of Social Security) (1998) *Households Below Average Income 1979–1996/7* (London, Stationery Office).

DTI (Department of Trade and Industry) (1998) *Home Accident Surveillance System: 20th Annual Report* (London, DTI).

Dugdill, L. and Springett, J (1994) 'Evaluation of Workplace Health Promotion: A Review', *Health Education Journal*, **53**, 337–47.

Duhl, L.J. (1986) 'The Healthy City: Its Function and its Future', *Health Promotion*, **1**, 55–60.

Dunnigan, M.G. (1993) 'The Problem with Cholesterol', *British Medical Journal*, **306**, 1355–6.

Durham, M. (1991) *Sex and Politics: The Family and Mortality in the Thatcher Years* (Basingstoke, Macmillan).

Edwards, G., Anderson, P., Babor, T. *et al.* (1994) *Alcohol Policy and the Public Good* (Oxford, Oxford University Press).

Edwards, G., Strang, J. and Jaffe, J. (1993) (eds) *Drugs, Alcohol and Tobacco: Making the Policy Connections* (Oxford, Oxford University Press).

Egger, G. and Swinburn, B. (1997) 'An Ecological Approach to the Obesity Pandemic', *British Medical Journal*, **315**, 477–80.

Ehiri, J., Morris, G. and McEwan, J. (1997) 'A Survey of HACCP Implementation in Glasgow: Is the Information Reaching the Target?', *International Journal of Environmental Health Research*, **7** (1), 71–84.

Ehiri, J.E. and Morris, G. (1998) 'Food Safety Control: Overcoming Barriers to Wider Use of Hazard Analysis', *World Health Forum*, **17** (3), 3013.

Elliott, P., Stamler, J., Nichols, R., Dyer, A. Kestlecoot, H. and Marmot, M. (1996) 'Intersalt Revisited: Further Analyses of 24 Hour Sodium Excretion and Blood Pressure Within and Across Populations', *British Medical Journal*, **312**, 1249–53.

Elmore, J.G., Barton, M.B., Moceri, V., Polk, S., Arena, P. and Fletcher, S. (1998) 'Ten Year Risk of False Positive Screening Mammograms and Clinical Breast Examinations', *New England Journal of Medicine*, **338**, 1089–96.

Elsom, D. (1987) *Atmospheric Pollution: Cause, Effect and Control Policies* (Oxford, Blackwell).

Emmott, S. (1998) 'Gene Food: The Legislative Mess', *Food Magazine*, **42**, 4–5.

Environment, Transport and Regional Affairs Committee (2000a) *Fourth Report Session 1999/2000: The Work of the Health and Safety Executive*, HC 31 (London, Stationery Office).

Environment, Transport and Regional Affairs Committee (2000b) *Fifth Report Session 1999/2000: UK Climate Change Programme*, HC 194 (London, Stationery Office).

Environmental Audit Committee (2000) *5th Report 1999/2000 The Greening Government Initiative: First Annual Report from the Green Ministers' Committee*, HC 341 (London, Stationery Office).

Environmental Health Commission (1997) *Agendas for Change* (London, Chadwick House).

Epstein, E. (1977) *Agency of Fear* (New York, G.P. Putnam).

Epstein, S.S. (1992) 'Mammography Radiates Doubts', *International Journal of Health Services*, **22** (3), 463–4.

Ettore, E. (1997) *Women and Alcohol* (London, Women's Press).

European Commission (1996) *Proposal for a Council Directive on the Assessment of Certain Plans and Programmes on the Environment*, Com (96) 511 (Luxembourg, Office for Official Publications of the European Communities).

European Commission (1997) *The European Union in Action Against Drugs* (Luxembourg, Office for Official Publications of the European Communities).

European Commission (1998) *Communication from the Commission to the Council, the European Parliament, the Economic and Social Committee and the Committee of the Regions*, COM (1998) 230 Final, (Luxembourg, Office for Official Publications of the European Communities).

European Commission (2000) *Health and Consumer Protection: General Information* www.europa.eu.int/comm/dg24/general_info/mission_en.html

European Parliament (1997) *Report on Alleged Contraventions or Maladministration in the Implementation of Community Law in Relation to BSE*, Committee of Inquiry into BSE, Europe Parliament, Session Documents DOC-EN/RR/3191/319544 and DOC-EN/RR/319/319579.

European Union (1997) *The Treaty of Amsterdam* (Luxembourg, European Commission, Office for Official Publications of the European Community).

Ewles, L. (1993) 'Hope Against Hype', *Health Service Journal*, 26 August, 30–1.

Faculty of Public Health Medicine/Royal College of Physicians (1991) *Alcohol and the Public Health* (Basingstoke, Macmillan).

Falck, P., Ricci, A., Wolff, M., Godbold, J. and Deckers, P. (1992) 'Elevated Levels of PCBs and Other Organochlorides, *Archives of Environmental Health*, **47** (2), 143–6.

Family Heart Study Group (1994) 'Randomised Controlled Trial Evaluating Cardiovascular Screening and Intervention in General Practice', *British Medical Journal*, **308**, 313–20.

Farrell, M., Ward, J. and Mattick, R. (1994) 'Methadone Maintenance Treatment in Opiate Dependence: A Review, *British Medical Journal*, **309**, 997–1001.

Fee, E. and Porter, D. (1992) 'Public Health, Preventive Medicine and Professionalisation: England and America in the Nineteenth Century'. In Wear, A. (ed.) *Medicine and Society: Historical Essays* (Cambridge, Cambridge University Press), pp. 249–75.

Fehily, J., Yarnell, J.W., Sweetnam, P.M. and Ellwood, P.C. (1993) 'Diet and Ischaemic Heart Disease: The Caerphilly Study, *British Journal of Nutrition*, **69** (2), 303–14.

Feinstein, A. (1999) 'Biases Introduced by Confounding and Imperfect Retrospective and Prospective Exposure Assessments. In Bate, R. (ed.) *What Risk* (London, Butterworth), pp. 37–48.

Fentem, P.H. (1994) 'Benefits of Exercise in Health and Disease, *British Medical Journal*, 308, 1291–5.

Ferrie, J.E., Shipley, M.J., Marmot, M.G., Stansfield, S. and Davey Smith, G. (1995) 'Health Effects of Anticipation of Job Change and Non-employment: Longitudinal Data from the Whitehall II Study', *British Medical Journal*, **311**, 1264–9.

Field, K., Thorogood, M., Silagy, C., Normand, C., O'Neill, C. and Muir, J. (1995) 'Strategy for Reducing Coronary Risk Factors in Primary Care: Which Is the Most Cost-effective?' *British Medical Journal*, **310**, 1109–12.

Fielder, H., Poon-King, C., Palmer, S., Moss, N. and Coleman, G. (2000) 'Assessment of Impact on Health of Residents Living Near the Nant-y-Gwyddon Landfill Site: Retrospective Analysis', *British Medical Journal*, **320**, 19–23.

Finer, S. (1952) *The Life and Times of Sir Edwin Chadwick* (London, Methuen).

Fischer, B. (1995) 'Drugs, Communities and Harm Reduction in Germany: The New Relevance of Public Health Principles in Local Responses', *Journal of Public Health Policy*, **16** (4), 389–411.

Fischer, B., Kendall, P., Rehm, J. and Room, R. (1997), 'Charting WHO – Goals for Licit and Illicit Drugs for the Year 2000: Are We on Track?', *Public Health*, **111** (5), 271–5.

Fischer, F. (1990) *Technocracy and the Politics of Expertise* (London, Sage).

Fisher, B., Neve, H. and Heritage, Z. (1999) 'Community Development, User Involvement and Primary Health Care', *British Medical Journal*, **314**, 1749–50.

Fisher, K. and Collins, J. (eds) (1993) *Homelessness, Health Care and Welfare Provision* (London, Routledge).

Fisher, R.B. (1991) *Edward Jenner* (London, André Deutsch).

Fleming, C., Wasson, J., Albertsen, P., Barry, M. and Wennberg, J. (1993) 'A Decision Analysis of Alternative Treatment Strategies for Clinically Localised Prostate Cancer. Prostate Patient Outcomes Research Team, *Journal of the American Medical Association*, **269** (20), 2650–8.

Flew, A. (1994) *Passive Smoking: Scientific Method or Corrupted Science* (London, FOREST).

Flinn, M.W. (ed.) (1965) *Report on the Sanitary Condition of the Labouring Population of Great Britain by Edwin Chadwick, 1842* (Edinburgh, Edinburgh University Press).

Flinn, M.W. (1968) *Public Health Reform in Britain* (London, Macmillan).

Florin, D. (1999) 'Scientific Uncertainty and the Role of Expert Advice: The Case of Health Checks for Child Protection by GPs in the UK', *Social Science and Medicine*, **49**, 1269–83.

Flynn, A., Marsden, T. and Harrison, M. (1999) 'The Regulation of Food in Britain in the 1990s', *Policy and Politics*, **27** (4), 435–46.

Flynn, R., Williams, G. and Pickard, S. (1996) *Markets and Networks: Contracting in Community Health Services* (Buckingham, Open University).

*Food Magazine* (1995) 'Irradiated Food – Where Is It Going?', **31**, October/December, p. 1.

*Food Magazine* (1997) 'Cyclamate Levels May Cause Testicular Atrophy', **36**, January/March, p. 3.

*Food Magazine* (1998) 'Olestra: Can They Make It Stick?', **40**, February, p. 4.

Forrest, P. (1990) *The Decision to Screen* (London, Nuffield Provincial Hospitals Trust).

Forrester, P. (1994) 'Housing Conditions and the Nation's Health', *Policy Studies*, **15** (3), 59–63.

Foster, P. (1995) *Women and the Health Care Industry* (Buckingham, Open University).

Fox, A.J. and Shewry, M. (1988) 'New Longitudinal Insights into Relationships Between Unemployment and Mortality', *Stress Medicine*, **4**, 11–19.

Fox, J. (ed.) (1989) *Health Inequalities in European Countries* (Aldershot, Gower).

Fox, J., Goldblatt, P. and Jones, D. (1990) 'Social Class Mortality Differentials: Artefact, Selection, or Life Circumstances?' In Goldblatt, P. (ed.) *Longitudinal Study: Mortality and Social Organization 1971–81*, OPCS LS 6 (London, HMSO), pp. 100–8.

Frankel, S., Gunnell, D.J., Peters, T.J., Maynard, M. and Davey Smith, G. (1998) 'Childhood Energy Intake and Adult Mortality from Cancer: the Boyd Orr Cohort Study', *British Medical Journal*, **316**, 499–504.

Fraser, D. (1973) *The Evolution of the British Welfare State: A History of Social Policy Since the Industrial Revolution* (London, Macmillan).

Frazer, W.M. (1950) *A Study of English Public Health 1834–1939* (London, Baillière Tindall & Cox).

Freeman, R. (1992) 'The Idea of Prevention: A Critical Overview'. In Scott, S., Williams, G., Platt, S. and Thomas, H. (eds) *Private Risks and Public Dangers* (Aldershot, Avebury), pp. 34–56.

Freeman, R. (1995) 'Prevention and Government: Health Policy Making in the UK and Germany', *Journal of Health Politics, Policy and Law*, **20** (3), 745–65.

Fuchs, C., Giovannucci, E., Colditz, G. *et al.* (1999) 'Dietary Fiber and the Risk of Colorectal Cancer and Adenoma in Women', *New England Journal of Medicine*, **340** (3), 169–76.

Fulop, N. and McKee, M. (1996) 'What Impact Do Annual Public Health Reports Have?', *Public Health*, **110** (5), 307–11.

Furedi, F. (1997) *Culture of Fear* (London, Cassell).

Gabe, J. and Williams, P. (1993) 'Women, Crowding and Mental Health'. In Burridge, R. and Ormandy, S. (eds) *Unhealthy Housing: Research, Remedies and Reform* (London, E. and F.N. Spon), pp. 191–208.

Gaesser, G. (1996) *Big Fat Lies* (New York, Fawcett Columbine).

Galbraith, J.K. (1992) *The Culture of Contentment* (London, Sinclair-Stevenson).

Gallerani, M., Manfredini, R., Caracuolo, S., Scapoli, C., Molinari, S. and Fersini, C. (1995) 'Serum Cholesterol Concentrations in Parasuicide', *British Medical Journal*, **310**, 1632–6.

Gamble, A. (1994) *The Free Economy and the Strong State: The Politics of Thatcherism*, 2nd edn (London, Macmillan).

Garfield, S. (1994) *The End of Innocence: Britain in the Time of Aids* (London, Faber).

Garrett, L. (1994) *The Coming Plague* (Harmondsworth, Penguin).

Garrow, J. (1988) *Obesity and Related Diseases* (London, Churchill Livingstone).

Garrow, J. (1991) 'The Importance of Obesity', *British Medical Journal*, **303**, 704–6.

Gatherer, A. (1991) 'Being Executive', *Public Health Physician*, 2 May, 2.

Gibbon, C., Smith, T., Egger, P., Betts, P. and Phillips, D. (1997) 'Early Infection and Subsequent Insulin-dependent Diabetes', *Archives of Diseases in Childhood*, **77** (5), 384–5.

Giddens, A. (1991) *Modernity and Self-identity: Self and Society in the Late Modern Age* (Cambridge, Polity Press).

Gilbert, B. (1970) *British Social Policy 1914–1939* (London, Batsford).

Gillman, M.W., Cupples, L.A., Millen, B.E., Ellison, R.C. and Wolf, P.A. (1997) 'Inverse associates of Dietary Fat with the Development of Ischaemic Stroke in Men', *Journal of the American Medical Association*, **278** (24), 2145–50.

Glantz, S.A., Slade, J., Bero, L., Hanaver, P. and Barnes, D.E. (1996) *The Cigarette Papers* (Los Angeles, University of California Press).

Glynn, M.K., Bopp, C., Dewitt, W., Dabney, P., Mokhtar, M. and Angulo, F.J. (1998) 'Emergence of Multidrug Resistant Salmonella Enterica Serotype Typhimurium DT104 Infections in the United States', *New England Journal of Medicine*, **338** (19), 1333–8.

Godber, G. (1986) 'Medical Officers of Health and Health Services', *Community Medicine*, **8** (1), 1–14.

Goddard, E. (1990) *Why Children Start Smoking*, OPCS (London, HMSO).

Goddard, E. (1996) *Teenage Drinking 1994*, OPCS Social Surveys Division (London, HMSO).

Godlee, F. (1992a) 'The Implications of Climatic Change'. In Godlee, F. and Walker, A. (eds) *Health and the Environment* (London, BMJ Publications), pp. 19–26.

Godlee, F. (1992b) 'The Dangers of Ozone Depletion'. In Godlee, F. and Walker, A. (eds) *Health and the Environment* (London, BMJ Publications), pp. 27–33.

Godlee, F. (1992c) 'Air Pollution II Road Traffic and Modern Industry'. In Godlee, F. and Walker, A. (eds) *Health and the Environment* (London, BMJ Publications), pp. 52–3.

Godlee, F. (1992d) 'Noise: Breaking the Silence'. In Godlee, F. and Walker, A. (eds) *Health and the Environment* (London, BMJ Publications), pp. 74–84.

Godlee, F. (1995) 'WHO in Europe: Does It Have a Role?', *British Medical Journal*, **310**, 389–93.

Goldblatt, P. (1989) 'Mortality by Social Class 1871–85'. In *Population Trends* (London, HMSO), pp. 6–15.

Goldblatt, P., Fox, J. and Leon, D. (1990) 'Mortality of Employed Men and Women'. In Goldblatt, P. (ed.), *Longitudinal Study: Mortality and Social Organization, 1971–81*, OPCS (London, HMSO), pp. 67–80.

Goldstein, A. and Kalant, H. (1993) 'Drug Policy: Striking the Right Balance'. In Bayer, R. and Oppenheim, G. (eds) *Confronting Drugs Policy* (Cambridge, Cambridge University Press), pp. 78–114.

Goodchild, B. (1998) 'Poor Housing: Poor Health', *International Journal of Health Promotion and Education*, **36** (3), 84–6.

Goodman, A., Johnson, P. and Webb, S. (1997) *Inequality in the UK* (Oxford, Oxford University Press).

Goraya, A. and Scambler, G. (1998) 'From Old to New Public Health: Role, Tensions and Contradictions', *Critical Public Health*, **8** (2), 141–51.

Gossop, M. (1996) *Living With Drugs* (4th edn) (Aldershot, Arena).

Gotzsche, P. and Olsen, O. (2000) 'Is Screening for Breast Cancer with Mammography Justifiable?', *Lancet*, **355**, 129–34.

Graffy, J. and Williams, J. (1994) 'Purchasing for All: An Alternative to Fundholding', *British Medical Journal*, **308**, 391–4.

Graham, H. (1993a) *When Life's a Drag: Women, Smoking and Disadvantage*, DoH (London, HMSO).

Graham, H. (1993b) *Hardship and Health in Women's Lives* (Brighton, Harvester Wheatsheaf).

Grant, W. (1989) *Pressure Groups, Politics and Democracy in Britain* (London, Philip Allan).

Gravelle, H. (1998) 'How Much of the Relation Between Population Mortality and Unequal Distribution of Income Is a Statistical Artefact?', *British Medical Journal*, **316**, 382–5.

Green, D. (1987) *The New Right: The Counter Revolution in Political, Economic and Social Thought* (Brighton, Wheatsheaf).

Green, G. (1992) 'Liverpool'. In Ashton, J. (ed.) *Healthy Cities* (Milton Keynes, Open University Press), pp. 88–95.

Green, T.H. (1911) 'Lecture on Liberal Legislation and Freedom of Contract'. In *Works*, Vol. 3 (London, Longmans Green).

Greenwood, D., Packham, C., Muir, K. and Madeley, R. (1995) 'How Do Economic Status and Social Support Influence Survival after the Initial Recovery from Acute Myocardial Infarction?', *Social Science and Medicine*, **40** (5), 639–47.

Griffiths, S. and Hunter, D. (eds) (1999) 'Introduction'. In *Perspectives in Public Health* (Oxford, Radical Medical Press), pp. 3–10.

Gronback, M., Deis, A., Sorenson, T.I.A., Becker, U., Schnohr, P. and Jenson, G. (1995) 'Mortality Associated with Moderate Intakes of Wine, Beer or Spirits', *British Medical Journal*, **310**, 1165–9.

Grubb, M., Koch, M., Munson, A., Sullivan, F. and Thomson, K. (1993) *The Earth Summit Agreements: A Guide and Assessment* (London, Carthscan).

Gruenewald, P., Ponicki, W. and Holder, H. (1993) 'The Relationship of Outlet Densities to Alcohol Consumption: A Time Series Cross Sectional Analysis', *Alcohol: Clinical and Experimental Research*, **17** (1), 38–47.

Gunnell, D.J., Davey Smith, G., Holly, J.M.P. and Frankel, S. (1998) 'Leg Length and the Risk of Cancer in the Boyd Orr Cohort', *British Medical Journal*, **317**, 1350–1.

Gunnell, D.J., Peters, T.J., Kammerling, R.M. and Brooks, J. (1995) 'Relation Between Parasuicide, Suicide, Psychiatric Admission and Socioeconomic Deprivation', *British Medical Journal*, **311**, 226–30.

Gwyn, R. (1999) '"Killer Bugs", "Silly Buggers" and "Politically Correct Pals": Competing Discourses in Health Care Reporting', *Health*, 3 March, 335–45.

Hackett, A.E., Kirby, S. and Howie, M. (1997) 'A National Survey of the Diet of Children aged 13–14 Years Living in Urban Areas of the UK', *Journal of Human Nutrition and Dietetics*, **10** (1), 37–51.

Hackshaw, A.K., Law, M.R. and Wald, N.J. (1997) 'The Accumulated Evidence on Lung Cancer and Environmental Tobacco Smoke', *British Medical Journal*, **315**, 980–8.

Haigh, N. (1992) *Manual of Environmental Policy in the EC and Britain* (London, Longman).

Hainsworth, P.J., Henderson, M.A. and Bennett, R.C. (1993) 'Delayed Presentation in Breast Cancer. Relationship to Tumour Stage and Survival', *Breast*, **2**, 37–41.

Hall, R. Hume (1990) *Health and the Global Environment* (Oxford, Polity Press).

Ham, C. and Mitchell, J. (1990) 'A Force To Reckon With', *Health Service Journal*, 1 February, 164–5.

Hammersley, R., Forsyth, A. and Morrison, V. (1989) 'The Relationship Between Crime and Opoid Use, *British Journal of Addiction*, **84**, 1029–43.

Hammond, R.J. (1951) *Food: The Growth of Policy,* Vol. 1 (London, HMSO).

Hancock, T. (1985) 'The Mandala of Health: A Model of the Human Ecosystem', *Family and Community Health*, **8**, 1–10.

Hancock, T. (1992) 'The Healthy City from Concept to Application: Implications for Research'. In Davies, J. and Kelly, M. (eds) *Healthy Cities* (Buckingham, Open University Press), pp. 14–24.

Hankinson, S.E., Willett, W., Colditz, G. *et al.* (1998) 'Circulating Concentrates of Insulin Like Growth Factor 1 and Risk of Breast Cancer', *Lancet*, **351**, 1393–6.

Hann, A. (1996) *The Politics of Breast Cancer Screening* (Aldershot, Avebury).

Hann, A. (1999) 'Cancer Test Smeared: Preventive Medicine or an Expensive Mistake?', *Critical Public Health*, 9 March, 251–5.

*Hansard* (1957) Session 1956/7, 1 March, column 1640.

Hansen, M (1998) *Potential Public Health Impacts of RBST in Dairy Products* (New York, Consumer Policy Institute).

Hardcastle, J.D., Chamberlain, J.O., Robinson, M.H. *et al.* (1996) 'Randomised Controlled Trial of Faecal Occult Blood Screening for Colorectal Cancer', *Lancet*, **348** (9040), 1472–7.

Harding, S. and Maxwell, R. (1997) 'Differences in the Mortality of Migrants'. In Drever, F. and Whitehead, M. (eds) *Health Inequalities: Decennial Supplement* (London, Stationery Office), pp. 108–21.

Harland, J., White, M., Drinkwater, C., Chinn, D., Farr, L. and Howel, D. (1999) 'The Newcastle Exercise Project: A Randomised Controlled Trial of Methods To Promote Physical Activity in Primary Care', *British Medical Journal*, **319**, 828–32.

Harman, R. (1999) 'The Transport White Paper: A Landmark in an Undefined Country', *Public Money and Management*, **19** (2), 5–6.

Harris, R.W., Brinton, L.A., Cowdell, R.H. *et al.* (1980) 'Characteristics of Women with Dysplasia or Carcinoma in Sites of the Cervix Uteri, *British Journal of Cancer*, **42** (3), 359–69.

Harrison, B. (1971) *Drink and the Victorians* (London, Faber and Faber).

Harrison, L. (1986) 'Tobacco Battered and the Pipes Shattered: A Note on the Fate of the First British Campaign Against Smoking', *British Journal of Addiction*, **81**, 553–8.

Harrison, S., Hunter, D., Johnson, I., Nicholson, N. and Thunhurst, C. and Wistow, G. (1994) *Health Before Healthcare*, Social Policy Paper No. 4 (London, Institute for Public Policy Research).

Harrow, J. (1991) 'Local Authority Health Strategies'. In McNaught, A. (ed.) *Managing Community Health Services* (London, Chapman & Hall), pp. 3–16.

Hart, C.L., Davey Smith, G. and Blane, D. (1998) 'Social Mobility and 21 Year Mortality in a Cohort of Scottish Men', *Social Science and Medicine*, **47** (8), 1121–30.

Hart, C.L., Smith, G.D., Hole, D.J. and Hawthorne, V.M. (1999) 'Alcohol Consumption and Mortality from all Causes, Coronary Heart Disease and Stroke: Results from a Prospective Cohort Study of Scottish Men with 21 Years of Follow-up', *British Medical Journal*, **318**, 1725–9.

Harvey, J. and Fralick, E. (1997) 'Targeting Neglect', *Health Service Journal*, 31 July, 26–7.

Hasler, J. (1992) 'The Primary Health Care Team: History and Contractual Farces', *British Medical Journal*, **305**, 232–4.

Hastings, G.B., Ruan, H., Teer, P. and MacKintosh (1994) 'Cigarette Advertising and Children's Smoking: Why Reg Was Withdrawn', *British Medical Journal*, **309**, 933–7.

Hattersley, L. (1997) 'Expectation of Life by Social Class'. In Drever, F. and Whitehead, M. (eds) *Health Inequalities: Decennial Supplement* (London, Stationery Office), pp. 73–82.

Hayek, F. (1976), *The Constitution of Liberty* (London, Routledge).

Hayek, F. (1988) *The Fatal Conceit: The Errors of Socialism* (London, Routledge).

He, J., Vupputuri, S., Allen, K., Prerost, M., Hughes, J. and Whelton, P.K. (1999) 'Passive Smoking and the Risk of Coronary Heart Disease – a Meta-analysis of Epidemiological Studies', *New England Journal of Medicine*, **340** (12), 920–6.

HEA (Health Education Authority) (1991) *The Smoking Epidemic: Counting the Costs in England* (London, HEA).

HEA (Health Education Authority) (1996) *Drug Realities: National Drugs Campaign Survey* (London, HEA).

HEA (Health Education Authority) (1997) *Guidelines: Promoting Physical Activity with Black and Minority Ethnic Groups* (London, HEA).

HEA (Health Education Authority) (1998) *Putting Health on the Regeneration Agenda* (London, HEA).

Health Committee (1990)*Food Poisoning: Listeria and Listeriosis*, 1st Report 1989/90, HC 93 (London, HMSO).

Health Committee (1993) *The European Commission's Proposed Directive on the Advertising of Tobacco Products*, 2nd Report 1992/3, HC 221 (London, HMSO).

Health Committee (1995) *Breast Cancer Services*, 3rd Report 1994/5, HC 324 (London, HMSO).

Health Visitors' Association (1996) *HVA Centenary Survey: Return of Diseases and Social Conditions of the Nineteenth Century* (London, HVA).

*Health and Safety Bulletin* (1998) 265, 13.

Heinz, J., Laumann, E., Nelson, R. and Salisbury, R. (1993) *The Hollow Core: Private Interests in National Policy Making* (Cambridge, MA, Harvard University Press).

Hemminki, E. (1996) 'Oral Contraception and Breast Cancer', *British Medical Journal*, **313**, 63–4.

Henderson, C.J., Smith, A.G., Ure, J., Brown, K., Bacon, E.J. and Wolf, C.R. (1998) 'Increased Skin Tumorigenesis in Mice Lacking pi Class Glutathione S-Transferases', *Proceedings of the National Academy of Sciences of the USA*, **95** (9), 5275–6.

Henderson, J., North, K., Griffiths, M., Harvey, I. and Golding, J. (1999) 'Pertussis Vaccination and Wheezing Illnesses in Young Children: Prospective Cohort Study: The Longitudinal Study of Pregnancy and Childhood Team', *British Medical Journal*, **318**, 1173–6.

Her, M. and Rehm, J. (1998) 'Alcohol and All Cause Mortality in Europe 1982–90: A Pooled Cross-section Time Series Analysis', *Addiction*, **93** (9), 1335–40.

Herbert, A. (1997) 'Effect of Screening May Be Being Underestimated', *British Medical Journal*, **314**, 1277–8.

Hewlett, S.A. (1993) *Child Neglect in Rich Nations* (New York, Unicef).

Hibbs, J., (1999) 'Review: A New Deal for Transport: Analysis of the Transport White Paper', *Public Policy and Management*, **19** (1), 70–2.

Highways Agency (1997) *West London Speed Camera Project: Analysis of Accident Data 36 Months Before and 36 Months After Implementation* (London, London Research Centre).

Hill, J.O. and Peters, J.C. (1998) 'Environmental Contributions to the Obesity Epidemic', *Science*, **280**, 1371–4.

Hillier, S., Inskip, H., Coggon, D. and Cooper, C. (1996) 'Water Flouridation and Osteoporotic Fracture', *Community Dental Health*, **13** (Supplement 2), 63–8.

Hills, J. (1997) *The Future of Welfare* (York, Joseph Rowntree Foundation).

Hirsch, J. (1998) 'Magic Bullet for Obesity', *British Medical Journal*, **317**, 1136–8.

Hodgett, G. (1998) 'Ethics, Science and the Social Management of Risk: The Bovine Spongiform Encephalopathy Epidemic', *Business and Law*, **1**, 359–86.

Hodgkinson, R. (1967) *The Origins of the NHS: The Medical Services of the New Poor Law* (London, Wellcome Foundation).

Holland, W. and Stewart, S. (1990) *Screening in Health Care: Benefit or Bane?* (London, NPHT).

Holland, W. and Stewart, S. (1998) *Public Health: The Vision and the Challenge* (London, Nuffield Trust).

Hollis, P. (1974) *Pressure from without in Early Victorian England* (London, Edward Arnold).

Holmes C. and Ward, T.M. (1996) 'Heart Well: Healthy Alliances in Action', *Nutrition and Food Science*, **6**, 25–8.

Holtzman, N.A. and Shapiro, D. (1998) 'Genetic Testing and Public Policy', *British Medical Journal*, **316**, 852–6.

Honingsbaum, F. (1970) *The Struggle for the Ministry of Health* (London, Social Administration Research Trust).

Hopkins, J. (1999) 'Apo E4 Gene Linked to Breast Cancer', *British Medical Journal*, **319**, 662.

Hopkins, T. (1997) 'Effectiveness is no Accident', *Health Lines*, June, 22–3.

Horlick-Jones, T. (1998) 'Meaning and Contextualisation in Risk Assessment', *Reliability Engineering and System Safety*, **59**, 79–89.

House of Lords Science and Technology Select Committee (1998a) *Resistance to Antibiotics and Other Microbial Agents*, 7th Report 1997/8, HL 81 (London, Stationery Office).

House of Lords Science and Technology Select Committee (1998b) *Cannabis: The Scientific and Medical Evidence*, 9th Report 1997/8, HL 151 (London, Stationery Office).

House of Lords Select Committee on European Communities (1990) *Irradiation of Foodstuffs*, 4th Report 1989/90, HL 13 (London, HMSO).

Howarth, C., Kenway, P., Palmer, G. and Miorelli, R. (1999) *Monitoring Poverty and Social Exclusion* (York, Joseph Rowntree Foundation).

Howlett, M. and Ramesh, A. (1995) *Studying Public Policy: Policy Cycles and Policy Subsystems* (Oxford, Oxford University Press).

Howson, A. (1999) 'Cervical Screening, Compliance and Moral Obligation', *Sociology of Health and Illness*, **21** (4), 401–25.

Hoyer, A.P., Grandjean, P., Jorgensen, T., Brock, J.W. and Hartvig, H.B. (1998) 'Organochloride Exposure and Risk of Breast Cancer', *Lancet*, **352**, 1816–20.

HSE (Health and Safety Executive) (1992) *Passive Smoking at Work* (London, HSE).

Hu, F.B., Stampfer, F.B., Manson, J. *et al.* (1998) 'Frequent Nut Consumption and Risk of Coronary Heart Disease in Women: Prospective Cohort Study', *British Medical Journal*, **317**, 1341–5.

Hudson, B. (1999) 'Decentralisation and Primary Care Groups: A Paradigm Shift for the National Health Service in England', *Policy and Politics*, **27** (2), 159–72.

Hughes, K., MacKintosh, A.M., Hastings, G., Wheeler, C., Watson, J. and Inglis, J. (1997) 'Young People, Alcohol and Designer and Drinks: Quantitative and Qualitative Study', *British Medical Journal*, **314**, 416–18.

Hunt, S. (1997) 'Housing-related Disorders'. In Charlton, J. and Murphy, M. (eds) *The Health of Adult Britain 1841–1994*, Vol. 1 (London, Stationery Office), pp. 156–70.

Hunter, D. (1996) 'Reinventing the Zeal', *Health Service Journal*, 29 August, 15.

Huntingdon, J. (1993) 'From FPC to FHSA to Health Commission?', *British Medical Journal*, **306**, 33–6.

Hutton, W. (1996) *The State We're In* (London, Vintage).

Hyde, H.M. (1976) *Neville Chamberlain* (London, Weidenfeld & Nicolson).

ISDD (Institute for Drug Dependence) (1995) *Drugs, Pregnancy and Children: A Guide for Professionals* (London, ISDD).

Illich, I. (1977) *Limits to Medicine* (Harmondsworth, Penguin).

Illsley, R. (1986) 'Occupation Class Selection and the Production of Inequalities in Health', *Quarterly Journal of Social Affairs*, **2** (2), 151–65.

Imperial Cancer Research Rund (1995) 'Effectiveness of Health Checks Conducted by Nurses in Primary Care', *British Medical Journal*, **310**, 1099–104.

*Independent* (1997) 'Cigarettes Set to Kill 10 Million by 2025', *Independent*, 25 August, p. 9.

*Independent* (1998) 'Brown is not such a Tory Chancellor after all', *Independent*, 19 March, 25.

*Independent* (1999) 'IFS Applauds Chancellor's Hat-trick', *Independent*, 11 March, p. 19.

*Independent* (2000a) 'Teenage Drug Use is Lowest for Nine Years', *Independent*, 6 March, p. 6.

*Independent* (2000b) ' Poverty Gap Widens Under Blair', *Independent*, 13 April, p. 1.

*Independent* (2000c) 'Mistake Allowed GM Seeds to be Sown Across Britain', *Independent*, 17 May, p. 1.

Independent Inquiry into Inequalities in Health (1998) Report (Acheson Report) (London, Stationery Office).

Independent Inquiry into the Misuse of Drugs Act 1971 (2000) *Drugs and the Law* (London, Police Foundation).

*Independent on Sunday* (1994) 'Drink Companies Pay Dons to Rubbish Alcohol Report', *Independent on Sunday*, 4 December, p. 1.

*Independent on Sunday* (1996) 'The Quiet Epidemic', *Independent on Sunday*, 7 April, p. 15.

Inglis, B. (1965) *A History of Medicine* (London, Weidenfield & Nicolson).

Interdepartmental Committee on Drug Addiction (1961) *Report* (London, HMSO).

Interdepartmental Committee on Drug Addiction (1965) *Report* (London, HMSO).

Intersalt Cooperative Research Group (1988) 'Intersalt: An International Study of Electrolyte Excretion and Blood Pressure. Results for 24 Hour Urinary Sodium and Postassium Excretion', *British Medical Journal*, **297**, 319–28.

Irwin, A. and Wynne, B. (1996) 'Conclusion'. In Irwin, A. and Wynne, B. (eds) *Misunderstanding Science? The Public Reconstruction of Science and Technology* (Cambridge University Press), pp. 214–21.

Jackson, R., Scragg, R. and Beaglehole, R. (1991) 'Alcohol Consumption and Risk of Coronary Heart Disease', *British Medical Journal*, **303**, 211–16.

Jacobs, D., Blackburn, H., Higgins, M., Reed, D., Iso, H. and McMillan, G. (1992) 'Report of the Conference on Low Blood Cholesterol: Mortality Associations', *Circulation*, **86**, 1046–60.

Jamdagni, L. (1996) *Purchasing for Black Populations* (London, King's Fund).

James, P. (1997) Food Standards Agency: An Interim Proposal (unpublished paper).

James, W.P., Nelson, M., Ralph, A. and Leather, S. (1997) 'The Contribution of Nutrition to Inequalities in Health, *British Medical Journal*, **314**, 1545–9.

Jansen, M.C., Bueno-de-Mesquista, H.B., Budna, R. *et al.* (1999) 'Dietary Fibre and Plant Foods in Relation to Colorectal Cancer Mortality: The 7 Countries Study', *International Journal of Cancer*, **81** (2) 174–9.

Jasanoff, S. (1990) *The Fifth Branch: Science Advisors as Policy Makers* (Cambridge, MA, Harvard University Press).

Jeffrey, D., McLellarn, R.W. and Fox, D.T. (1982) *Health Education Quarterly*, **9** (2–3), 174–89.

Jenkins, R. (1993) 'Defining the Problem. Stress, Depression and Anxiety: Causes, Prevalence and Consequences'. In Jenkins, R. and Warman, D. (eds) *Promoting Mental Health Policies in the Workplace* (London, HMSO), pp. 32–49.

Jenkins-Smith, H. and Sabatier, P. (1993) 'Evaluating the Advocacy Coalition Framework', *Journal of Public Policy*, **14** (2), 175–203.

Joffe, M. and Sutcliffe, J. (1997) 'Developing Policies for a Healthy Environment', *Health Promotion International*, **12** (2), 169–73.

John, P. (1998) *Analysing Public Policy* (London, Pinter).

Johnson, A.P., Speller, D.C., George, R.C., Warner, M., Domingue, G. and Efstratiou, A. (1996) 'Prevalence of Antibiotic Resistance and Serotypes in Pneumococci in England and Wales. Results of Observational Studies in 1990 and 1995', *British Medical Journal*, **312**, 1434–6.

Johnson, M. (1993) 'Equal Opportunities in Service Delivery. Responses to a Changing Population?' In Ahmad, W. (ed.) *Race and Health in Contemporary Britain* (Buckinham, Open University Press), pp. 183–200.

Jones, C., Taylor, G., Whittle, J., Evans, D. and Trotter, D. (1997) 'Water Flouridation: Tooth Decay in 5 Year Olds and Social Deprivation Measured by the Jarman Scale Analysis of Data from British Surveys', *British Medical Journal*, **315**, 514–17.

Joossens, L. and Raw, M. (1995) 'Smuggling and Cross-border Shopping of Tobacco in Europe', *British Medical Journal*, **310**, 1393–7.

Jordan, A. (1998) 'Step Change or Stasis? EC Environmental Policy After the Amsterdam Treaty', *Environmental Politics*, **7** (1), 227–36.

Jordan, A.G. and Maloney, W. (1997) *The Protest Business* (Manchester, Manchester University Press).

Joseph Rowntree Foundation (1994) *Disadvantage in Rural Scotland* (York, Joseph Rowntee Foundation).

Joseph Rowntree Foundation (1995) *Income and Wealth* (York, Joseph Rowntree Foundation).

Judd, D. (1977) *Radical Joe: A Life of Joseph Chamberlain* (London, Hamish Hamilton).

Judge, K. (1995) 'Income Distribution and Life Expectancy: A Critical Appraisal', *British Medical Journal*, **311**, 1282–5.

Juniper, T. (1999) 'Unfair Trade Sparks New World War', *Guardian*, 17 August, p. 14.

Kalkstein, L.S. (1993) 'Health and Climate Change: Direct Impacts on Cities', *Lancet*, **342**, 1377–9.

Kalkstein, L.S. (1995) 'Lessons from a Very Hot Summer', *Lancet*, **346**, 857–9.

Kammerling, R. and Kinnear, D. (1996) 'The Extent of the Two Tier Service for Fundholders', *British Medical Journal*, **312**, 1399–401.

Kaplan, G.A., Pamuk, E.R., Lynch, J.W., Cohen, R.D. and Balfour, J.L. (1996) 'Inequality in Income and Mortality in the United States: Analysis of Mortality and Potential Pathways', *British Medical Journal*, **312**, 999–1003.

Kawachi, I. and Kennedy, B. (1997) 'Health and Social Cohesion. Why Care about Income Inequality?', *British Medical Journal*, **314**, 1037–40.

Kawachi, I., Kennedy, B. Lochner, K. and Prothrow-Stith, D. (1997) 'Social Capital, Income Inequality and Mortality', *American Journal of Public Health*, **87** (9), 1491–8.

Kay, J. (1832) *The Moral and Physical Condition of the Working Classes of Manchester* (London, Ridgeway).

Kehner, B.H. and Wolin, C.M. (1979) 'Impact of Income Maintenance on Low Birthweight: Evidence from the Gary Experiment', *Journal of Human Resources*, **14**, 434–62.

Kelleher, D. and Hillier, S. (1996) *Researching Cultural Differences in Health* (London, Routledge).

Kelly, M.P., Davies, J.K. and Charlton, B.G. (1992) 'Healthy Cities?' In Davies, J. and Kelly, M. (eds) *Healthy Cities: Policy and Practice* (London, Routledge), pp. 1–14.

Kemp, T., Pearce, N., Fitzharris, P. *et al.* (1997) 'Is Infant Immunisation a Risk Factor for Childhood Asthma or Allergy?', *Epidemiology*, **8** (6), 678–80.

Kendall, L. (1999) *Local Inequalities Targets* (London, King's Fund).

Kennedy, B.P., Kawachi, I. and Prothrow-Stith, D. (1996) 'Income Distribution and Mortality: Cross-sectional Ecological Study of the Robin Hood Index in the United States', *British Medical Journal*, **312**, 1004–7.

Key, T., Thorogood, M., Appleby, P. and Burr, M. (1996) 'Dietary Habits and Mortality in 11,000 Vegetarians and Health Conscious People: Results of a 17 Year Follow Up', *British Medical Journal*, **313**, 775–9.

Keys, A. (1980) *Seven Countries: A Multi Analysis of Death and CHD* (Cambridge, MA, Harvard University Press).

Kickbusch, I. (1986) 'Health Promotion Strategies for Action', *Canadian Journal of Public Health*, **77**, 321–6.

Kilduff, A., McKeown, K. and Crowther, A. (1998) 'Heath Needs Assessment in Primary Care: The Evolution of a Practical Public Health Approach', *Public Health*, **112** (3), 175–81.

King James I (1616) 'A Counterblaste to Tobacco'. In James I (ed.) *The Workes of the Most High and Mighty Prince, James*, (London, Barker & Bill), pp. 214–22.

King, D. (1987) *The New Right: Politics, Markets and Citizenship* (London, Macmillan).

Kingdon, J. (1984) *Agendas, Alternatives and Public Policy* (Boston, MA, Little, Brown).

Kingsnorth, P. (1998) 'Bovine Growth Hormones', *Ecologist*, **28** (5), 266–9.

Kinlen, L. (1988) 'Evidence for an Infective Cause of Childhood Leukaemia', *Lancet*, **2**, 1323–7.

Kinlen, L. (1995) 'Epidemiological Evidence for and Infective Basis in Childhood Leukaemia', *British Journal of Cancer*, **71**, 1–5.

Kinnersley, D. (1994) *Coming Clean* (London, Penguin).

Kisely, S. and Jones, J. (1997) 'Acheson Revisited: Public Health Medicine Ten Years After the Acheson Report', *Public Health*, **111** (6), 361–4.

Kitto, H.D.F. (1957) *The Greeks* (London, Pelican).

Kjaer, K., Dahl, C., Engholm, G., Bock, J.E., Lynge, E. and Jensen, O.M. (1992) 'Case Control Study of Risk Factors for Cervical Neoplasia in Denmark: II. Role of Sexual Activity, Reproductive Factors and Venereal Infections', *Cancer Causes Control*, **3** (4), 339–48.

Klein, R. (1980) 'Between Nihilism and Utopia in Health Care' (unpublished lecture, Yale University, New Haven, CT).

Klein, R. (1991) 'Making Sense of Inequalities: A Response to Peter Townsend', *International Journal of Health Services*, **21** (1), 175–81.

Knowles, R. (1999) 'How We Can Improve Our Buses', *Independent*, 7 January, p. 4R

Kogevinas, E. (1990) *1971–83 England and Wales: Longitudinal Study: Socio-demographic Differences in Cancer Survival* (London, HMSO).

Kohlmeier, L., Simonsen, N., Van't Veer, P. *et al.* (1997) 'Adipose Tissue, Transfatty Acids and Breast Cancer in the European Community Multicenter Study on Antioxidants, Myocardial Infarction and Breast Cancer', *Cancer Epidemiology, Biomarkers, Prevention*, **6** (9), 705–10.

Kolata, G. (2000) *Flu: The Story of the Great Influenza Pandemic of 1918 and the Search for the Virus that Caused It* (Basingstoke, Macmillan).

Kramer, A., Hahn, S., Cohen, N. *et al.* (1999) 'Ageing, Fitness and Neurocognitive Function', *Nature*, **400**, 418–19.

Krause, R. (ed.) (1998) *Emerging Infections* (New York, Academy Press).

Krieger, N., Wolff, M.S., Hiatt, R., Rivera, M., Vogelman, J. and Orentreich, N. (1994) 'Breast Cancer and Serum Organochlorines: A Prospective Study among White, Black and Asian Women', *Journal of the National Cancer Institute*, **86**, 589–99.

Kronborg, O., Fenger, C., Olsen, J., Jorgensen, O.D. and Sondergaard, O. (1996) 'Randomised Study of Screening for Colorectal Cancer with Faecal Occult Blood Test', *Lancet*, **348**, 1467–71.

Kunst, A.E., Groenhof, F. and Machenbach, J. (1998) 'Occupational Class and Cause Specific Mortality in Middle Aged Men in 11 European Countries: Comparison of Population Based Studies', *British Medical Journal*, **316**, 1636–42.

Labonte, R. (1998a) 'Healthy Public Policy and the World Trade Organization: A Proposal for an International Health Presence in Future Trade/Investment Talks', *Health Promotion International*, **13** (3), 245–55.

Labonte, R. (1998b) 'Health Promotion and the Common Good: Towards a Politics of Practice', *Critical Public Health*, **8** (2), 107–23.

Labrie, F., Cusan, L., Diamond, P. *et al.* (1999) 'Screening Decreases Prostate Cancer Death: First Analysis of the 1988 Quebec Prospective RCT', *Prostate*, **38** (2), 83–91.

Lalonde, M. (1974) *A New Perspective on the Health of Canadians* (Ottawa, Ministry of National Health and Welfare).

Lambert, R. (1963) *Sir John Simon* (London, Magibbon & Kee).

Lash, M., Szerszynski, S., and Wynne, B. (1996) *Risk, Environment and Modernity* (London, Sage).

Last, J. (1987) *Public Health and Human Ecology* (Connecticut, Appleton & Lange).

Law, M. and Wald, N. (1999) 'Why Heart Disease Mortality is Low in France: The Time Lag Explanation', *British Medical Journal*, **318**, 1471–6.

Law, M.R., Morris, J.K. and Wald, N.J. (1997) 'Environmental Tobacco Smoke Exposure and Ischaemic Heart Disease: An Evaluation of the Evidence', *British Medical Journal*, **315**, 973–80.

Law, M.R., Thompson, S.G. and Wald, N.J. (1994a) 'Assessing Possible Hazards of Reducing Serum Cholesterol', *British Medical Journal*, **308**, 373–9.

Law, M.R., Wald, N.J. and Thompson, S.G. (1994b) 'By How Much and How Quickly Does Reduction in Serum Cholesterol Concentration Lower Risk of Ischaemic Heart Disease?', *British Medical Journal*, **308**, 367–73.

Lawrence, M. (ed.) (1987) *Fed Up and Hungry: Women, Oppression and Food* (London, Women's Press).

Lawson, P. and Emerson, P. (1995) 'Nurse Practitioners: Agents of Change', *Health Visitor*, **68**, 244–5.

Lawson, R. (1997) *Bills of Health* (Oxford, Radcliffe Medical Press).

Lawton, J. (1989) 'Alcohol, Tobacco and Illicit Drugs', *Policy Studies* (3), 27–32.

Le Fanu, J. (ed.) (1994a) 'Prevention: Wishful Thinking of Hard Science: The Exaggerated Claims of Health Promotion'. In Le Fanu, J. (ed.) *Preventionitis* (London, Social Affairs Unit), pp. 23–35.

Le Fanu, J. (ed.) (1994b) *Preventionitis* (London, Social Affairs Unit).

Le Grand, J. (1987) 'Equity, Health and Healthcare', *Social Justice Research*, **1**, 257–74.

Le Touze, S. and Calnan, M. (1996) 'The Banding Scheme for Health Promotion in General Practice', *Health Trends*, **28** (3), 100–5.

Lear, J., Lawrence, I., Pohl, J. and Burden, A. (1994) 'Myocardial Infarction and Thrombolysis: A Comparison of the Indian and European Populations on a Coronary Care Unit', *Journal of Royal College of Physicians*, **28**, 143–7.

Lee, C.D., Blair, S.N. and Jackson, A.J. (1999) 'Cardiorespiratory Fitness, Body Composition, and All Cause and Cardiovascular Disease Mortality in Men', *American Journal of Clinical Nutrition*, **69** (3), 373–80.

Lee, P. (1994) 'The Need for Caution in Interpreting Low Level Risks Reported by Epidemiologists'. In Le Fanu, J. (ed.) *Preventionitis* (London, Social Affairs Unit), pp. 36–45.

Leggett, J. (1999) *The Carbon War* (London, Allen Lane).

Lehtinen, M., Dillner, J., Knekt, P. *et al.* (1996) 'Serologically Diagnosed Infection with Human Papillomavirus Type 16 and Risk for Subsequent Development of Cervical Carcinoma: Nested Case Control Study', *British Medical Journal*, **312**, 537–9.

Leicester City Council (1998) *Leicester's Local Agenda 21: Action Plans* (Leicester, Leicester City Council).

Leichter, H. (1991) *Free To Be Foolish: Politics and Health Promotion in the United States and Great Britain* (Oxford, Oxford University Press).

Leitner, M., Shapland, J. and Wiles, P. (1993) *Drug Usage and Drug Prevention: The Views and Habits of the General Population* (London, HMSO).

Lemmens, P.H.H.M. and Garretson, H.F.L. (1998) 'Unstable Pragmatism: Dutch Drug Policy Under National and International Pressure', *Addiction*, **93** (2), 157–62.

Leung, W.C. (1999) 'Effect of Screening on Cervical Cancer Mortality in England and Wales', *British Medical Journal*, **319**, 581.

Levenson, R., Joule, N. and Russell, J. (1997) *Developing Public Health in the NHS – the Multidisiplinary Contribution* (London, King's Fund).

Lewis, J. (1986) *What Price Community Medicine?* (Brighton, Wheatsheaf).

Lewis, J. (1992) 'Providers, "Consumers": the State and the Delivery of Health-care Services in Twentieth Century Britain'. In Wear, A. (ed.) *Medicine in Society: Historical Essays* (Cambridge, Cambridge University Press), pp. 317–45.

Lewis, S.A. and Britton, J.R. (1998) 'Measles Infection, Measles Vaccination and the Effect of Birth in the Aetiology of Hay Fever', *Clinical and Experimental Allergy*, **28** (12), 1493–500.

Lichtman, S.W., Pisarska, K., Berman, E.R. *et al.* (1992) 'Discrepancy Between Self-reported and Actual Calorie Intake Exercise in Obese Subjects', *New England Journal of Medicine*, **327**, 893–8.

Lidbrink, E., Elfving, J., Frisell, J. and Jonsson, E. (1996) 'Neglected Aspects of False Positive Findings of Mammography in Breast Cancer Screening: Analysis of False Positive Cases from the Stockholm Trial', *British Medical Journal*, **312**, 273–6.

Lindheim, R. and Syme, S. (1983) 'Environment, People and Health', *Annual Review of Public Health*, **4**, 335–59.

Lister Sharp, D. (1994) 'Underage Drinking in the UK since 1970: Public Policy, the Law and Adolescent Drinking Behaviour', *Alcohol and Alcoholism*, 55–63.

Littlewood, S. and While, A. (1997) 'A New Agenda for Governance? Local Agenda 21 and the Prospects for Holistic Local Decision Making', *Local Government Studies*, **23** (4), 111–23.

Lobstein, T. (1998) 'The Common Agricultural Policy: A Dietary Disaster?', *Consumer Policy Review*, **8** (2), 83–87.

Lobstein, T. (1999) 'Agenda 2000 Hits the Rocks', *Food Magazine*, **45** April/June, pp. 14–15.

Logan, W.P.D. (1950) 'Mortality in England and Wales from 1848–1947', *Population Studies*, **4**, 132–78.

Longmate, N. (1966) *King Cholera: The Biography of a Disease* (London, Hamish Hamilton).

Lovestone, S. and Fahey, T. (1991) 'Psychological Factors in Breast Cancer', *British Medical Journal*, **302**, 1219–20.

Lowry, S. (1991) *Housing and Health* (London, BMJ Publications).

Luke, C. (1998) 'Accident and Emergency', *Alcohol Alert*, **3**, 2–4.

Lundberg, O. (1993) 'The Impact of Childhood Living Conditions on Illness and Mortality in Adulthood', *Social Science and Medicine*, **36**, 1047–52.

Lupton, D. (1995) *The Imperative of Public Health: Public Health and the Regulated Body* (London, Sage).

Lynch, J. and Kaplan, G. (1997) 'Understanding How Inequality in the Distribution of Income Affects Health', *Journal of Health Psychology*, **2** (3), 297–314.

Lyon, J.L., Gardner, J.W., West, D.W., Stanish, W.M. and Herbertson, R.M. (1983) 'Smoking and Carcinoma in situ of the Uterine Cervix', *American Journal of Public Health*, **73** (5), 558–62.

McCallum, A. (1997) 'Public Health, Health Promotion and Broader Health Strategy'. In Iliffe, S. and Munro, J. (eds) *Healthy Choices: Future Options for the NHS* (London, Lawrence & Wishart), pp. 94–119.

McCarthy, A. (1996) 'Protecting the Public Health: The Role of Environmental Health', *Public Health*, **110** (2), 77–80.

McCarthy, M. and Rees, S. (1992) *Health Systems and Public Health Medicine in the European Community* (London, Royal College of Physicians/Faculty of Public Health Medicine).

McCormick, A., Fleming, D. and Charlton, J. (1995) *Morbidity Statistics from General Practice*, 4th National Study 1991/2 (London, HMSO).

McCormick, J. (1991) *British Politics and the Environment* (London, Earthscan).

McCormick, J.S. (1989) 'Cervical Smears: A Questionable Practice?', *Lancet*, **2**, 207.

MacDonagh, O. (1977) *Early Victorian Government* (London, Weidenfield & Nicolson).

McDonald, A., Langford, I. and Scott, N. (1997) 'The Future of Community Nursing in the UK: District Nursing, Health Visiting and School Nursing', *Journal of Advanced Nursing*, **26**, 257–65.

McGoogan, E. (1993) *Report of the Committee of Inquiry into Cervical Cytopathology At Inverclyde Royal Hospital, Greenock* (Edinburgh, HMSO).

McGurk, H. and Hurry, J. (1995) *Project Charlie: An Evaluation of a Life Skills Drug Education Programme for Primary Schools: Paper 1. Drugs Prevention Initiative* (London, Home Office).

McGurk, H. and Hurry, J. (1997) *Drugs Prevention Initiative Paper 1. Project Charlie: An Evaluation of a Life Skills Drug Education Programme for Primary Schools* (London, Home Office).

MacIntyre, S. and Hunt, K. (1997) 'Socioeconomic Position, Gender and Health', *Journal of Health Psychology*, **2**, 315–34.

MacIntyre, S., McIver, and Soomans, A. (1993) 'Area, Class and Health: Should We Be Focusing on Places or People?', *Journal of Social Policy*, **22**, 213–34.

McKeganey, N., Forsyth, A., Barnard, M. and Hay, G. (1996) 'Designer Drinks and Drunkenness amongst a Sample of Scottish Schoolchildren', *British Medical Journal*, **313**, 401.

McKeown, T. (1976) *The Role of Medicine: Dream, Mirage or Nemesis* (London, Nuffield Provincial Hospital Trust).

McKinlay, J.B. (1979) 'Epidemiological and Political Developments of Social Policies Regarding Public Health', *Social Science and Medicine*, **13A**, 541–8.

McLoone, P. and Boddy, F.A. (1994) 'Deprivation and Mortality in Scotland 1981 and 1991', *British Medical Journal*, **309**, 1465–70.

McMichael, A.J. and Haines, A. (1997) 'Global Climate Change: The Potential Effects on Health', *British Medical Journal*, **315**, 805–9.

McNeill, W.H. (1976) *Plagues and People* (Oxford, Blackwell).

MacRae, K. (1994) 'Social Deprivation in Britain: Commentaries on Socioeconomic Deprivation and Health and the Ecological Fallacy', *British Medical Journal*, **309**, 1478–9.

Mackenbach, J.P., Kunst, A., Cavelaars, A., Groenhof, F., Guerts, J. and the EU Working Group on Socioeconomic Inequalities in Health (1997) 'Socioeconomic Inequalities in Morbidity and Mortality in Western Europe', *Lancet*, **349**, 1655–59.

Macran, S., Clark, L. and Joshi, H. (1996) 'Women's Health: Dimensions and Differentials', *Social Science and Medicine*, **42**, 1203–16.

MAFF (Ministry of Agriculture Fisheries and Food) (1998a) *A Review of Antimicrobial Resistance in the Food Chain. A Technical Report for MAFF* (London, MAFF).

MAFF (Ministry of Agriculture, Fisheries and Food) (1998b) *National Food Survey 1997* (London, Stationery Office).

MAFF/HSE (Ministry of Agriculture Fisheries and Food/Health and Safety Executive) (1999) *Annual Report of the Working Party on Pesticide Residues* (London, MAFF).

Maga, J. and Tu, A.T. (eds) (1994) *Food Additive Toxicology* (New York, Marcel Dekker).

Majeed, F., Cook, D., Anderson, H., Hilton, S., Bunn, S. and Stones, C. (1994) 'Using Patients and General Practice Characteristics to Explain Variations in Cervical Smear Uptake Rates', *British Medical Journal*, **308**, 1272–6.

Majone, G. (1989) *Evidence, Argument and Persuasion in the Policy Process* (New Haven, CT, Yale University Press).

Maloney, W., Jordan, G. and McLaughlin, A. (1994) 'Insider Groups and Public Policy', *Journal of Public Policy*, **14** (1), 17–38.

Malpass, P. (1999) 'Housing Policy: Does It Have a Future?', *Policy and Politics*, **27** (2), 217–28.

Mangtani, P., Jolly, D., Watson, J. and Rodrigues, L. (1995) 'Socioeconomic Deprivation and Notification Rates for Tuberculosis in London During 1982–91', *British Medical Journal*, **310**, 963–6.

Marks, D. (1995) 'A Balancing Act', *Health Service Journal*, 13 April, 26–7.

Marmot, M.G. and Shipley, M.J. (1996) 'Do Socioeconomic Differences in Mortality Persist After Retirement? 25 Year Follow Up of Civil Servants from the First Whitehall Study', *British Medical Journal*, **313**, 1177–80.

Marmot, M.G., Davey Smith, G., Stansfield, S. *et al.* (1991) 'Health Inequalities Among British Civil Servants: The Whitehall II Study', *Lancet*, **337**, 1387–93.

Marmot, M.G., Shipley, M.J. and Rose, G. (1984) 'Inequalities in Death: Specific Explanations of a General Pattern', *Lancet*, **1**, 1003–6.

Marquand, D. (1988) *The Unprincipled Society* (London, Fontana).

Marsden, T. and Flynn, A. (1997) *Constructing Consumer Interest: Retailing Regulation and Food Quality* (Cardiff, University of Wales).

Marsh, A. and McKay, S. (1994) *Poor Smokers* (London, Policy Studies Institute).

Marsh, A., Gordon, D., Pantazis, C. and Heslop, P. (1999) *Home Sweet Home: The Impact of Poor Housing on Health* (Bristol, Policy Press).

Marsh, D. (1998a) 'The Development of the Policy Network Approach'. In Marsh, D. (ed.) *Comparing Policy Networks* (Buckingham, Open University Press), pp. 3–20.

Marsh, D. (ed.) (1998b) *Comparing Policy Networks* (Buckingham, Open University Press).

Marsh, D. and Rhodes, R. (1992) *Policy Networks in British Government* (Oxford, Clarendon).

Mayor, S. (1999) 'Swedish Study Questions Mammography Screening Programmes', *British Medical Journal*, 6 March, 621.

Mazey, S. and Richardson, J. (eds) (1992) *Lobbying in the European Union* (Oxford, Oxford University Press).

Meads, G., Killoran, A., Ashcroft, J. and Cornish, Y. (1999) *Mixing Oil and Water* (London, HEA).

Measham, F., Palmer, H. and Aldridge, J. (1998) *Starting, Switching, Slowing and Stopping* (London, Home Office).

Meltzer, H., Gill, B., Petticrew, M. and Hinds, K. (1995) *The Prevalence of Psychiatric Morbidity among Adults Living in Private Households* (London, HMSO).

Mendelson, J. (1998) 'Roundup: The World's Biggest-selling Herbicide', *Ecologist*, **28** (5), 270–5.

Mental Health Foundation (1999) *The Big Picture: Promoting Children and Young People's Mental Health* (London, Mental Health Foundation).

*Men's Health* (1996) 'A Comprehensive Guide to Your Health and Wellbeing' (London, Wallace Press).

Mepham, T.B., Schofield, P., Zumkeller, W. and Cotterill, A. (1994) 'Safety of Milk from Cows Treated with BST', *Lancet*, **334**, 1445–1.

Milburn, K. and MacAskill, S. (1994) 'Cervical Screening: Continuing Concerns in the 1990s', *Health Education Journal*, **53**, 201–13.

Miles, A. (1991) *Women, Health and Medicine* (Buckingham, Open University Press).

Milio, N. (1986) *Promoting Health Through Public Policy* (Ottowa, Canadian Public Health Association).

Mill, J.S. (1974) *On Liberty* (Harmondsworth, Pelican).

Miller, A. (1980) 'The Canadian National Breast Cancer Screening Study', *Clinical Investigative Medicine*, **4**, 227–58.

Miller, P. and Plant, M. (1996) 'Drinking, Smoking and Illicit Drug Use Among 15 and 16 Year Olds in the UK', *British Medical Journal*, **313**, 394–7.

Mills, M. (1992) *The Politics of Dietary Change* (Aldershot, Dartmouth).

Mills, M.P. (1993) *Prevention, Health and British Politics* (Aldershot, Avebury).

Mills, M.P. and Saward, M. (1993) 'Liberalism, Democracy and Prevention'. In Mills M.P. (ed.) (1993) *Prevention, Health and British Politics* (Aldershot, Avebury), pp. 161–73.

Millstone, E. (1986) *Food Additives* (Harmondsworth, Penguin).

Mishan, E.J. (1990) 'Narcotics: The Problem and the Solution', *Political Quarterly*, **61** (4), 441–62.

Montz, F.J., Monk, B.J., Fowler, J.M. and Nguyen, L. (1992) 'Natural History of the Minimally Abnormal Papanicolaou Smear', *Obstetrics and Gynaecology*, **80** (3) Part 1, 385–8.

Mooney, G. and Healey, A. (1991) 'Strategy Full of Good Intentions', *British Medical Journal*, **303**, 1119–20.

Moore, W. (1991) 'Green Paper Fudges Health and Housing Link', *Health Service Journal*, 6 June, 3.

Moran, G. (1989) 'Public Health at Risk', *Health Service Journal*, 1 June, 668–9.

Moritz, S., Bates, T., Henderson, S. Humphreys, S. and Mitchell, M. (1997) 'Variations in Management of Small Invasive Breast Cancers Detected on Screening in the Former SE Thames Region: Observational Study', *British Medical Journal*, **315**, 1266–72.

Morris, J.K. (1980) 'Are Health Services Important to People's Health?', *British Medical Journal*, **280**, 167–8.

Morris, J.K., Cook, D.G. and Shaper, A.G. (1994) 'Loss of Employment and Mortality', *British Medical Journal*, **308**, 1135–9.

Morris, R.J. (1976) *Cholera 1832: A Social Response to an Epidemic* (London, Croom Helm).

Morrison, C. Woodward, M., Leslie, W. and Tunstall-Pedoe, H. (1997) 'Effect of Socioeconomic Group on Incidence of Management of, and Survival after Myocardial Infarction and Coronary Death: Analysis of Community Coronary Events', *British Medical Journal*, **314**, 541–6.

Moser, K., Goldblatt, P., Fox, J. and Jones, D. (1990) 'Unemployment and Mortality'. In Goldblatt, P (ed.) *Longitudinal Study, Mortality and Social Organization 1971–81*, OPCS (London, HMSO), pp. 81–97.

Muntaner, C. and Lynch, J. (1999) 'Income Inequality, Social Cohesion and Class Relations: A Critique of Wilkinson's Neo-Durkheimian Research Programme, *International Journal of Health Studies*, **29** (1), 59–81.

Murphy, M.F.G., Campbell, M.J. and Goldblatt, P.O. (1987) 'Twenty Year Screening for Cancer of the Uterine Cervix in Great Britain 1964–84: Further Evidence of its Ineffectiveness', *Journal of Epidemiology and Community Health*, **42**, 49–53.

Murray, M. (1999) *Health and Safety Legislation in the European Union: Croner's Health and Safety Special Report* (London, Croner Publications).

NACNE (National Advisory Committee on Nutrition Education) (1983) *A Discussion Paper on Proposals for Nutrition Guidelines for Health Education in Britain* (London, HEA).

NAO (National Audit Office) (1986) *NHS: Preventive Medicine*, HC 229 1985/6, HC 656 Session 1995/6 (London, HMSO).

NAO (National Audit Office) (1989) *NHS: Coronary Heart Disease*, HC 208 Session 1988/9 (London, HMSO).

NAO (National Audit Office) (1996a) *Health of the Nation: A Progress Report*, HC 656 Session 1995/6 (London, HMSO).

NAO (National Audit Office) (1996b) *Improving Health in Wales*, HC 633 Session 1995/6 (London, HMSO).

NAO (National Audit Office) (1998a) *Performance of the NHS Cervical Screening Programme*, HC 678 Session 1997/8 (London, Stationery Office).

NAO (National Audit Office) (1998b) *BSE: The Cost of the Crisis*, HC 853 1997/8 (London, Stationery Office).

NHSE (NHS Executive) (1999) *Leadership for Health: The Health Authority Role* (London, DoH).

Nagle, D., McGrail, S., Vitale, J. *et al.* (1999) 'The Mahogany Protein is a Receptor Involved in the Suppression of Obesity', *Nature*, **398**, 11 March, pp. 148–52.

National Assembly for Wales (1998) *Strategic Framework: Better Health, Better Wales* (Cardiff, NAW).

National Heart Forum (1998) *Social Inequalities in Heart Disease* (London, Stationery Office).

National Housing Forum (1994) *Papering Over the Cracks* (London, National Housing Forum).

Navarro, V. (1976) *Medicine Under Capitalism* (London, Croom Helm).

Nazroo, J.Y. (1997a) *The Health of Britain's Ethnic Minorities: Findings from a National Survey* (London, Policy Studies Institute).

Nazroo, J.Y. (1997b) *Ethnicity and Mental Health: Findings from a Community Sruvey* (London, Policy Studies Institute).

Nazroo, J.Y. (1998) 'Genetic, Cultural or Socio-economic Vulnerability? Explaining Ethnic Inequalities in Health', *Sociology of Health and Illness*, **20** (5) 710–30.

Neal, M. and Davies, C. (1998) *The Corporation Under Siege?*(London, Social Affairs Unit).

Needle, C. (1999) *Public Health Policy*, European Parliament Minutes, 10 March 1999, A4–0082/99.

Nettleton, S. and Burrows, R. (1997) 'Knit Your Own Without a Pattern: Health Promotion Specialists in an Internal Market', *Social Policy and Administration*, **31** (2), 191–201.

*New Scientist* (1998) 'A Safe High', *New Scientist*, 21 February, pp. 24–9.

Newburn, T. and Elliott, J. (1998) *Police Anti-drugs Strategies: Tackling Drugs Three Years On*, Crime Detection and Prevention Series 89 (London, Home Office).

Newcombe, R. (1996) 'Live and Let Die: Is Methadone More Likely to Kill You Than Heroin?', *ISDD Druglink*, **11** (1), 9–12.

Newcombe, R., Measham, F. and Parker, H. (1995) 'A Survey of Drinking and Deviant Behaviour Among 14–15 Year Old Girls in North West England', *Addiction Research*, **2** (3), 19–41.

Newman, T.B. and Hulley, S.B. (1996) 'Carcinogenicity of Lipid Lowering Drugs', *Journal of American Medical Association*, **275** (1), 55–60.

Nilson, R. (1999) 'Is Environmental Tobacco Smoke a Risk Factor for Lung Cancer?' In Bate, R. (ed.) *What Risk: Science, Politics and Public Health* (London, Butterworth Heinemann), pp. 96–150.

Nilsson, L., Kjellman, N. and Bjorkstein, B. (1998) 'A Randomised Controlled Trial of the Effect of Pertussis Vaccines on Atopic Disease', *Archives of Paediatric and Adolescent Medicine*, **152** (8), 734–8.

Nocon, A. (1993) 'Made in Heaven', *Health Service Journal*, 2 December, 24–6.

Noise Review Working Party (1990) *Report of the Noise Review Working Party* (London, HMSO).

Noppa, H., Gengtsson, C., Wedel, H. and Wilhemson, L. (1980) 'Obesity in Relation to Morbidity and Mortality from Cardio-vascular Disease', *American Journal of Epidemiology*, **111**, 682–92.

Northern Ireland Department of Health and Social Services (1996) *Health and Wellbeing: Into the Next Millennium* (Belfast, DHSS).

Northern Ireland Department of Health and Social Services (1997) *Well into 2000: A Positive Agenda for Health and Wellbeing* (Belfast, DHSS).

Nottingham, C. (1999) *The Pursuit of Serenity: Havelock Ellis and the New Politics* (Amsterdam University Press).

Nottingham, S. (1998) *Eat Your Genes* (London, Zed).

O'Connor, I.F., Shembekar, M.V. and Shousha, S. (1998) 'Breast Carcinoma Developing in Patients on Hormone Replacement Therapy: A Histological and Immunohistological Study', *Journal of Clinical Pathology*, **51** (12), 935–8.

O'Riordan, T. and Cameron, J. (1994) *Interpreting the Precautionary Principle* (London, Earthscan).

O'Riordan, T. and Weale, A. (1989) 'Administrative Reorganisation and Policy Change: The Case of Her Majesty's Inspectorate of Pollution', *Public Administration*, **67**, 277–94.

Office for Standards in Education (1997) *Drug Education in Schools* (London, Stationery Office).

Office of Health Economics (1994) *Obesity* (London, OHE).

Office of Health Economics (1995) *Diseases of the Prostate* (London, OHE).

Office of Population Censuses and Surveys (1992) *Mortality Statistics: Perinatal and Infant Mortality. Sociological and Biological Factors England and Wales 1990* (London, HMSO).

Office of Population Censuses and Surveys (1996) *General Household Survey 1994* (London, HMSO).

*Official Journal of the European Communities* (1985) *Council Directive 85/337/EEC on the Assessment of the Effects of Certain Public and Private Projects on the Environment*, L175/40.

*Official Journal of the European Communities* (1989) *Council Directive 89/391/EEC on the Introduction of Measures to Encourage Improvements in the Safety and Health of Workers at Work*, L183/1.

*Official Journal of the European Communities* (1993) *Council Directive 93/43/EEC on Hygiene of Foodstuffs*, L175/1.

*Official Journal of the European Communities* (1996) *Council Directive 96/61/EC Concerning Integrated Pollution Prevention and Control*, L257/27.

*Official Journal of the European Communities* (1997) *Council Directive 97/11/EC on the Assessment of the Effects of Certain Public and Private Projects on the Environment*, L073/5–15.

*Official Journal of the European Communities* (1999) *Council Directive on the Landfill of Waste 99/31/EC*, L182/1–19.

Olson, N. (1997) 'At Last a Public Health Minister', *British Medical Journal*, **314**, 1498–9.

ONS (Office for National Statistics) (1997a) *Cancer Statistics: Registrations England and Wales 1991* (London, Stationery Office).

ONS (Office for National Statistics) (1997b) *Social Trends* (London, Stationery Office).

ONS (Office for National Statistics) (1998) *Social Trends 1997* (London, Stationery Office).

ONS (Office for National Statistics) (1999) *Social Trends 1998* (London, Stationery Office).

ONS (Office for National Statistics)(1997c) *Smoking Among Secondary Schoolchildren in 1996* (London, Stationery Office).

ONS (Office for National Statistics)/Cancer Research Campaign/London School of Hygiene and Tropical Medicine (1999) *Cancer Survival Trends in England and Wales 1971–95* (London, Stationery Office).

ONS/HEA (Office for National Statistics/Health Education Authority (1997) *Health in England 1996* (London, Stationery Office).

Orbach, S. (1978) *Fat is a Feminist Issue* (London, Hamlyn).

Orr, J. Boyd (1936) *Food, Health and Income* (London, Macmillan).

Ottewill, R. and Wall, A. (1990) *The Growth and Development of the Community Health Services* (Sunderland, Business Education Publishers).

Pamuk, E.R. (1985) 'Social Class Inequality in Mortality from 1921–72 in England and Wales', *Population Studies*, **39**, 17–31.

Parazzini, K., La Vecchia, A., Negri, E., Franceschi, S., Moroni, S. and Chatenoud, L. (1997) 'Case Control Study of Oestrogen Replacement Therapy and Risk of Cervical Cancer', *British Medical Journal*, **315**, 85–8.

Parker, H., Aldridge, J. and Measham, F. (1998) *Illegal Leisure: The Normalisation of Adolescent Recreational Drug Use* (London, Routledge).

Parker, H., Measham, F. and Aldridge, J. (1995) *Drug Futures: Changing Patterns of Drug Use Among English Youth* (London, Institute for Drug Dependency).

Parliamentary Commissioner for Administration (1976) 3rd Report 1975/6 (London, HMSO).

Parry, N. and Parry, J. (1976) *The Rise of the Medical Profession* (London, Croom Helm).

Parsonnet, J. (1999) *Microbes and Malignancy* (Oxford, Oxford University Press).

Parsonnet, J., Friedman, G.D., Vandersteen, D.P. *et al.* (1991) 'Helicobacter Pylori Infection and the Risk of Gastric Carcinoma', *New England Journal of Medicine*, **325** (16), 1127–31.

Parsons, W. (1995) *Public Policy* (Aldershot, Edward Elgar).

Paterson, M. (1996) *Global Warming and Global Politics* (London, Routledge).

Patterson, R.G. (1948) 'The Health of Towns Association in Great Britain 1844–9', *Bulletin of the History of Medicine (USA)*, **22** (4), 373–402.

Payer, L. (1989) *Medicine and Culture* (London, Gollancz).

Pearce, F. (1998) 'A Wasted Chance', *New Scientist*, **158** (2132), 22–3.

Pelling, M. (1978) *Cholera, Fever and English Medicine 1825–65* (Oxford, Oxford University Press).

Pereira, J. (1993) 'What Does Equity in Health Mean?', *Journal of Social Policy*, **22** (1), 19–48.

Petersen, A. (1997) 'Risk, Governance and the New Public Health'. In Petersen, A. and Bunton, R. (eds) *Foucault, Health and Medicine* (London, Routledge), pp. 189–206.

Petersen, A. and Lupton, D. (1996) *The New Public Health: Health and Self in the Age of Risk* (London, Sage).

Petersen, A. and Lupton, D. (1996) *The New Public Health; Health and Self in the Age of Risk* (London, Sage).

Phillimore, P. and Reading, R. (1992) 'A Rural Advantage? Urban/Rural Health Difference in Northern England', *Journal of Public Health Medicine*, **14**, 290–4.

Phillimore, P., Beattie, A. and Townsend, P. (1994) 'Widening Inequality of Health in Northern England 1981–91', *British Medical Journal*, **308**, 1125–8.

Pianezza, M., Sellers, G.M. and Tyndale, R.F. (1998) 'Genetics and Cancer', *Nature*, **393**, 750.

Pietroni, P. (1991) *The Greening of Medicine* (London, Gollancz).

Platt, S.D., Martin, C.J. and Hunt, S.M. (1989) 'Damp Housing, Mould Growth and Symptomatic Health State', *British Medical Journal*, **298**, 1673–78.

Platz, E.A., Giovannuci, E., Rumm, E.B. *et al.* (1997) 'Dietary Fibre and Distal Colorectal Adenoma in Men', *Cancer Epidemiology Biomakers Preview*, **6**, 661–70.

Plowden, S. and Hillman, M. (1996) *Speed Control and Transport Policy* (London, Policy Studies Institute).

Political and Economic Planning (1937) *Report on the British Health Services* (London, PEP).

Pollock, D. (1999) *Denial and Delay: The Political History of Smoking and Health 1951–64* (London, ASH).

Popay, J. and Williams, G. (eds) (1994) *Researching the People's Health* (London, Routledge).

Popay, J., Williams, G., Thomas, C. and Gatrell, T. (1998) 'Theorising Inequalities in Health: The Place of Lay Knowledge', *Sociology of Health and Illness*, **20** (5), 619–644.

Popham, G.T. (1981) 'Government and Smoking: Policymaking and Pressure Groups', *Policy and Politics*, **9** (3), 331–47.

Porritt, J. and Winner, M. (1989) *The Coming of the Greens* (London, Fontana).

Porter, D. (1990) 'How Soon Is Now? Public Health and the BMJ', *British Medical Journal*, **301**, 738–40.

Porter, R. (1995) *Disease, Medicine and Society in England 1550–1880* (Cambridge, Cambridge University Press).

Posner, T. and Vessey, M. (1988) *Prevention of Cervical Cancer: The Patient's View* (London, King's Fund).

Potts, L. (1999) 'Breast Cancer on the Map', *Health Matters*, **35**, 10–11.

Powell, K.E., Thompson, P.D., Caspersen, C.J. and Kendrick, J.S. (1987) 'Physical Activity and the Incidence of CHD', *Annual Review of Public Health*, **8**, 253–87.

Power, C. (1994) 'Health and Social Inequality in Europe', *British Medical Journal*, **308**, 1153–6.

Power, C., Matthews, S. and Manor, O. (1996) 'Inequalities in Self-related Health in the 1958 Birth Cohort: Lifetime Social Circumstance or Social Mobility?', *British Medical Journal*, **313**, 449–53.

Powles, J. (1973) 'On the Limitations of Modern Medicine', *Science, Medicine and Man*, **1**, 1–30.

Prentice, A. and Jebb, S. (1995) 'Obesity in Britain: Gluttony or Sloth?', *British Medical Journal*, **311**, 437–9.

Prentice, A., Black, A., Coward, W. *et al.* (1986) 'High Levels of Energy Expenditure in Obese Women', *British Medical Journal*, **292**, 983–7.

Preston, R. (1994) *The Hot Zone* (New York, Doubleday).

PRISMATIC Project Management Team (1999) 'Assessment of Automated Primary Screening on PAPNET of Cervical Smears in the PRISMATIC Trial', *Lancet*, **353**, 1381–5.

Proctor, R. (1988) *Racial Hygiene: Medicine Under the Nazis* (Cambridge, MA, Harvard University Press).

Protheroe, D., Turvey, K., Morgan, K., Benson, E., Bowers, D. and House, A. (1999) 'Stressful Life Events and Difficulties and Onset of Breast Cancer: Case-control Study', *British Medical Journal*, **319**, 1027–30.

Public Accounts Committee (1986) *Preventive Medicine*, 44th Report 1985/6, HC 413 (London, HMSO).

Public Accounts Committee (1989) *Coronary Heart Disease*, 26th Report 1988/9, HC 249 (London, HMSO).

Public Accounts Committee (1992) *Cervical and Breast Screening in England,* 2nd Report 1992/3, HC 58 (London, HMSO).

Public Accounts Committee (1997) *The Health of the Nation: A Progress Report,* 17th Report 1996/7, HC 85 (London, HMSO).

Public Accounts Committee (1998) *The Performance of the NHS Cervical Cancer Screening Programme in England,* 69th Report 1997/8, HC 757 (London, Stationery Office).

Public Health Alliance (1988) *Beyond Acheson* (Birmingham, PHA).

Purdey, M. (1996) 'Mandarins Who Fail To Ask the Right Questions', *Parliamentary Brief,* **4** (6), 36–9.

Quick, A. (1991) *Unequal Risk: Accidents and Social Policy* (London, Socialist Health Association).

Quinn, M. and Allen, E. (1995) 'Changes in Incidence of and Mortality from Breast Cancer in England and Wales Since Introduction of Screening', *British Medical Journal,* **311**, 1391–5.

Quinn, M., Babb, P., Jones, J. and Allen, E. (1999) 'Effect of Screening on Incidence of an Mortality from Cancer of the Cervix in England: Evaluation Based on Routinely Collected Statistics', *British Medical Journal,* **318**, 404–8.

Radical Statistics Health Group (1991) 'Missing – a Strategy for the Health of the Nation', *British Medical Journal,* **303**, 299–302.

Raffle, A.G. (1997) 'Deaths from Cervical Cancer Began Falling Before Screening Programmes Were Established', *British Medical Journal,* **315**, 953–4.

Raistrick, D., Hodgson, R. and Ritson, B. (eds) (1999) *Tackling Alcohol Together: The Evidence Base For a UK Alcohol Policy* (London, Free Association Books).

Raleigh, V. Soni and Kiri, V. (1997) 'Life Expectancy in England: Variations and Trends by Gender, Health Authority and Level of Deprivation', *Journal of Epidemiology and Community Health,* **51** (6), 649–58.

Ramsay, L.E., Yeo, W.W. and Jackson, P.R. (1994) 'High Blood Cholesterol: A Problem With No Ready Solution'. In Le Fanu, J. (ed.) *Preventionitis* (London, Social Affairs Unit), pp. 64–80.

Ramsay, M. and Spiller, J. (1997) *Drug Use Declared: Results of the 1996 Brirish Crime Survey* (London, Home Office).

Rathwell, T. (1992) 'Pursuing Health for All in Britain: An Assessment', *Social Science and Medicine,* **34** (2), 169–82.

Ratzan, S. (ed.) (1998) *The Mad Cow Crisis: Health and the Public Good* (London, UCL Press).

Razay, G., Heaton, K.W., Bolton, C.H. and Hughes, A.O. (1992) 'Alcohol Consumption and its Relation to Cardiovascular Risk Factors in British Women', *British Medical Journal,* **304**, 80–3.

RCGP (Royal College of General Practitioners) (1986) *Alcohol: A Balanced View* (London, RCGP).

RCP (Royal College of Physicians) (1962) *Smoking and Health* (London, Pitman).

RCP (Royal College of Physicians) (1971) *Smoking and Health Now* (London, Pitman).

RCP (Royal College of Physicians) (1977) *Smoking or Health?* (London, Pitman).

RCP (Royal College of Physicians) (1981) *Medical Aspects of Dietary Fibre* (London, Pitman).

RCP (Royal College of Physicians) (1983a) *Health or Smoking?* (London, Pitman).

RCP (Royal College of Physicians) (1983b) 'Obesity', *Journal of the Royal College of Physicians,* **17**, 5–64.

RCP (Royal College of Physicians) (1987) *Medical Consequences of Alcohol Misuse: A Great and Growing Evil* (London, Tavistock).

RCP (Royal College of Physicians) (1991) 'Medical Aspects of Exercise: Benefits and Risks', *Journal of the Royal College of Physicians,* **25**, 193–6.

RCP (Royal College of Physicians) (1995) *Alcohol and the Heart in Perspective: Sensible Limits Reaffirmed* (London, RCP).

RCP (Royal College of Physicians) (2000) *Nicotine Addiction in Britain* (London, RCP).

RCP (Royal College of Physicians)/British Cardiac Society (1976) 'The Prevention of Coronary Heart Disease', *Journal of the Royal College of Physicians,* **10** (3), 213–75.

Reed, H. (2000) *Post-budget Analysis: Personal Tax and Benefits Issues* (London, Institute for Fiscal Studies) (www.ifs.org.uk/research).

Regional Policy Commission (1996) *Reviewing the Region's Strategies for Regional Economic Development* (Sheffield Hallam University, PAVIC Publications).

Research Bureau Ltd (1986) *Heroin Misuse Campaign Evaluation: Report and Findings* (London, DHSS).

Rhodes, G. (1981) *Inspectorates in British Government* (London, Allen & Unwin).

Richards, M.A., Westcombe, A.M., Love, S.B., Littlejohns, P. and Ramirez, A.J. (1999) 'Influence of Delay on Survival in Patients with Breast Cancer: A Systematic Review', *Lancet*, **353**, 1119–26.

Ridley, F. and Jordan, G. (eds) (1998) *Protest Politics: Cause Groups and Campaigns* (Oxford, Oxford University Press).

Rimm, E.B., Klatsky, A., Grobbee, D. and Stampfer, M.J. (1996) 'Review of Moderate Alcohol Consumption and Reduced Risk of Coronary Heart Disease: Is the Effect Due to Beer, Wine or Spirits?', *British Medical Journal*, **312**, 731–6.

Roberts, H. (1997) 'Children, Inequalities and Health', *British Medical Journal*, **314**, 1122–3.

Roberts, I. and Di Guiseppe, C. (1997) 'Children in Cars', *British Medical Journal*, **314**, 392.

Roberts, I. and Power, C. (1996) 'Does the Decline in Child Injury Mortality Vary by Social Class? A Comparison of Class Specific Mortality in 1981 and 1991', *British Medical Journal*, **313**, 784–6.

Roberts, M. (1989) 'Breast Screening: Time for a Rethink', *British Medical Journal*, **299**, 1153–5.

Roberts, S.B. and Greenberg, A.S. (1996) 'The New Obesity Genes', *Nutrition Review*, **54** (2), Part 1, 41–9.

Robinson, F., Keithley, J., Robinson, S. and Childs, S. (1998) *Exploring the Impacts of Crime on Health Services: A Feasibility Study* (Durham, Department of Sociology and Social Policy, University of Durham).

Robinson, M.H., Hardcastle, J.D., Moss, S.M. *et al.* (1999) 'The Risks of Screening: Data from the Nottingham Randomised Controlled Trial of Faecal Occult Blood Screening for Colorectal Cancer', *Gut*, **45** (4), 588–92.

Robinson, W.S. (1950) 'Ecological Correlations and the Behaviour of Individuals', *American Sociological Reviews*, **15**, 351–7.

Rodgers, A. (1990) 'The UK Breast Cancer Screening Programme: An Expensive Mistake', *Journal of Public Health Medicine*, **12** (3, 4), 197–204.

Rodriguez, E. (1995) 'Global Environmental Change: Preventive Measures to Reduce the Impact on Human Health', *Health Promotion International*, **10** (3), 239–45.

Rogers, A. and Pilgrim, D. (1996) *Mental Health Policy in Britain: A Critical Introduction* (Basingstoke, Macmillan).

Rorsman, B., Grasbeck, A., Hagnell, O. *et al.* (1990) 'A Prospective Study of First Incidence Depression', *British Journal of Psychiatry*, **156**, 336–42.

Rose, G. (1985) 'Sick Individuals and Sick Populations', *International Journal of Epidemiology*, **14** (1), 132–8.

Rosen, F. and Burns, J.N. (eds) (1983) *The Collected Works of Jeremy Bentham: Constitutional Code* Vol. 1 (Oxford, Oxford University Press).

Rosen, G. (1993) *A History of Public Health* (New York, John Hopkins University Press), edited by E. Fee.

Rosen, M. and Rehnquist, N. (1999) 'Breast Screening: No Need To Reconsider Breast Screening Programmes on Basis of Results from Defective Study', *British Medical Journal*, **318**, 809–10.

Royal College of Psychiatrists (1979) *Alcohol and Alcoholism* (London, Tavistock).

Royal College of Psychiatrists (1986) *Our Favourite Drug* (London, Tavistock).

Royal Commission on the State of Large Towns and Populous Districts (1844/1970) *First Report*, HC 572, House of Commons Sessional Papers, Vol. 17, p. 1. (Shannon, Irish University Press).

Royal Commission on the State of Large Towns and Populous Districts (1845/1970) *Second Report*, HC 602 and 610, House of Commons Sessional Papers, Vol. 18, pp. 1, 299. (Shannon, Irish University Press).

Rugg-Gunn, A.J. and Edgar, W.M. (1984) 'Sugar and Dental Cavities. A Review of the Evidence', *Community Dental Health*, **1**, 85–92.

Rush, M. (ed.) (1990) *Parliament and Pressure Groups* (Oxford, Oxford University Press).

Ryle, M. (1988) *Ecology and Socialism* (London, Rodins).

Sabatier, P. (1987) 'Knowledge, Policy-oriented Learning and Change: An Advocacy Coalition Framework', *Knowledge: Creation, Diffusion and Utilisation*, **8** (4), 649–92.

Sadler, M. (1998) 'Labelling Genetically Modified Soya and Maize in the EU', *Nutrition and Food Science*, **6**, 306–9.

Sagan, L. (1987) *The Health of Nations* (New York, Basic Books).

Saidi, S. (1993) 'Off Screen Blues?', *Health Service Journal*, 4 November, 26–7.

Sainsbury, R., Johnston, C. and Haward, B. (1999) 'Effect on Survival of Delays in Referral of Patients with Breast Cancer Symptoms: A Retrospective Analysis', *Lancet*, **353**, 1132–5.

Salter, B. (1993) 'Public Image Limited', *Health Service Journal*, 15 July, 28–9.

Sashidaran, S. and Francis, E. (1993) 'Epidemiology, Ethnicity and Schizophrenia'. In Ahmad, W. (ed.) *Race and Health in Contemporary Britain* (Buckingham, Open University Press), pp. 96–113.

Sasieni, P. and Adams, J. (1999) 'Effect of Screening on Cervical Cancer Mortality in England and Wales: Analysis of Trends with an Age Period Cohort Model', *British Medical Journal*, **318**, 1244–5.

Scally, G. (1996) 'Public Health Medicine in a New Era', *Social Science and Medicine*, **42** (5), 777–80.

Schenker, S. (1999) 'Colon Cancer and Fibre', *BNF Nutrition Bulletin*, **24**, 5–6.

Schiffman, M.H. and Brinton, L.A. (1995) 'The Epidemiology of Cervical Carcinogenesis', *Cancer*, **76** (10, Supplement), 1888–901.

Schiffman, M.H., Bauer, H.M., Hoover, R.N., Glass, A.G. and Cadell, D.M. (1993) 'Epidemiologic Evidence Showing that Human Papillomavirus Infection Causes Most Cervical Intraepithelial Neoplasia', *Journal of the National Cancer Institute*, **85**, 958–64.

School Travel Advisory Group (2000) *Report 1998–9* (London, DETR).

Scott-Samuel, A. (1996) 'Health Impact Assessment: An Idea Whose Time Has Come', *British Medical Journal*, **313**, 183.

Scott-Samuel, A. (1998) 'Concepts of Health and Regeneration'. In Health Education Authority *Health and Regeneration*, (London, HEA), pp. 4–6.

Scottish Office (1997) *The Pennington Group Report* (Edinburgh, Stationery Office).

Scriven, A. (ed.) (1998) *Alliances in Health Promotion Theory and Practice* (London, Macmillan).

Searle, G.R. (1971) *The Quest for National Efficiency. A Study in British Politics and British Political Thought 1899–1914* (Oxford, Blackwell).

Searle, G.R. (1976) *Eugenics and Politics in Britain 1900–14* (Leydon, Noordhoff International).

Sears, A. (1992) 'To Teach Them How To Live. The Politics of Public Health from TB to AIDS', *Journal of Historical Sociology*, **5** (1), 61–83.

Select Committee on Drunkenness (1834/1968) *Report*, HC 559/1834 (Shannon, Irish University Press).

Select Committee on Expenditure (1977) *First Report for the Expenditure Committee, Session 1976/77: Preventive Medicine*, HC 169 (London, HMSO).

Self, P. and Storing, H. (1962) *The State and the Farmer* (London, Allen & Unwin).

Selly, S., Donovan, J., Faulkner, A., Coast, J. and Gilliat, D. (1996) *Diagnosis, Management and Screening of Early Localised Prostate Cancer: A Systematic Review* (Bristol, Health Care Evaluation Unit, University of Bristol).

Sen, A. (1985) *Commodities and Capabilities* (Amsterdam, North Holland).

Shaheen, S.O., Aaby, P., Hall, A.J. *et al.* (1996) 'Measles and Atopy in Guinea-Bissau', *Lancet*, **347**, 1792–6.

Shanks, N.J. and Smith, S.J. (1992) 'Public Policy and the Health of Homeless People', *Policy and Politics*, **20** (1), 35–46.

Shapiro, S., Venet, W., Strax, P., Venet, L. and Roeser, R. (1982) 'Ten to Fourteen Year Effect of Breast Cancer Screening on Mortality', *Journal of the National Cancer Institute*, **69** (2), 349–55.

Shaw, M., Dorling, D. and Brimblecombe, N. (1998) 'Changing the Map: Health in Britain 1951–91', *Sociology of Health and Illness*, **20** (5), 694–709.

Shaw, M., Dorling, D., Gordon, D. and Davey Smith, G. (1999) *The Widening Gap: Health Inequalities and Policy in Britain* (Bristol, Policy Press).

Sheiham, A., Marmot, M., Rawson, D. and Ruck, N. (1987) 'Food Values: Health and Diet'. In Jowell, R., Witherspoon, S. and Brook, L. (eds) *British Social Attitudes, The 1987 Report*, Social and Community Planning Research (Aldershot, Gower), pp. 97–112.

Sheldon, T. (1997) 'Failing the Screen Test', *Nursing Times*, **93** (28), 32–3.

Sheldon, T. (1998) 'Ashes to Ashes', *Health Service Journal*, 12 February, 18.

Shryock, R. (1979) *The Development of Modern Medicine* (Madison, WI, University of Wisconsin Press).

Siddall, R. (1998) 'Lifting the Burden', *Health Service Journal*, 26 November, 9–10.

Signal, L. (1998) 'The Politics of Health Promotion: Insights from Political Theory', *Health Promotion International*, **13** (3), 257–63.

Simon, J. (1890) *English Sanitary Institutions* (London, Cassell).

Sjonell, G. and Stahle, L. (1999) 'Mammographic Screening Does Not Reduce Breast Cancer Mortality', *Lakartidningen*, **96** (8), 904–5, 908–13.

Skegg, D. (1991) 'Multiple Sclerosis: Nature or Nuture?', *British Medical Journal*, **302**, 247–8.

Skrabanek, P. (1987) 'Cervical Cancer Screening', *Lancet*, **1**, 1432.

Skrabanek, P. (1988a) 'The Debate Over Mass Mammography in Britain', *British Medical Journal*, **297**, 970–1.

Skrabanek, P. (1988b) 'The Physician's Responsibility to the Patient', *Lancet*, **1**, 1155–7.

Skrabanek, P. (1994) *The Death of Humane Medicine* (London, Social Affairs Unit).

Slater, D.N., Milner, P.C. and Radley, H. (1994) 'Audit of Deaths from Cervical Cancer: Proposal for an Essential Component of the National Screening Service', *Journal of Clinical Pathology*, **47**, 27–8.

Sloggett, A. and Joshi, H. (1994) 'High Mortality in Deprived Areas: Community or Personal Disadvantage?', *British Medical Journal*, **309**, 1470–4.

Smaje, C. (1995) *Health, 'Race' and Ethnicity: Making Sense of the Evidence* (London, King's Fund).

Smaje, C. and Le Grand, J. (1997) Ethnicity, Equity and the Use of Health Services in the British National Health Service (London, LSE Health).

Smart, C. (1984) 'Social Policy and Drug Addiction: A Critical Study of Policy Development', *British Journal of Addiction*, **79**, 31–9.

Smith, A. and Jacobson, B. (1988) *The Nation's Health: A Strategy for the 1990s* (London, King Edward's Hospital Fund).

Smith, F.B. (1979) *The People's Health 1830–1910* (London, Croom Helm).

Smith, M.J. (1993) *Pressure, Power and Policy* (Hemel Hempstead, Harvester Wheatsheaf).

Smith, P. (1967) *Disraelian Conservatism and Social Reform* (London, Routledge & Kegan Paul).

Smith, S.J. and Mallinson, S. (1997) 'Housing for Health in a Post-welfare State', *Housing Studies*, **12** (2), 173–200.

Snow, J. (1936) *On Cholera* (New York, Commonwealth Fund).

Spencer, N. (1996) *Poverty and Child Health* (London, Radcliffe).

Spruit, I. (1998) 'Deviant or Just Different? Dutch Alcohol and Drug Policy'. In Bloor, M. and Wood, F. (eds) *Addictions and Problem Drug Use: Issues in Behaviour, Policy and Practice* (London, Jessica Kingsley), pp. 107–21.

Sram, I. and Ashton, J. (1998) 'Millennium Report to Sir Edwin Chadwick', *British Medical Journal*, **317**, 592–5.

Stallibrass, A. (1989) *Being Me and Also Us: Lessons from the Peckham Experiment* (Edinburgh, Scottish Academic Press).

Standing Conference on Public Health (1994) *Housing, Homelessness and Health* (London, Nuffield Provincial Hospitals Trust).

Stanistreet, D., Scott-Samuel, A. and Bellis, M.A. (1999) 'Income Inequality and Mortality in England', *Journal of Public Health Medicine*, **21** (2), 205–7.

Starr, P. (1982) *The Social Transformation of American Medicine* (New York, Basic Books).

Stern, J. (1983) 'Social Mobility and the Interpretation of Social Class Mortality Differentials', *Journal of Social Policy*, **12** (1), 27–49.

Stevens, A. and Gillam, S. (1998) 'Needs Assessment from Theory to Practice', *British Medical Journal*, **316**, 1448–52.

Stevens, A. and Raftery, J. (eds) (1994) *Health Care Needs Assessment: The Epidemiologically-based Needs Assessment Reviews* (Oxford, Radcliffe Medical Press).

Stevens, A. and Raftery, J. (eds) (1997) *Health Care Needs Assessment: The Epidemiologically-based Needs Assessment Reviews*, second series (Oxford, Radcliffe Medical Press).

Stewart-Brown, S. and Farmer, A. (1997) 'Screening Could Seriously Damage Your Health', *British Medical Journal*, **314**, 533–4.

Stiller, C.A. and Boyle, P.J. (1996) 'Effect of Population Mixing and Socioeconomic Status in England and Wales 1979–85 on Lymphoblastic Leukaemia in Children', *British Medical Journal*, **313**, 1297–300.

Stimson, G.V. (1987) 'British Drug Policies in the 1980s: A Preliminary Analysis and Suggestions for Research', *British Journal of Addiction*, **82**, 477–88.

Stimson, G.V. (1995) 'AIDS and Injecting Drug Use in the UK 1987–93: The Policy Response and the Prevention of the Epidemic', *Social Science and Medicine*, **41** (5), 699–716.

Stimson, G.V. and Oppenheimer, E (1982) *Heroin Addiction: Treatment and Control in Britain* (London, Tavistock).

Stimson, G.V., Hickman, M. and Turnbull, P.J. (1998) 'Statistics on Misuse of Drugs Have Been Misused', *British Medical Journal*, **317**, 1388.

Stockwell, T., Somerford, P. and Lang, E. (1992) 'The Relationship between License Type and Alcohol Related Problems in Perth, Western Australia', *Journal of Studies on Alcohol*, **53**, 495–8.

Stone, D. (1989) 'At Risk in the Welfare State', *Social Research*, **56**, 591–633.

Stone, K.M., Zaidi, A., Rosero-Bixby, L. *et al.* (1995) 'Sexual Behaviour, Sexually Transmitted Diseases and Risk of Cervical Cancer', *Epidemiology*, **6** (4), 409–14.

Storey, A., Thomas, M., Kalita, A. *et al.* (1998) 'Role of a p53 Polymorphism in the Development of Human Papillomavirus Associated Cancer', *Nature*, **393**, 229–34.

Stowe, K. (1989) *On Caring for the National Health* (London, Nuffield Provincial Hospitals Trust).

Strang, J. and Gossop, M. (eds) (1994) *Heroin Addiction and Drug Policy: The British System* (Oxford, Oxford University Press).

Strong, P. and Robinson, J. (1990) *The NHS: Under New Management* (Buckingham, Open University Press).

Strugnell, C.J. (1996) 'Food Deserts: Fact of Fiction?', *Nutrition and Food Science*, **6**, 349–63.

Stuttaford, T. (1997) 'To Treat or Not To Treat? That is the Question', *The Times*, 20 February, p. 18.

Szarewski, A., Jarvis, M.J., Sasieic, P. *et al.* (1996) 'Effect of Smoking Cessation on Cervical Lesion Size', *Lancet*, **347**, 941–3.

Szreter, S. (1988) 'The Importance of Social Intervention in Britain's Mortality Decline c1850–1914', *Social History of Medicine*, **1** (1), 1–38.

Tabar, L., Gad, A., Holmberg, L.H. *et al.* (1985) 'Reduction on Mortality from Breast Cancer after Mass Screening with Mammography. Randomised Trial from the Breast Cancer Screening Working Group of the Swedish National Board of Health and Welfare', *Lancet*, **i**, 829–32.

Tall, A.R. (1990) 'Plasma High Density Lipoprotein: Metabolism and the Relationship to Atherogenesis', *Journal of Clinical Investigation*, **86** (2), 379–84.

Tam, H. (1998) *Communitarianism: A New Agenda for Politics and Citizenship* (London, Macmillan).

Tansey, G. and Worsley, T. (1995) *The Food System: A Guide* (London, Earthscan).

Taras, H.L., Sallis, J.F., Patterson, T.L., Nader, P.R. and Nelson, J.A. (1989) 'Television's Influence on Children's Diet and Physical Activity', *Journal of Development and Behavioural Paediatrics*, **10** (4), 176–80.

Tarimo, E. and Creese, A. (eds) (1990) *Achieving Health for All by the Year 2000* (Geneva, WHO).

Taubert, K.A., Shulman, S.T. (1999) 'Kawasaki Disease', *American Family Physician*, **59** (11), 3093–102, 3107–8.

Taylor, B., Miller, E., Farrington, C.P. *et al.* (1999) 'Autism and Measles, Mumps and Rubella Vaccine?: No Epidemiological Evidence for a Causal Association, *Lancet*, **353**, 2626–9.

Taylor, P. (1984) *The Smoke Ring: Tobacco, Money and Multi-national Politics* (London, Bodley Head).

Taylor, P., Peckham, S. and Turton, P. (1998) *A Public Health Model of Primary Care: From Concept to Reality* (Birmingham, Public Health Alliance).

Tesh, S. (1982) 'Political Ideology and Public Health in the Nineteenth Century', *International Journal of Health Services*, **12** (2), 321–42.

Tether, P. and Godfrey, C. (1990) 'Liquor Licencing'. In Godfrey, C. and Robinson, D. (eds) *Preventing Alcohol and Tobacco Problems*, Vol. 2 (Aldershot, Avebury), pp. 116–38.

Thames Cancer Registry (1994) *Cancer in South East England* (Sutton, Thames Cancer Registry).

*The BSE Inquiry* (2000) www.bse.org.uk

Thom, B. (1999) *Dealing with Drink* (London, Free Association Books).

Thompson, J.A. (1991) *Child Pedestrian Accidents* (London, Cassell Education).

Thoms, G. (1992) 'Sheffield'. In Ashton, J. (ed.) *Healthy Cities* (Milton Keynes, Open University Press), pp. 96–107.

Tinsley, R. and Luck, M. (1998) 'Fundholding and the Community Nurse', *Journal of Social Policy*, **27** (4), 471–87.

Tobutt, C., Oppenheimer, E. and Laranjeira, R. (1996) 'Health of the Cohort of Heroin Addicts from London Clinics: 22 Year Follow Up', *British Medical Journal*, **312**, 1458.

Townsend, J., Roderick, P. and Cooper, J. (1994) 'Cigarette Smoking by Socioeconomic Group, Sex and Age: Effects of Price Income and Health Publicity', *British Medical Journal*, **309**, 923.

Townsend, P. (1990) 'Individual or Social Responsibility for Premature Death? Current Controversies in the British Debate about Health', *International Journal of Health Services*, **20** (3), 373–92.

Townsend, P., Davidson, N. and Whitehead, M. (eds) (1992) *Inequalities in Health* (Harmondsworth, Penguin).

Transport and Health Study Group (1991) *Health on the Move* (Birmingham, Public Health Alliance).

Travis, A. (1999) 'Scientists Take Flack over Food Scares', *Guardian*, 8 June, p. 7.

Trayhurn, P (1997) 'Leptin – The 'New' Player in Energy Balance and Obesity', *BNF Nutritional Bulletin*, **22**, Spring, 7–22.

Trevelyan, G.M. (1973) *English Social History: A Survey of Six Centuries* (London, Longman).

Trevethan, E., Layde, P., Webster, L.A., Adams, J.B., Benigno, B.B. and Ory, H. (1983) 'Cigarette Smoking and Dysplasia and Carcinoma in Situ of the Uterine Cervix', *Journal of the American Medical Association*, **250** (4), 499–502.

Trevett, N. (1997) 'Injecting New Life into the Wirral', *Healthlines*, **39**, February, 20–1.

Tsouros, A. (1990) *World Health Organization Healthy Cities Project. A Project Becomes a Movement (Review of Progress 1987–1990)* (Copenhagen, WHO).

Tsouros, A. and Draper, R. (1992) 'The Healthy Cities Project: New Development and Research Needs'. In Davies, M.P. and Kelly, J.K. (eds) *Healthy Cities* (London, Routledge), pp. 25–33.

Tudor, K. (1996) *Mental Health Promotion* (London, Routledge).

Tuxworth, B. and Thomas, E. (1996) *Local Agenda 21 Survey 1996: Results* (Luton, Local Government Management Board).

UK Climate Change Impacts Group (1996) *Review of the Potential Effects of Climate Change in the UK* (London, HMSO).

UK Scientific Committee on Tobacco and Health (1998) *1st Report* (London, HMSO).

UK Trial of Early Detection Cancer Group (1988) 'First Results on Mortality Reduction in the UK Trial of Early Detection of Breast Cancer', *Lancet*, **2**, 411–16.

UK Trial of Early Detection Cancer Group (1999) '16 Year Mortality from Breast Cancer in the UK Trial of Early Detection of Breast Cancer', *Lancet*, **353**, 1909–14.

UN (United Nations) Commission for Narcotic Drugs (1999) *Report of the Meeting of the High Level Expert Group to Review the UN International Drug Control Program and to Strengthen the UN Machinery for Drug Control* (Vienna, Commission for Narcotic Drugs).

UN (United Nations) Development Programme (1996) *Human Development Report* (New York, Oxford University Press).

UN (United Nations) Environment Programme (1999) *Global Environment Outlook 2000* (Nairobi, UNEP).

UN (United Nations) Environment Programme (1992) *Environmental Effects of Ozone Regulation: 1991 Update* (Nairobi, UNEP).

UN (United Nations)/World Health Organization (1998) *AIDS Epidemic Update* (Geneva, Joint UN/WHO HIV/AIDS Programme).

US Environmental Protection Agency (1992) *Respiratory Effects of Passive Smoking, Lung Cancer and Other Disorders* (Washington, DC, Office of Health and Environment Assessment/Office of Research & Development, USEPA).

Vaidya, J.S. and Baum, M. (1999) 'Screening and Mortality from Cervical Cancer. Does Screening Really Reduce Mortality?', *British Medical Journal*, **319**, 642.

Van't Veer, P., Lobbezoo, I., Martin-Moreno. J. *et al.* (1997) 'DDT (Dicophane) and Post-menopausal Breast Cancer in Europe: A Case Control Study', *British Medical Journal*, **315**, 81–5.

Verbeek, A., Holland, R., Sturmans, F., Hendrick, J., Mrauenac, M. and Day, N. (1984) 'Reduction of Breast Cancer Mortality through Mass Screening with Modern Mammography', *Lancet*, **i**, 1222–6.

Verschuren, W., Jacobs, D., Bloemberg, B. *et al.* (1995) 'Serum Total Cholesterol and Long Term Coronary Heat Disease Mortality in Different Cultures. Twenty-five Year Follow Up of the 7 Countries Study', *Journal of the American Medical Association*, **274** (2), 131–6.

Vetter, N. (1998) *The Public Health and the NHS* (Oxford, Radcliffe Medical Press).

Vogel, D. (1986) *National Styles of Regulation. Environmental Policy in Great Britain and the US* (New York, Cornell University Press).

Voisey, H. and O'Riordan, T. (1997) 'Governing Institutions for Sustainable Development: The UK's National Level Approach', *Environmental Politics*, **6** (1), 24–53.

Voisey, H., Beuerman, C., Sverdrup, L. and O'Riordan, T. (1996) 'The Political Significance of Local Agenda 21: The Early Stages of Some European Experiences', *Local Environment*, **1** (1), 33–50.

Wakefield, A.J., Murch, S.H., Anthony, A. *et al.* (1998) 'Ileal-lymphoid-nodular Hyperplasia, Non-specific Colitis, and Pervasive Development Disorder in Children', *Lancet*, **351**, 637–41.

Wald, N.J., Murphy, P., Major, P., Parkes, C., Townsend, J. and Frost, C. (1995) 'UK CCCR Multi-centre Randomised Controlled Trial of One and Two View Mammography in Breast Cancer Screening', *British Medical Journal*, **311**, 1189–93.

Walker, A. (1992) 'Waste Disposal: Fresh Looks at a Rotting Problem'. In Godlee, F. and Walker, A. (eds) *Health and the Environment* (London, BMJ Publications), pp. 34–43.

Waller, T. and Holmes, R. (1995) 'The Sleeping Giant Awakes: Hepatitis C and its Impact in Britain', *Druglink*, **10** (5), 8–11.

Wallin, K., Wiklund, F., Angstrom, T. *et al.* (1999) 'Type-specific Persistence of Human Papillomavirus DNA Before the Development of Invasive Cervical Cancer', *New England Journal of Medicine*, **341** (22), 1633–8.

Walt, G. (1993) 'The WHO Under Stress: Implications for Policy', *Health Policy*, **24**, 125–44.

Walt, G. (1996) *Health Policy: An Introduction to Process and Power* (London, Zed).

Walvin, J. (1987) *Victorian Values* (London, Deutsch).

Wang, J., Liu, R., Liu, L. *et al.* (1999) 'The Effect of Leptin on Lep Expression is Tissue-specific and Nutritionally Regulated', *Nature Medicine*, **5** (8), 895–8.

Wannamethee, G., Shaper, A.G., Whincup, P.H. and Walker, M. (1995) 'Low Serum Total Cholesterol Concentrations and Mortality in Middle-aged British Men', *British Medical Journal*, **311**, 409–13.

Ward, S. (1997) 'The IGC and the Current State of EU Environmental Policy: Consolidation or Roll Back', *Environmental Politics*, **6** (1), 178–84.

Watmough, D., Bhargava, A., Syed, S.R. and Sharma, P. (1997) 'For Debate: Does Breast Cancer Screening Depend on a Wobbly Hypothesis?', *Journal of Public Health Medicine*, **19** (4), 375–9.

Watt, I. and Freemantle, N. (1994) 'Purchasing and Public Health: The State of the Union', *Journal of Management in Medicine*, **8** (1), 6–11.

Watterson, A. (1994a) 'Threats to Health and Safety in the Workplace in Britain', *British Medical Journal*, **308**, 1115–16.

Watterson, A. (1994b) 'British and Related European Workplace Health and Safety Policies and Practices: No Major Changes Likely', *New Solutions*, Fall, 62–70.

Watterson, A. (1994c) 'Whither Lay Epidemiology in UK Public Health Policy and Practice? Some Reflections on Occupational and Environmental Health Opportunities', *Journal of Public Health Medicine*, **16** (3), 270–4.

Watterson, A. (1995) *Breast Cancer and the Links with Exposure to Environmental and Occupational Carcinogens* (Leicester, Centre for Occupational and Environmental Health Policy Research).

Weale, A. (1983) 'Invisible Hand or Fatherly Hand? Problems of Paternalism in the New Perspective on Health', *Journal of Health Politics, Policy and Law*, **7** (4), 784–807.

Weale, A. (1992) *The New Politics of Pollution* (Manchester, Manchester University Press).

Webb, T. and Lang, T. (1990) *Food Irradiation: The Myth and the Reality* (Wellingborough, Thorsons).

Webster, C. (1986) 'MoHs – for the Record', *Radical Community Medicine*, Autumn (3), 10–14.

Webster, C. (1988) *Health Services Since the War: Volume 1. Problems of Health Care. The National Health Service Before 1957* (London, HMSO).

Webster, C. (1990) *The Victorian Public Health Legacy: A Challenge to the Future* (London, Public Health Alliance).

Webster, C. (1996) *Government and Health Care: Volume II. The National Health Service 1958–79* (London, HMSO).

Webster, D. and Mackie, M. (1996) *Review of Traffic Calming Schemes in 20 mph Zones*, Transport Research Laboratory Study No. 215 (London, DoE).

Weinser, R.L., Hunter, G.R., Hevic, A.F., Goran, M.I. and Sell, S.M. (1998) 'The Etiology of Obesity: Relative Contribution of Metabolic Factors, Diet and Physical Activity', *American Journal of Medicine*, **105** (2), 145–50.

Wells, W. (1997) *Review of Cervical Cancer Screening Service at Kent and Canterbury Hospital NHS Trust* (London, NHSE South Thames).

Welsh Office (1997) *Health Gain Targets for Wales*, DGM (97) 50 (Cardiff, Welsh Office).

Welsh Office, NHS Directorate (1989) *Welsh Health Planning Forum: Strategic Intent and Direction for the NHS in Wales* (Cardiff, Welsh Office).

Welshman, J. (1997) 'The Medical Officers of Health in England and Wales 1900–74: Watchdog or Lapdog?', *Journal of Public Health and Medicine*, **19** (4), 443–50.

Westin, J.B. (1993) 'Carcinogens in Israeli Milk: A Study in Regulatory Failure', *International Journal of Health Services*, **23** (3), 497–517.

Wheelock, V. (1986) *Food Additives in Perspective* (Bradford, University of Bradford).

While, D., Kelly, S., Huang, W. and Charlton, A. (1996) 'Cigarette Advertising and Onset of Smoking in Children: Questionnaire Survey', *British Medical Journal*, **313**, 398–9.

White, D., Leach, K. and Christensen, L. (1996) 'Self Fulfilling Prophecies', *Health Service Journal*, 23 May, 31.

Whitehead, M. (1987) *The Health Divide* (London, Health Education Council).

Whitehead, M. (1989a) 'Time for a New Agenda', *Health Service Journal*, 5 October, 1220–1.

Whitehead, M. (1989b) *Swimming Upstream – Trends and Prospects in Health Education* (London, King's Fund).

Whitehead, M. (1992) 'The Concepts and Principles of Equity and Health', *International Journal of Health Services*, **22** (3), 429–46.

Whitehead, M. (1995) 'Tackling Inequalities: A Review of Policy Initiatives'. In Benzeval, M., Judge, K and Whitehead, M. (eds) *Tackling Inequalities in Health: An Agenda for Action* (London, King's Fund), pp. 22–52.

Whitehead, M. and Drever, M. (1997) 'Health Inequalities: Main Findings and Implications for the Future'. In Drever, M. and Whitehead, M. (eds) *Health Inequalities* (London, Stationery Office), pp. 224–36.

Whitty, P. and Jones, I. (1992) 'Public Health Heresy: A Challenge to the Purchasing Orthodoxy', *British Medical Journal*, **304**, 1039–41.

WHO (World Health Organization) (1946) *Constitution: Basic Documents* (Geneva, WHO).

WHO (World Health Organization) (1978) *Declaration of Alma Ata. Report of the International Conference on Primary Health Care* (Geneva, WHO/Unicef).

WHO (World Health Organization) (1981) *Global Strategy for Health for All by the Year 2000* (Geneva, WHO).

WHO (World Health Organization) (1982) *Prevention of Coronary Heart Disease*, WHO Expert Committee, Technical Report 678 (Geneva, WHO).

WHO (World Health Organization) (1986a) First International Conference on Health Promotion. The Move Towards a New Public Health: Ottawa Charter for Health Promotion, Ottawa, Nov 17–21 (Ottawa, WHO/Health and Welfare Canada/Canadian Association for Public Health).

WHO (World Health Organization) (1986b) *Health and the Environment* (Geneva, WHO).

WHO (World Health Organization) (1988) *Second International Conference on Health Promotion: Adelaide Recommendations* (Adelaide, WHO/Australian Department of Community Services and Health).

WHO (World Health Organization) (1990) *Diet, Nutrition and the Prevention of Chronic Diseases.* Report of a WHO Study Group on Diet, Nutrition and Prevention of Non-communicable Diseases (Geneva, WHO).

WHO (World Health Organization) (1991) *Third International Conference on Health Promotion: Sundsvall Statement on Supportive Environments for Health* (Sundsvall, WHO/UNEP/Nordic Council of Ministers).

WHO (World Health Organization) (1992) *Our Planet, Our Health.* Report of the WHO Commission on Health and the Environment (Geneva, WHO).

WHO (World Health Organization) (1993) *The Application of HACCP System for the Improvement of Food Safety* (Geneva, WHO Food Safety Unit).

WHO (World Health Organization) (1995) *Implementation of the Global Strategy for Health For All by the Year 2000, Second Evaluation* (Geneva, WHO).

WHO (World Health Organization) (1996) *International Strategy for Tobacco Control* (Geneva, WHO).

WHO (World Health Organization) (1997a) *Fourth International Conference on Health Promotion: The Jakarta Declaration* (WHO, Jakarta).

WHO (World Health Organization) (1997b) *Health and Environment in Sustainable Development: 5 Years after the Earth Summit* (Geneva, WHO).

WHO (World Health Organization) (1997c) *Tobacco or Health: A Global Status Report 1997* (Geneva, WHO).

WHO (World Health Organization) (1997d) *Cannabis* (Geneva, WHO).

WHO (World Health Organization) (1998a) *Health For All for the 21st Century* (Geneva, WHO).

WHO (World Health Organization) (1998b) *Passive Smoking Does Cause Lung Cancer*, Press Release WHO/29, (Geneva, WHO).

WHO (World Health Organization) (1998c) *Obesity and Diet Related Non-Communicable Diseases: Obesity, Preventing and Managing the Global Epidemic* (Geneva, WHO).

WHO (World Health Organization) (1999a) *World Health Report 1998: Life in the 21st Century: A Vision For All* (Geneva, WHO).

WHO (World Health Organization) (1999b) *Health Costs due to Road Traffic-related Air Pollution* (Geneva, WHO).

WHO (World Health Organization) Regional Office for Europe (1985a) *Health Implications of Unemployment* (Copenhagen, WHO Regional Office for Europe).

WHO (World Health Organization) Regional Office for Europe (1985b) *Targets for Health for All: Targets in Support of the European Regional Strategy for Health for All* (Copenhagen, WHO).

WHO (World Health Organization) Regional Office for Europe (1988) *Healthy Nutrition: Preventing Nutrition-related Disease in Europe* (Copenhagen, WHO).

WHO (World Health Organization) Regional Office for Europe (1989) *European Charter on Environment and Health. Document for 1st European Conference on Environmental Health* (Frankfurt, WHO).

WHO (World Health Organization) Regional Office for Europe (1990) *Environment and Health: The European Charter and Commentary* (Copenhagen, WHO).

WHO (World Health Organization) Regional Office for Europe (1993a) *Health for All Target: The Health Policy for Europe* (Copenhagen, WHO).

WHO (World Health Organization) Regional Office for Europe (1993b) *Action Plan for a Tobacco Free Europe* (Copenhagen, WHO Regional Office for Europe).

WHO (World Health Organization) Regional Office for Europe (1993c) *European Alcohol Action Plan* (Copenhagen, WHO).

WHO (World Health Organization) Regional Office for Europe (1994) *Environmental Health Action Plan for Europe* (Copenhagen, WHO).

WHO (World Health Organization) Regional Office for Europe (1996) *Alcohol: Less is Better* (Copenhagen, WHO).

WHO (World Health Organization) Regional Office for Europe (1998a) *Health 21: The Health for All Policy Framework for the Twenty First Century* (Copenhagen, WHO).

WHO (World Health Organization) Regional Office for Europe (1998b) *Comparative Analysis of Nutrition Policies in WHO Member States* (Copenhagen, WHO).

WHO (World Health Organization) Regional Office for Europe (1999) *Access to Information, Public Participation and Access to Justice in Environment and Health Matters* (Copenhagen, WHO).

Whynes, D.K., Neilson, A.R., Walker, A.R. and Hardcastle, J.D. (1998) 'Faecal Occult Blood Screening for Colorectal Cancer: Is it Cost Effective?', *Health Economics*, **7** (1), 21–9.

Wild, S. and McKeigue, P. (1997) 'Cross-sectional Analysis of Mortality by Country of Birth in England and Wales 1970–92', *British Medical Journal*, **314**, 305–10.

Wildavsky, A. (1988) *Searching for Safety* (New Brunswick, Transaction).

Wildavsky, A. (1991) 'If Claims of Harm from Technology Are False, Mostly False or Unproven, What Does That Tell Us About Science?' In Berger, P. (ed.) *Health, Lifestyle and Environment* (London, Social Affairs Unit), pp. 111–45.

Wilding, J. (1997) 'Obesity Treatment', *British Medical Journal*, **315**, 997–1000.

Wiles, R. and Robison, J. (1994) 'Teamwork in Primary Care: The Views and Experience of Nurses, Midwives and Health Visitors', *Journal of Advanced Nursing*, **20**, 324–30.

Wilkinson, R. (1994) *Unfair Shares* (Ilford, Barnardo's).

Wilkinson, R. (1995) 'Commentary: A Reply to Ken Judge: Mistaken Criticism Ignores Overwhelming Evidence', *British Medical Journal*, **311**, 1285–7.

Wilkinson, R.G. (1992) 'Income Distribution and Life Expectancy', *British Medical Journal*, **304**, 165–8.

Wilkinson, R.G. (1996) *Unhealthy Societies: The Afflictions of Inequality* (London, Routledge).

Wilkinson, R.G. (1997) 'Health Inequalities: Relative or Absolute Material Standards?', *British Medical Journal*, **314**, 591–5.

Williams, D.R., Lavizzo-Mourey, R. and Warren, R.C. (1994) 'The Concept of Race and Health Status in America', *Public Health Reports*, **109** (1), 26–41.

Williams, G., Popay, J. and Bissell, P. (1995) 'Public Health Risks in the Material World: Barriers to Social Movements in Health'. In Gabe, J. (ed.) *Medicine, Health and Risk*, (Oxford, Blackwell), pp. 113–32.

Willis, E. (1998) 'Public Health, Private Genes: The Social Contract and Genetic Biotechnologies', *Public Health*, **8** (2), 131–9.

Wilson, D. and Game, C. (1994) *Local Government in the United Kingdom* (London, Macmillan).

Wilson, J.M.G. and Jungner, G. (1968) *Principles and Practice of Screening for Disease* (Geneva, WHO).

Wilson, M.E. (1995) 'Infectious Diseases: An Ecological Perspective', *British Medical Journal*, **311**, 1681–4.

Winslow, C.E.A. (1920) 'The Untilled Fields of Public Health', *Science*, **51**, 23.

Wisotsky, S. (1986) *Breaking the Impasse on the War on Drugs* (London, Greenwood Press).

Witcombe, J. (1988) 'A Licence for Breast Cancer Screening', *British Medical Journal*, **296**, 909–12.

Wohl, A.S. (1984) *Endangered Lives, Public Health in Victorian Britain* (London, Unwin Methuen).

Wolff, M.A., Toniolo, P.G., Lee, E., Rivera, M. and Dublin, N. (1993) 'Blood Levels of Organochlorine Residues and Risk of Breast Cancer', *Journal of the National Cancer Institute*, **85**, 648–52.

Wolfson, M., Kaplan, G., Lynch, J., Ross, N. and Backlund, E. (1999) 'Relation Between Income Inequality and Mortality: Empirical Demonstration', *British Medical Journal*, **319**, 953–7.

Wolk, A., Manson, J.E., Stampfer, M.J. *et al*. (1999) 'Long-term Intake of Dietary Fibre and Decreased Risk of Coronary Heart Disease Among Women', *Journal of the American Medical Association*, **281** (21), 1990–2004.

Wood, F. (1998) 'Injecting Drug Use and the HIV Epidemic'. In Bloor, M. and Wood, F. (eds) *Addictions and Problem Drug Use: Issues in Behaviour Policy and Practice* (London, Jessica Kingsley), pp. 125–38

Woodman, C.B.J., Threlfall, A.G., Boggis, C.R.M. and Prior, P. (1995) 'Is the Three-year Breast Screening Interval Too Long? Occurrence of Interval Cancers in NHS Breast Screening Programme's NorthWest Region', *British Medical Journal*, **310**, 224–6.

Woodward, L. (1962) *The Age of Reform 1815–1870*, 2nd edn (Oxford, Oxford University Press).

World Commission on Environment and Development (1987) *Our Common Future* (Oxford, Oxford University Press).

Wright, C.J. (1986) 'Breast Cancer Screening. A Different Look at the Evidence', *Surgery*, **100** (4), 594–8.

Wright, J., Williams, R. and Wilkinson, J.R. (1998) 'Development and Importance of Health Needs Assessment', *British Medical Journal*, **316**, 1310–13.

Wrigley, N. (1998) 'How British Retailers Have Shaped Food Choice'. In Murcott, A. (ed.) *The Nation's Diet: The Social Science of Food Choice* (London, Longman), pp. 112–18.

Wynne, B. (1996) 'May the Sheep Safely Graze?'. In Lash, S., Szerszynski, B. and Wynne, B. (eds) *Risk, Environment and Modernity*, (London, Sage), pp. 44–83.

Yarrow, A. (1986) *Politics, Society and Preventive Medicine*, Occasional Paper 6 (London, Nuffield Provincial Hospitals Trust).

Yates, J. (1996) 'Medical Genetics', *British Medical Journal*, **312**, 1021–5.

Yeoman, L. Wilson, A. and Evans, A. (1994) 'Screening for Breast Cancer', *British Medical Journal*, **308**, 792.

Young, B. and Hetherington, M. (1996) 'The Literature on Advertising and Children's Food Choice', *Nutrition and Food Science*, **5**, 15–18.

Young, K. (1985) 'Local Government and the Environment'. In Jowell, R. and Witherspoon, S. (eds) *British Social Attitudes: The 1985 Report* (Aldershot, Gower), pp. 158–63.

Young, K. (1991) 'Shades of Green'. In Jowell, R., Brook, L., Taylor, B. and Prior, G. (eds) *British Social Attitudes the 8th Report* (Aldershot, Dartmouth), pp. 107–30.

Young, S. (1996) 'Stepping Stones to Empowerment?: Participation in the Context of Local Agenda 21', *Local Government Policy Making*, **22** (4), 25–31.

Zunzunegui, M.V., King, M.C., Coria, C.F. and Charlet, J. (1986) 'Male Influences on Cervical Cancer Risk', *American Journal of Epidemiology*, **123** (2), 302–7.

# Index